Representations of Slave Women in Discourses on Slavery and Abolition, 1780–1838

Routledge Studies in Slave and Post-Slave Societies and Cultures
EDITED BY GAD HEUMAN

1. Abolition and Its Aftermath in Indian Ocean Africa and Asia
edited by Gwyn Campbell

2. Resisting Bondage in Indian Ocean Africa and Asia
edited by Edward Alpers, Gwyn Campbell and Michael Salman

3. Representations of Slave Women in Discourses on Slavery and Abolition, 1780–1838
Henrice Altink

Previous titles to appear in Studies in Slave and Post-Slave Societies and Cultures include

The Structure of Slavery in Indian Ocean Africa and Asia
edited by Gwyn Campbell

Representing the Body of the Slave
edited by Thomas Wiedemann and Jane Gardner

Rethinking the African Diaspora
The Making of a Black Atlantic World in the Bight of Benin and Brazil
edited by Kristin Mann and Edna G. Bay

After Slavery
Emancipation and its Discontents
Edited by Howard Temperley

From Slavery to Emancipation in the Atlantic World
edited by Sylvia R. Frey and Betty Wood

Slavery and Colonial Rule in Africa
edited by Suzanne Miers and Martin A. Klein

Classical Slavery
edited by M. I. Finley

Popular Politics and British Anti-Slavery
The Mobilisation of Public Opinion against the Slave Trade, 1787–1807
J. R. Oldfield

Routes to Slavery
Direction, Ethnicity and Mortality in the Transatlantic Slave Trade
edited by David Eltis and David Richardson

Representations of Slave Women in Discourses on Slavery and Abolition, 1780–1838

Henrice Altink

Routledge
Taylor & Francis Group
New York London

Routledge
Taylor & Francis Group
270 Madison Avenue
New York, NY 10016

Routledge
Taylor & Francis Group
2 Park Square
Milton Park, Abingdon
Oxon OX14 4RN

© 2007 by Taylor & Francis Group, LLC
Routledge is an imprint of Taylor & Francis Group, an Informa business

Printed in the United States of America on acid-free paper
10 9 8 7 6 5 4 3 2 1

International Standard Book Number-10: 0-415-35026-3 (Hardcover)
International Standard Book Number-13: 978-0-415-35026-6 (Hardcover)

No part of this book may be reprinted, reproduced, transmitted, or utilized in any form by any electronic, mechanical, or other means, now known or hereafter invented, including photocopying, microfilming, and recording, or in any information storage or retrieval system, without written permission from the publishers.

Trademark Notice: Product or corporate names may be trademarks or registered trademarks, and are used only for identification and explanation without intent to infringe.

Library of Congress Cataloging-in-Publication Data

Altink, Henrice.
  Representations of slave women in discourses on slavery and abolition, 1780-1838 / Henrice Altink.
      p. cm. -- (Routledge studies in slave and post-slave societies and cultures ; 3)
    Includes bibliographical references and index.
    ISBN-13: 978-0-415-35026-6 (hardback : alk. paper)
    1. Women slaves--Jamaica--History. 2. Slavery--Jamaica--History. I. Title.

HT1096.A748 2007
306.3'62082097292--dc22   2006033882

Visit the Taylor & Francis Web site at
http://www.taylorandfrancis.com

and the Routledge Web site at
http://www.routledge-ny.com

Contents

Acknowledgments vii

   Introduction 1

1 Belly women: Slave women's childbirth practices 11

2 Pickeniny mummas: Slave women's childrearing practices 39

3 Deviant and dangerous: Slave women's sexuality 65

4 Till death do us part: Slave wives and slave husbands 91

5 The indecency of the lash 129

6 Slavery by another name 147

   Conclusion 169

Notes 177
Bibliography 237
Index 253

Acknowledgments

I have incurred many debts while researching and writing this book. My gratitude goes especially to David Richardson and Keith Nield for supervising the Ph.D. dissertation that led to this book. Thanks also to Judith Spicksley, Neil Wynn, David Turner, Norry La Porte, Christer Petley, and Miles Taylor for reading chapters and making helpful suggestions. I also want to thank the Gender Studies and Philosophy Reading Group at the University of Hull for introducing me to new and relevant approaches to my primary sources. Parts of the book were presented at conferences and seminars at the University of Hull, the University of Liverpool, the University of London, the International Centre for the History of Slavery, the Society for Caribbean Studies, the Economic History Society, and the Social History Society. I am grateful for the useful comments received from those who participated in them. Thanks also to the anonymous reader for Taylor and Francis, who gave me invaluable comments on the manuscript.

Versions of some of the material presented here have already been published. The first section of chapter three appeared as 'Deviant and Dangerous: Pro-Slavery Representations of Jamaican Slave Women's Sexuality, c. 1780-1834', *Slavery and Abolition*, 26, 2 (2005), pp. 271–88. An earlier version of the antislavery debate about female flogging in chapter five appeared as '"An Outrage on All Decency": Abolitionist Reactions to Flogging Jamaican Slave Women, 1780-1834', *Slavery and Abolition*, 23, 2 (2002), pp. 107–22. And the examination of attempts to end the practice of female flogging in Jamaican workhouses draws on my article 'Slavery by Another Name: Apprenticed Women in Jamaican Workhouses in the Period 1834-1838', *Social History*, 26, 1 (2001), pp. 40–59. I am grateful to the publishers for allowing me to reprint this material.

Thanks are also due to the University of Hull for providing me with the funds to carry out the research and to my former colleagues at the University of Glamorgan and my colleagues at the University of York for their interest in my project and their encouragement to bring it to completion. Staff at the following libraries and archives have been most helpful: the Brynmor Jones Library (University of Hull), the University of London

Library, the British Library, the Institute of Commonwealth Studies, the Public Record Office, and the Jamaica Archives.

The project would not have been completed without the consistent support of my friends Sue Wright, Simon Topping, and Martina Kunnecke; my parents Hendrik-Jan and Jo Altink; my sisters Johanna, Wilmien and Annet; my nieces and nephews, and my uncle Gerrit Altink.

Introduction

> But sir, the whole slave system with respect to women in our West India colonies is abominable, and must excite horror and disgust in every well-regulated mind. They are considered as beings created solely to gratify the avarice or the brutal appetites of their masters — indeed, never treated as women, except for some vile purpose. (James Losh, speech in the Guildhall at Newcastle, 31 March 1824)[1]

British abolitionism emerged as a mass movement in the late 1780s. The Committee for the Abolition of the Slave Trade was set up in 1787 by Quakers, evangelical Christians and other supporters of social reform, which presented petitions and parliamentary motions against the slave trade. It was not until 1807, however, that it achieved its aim of a legal prohibition of the slave trade to the British colonies. In the years following, the antislavery movement regularly called upon the government to enforce British abolition of the slave trade and encourage other nations to withdraw from the trade. It also introduced a bill in 1815 to assess the impact of the abolition of the slave trade on the slave populations in the Caribbean by means of a Central Register of slaves. Although the bill was not passed, it encouraged most colonial legislatures to pass slave registration acts of their own. Antislavery advocates assumed that these acts and the abolition of the slave trade in itself would encourage slaveholders to adopt ameliorative practices, such as reducing the working hours of the slaves and allowing them to attend missionary churches. Such practices, it was argued, would improve the slaves' physical wellbeing and enhance their moral condition to such an extent that they would become capable of full freedom.

By the early 1820s, the returns of the slave registers and other evidence showed that the slave populations in the British Caribbean were declining and that the slaves' moral condition had far from improved. As a result, several antislavery activists set up the Anti-Slavery Society in 1823, which aimed to bring about the gradual emancipation of the slaves through ameliorative legislation. By May 1830, however, the Society realized that colonial legislatures, which were mainly made up of planters, were unwilling to implement ameliorative measures and dedicated itself to immediate freedom. Two years later, Thomas Buxton, the parliamentary leader of the abolitionists, introduced a resolution that would commit the government to immediate emancipation. The resolution was voted down but as a compromise it was agreed that a parliamentary committee would be set up to consider the best way of abolishing slavery. The Select Committee on the Extinction of Slavery throughout the British Dominions (hereafter, 1832 Select Committee) listened to 33 witnesses and published a report in August 1832 which failed to reach a conclusion. When the King's speech on February 1833 did not mention emancipation, abolitionists launched their most far-reaching campaign. Some 5,000 petitions were presented to Parliament and numerous pamphlets depicting the horrors of slavery were published. This agitation along with various other factors led Parliament to pass the Abolition of Slavery Act (hereafter, 1833 Abolition Act) which stipulated that from August 1834 onwards all children under six would be free, that the other slaves would be apprenticed part-time to their former master for a period of four to six years depending on whether they were house or field slaves, and that planters would be given 20 million pounds to compensate for their future loss of labour. When abolitionists learned from 1835 onwards that planters abused apprenticeship, they launched a national campaign for the ending of the system. Largely as a result of this campaign, apprenticeship was prematurely abolished in 1838.[2]

The reformer and philanthropist James Losh was not the only antislavery advocate who conveyed the horrors of slavery through the treatment of slave women. Supporters of both gradual and immediate abolition focussed in their writings and speeches on the harm done to the enslaved female body. They pointed out that slave women had to endure sexual abuse and also excessive physical punishments, even when they were pregnant. This was a most effective means to arouse audiences because this treatment was diametrically opposed to the gender order of the metropolitan society,[3] which assumed that women were the gentler sex in need of male protection. To effectively counter antislavery attacks, proslavery advocates had thus little choice but to address the working and living conditions of slave women. Writing a year after the launch of the abolitionist campaign for emancipation, James McQueen, a metropolitan-based defender of slavery, published a pamphlet entitled *The West India Colonies* (1824) in which he argued that 'women who are bearing children are most carefully and tenderly treated. From the third month of pregnancy, they are exempted from labour, a proper midwife and nurse are appointed to attend them at the time of delivery, and a medical man is within call, in case of necessity.'[4] It was, however, not only antislavery attacks that led proslavery advocates to centralize slave women in their writings but also various socio-economic factors that threatened the viability of the plantation system, including the natural decrease of the slave population and the growth of the free(d) population. The former factor largely accounts for the dominance of the slave mother in early proslavery writings, while the latter explains the centrality of the naturally promiscuous slave woman in proslavery writings published after the abolition of the slave trade in 1807.

Images of slave women, then, were central to what Catherine Hall has called 'the war of representation'; that is, the struggle to depict the truth about the system of slavery in the British Caribbean. Various people other than planters and committed abolitionists played a prominent role in this 'war', which took place in many sites in both the metropole and the colonies.[5] This study examines textual representations of Jamaican slave women in three contexts — motherhood, intimate relationships, and work — in a wide range of materials produced by pro- and antislavery advocates from the 1780s till 1838.[6] It first of all aims to show *how* both sides represented slave women to their audiences and explain *why* they created their negative and positive images of Jamaican slave women. This implies not only that it will devote considerable attention to the strategies used by both sides to appeal to their audiences, but also that it will examine the interplay of pro- and antislavery images of slave women and explore their reliance upon a variety of metropolitan discourses.[7] Both sides measured slave women against the metropolitan norm of womanhood. As they were not only concerned with slave women, however, but also with their partners and children, their owners, and the black and white men who supervised them in the field, both sides invoked also metropolitan ideas about masculinity, race, sexuality, marriage, punishment, and the rule of law. By examining the images of slave women within their socio-economic, cultural, and political context, this book will try to pinpoint the factors that gave rise to and/or changed the images of Jamaican slave women and will also unravel more specific political concerns than the prolongation or the abolition of slavery that were contained within or furthered by the imagery of slave women. We shall see, in fact, that the slave woman, and in particular her body, was essentially a site where important political and cultural contests were enacted.

A second aim of this study is to explore some of the political, cultural, and intellectual work done by the representations of Jamaican slave women. It mentions (implemented and proposed) local and imperial legislation and plantation practices that engaged with specific ideas about slave women and which had both (real and intended) enabling and limiting effects on slave women, such as the provision in the 1833 Abolition Act that forbade the flogging of female apprentices and the practice adopted on some estates in the early nineteenth century to offer slave women a monetary reward for weaning their children early. It furthermore demonstrates that by characterizing and defining slave women and those who interacted with them on the estates, pro- and antislavery activists could identify themselves as white, male, civilized, Jamaican, or English, and that these identities helped to instil in them a feeling of superiority. And it also tries to show that the pro- and antislavery discussion about Jamaican slave women drew not only upon various metropolitan discourses but also helped to reinforce and even change them, in particular those on gender, race, and sexuality. What this study does not try to do, however, is to answer the question how the objects of representation responded to the identities imposed upon them by pro- and antislavery advocates. To examine whether slave women internalized the images that defined them as indifferent and caring mothers, adulterous and loving wives, and obedient and unruly workers, we need accounts in which the women responded to the practices that were informed by these images. This is an almost impossible task because we lack sources in which Jamaican slave women voice their own opinion.[8]

This book is not the first to examine images of slave women in discourses of slavery and abolition. In the 1980s and early 1990s, several feminist scholars examined stereotypes of slave women in the Antebellum South which, according to them, formed the basis of contemporary controlling images of African American women. They focussed in particular on the scheming Jezebel (the sexually aggressive woman) and the Mammy (the faithful, obedient domestic servant) and were concerned to show the plantation practices that helped to sustain these stereotypical images in the white mind and the ways in which these images enabled planters to control their female slaves.[9] Following this pioneering work on imagery of slave women, several articles were published in the 1990s by scholars working on the British Caribbean that examined stereotypes of slave women in a small range of well-known proslavery writings. Based on the assumption that these images, in particular that of the sexually promiscuous slave woman, inform the treatment of African Caribbean women today and that they need to be debunked in order for African Caribbean women to progress in society, the authors provide counter-images of slave women drawn from other contemporary writings, including antislavery accounts.[10]

As this book does not aim to provide a more positive reconstruction of slave women's lives but to further our understanding of the discourses of slavery and abolition, it deviates in some important respects from existing work on the imagery of slave women in the British Caribbean. First, it scrutinizes images of slave women in pro- and antislavery writings to the same extent and explores the interaction between the two sets of images.[11] Second, it is based on a wider range of primary materials and includes both well-known and lesser-known texts.[12] Hence, it uses alongside works that have received considerable scholarly attention, such as Matthew Gregory Lewis' *Journal of a West India Proprietor* (1818), also travel accounts, slave management manuals, published speeches, anonymously written pamphlets, reports of parliamentary committees, and official correspondence. Third, it is not only concerned with negative stereotypes of slave women but also with sympathetic and even idealizing images of slave women. And fourth, it is only concerned with the work done by the images at the time that they were produced.

Because both the pro- and antislavery debate centred on slave women, an analysis of the construction of images of a particular group of slave women can yield rich insights into these two discourses, which thus far have been mainly studied in isolation.[13] They were part of a wider discourse that presented images of British colonial subjects. In recent decades, there has been an outpouring of studies on 'colonial discourse'; that is, the language that was part of the historical process of colonisation. This work has demonstrated that colonialism was not just a political or an economic relationship but also a cultural process in that it was 'imagined and energized through signs, metaphors and narratives'.[14] Most studies on 'colonial discourse' have failed to understand the diversity and conflict amongst colonizers. By exploring the writings of a diverse group of people situated in both the metropole and the colony who did not seriously question the colonial project, this book tries to demonstrate that 'colonial discourse' was a highly complex discourse marked by heterogeneity, contradiction, and ambivalence.[15]

It was not until the early 1990s that scholars began to examine in detail proslavery writings. They have either explored writings by defenders of slavery located in the metropolitan society, many of whom had experiences of plantation life, including several absentee proprietors, or they have examined the ways in which planters and other local residents responded to abolitionist attacks.[16] Those who adopted the latter approach, such as David Lambert in his work on Barbados, have been more concerned with demonstrating that the production of images of slaves as lesser human beings enabled local residents to identify themselves as white, male, and English than with examining the controlling effects that the images exerted on the slaves' lives. Like those who took up the first approach, they have suggested that the proslavery debate changed little over time.[17] As existing work on proslavery discourse has studied local and metropolitan defenders of slavery separately and has tended to concentrate on a small period of time, it has suggested that proslavery discourse was relatively monolithic and static. This study examines the writings of local residents alongside those of metropolitan defenders of slavery over a 50-year period and argues that proslavery discourse was varied, changing, inconsistent, and contradictory. Jamaican and metropolitan-based defenders of slavery had very different opinions about the best way to prolong slavery. This along with their different degrees of exposure to metropolitan debates other than slavery largely explains why they presented at times very different images of slave women. A changing socio-economic, cultural, and political context, on the other hand, accounts for the rise and fall of particular images of Jamaican slave women in proslavery writings. The 'indifferent mother', for example, featured prominently in late eighteenth- and early nineteenth-century proslavery writings because it resonated well with the concern about natural decrease. She was pushed to the background by the 'caring mother' in the 1820s and early 1830s, whose main aim it was to deny the abolitionist charge that Jamaican planters were unwilling to ameliorate the condition of the slaves. The 'indifferent mother' surfaced again between 1834 and 1838 in order to excuse planters for the deteriorating condition of young children. It will also be shown in this book that proslavery activists, especially those who resided in Jamaica, often contradicted themselves. In the space of one work, they could present the slave woman as an 'indifferent mother' on the one hand and a 'caring mother', on the other. It will be argued that the contradictions in proslavery discourse stemmed largely from its dual aim: averting antislavery attacks and justifying (far-reaching) interventions in the lives of the slaves.

Since the 1970s, there has been an increased output of studies on organized antislavery, which have tried to transcend older interpretations of the movement as either a humanitarian crusade or as an economically determined movement that facilitated the advancement of industrial capitalism.[18] Although several anthologies of antislavery writings have been published in recent years, scholarship on antislavery has continued to be more concerned with the origins, makeup and activities of the movement than with its ideas.[19] Most of the work thus far done on antislavery writings has been carried out by literary scholars.[20] This scholarship has demonstrated the centrality of slave women to antislavery writings, most notably Moira Ferguson's pioneering work *Subject to Others: British Women Writers and Colonial Slavery, 1670–1834* (1992). It has furthermore demonstrated the contradictory nature of antislavery discourse, that is the coexistence of a belief in human equality with imagery of slaves that left in place the differential status of blacks vis-à-vis whites; shown its engagement with metropolitan ideas about race; and listed the main strategies employed by antislavery activists to arouse their audiences, such as the use of highly sentimental language.

This study builds on and adds to the scholarship on antislavery writing. First, it also illustrates the contradictory nature of antislavery writings. It mentions some of the ways in which antislavery writers undermined their belief in the equality of the slaves, such as attributing them with a humanity that was more potential than real. Second, it confirms that antislavery discourse engaged with metropolitan ideas about race. As it examines antislavery writings firmly within their historical context, however, this book is also able to demonstrate their reliance on and contribution to various other metropolitan debates and to mention some other methods used by antislavery writers to appeal to their audiences. Third, it shows more clearly than earlier work that antislavery discourse was a changing discourse. Previous work has largely concentrated on writings produced during the campaign to abolish the slave trade. As this study is based on writings mobilized in all the abolitionist campaigns, it is able to show some important changes in the antislavery discussion, such as a stronger condemnation of the planting class from the mid-1820s onwards. And finally, it corrects the bias in earlier work towards fictive writings. It analyzes a large number of non-fictive writings that were produced not only by committed abolitionists but also by various other individuals who deplored the institution of slavery, including (former) missionaries and colonial officials.[21] While some of these antislavery advocates favoured immediate abolition of slavery, others supported gradual emancipation. Their different opinions about abolition and the extent to which they had experienced plantation life led them to portray slave women in different ways and propose different solutions to enhance the quality of their lives. Thus by including non-fictive writings, this book will demonstrate more clearly than earlier studies, the varied nature of antislavery discourse.

By examining the method, aims, and effects of representations of Jamaican slave women this study will provide a deeper insight into the nature of pro- and antislavery discourse and their mutual influence, and also shed some light on the complex relation of the two discourses to the exercise of power in the slave societies in the British Caribbean and on the construction of British identities at the time. This work does not only contribute, however, to the scholarship on the pro- and antislavery debates but also to that on Caribbean slave women. In the late 1980s and early 1990s, three monographs on slave women's lives were published that built on the pioneering work of Lucille Mathurin Mair[22] and demographic and medical histories of Caribbean slavery[23] and concentrated on the British Caribbean: Hilary McD. Beckles, *Natural Rebels: A Social History of Enslaved Black Women in Barbados* (1989); Barbara Bush, *Slave Women in Caribbean Society, 1650–1838* (1990); and Marietta Morrissey, *Slave Women in the New World: Gender Stratification in the Caribbean* (1989). By examining not only slave women's working lives but also their family and domestic lives and their role in slave resistance, these studies have done much to make the slave woman visible in Caribbean history. A serious gap in these works, however, is their lack of attention to the period of apprenticeship.[24] Apprenticeship aimed to create a smooth transition from slavery to a free-labour economy by instilling in the ex-slaves the skills and habits expected of wage labourers and by making planters fair employers. The administration of the system was given to a corps of Special Magistrates (S.M.s), who were to stand between the planters and the apprentices and facilitate a mutual understanding that would last beyond the period of apprenticeship. They were given the weighty task of punishing apprentices who failed to carry out their duties. As they were not allowed to flog female apprentices, S.M.s usually sent recalcitrant female apprentices to the workhouse where they had to work in the penal gang and/or dance the treadmill.[25]

This book is as much concerned with images of apprenticed women as with images of slave women. As it integrates the analysis of images of apprenticed women with an analysis of plantation practices, it will provide information about the working lives and domestic arrangements of apprenticed women and thus complement the three monographs on Caribbean slave women. It will illustrate that apprenticed women faced a variety of legal and illegal practices after August 1834 that reversed the improvements that planters had brought about in the lives of their female labour force since the 1780s and which also in other ways increased their burden. As this book pays considerable attention to the motives underpinning these practices and the way in which they were put in place, it will also make a contribution to a growing scholarship on the workings of apprenticeship. The first studies on apprenticeship were published in the 1920s and 1930s and presented it as a marked and successful deviation from slavery. Scholars reiterated this view until the 1980s when they began to examine more carefully the ex-slaves' experiences of apprenticeship. Their analyses led them to conclude that there were more continuities than discontinuities between slavery and apprenticeship.[26] More recently, a third interpretation has emerged which acknowledges the similarities between slavery and apprenticeship but is more concerned to show that apprenticeship differed from both what went on before and what came after.[27]

As apprenticeship showed many similarities with the system of slavery, its abolition in 1838 forms a logical end for this study. It begins in the 1780s because this decade witnessed the gradual rise of organized abolitionism, which, alongside other factors that threatened the plantation economy, triggered a spate of writings that defended the institution of slavery in the British Caribbean.[28] The locus of the book is Jamaica because the island formed the basis of British policy relating to the slave colonies and dominated the public debate about slavery and abolition.[29] The 1832 House of Commons Select Committee that aimed to establish whether slavery could be safely abolished in the near future, for instance, restricted itself to Jamaica, while antislavery advocates supported their demands primarily with evidence relating to this island.

For most English men and women in the 1780s till 1830s, then, Jamaica was synonymous with the West Indies. The island was the largest slave colony in the British Caribbean. On the eve of apprenticeship, there were 311,070 slaves (152,000 men and 161,000 women) in Jamaica, constituting 46.8 per cent of all the slaves in the British Caribbean.[30] Although the enslaved population declined by 10.8 per cent between 1807 and 1834, it far outnumbered the whites and the free blacks and coloureds in the island.[31] In 1830, these two groups only made up respectively 5.0 and 10.6 per cent of the total population.[32] About 53 per cent of the slaves were engaged in the production of sugar, the island's main cash crop throughout the period under discussion.[33] As slave men were put to a wide range of (skilled) occupations around the sugar plantation, slave women outnumbered male slaves in the field. By the late 1820s, almost two-thirds of the field labour force was made up of slave women.[34] The field labour force was divided into three gangs. The first was employed in hard work in the field, such as digging holes and cutting cane, and also had to perform hard labour in the mill during crop season. The slaves in this gang usually worked 12 hours a day, six days a week. The second gang carried out lighter tasks in the field and the mill and was largely made up of adolescents and lesser-able slaves, such as nursing slave women. Like the second gang, the third also worked shorter hours and consisted mainly of slave children aged five and older, whose main task it was to collect grass for the estate's livestock.[35] The daily management of the slaves was in the hands of an overseer, who supervised a small number of white officers and several slave drivers.

A fall in the price of sugar on the London market caused by increased competition and a rise in sugar duties squeezed profit margins in sugar production in the 1820s.[36] The relentless pressure that planters put on their enslaved workforce in order to sustain their profit levels is one of the main factors behind the rebellion that broke out in Jamaica on Christmas Day 1831 and which lasted for two weeks. This rebellion, in which some 25,000 slaves took part, helped to speed up the abolition of slavery in the British Caribbean.[37] As planters and other white islanders were convinced that the rebellion was triggered by Baptist and Methodist missionaries, they burned down chapels, imprisoned several missionaries, and threatened the lives of many others. Some of the persecuted missionaries went to Britain where they gave lectures in spring and summer 1832, conveying their sufferings at the hands of the white population. These lectures did much to increase nonconformist support for the abolitionist cause and convince existing abolitionists of the necessity of immediate emancipation.[38]

The analysis of the images of slave and apprenticed women is organized in six chapters. The first two explore the debate about slave motherhood. The first chapter concentrates on the discussion about pregnant and lying-in women, which emerged in the late eighteenth century and lasted until 1838. During slavery, only proslavery advocates took an active part in this debate. The chapter is particularly concerned with their proposals to encourage slave women to give birth more often and enhance the survival rate of newborn slave infants. It examines the images of slave women that underpinned these proposals and explores the degree to which the proposals were implemented in order to assess their impact on slave women's lives. The second chapter compares the extent to which proslavery and antislavery advocates and also critics and opponents of apprenticeship measured slave and apprenticed women against the metropolitan ideal of motherhood in their accounts of the ways in which female plantation workers took care of their young infants.[39] This chapter illustrates that their different projects and the realities of plantation life led the participants in this debate not only to emphasize different attributes of the metropolitan motherhood ideal but also to interpret the attributes differently.

Chapters three and four explore the debate about slave and apprenticed women's intimate relationships. Chapter three is concerned with slave women's sexual relationships, especially with white men. This issue proved an excellent means for antislavery writers to arouse their audiences because female purity was deemed a priceless possession in metropolitan society at the time, while it allowed proslavery writers to shift the blame for the socio-economic factors that affected the viability of the plantation economy, such as natural decrease and the growth of the free(d) population, away from the planters. Both sides presented slave women's sexuality as a marked deviation from the metropolitan ideal of female purity. Antislavery writers and also many defenders of slavery suggested that slave marriage was a means to bring slave women closer to this ideal. Chapter four analyzes the debate about slave and apprenticed marriage. It is especially interested in the roles that the participants in the debate expected of slave and apprenticed wives and the place that they wanted them to occupy. The 1833 Abolition Act held out the promise of marriage becoming a voluntary and binding contract between two parties. Various legal and illegal practices adopted by planters, however, ensured that apprenticed marriage differed little from slave marriage. An analysis of writings that defended or criticized these practices will demonstrate that the discourses of slavery and abolition used the African Jamaican woman as a vehicle to articulate a variety of concerns, including the question whether white and black islanders would commit themselves to the rule of law upon freedom.

The last two chapters look at the debate about female flogging. Chapter five argues that this issue dominated in later antislavery writings not only because of its potential to arouse audiences but also because it enabled the authors to convince the public that the abolition of slavery had to be part of a bigger project, namely the transformation of West Indian societies. They not only described how the practice of female flogging debased slave women and their partners but also outlined its negative effects on the black and white men who inflicted the punishments and the white men and women who issued them. Locally-based proslavery writers responded fiercely to the antislavery attack on white Jamaican society. By invoking the metropolitan debate about penal reform, these men tried to counteract the antislavery representation of them as men beyond the pale of Englishness. Although the Abolition Act specifically forbade female flogging, female apprentices who were sent to the workhouse were subject to flogging. Chapter six examines the debate about female flogging and some other forms of female abuse in the workhouse during apprenticeship. This chapter provides an insight into the ways in which planters tried to counteract the decline in their arbitrary and proprietary power brought about by the Abolition Act and illustrates that not only during slavery but also during apprenticeship, the Imperial Government and the Jamaican legislature regularly and fiercely clashed.

By exploring the various and complicated ways in which race, gender, sexuality and other categories of difference intersected in the discussion about slave and apprenticed women in Jamaica, the six chapters will demonstrate that the discourses of slavery and abolition identified not just the slaves but also white men and women in the slave colonies as falling short of a canonised set of cultural values, and that as a result these groups were treated as different. As such, they will try to shed some light on the complex process by which differences among people have been constructed in such a way as to give some people power and privilege over others.[40]

1 Belly women
Slave women's childbirth practices

In his *History of Jamaica,* which was published in 1774, the planter and leading contemporary commentator on Jamaican affairs, Edward Long, attributed the high slave infant mortality rate amongst others to the 'unskilfulness or absurd management of the negroe midwives' and put forward some basic measures to enhance the survival rate of newborn slaves, such as a reduction in the workload of pregnant slave women.[1] It was not until the late 1780s, however, that defenders of slavery seriously began to examine childbirth practices on the estates and proposed methods to improve them. This change was largely triggered by abolitionist pressure. In 1784, James Ramsay, an Anglican missionary who had lived and worked in St. Kitts for 19 years, published his *Essay on the Treatment and Conversion of African Slaves*, which played a crucial role in arousing public concern about the horrors of the Atlantic slave trade. A former surgeon in the Royal Navy, Ramsay devoted considerable attention to the treatment of pregnant slave women. His account of slave women working until the last stages of their pregnancy, giving birth in 'dark, damp, smoky' huts and returning to work three weeks after the delivery, was strongly attacked by proslavery writers.[2] The absentee Nevis planter and proslavery campaigner James Tobin, for instance, wrote in his *Cursory Remarks upon the Rev Mr. Ramsay's Essay on the Treatment and Conversion of African Slaves in the British Sugar Colonies* (1785), that slave women were exempted from hard labour during the last months of their pregnancy, had access to a well-equipped lying-in room, were given baby clothes and a nurse to take care of them while lying-in, and generally did not return to work until four months after the delivery.[3] Similar rose-coloured accounts of slave women's childbearing experiences were provided throughout the period 1780–1834 and served mainly to counteract the abolitionist accusation that planters and their white employees failed to elevate slave women and thus lacked sensibility; that is, they failed to display the moral qualities of compassion, self-control, sympathy, and benevolence which were used in metropolitan society as markers of a civilized nature.[4] The abolitionist emphasis on slave women as mothers is not surprising, considering that metropolitan society at the time increasingly defined women as natural maternal beings and also came to see childhood as a stage in life in its own right.[5] Apart from Ramsay, however, few antislavery writers addressed slave women's childbearing practices.[6] They concentrated more on slave women's nursing practices, as these enabled them better to demonstrate that slavery did not recognize the most important role that nature had bestowed on women and which was essential for the moral development of any society.

Another and more important factor that explains the proslavery focus on slave women's childbearing practices is the natural decrease of the Jamaican slave population. In the 1770s, the Jamaican slave population declined by 2 per cent per year.[7] This demographic pattern contrasted sharply with that in the metropolitan society at the time. Between 1751 and 1821, the population in England rose from nearly 6 to 11 million as a result of earlier and more marriage and a rise in birth rates.[8] It was, however, not until the emergence of organized abolitionism in Britain in the late 1780s that defenders of slavery, including those who resided in the metropolitan society, began to express a concern about this evident infertility. Antislavery writers argued that the planters' wanton and improper exercise of the power that slavery gave them over the bodies they owned caused the population to decline. Proslavery writers responded by putting forward various causes that laid the blame with the slave population. They not only singled out slave women's childbearing and childrearing practices but also their sexual behaviour, which will be discussed in chapter three.[9] Various proslavery writers, however, feared that the abolitionists would succeed to ban the international slave trade and therefore argued that it was essential for planters to adopt measures on their estates to achieve natural increase. Amongst the various pronatalist proposals were not only measures to 'bribe' slave women into giving birth more often but also methods to relieve pregnant slave women and changes in delivery and lying-in practices.[10] These proposals, which were predominantly articulated by planters who resided in England, were not only shaped by metropolitan medical literature on childbirth and metropolitan gender ideals but also by various concerns that preoccupied planters besides natural decrease and abolitionist attacks, most notably the profitability and stability of their estates.

After the abolition of the slave trade in 1807, various proslavery writers continued to deflect blame for natural decrease by providing negative accounts of slave women's childbearing practices and/or by proposing measures to improve the lives of pregnant slave women. When the abolitionists stepped up their campaign to abolish slavery in the late 1820s, these accounts became overshadowed by rose-coloured pictures of slave women's childbearing practices. Opponents of apprenticeship used none of these three approaches to childbirth practices. Their discussion was a highly legalistic one, as it mainly aimed to account for changes in childbirth practices which, according to antislavery writers and many S.M.s, went against the spirit and letter of the 1833 Abolition Act.

The first two sections of this chapter concentrate on the proslavery debate about childbirth practices. The first examines accounts of childbirth practices in the slave community, which were as concerned with the behaviour of slave women as with that of the planters and their estate officers, and demonstrates that they conveyed three overlapping opinions about slave women's childbirth methods. The second section examines proposals that were put forward to make slave women change their childbirth practices and also looks at measures that were suggested to encourage slave women to give birth more often. The final section determines the extent to which these two sets of proposals to achieve natural increase were implemented on the estates and poses the question what happened to the implemented proposals during apprenticeship.

The chapter demonstrates that a concern about natural decrease and the possible abolition of the slave trade led planters and their white estate officers to develop a paternalistic attitude towards slave women. This attitude was expanded in the late 1820s and early 1830s as a result of increased abolitionist attacks on the slave system, but was largely undone after August 1834, when children born on the estates were no longer the property of the planters. The term 'paternalism' in slave studies is generally associated with the work of Eugene D. Genovese on the Antebellum South. Genovese used the term to refer not only to the set of punishments, allowances and privileges that planters bestowed upon their slaves but also to the planters' view of themselves as benevolent protectors of their enslaved labour force.[11] We shall see in this chapter and the next that resident and absentee Jamaican planters also adopted a paternalistic worldview; they often justified the institution of slavery with the argument that they did their utmost to raise the slaves up from a childlike status.

Before we explore the paternalism that underpinned the proslavery debate about childbirth, it needs to be stressed that we know relatively little about childbirth practices on Jamaican estates prior to the emergence of this debate. The first two sections may therefore present the paternalist attitude towards pregnant slave women in the late eighteenth and early nineteenth centuries as too much of a deviation from what went on before. The few sources that provide us with clues about childbirth practices before the rise of organized abolitionism, such as statements made in 1788 before a committee of the Privy Council that explored the volume and nature of the slave trade and its effects on Africa and the West Indies (hereafter, the Slave Trade Committee), suggest that on most estates pregnant and lying-in slave women were not singled out for special treatment.[12] Pregnant slave women were not exempted from flogging, although most were allowed to lie down on the ground with their belly in a specially-dug hole rather than being flogged in the usual way (hands tied to a tree and feet a few inches from the floor); were kept at work until the last weeks of their pregnancy; and gave birth in their own hut assisted by a part-time slave midwife who was seldom provided with bed linen or with clothes for the infant. The white estate doctor would only make his appearance during a slave delivery if there were complications and usually did not check upon lying-in slave women, who received the same allowances of food as other slave women and were expected to return to the field within three weeks after the delivery.[13]

CHILDBIRTH PRACTICES

Proslavery writers expressed three opinions about the treatment of pregnant and lying-in slave women: planters and their white employees cared excellently and disinterestedly for pregnant and lying-in women; slave women were given all the help to deliver healthy babies but Jamaican plantations failed to achieve natural increase because the women stubbornly clung to their own childbirth practices; and planters and estate officers seriously neglected the interests of pregnant and lying-in slave women. Considering the abolitionists' accusation that planters were to blame for the natural decrease of the Jamaican slave population and that white Jamaican men fell beyond the pale of civilization, it is no surprise that the first two opinions were mostly expressed by resident defenders of slavery. It needs to be mentioned, however, that some proslavery writers expressed more than one opinion in their works, such as the absentee planter and philanthropist Robert Hibbert. In his *Hints to the Young Jamaica Sugar Planter* (1825), which was a response to a pamphlet written by the former missionary Thomas Cooper that painted a very negative picture of slave life on Hibbert's estate, he argued that during the delivery slave women were always assisted by a midwife and nurse and supplied with abundant amounts of food, clothes and medicine. He also mentioned in this text, however, that planters could do more to alleviate pregnant and lying-in slave women and that many newborn infants died because of their mothers' ignorance.[14]

Like Tobin, various proslavery writers tried to deflect the planters' blame for the natural decrease by listing practices which allegedly had been universally adopted on plantations to relieve pregnant and lying-in slave women. They emphasized in particular the provision of adequate medical care during the delivery and the lying-period and the time off that slave women were given before and after the delivery.[15] While some of these practices could be found on Jamaican estates after the turn of the century, such as the practice of giving birth in a lying-in room in the estate hospital or in the hut assisted by a full-time midwife and nurse, the majority were never implemented, especially those put forward in the late 1820s when more and more abolitionists called for immediate abolition. It is unlikely, for example, that James McQueen, who defended the West India interest in his editorials in the *Glasgow Herald* and in various other publications, spoke the truth in 1824 when he stated that slave women were excused from all work from the third month onwards, especially if we take into account that sugar profit rates by this time had dropped considerably and that planters therefore looked for ways to increase output levels.[16]

Some proslavery writers excused the planters further by adding that as a result of the various indulgences[17] bestowed upon them, pregnant and lying-in slave women were as well-off, if not better off, than their lower-class counterparts in the mother country. James Tobin stated, for example, in 1785 that rural English women often gave birth while at work and that they returned to their domestic and other chores within three or four days.[18] As we shall see in the final section, Tobin largely exaggerated his account of slave women's childbirth practices. His remarks about the childbirth practices of rural English women, however, were fairly accurate. Many rural English women at the time worked until the onset of labour and few were able to follow the nine-day bed rest recommended by the midwife.[19] His argument, then, was a most powerful tool to combat abolitionist accusations regarding the planters' maltreatment of pregnant and lying-in slave women.

Writers who presented rose-coloured pictures of slave women's childbirth practices realized that their opponents could easily argue that some of these practices did not go far enough to facilitate natural increase, in particular the time off that women were given before and after their delivery. To prevent such criticism, they tried to justify these more limiting childbirth practices. Although some proslavery writers argued, like McQueen, that slave women did hardly any work from the moment that they were visibly pregnant, most pointed out that slave women were taken to the second gang soon after they were reported pregnant and were kept there till six or eight weeks before the delivery.[20] They justified this limited period of 'maternity leave' by arguing that it benefited the health of both the pregnant slave woman and her unborn child. This justification relied upon images of ignorant and indolent pregnant slave women. According to the planters Robert Hibbert and Gilbert Francklyn, pregnant slave women would not do any work after five months if given the choice, while another planter mentioned in 1825 that it was only by keeping pregnant women at work till the seventh month that estate officers could prevent them from 'carrying heavy loads' and doing other things that were not conducive to the health of their unborn infant.[21]

To justify and sustain the enslavement of men and women of African descent, it was essential for proslavery writers to portray the slaves as different from white men and women in the metropolitan society, preferably as naturally different. The justifications for a lying-in period of up to three weeks and the employment of full-time midwives rather than white estate doctors to deliver slave women did this indirectly by arguing that black women, who constituted the bulk of the female slave population, gave birth more easily and recovered more quickly after the delivery than white or (free or enslaved) coloured women.[22] Some justifications for the more limited childbirth practices undermined rather than enhanced the proslavery project of sustaining or prolonging slavery, as they assumed a degree of similarity between slave and white women. The anonymous author of the pamphlet *The Edinburgh Review and the West Indies* (1816) who had been 'long resident in the West Indies' used, for example, not only images of indolent and ignorant pregnant slave women to justify the relatively short period of 'maternity leave' but also the claim that distinguished metropolitan medical authors were convinced that pregnant women should be kept active until the very last stages of their pregnancy.[23] Following chapters will demonstrate more clearly that the proslavery writers' engagement with metropolitan discourses could both support and undermine their project and will also provide some tentative conclusions as to why this engagement was so complex.

The idea that planters and their white employees cared excellently and disinterestedly for pregnant and lying-in women was articulated throughout the period 1780–1834. The suggestion that Jamaican plantations failed to achieve natural increase because slave women stubbornly clung to their own childbirth practices, on the other hand, was mostly expressed in the late eighteenth and early nineteenth centuries and focussed predominantly on the delivery and lying-in period. The writers who expressed this opinion depicted planters as sensitive men by listing the changes that they had brought about in childbirth practices and excused them for not achieving natural decrease by arguing that slave women neglected their newborn infants and were ignorant of proper childcare practices. Or as Jesse Foot, a former estate doctor and staunch metropolitan supporter of West Indian planters, argued in 1805, there was 'no greater check to population than wrong treatment or deserted attention to an infant of the mother at that very time when of all others it stands most in need of its fostering care.'[24] Some authors presented slave women's 'deserted attention' of their newborn infants as an innate condition. James Adair, another former estate doctor, acknowledged in his 1790 defence of the planters, for instance, that the high slave infant mortality rate was largely the result of the 'inattention of the mother, whose *natural* affection for her offspring, does not seem in general to be so ardent as that of white women.'[25] Others, however, attributed slave women's motherly neglect to factors external of slave women, most notably the indulgences that planters bestowed on pregnant and lying-in slave women.[26] The novelist, playwright, and absentee planter Matthew Gregory [Monk] Lewis narrated, for example, in his account of two visits to his Jamaican estates entitled *Journal of a West India Proprietor* (1818), the case of a slave woman who, after having received an allowance of clothes and some other goods on the ninth day after the delivery, had left her infant 'without food for so long' while she had attended a dance on a neighbouring estate that it had died.[27] Lewis, however, also mentioned some cases which located slave women's motherly neglect in nature. After listing the various indulgences that he had bestowed on his pregnant and lying-in slave women, including a lying-in hospital where women were given the most 'nourishing and palatable food' and were daily visited by the white estate doctor, he attributed the high death rate of infants born in the hospital to the fact that even the best-intentional slave mothers were 'heedless and inattentive'.[28] He mentioned, for instance, a lying-in woman who had become so worried about her child's 'apparent sleepiness' that she had shaken it until it was wet with perspiration. Because she had taken the child to the window, it had caught a cold and, the next morning, was diagnosed with symptoms of lockjaw, a tetanus-like disease from which many young slave children died.[29] In following chapters, we shall see that various other writers with a vested interest in the continuation of the slave system attributed slave women's deviation from metropolitan norms of womanhood simultaneously to their nature and the system of slavery. Their remarks about slave women's natural difference aimed largely to excuse the planters for not achieving natural increase and other aims set by the abolitionists, while those that linked slave women's difference to the slave system served to support the often far-reaching real and proposed changes in the treatment of slave women.

The two examples of ignorant and neglectful mothers indicate that Lewis shifted in his journal between self-justification as a slaveholder on the one hand, as illustrated by his emphasis on the (natural) difference of the slave women, and as a man of sensibility on the other, which can be deduced from his account of the changes that he had implemented in childbirth practices.[30] Like most resident and absentee planters, Lewis struggled to weigh up his long-term and short-term economic interests. Although he was convinced that certain changes in childbirth practices would enhance the survival rate of slave infants and thus safeguard the long-term economic interests of his estates, he did not adopt all of them because some practices had the potential to cause social instability, which in turn could lead to a decline in output levels and hence, a drop in short-term profits. He had learnt this the hard way when he had ordered the nurses in the lying-in hospital to plunge babies into cold water immediately upon birth as a method to prevent lockjaw. As the lying-in women were so 'obstinate in their opposition' to this practice, he had been forced to discontinue it. His remark that the women 'took a prejudice against it into their heads', shows that he excused himself for the lack of natural increase and presented himself as a civilized man by accusing slave women not only of neglecting their newborn infants but also of not knowing, or not wanting to know, the proper way to care for their infants.[31]

Slave women were not only presented as ignorant and stubborn mothers in accounts of their opposition to new childbirth practices but also in stories about their preferred childbirth practices. Various proslavery writers criticized the women's preference to give birth in their own huts rather than in the lying-in rooms, which had been added to various estate hospitals from the late eighteenth century onwards, on the grounds that slave children born in slave huts were exposed to factors that could trigger such mortal diseases as lockjaw. In his statement before the 1832 Select Committee, former estate manager William Sand mentioned, for instance, that the smoke caused by the cooking that went on in the huts was 'very prejudicial to infant children', while others added that the huts were exposed to rain and draughts and were dirty.[32] In metropolitan society at the time there was also a concern about the lack of hygiene during home deliveries. Metropolitan medical writers, however, were more concerned about the impact that this could have on the health of the mother than on that of the infant. They were especially worried about the post-delivery infections that could result from a septic environment and which were a main cause of maternal mortality.[33] The proslavery writers' focus on the newborn infants stems, of course, from the fact that they were more valuable for the planters than their mothers.

The former estate doctors David Collins and James Grainger were equally critical of slave women's practice not to breastfeed their infants for the first nine days after the delivery. The women either used a slave wet-nurse or handfed their infant during that period. Collins pointed out in 1803 that 'nature disposes [the child] to suck and we should pursue her inclination', while Grainger mentioned ten years later that slave women were 'in general abundantly supplied with milk' and could thus immediately breastfeed their infants.[34] Both men, then, dismissed this practice as an irrational prejudice and proposed that slave women breastfeed as soon as possible. This recommendation should not surprise us considering the medical debate about breastfeeding at the time. Based on experiments conducted in lying-in hospitals, this debate argued that immediate breastfeeding not only strengthened the bond between mother and child but was also beneficial for both their health. As a mother's first milk contained important protective and nutritive functions, children who were immediately upon birth put to the mother's breast suffered less from colic, a common illness amongst newborn infants, while their mothers were protected from contracting milk fever, one of the main post-delivery infections.[35]

The childbirth practice that was most criticized, however, was slave women's reliance upon old and untrained midwives. Like Edward Long, the planter-dominated Jamaican legislature (House of Assembly) attributed in 1803 the lack of natural decrease largely to the 'ignorance of and want of skill in the midwives.'[36] Only two authors tried to explain in some detail how the slave midwife's lack of skill helped to cause a slave infant mortality rate of 275 per 1,000.[37] The historian Robert Renny and absentee planter Gilbert Mathison argued in the first decade of the nineteenth century that slave midwives made newborn infants susceptible to lockjaw because they neglected to purge the meconium (a baby's first stool which may be passed before birth); used a blunt lacerating instrument to cut the umbilical cord; left newborn infants exposed to the cold; did not change an infant's clothes during the first nine days; and applied 'leaves of some astringent plant's on ulcerated parts.[38] Contrary to most authors who expressed the second opinion about childbirth practices, these men suggested that slave women were not that different from white women and could even become like them. Renny, for example, argued that slave midwives should not be judged too harshly because they did not differ that much from 'their fairer sisters in Europe', who were also 'illiterate, generally careless, and often intoxicated', while Mathison recommended in his account of his four-year stay on his Jamaican property that planters should instruct young, locally-born slave women in proper midwifery skills by letting them live 'in families of white people'.[39]

Proslavery writers who presented rose-coloured pictures of childbirth practices or who blamed the lack of natural increase on slave women's neglect of their newborn infants and their irrational childbirth practices were thus not completely uncritical of Jamaican planters. Their remarks about the planters, however, are nothing compared to the fierce attacks issued by a few proslavery writers with experience of plantation life in the years immediately preceding and following the abolition of the slave trade and which were strikingly similar to those expressed by abolitionists. These men argued, for instance, that planters refrained from improving the condition of pregnant and lying-in slave women because they deemed it more expensive to keep up the numbers of their labour force through 'breeding' than through imports, not only because such improvements as the establishment of a lying-in room increased their costs but also because improvements interfered with the work that they could extract from slave women.[40] These men, however, not only attacked the planters but also tried to convince them to change the childbirth practices on their estates. They pointed out that implementing changes in childbirth practices would impact very little upon output levels and that the changes would aid the stability of the estates. The planter and historian William Beckford mentioned in 1788, for instance, that he had observed that slaves with children were 'the most steady, the most quiet and the most obedient' slaves on the estates.[41] It was furthermore suggested that improvements in the condition of pregnant and lying-in slave women could enable planters and their white estates officers to counteract the abolitionist criticism that they were insensitive and uncivilized men: 'pregnant women will be the object of peculiar care of the overseer, whose character as a humane and judicious manager, mainly depends on the natural increase of his negroes.'[42] Some writers also used the 'tried-and-tested' method to convince planters to adopt changes in childbirth practices. Gilbert Mathison suggested, for example, that planters should adopt the method to combat lockjaw which had been successfully pioneered by Dr Perkins in the lockjaw hospital in Falmouth and which consisted of a mixture of medicines containing antimonial lead (herbs that caused perspiration) and tepid baths.[43]

Proslavery writers, then, used two strategies to excuse planters for the lack of natural increase, while simultaneously presenting them as civilized men: exaggerating the real conditions of childbirth on estates and shifting the blame for natural decrease away from the planters onto slave women.

Both strategies depended heavily on images of slave women as different from white metropolitan women. Slave women's difference, however, was not only presented as a negative but also as a positive feature, as we have seen, for instance, in the comparisons that some authors drew between the condition of pregnant and lying-in women in the island and those in the mother country. To lend credibility to their statements, the writers invoked relatively accurate information and drew upon metropolitan medical texts.

PROPOSALS TO CHANGE CHILDBIRTH PRACTICES

The previous section has not only set out some of the more common rhetorical strategies used by proslavery writers but has also hinted at a problem with which many proslavery writers, especially resident planters, struggled in their accounts of slave women: regarding slave women as both producers and reproducers. Writers who were more concerned about the short-term profits of the estates were more likely to emphasize slave women's identity as producers, while those who were worried about the future prosperity of the estates gave more weight to the women's identity as reproducers. This struggle can also be seen in the various proposals that were put forward in the years leading up to the abolition of the slave trade to encourage slave women to give birth more often and to enhance the survival rate of newborn slave infants. While many proposals were based on and helped to reinforce the assumption that slave women were (naturally) different from white metropolitan women, there were also those that assumed a degree of similarity between slave and white women. This section is not only concerned, however, with the assumptions about slave women that underpinned the proposals but also with the factors that helped to shape them.

A monetary reward for successful deliveries and the release from hard labour for exceptionally fertile slave women were put forward as a means to encourage slave women to give birth more often. Most proslavery writers meant by a monetary reward not only a cash payment to slave women for every successful birth but also an annual sum of money handed out to slave mothers, depending on the number of their living children. Based on his experiences of plantation life in Barbados, Philip Gibbes suggested in 1788 that planters should award five shillings for every child born and that each Christmas they should give ten shillings to mothers with four or more children and five shillings to those with two to four children.[44] Annual cash payment schemes such as this one were based on the assumption that slave women lacked natural affection for their children and that they would only care well for their infants if they were generously compensated for their efforts. They aimed not just to increase slave women's fertility rate but also to make slave women more attentive mothers. The Bristol MP John Baker

Holroyd, who played a prominent role in defending his city's interests in the slave trade, suggested, for example, in 1790 that planters should only give slave women their reward of 20 shillings upon the child's first birthday.[45] Another assumption about slave women that informed the monetary reward schemes was that the women possessed, like white, middle-class metropolitan women, an innate desire for material, consumer pleasures.[46] This assumption about slave women's nature was also expressed in the debate about slave women's sexuality (see chapter three) and in various proslavery accounts about slave women's leisure activities.[47] While this innate quality was seen as dangerous for white, middle-class metropolitan women because it diverted their attention away from their role as homemakers, in the case of slave women it was presented not as a danger to be controlled but as an opportunity to be exploited. As we shall see in the next section, the proposal to reward women for births was wholeheartedly welcomed by the local planting class.

The proposals to exempt exceptionally fertile slave women from hard work used different measures of exceptional fertility. Some proposals only defined slave women with six or more living children as exceptionally fertile, while others regarded women with three children already as such. They also differed in terms of the release from labour offered. The most generous schemes were those that gave each slave mother an amount of time off during the week, increasing with the number of their living children. Robert Hibbert, for example, suggested in 1825 that slave mothers should be given a day off in the week for each of their living children, so that slave women with six or more children would be completely released from work. He seems to have built his proposal on the Trinidad Ordinance of 1800 which stipulated that mothers of three children were to have an additional free day out of crop and that those with seven or more were to be completely exempted from labour.[48] The least generous scheme was the one proposed by John Baker Holroyd in his *Observations on the Project for Abolishing the Slave Trade* (1790). He suggested that women who had brought up 'a specified number of children to the age of seven or eight years' should be given 'only certain exemptions from labour.'[49] Dr David Collins agreed with him that only slave women whose children were enrolled in the third gang should be released from work. Contrary to Baker Holroyd, Collins specified the number of children — six — and advocated a complete rather than a partial release from work.[50] By setting the number of children for the reward relatively high and stipulating that the reward was to be paid for by the slave mother's children, both schemes aimed to keep the planters' costs as low as possible and not to affect a drastic decline in output levels. Statistical information about the number of children that slave women gave birth to and managed to keep alive suggests that Baker Holroyd and Collins' proposals served more to convince the Imperial Government and the abolitionists (some of whom advocated a labour release scheme for women with three or more children), that planters took the natural decrease of the slave population seriously and elevated their slave women than as a practical solution to the problem of natural decrease.[51] When planter Rose Price conducted an inquiry into the fertility of the slaves on his Worthy Park estate in 1794–95, he found that only 89 of his 240 female slaves had given birth and that of these only 19 had managed to keep all of their children alive; 15 slave women had given birth to 1 child, 2 slave women to 2 children, and 2 slave women to 3 children.[52] In other words, very few Jamaican slave women would have qualified for release from hard labour under the schemes proposed by Baker Holroyd and Collins.

Concerns about the productivity and profitability of the estates also explain why proslavery writers dismissed the proposal of manumitting exceptionally fertile slave women as an incentive to childbirth. Dr Collins, for instance, pointed out that children born after their mother's manumission would be free and thus not add to the slave labour force.[53] William Beckford masked this long-term economic interest in his variation on the proslavery idea that African Jamaican people were better off in a state of slavery than freedom: 'To the absolute liberation of the slaves who shall brought up a number of children upon an estate, I must for the sake of *humanity* object; for when she shall become unable to work for her family, she will be unable to work for herself, and therefore will stand in need of double support.'[54] Interestingly, none of the early proslavery writers objected to manumission as an incentive to childbirth on the grounds that it would upset the social stability in the island because it would lead to an increase in the free population, a concern which was widely articulated in the proslavery debate about slave women's sexuality.

The proposals to enhance the survival rate of newborn slave infants fall into two categories: time off before and after the delivery and measures to improve the quality of the delivery. That proslavery writers did not put forward any proposals to provide slave women with some basic antenatal care, such as regular check-ups by the white estate doctor and extra allowances of food, is not surprising, as there was generally little known at the time about the impact of a pregnant woman's diet and other factors on the health of her unborn infant.[55] As for the proposals to reduce the workload of pregnant women and extend the lying-in period, these were less often articulated than the other set of proposals because their implementation had a greater impact on the estates' profitability, as they resulted in a marked decline in output levels. In 1798 the Colonial Secretary, the Duke of Portland, asked the Assembly to consider a law that would exempt slave women from field labour during the last six to eight weeks of their pregnancy and allow them the same time to recover from the delivery.[56] Several proslavery writers who had experience of plantation life strongly disapproved of his suggestion to withdraw heavily pregnant women from the field. They proposed instead that pregnant women should be given a lighter load when visibly pregnant but work up till the delivery. Like those writers who justified the limited period of 'maternity leave' in their otherwise rose-coloured pictures of slave women's pregnancy experiences, they pointed out that their proposal benefited the health of slave mother and child. To hide the economic concerns that underpinned their proposal, they not only supported it with images of naturally indolent and ignorant slave mothers but also with the remark that the work required of pregnant women benefited the estates 'very little'.[57] It was also concerns about the stability of the estates that led some writers to suggest that slave women should work until the very last stage of their pregnancy. Philip Gibbes, for instance, saw this as a means to prevent pregnant slave women from 'rambling' over, and even out of, the plantation.[58]

Several improvements in the quality of the delivery were put forward, which would significantly increase an estate's costs: the addition of a lying-in room to the estate hospital or the establishment of a special lying-in house separate from the hospital; a training and reward scheme for midwives; and an increased role of the white estate doctor in the delivery. The first proposal drew upon the various success stories of lying-in hospitals in the metropolitan society, which had been established since the 1740s and catered mainly for the lower classes.[59] It was not only informed by the idea that a lying-in room or special lying-in hospital provided a less septic environment than the hut and was thus more conducive to the health of newborn infants but also by a desire to control the slave population. Dr William Sells remarked, for example, in a statement before a committee of the Assembly in November 1815 that in lying-in rooms slave women could get 'better attention than in their own houses from the manager and the medical practitioner.'[60] Read alongside the dismissive remarks about the slave midwife mentioned in the previous section and the proposals to train the midwife mentioned further on, Sells' remark seems to suggest that it was not so much the pregnant or the lying-in slave woman who posed a threat for the estate management and who had to be controlled, but the slave midwife.

Slaves valued a space that was free from white interference. Their quarters and their provision grounds, that is the land on which they produced their own food, were far removed from the white residential buildings on the estate and were seldom visited by the planter and his white employees. Any attempts to increase white control over their semi-autonomous spaces were usually met with fierce opposition. It is no surprise, then, that those who were keen to see the delivery move from the hut to the lying-in room or lying-in hospital feared that few slave women would avail themselves of these new facilities that included a high degree of white control. James Adair therefore suggested in 1790 that, if necessary, slave women should be forced to use them.[61] Gilbert Mathison was convinced that such a policy would increase the threat of slave resistance and suggested instead that planters bribe both the midwife and pregnant slave women to give birth in the lying-in room or hospital. He mentioned that during his four-year stay on his estate, he had managed to persuade the midwife to use the lying-room through 'a very good, though gentle mode of reasoning' and also by increasing her fee for successful deliveries and that he had convinced pregnant slave women to give birth in the lying-room by offering them cloth upon the delivery.[62] Thus like the proposal to offer slave women cash payments for successful births, Mathison's was based on the idea that slave women were naturally ignorant of proper childcare skills and would only care well for children if their innate appetite for consumer goods was satisfied.

Robert Hibbert doubted whether Mathison's method could sufficiently counteract the ignorance and obstinacy of both the midwife and the mothers-to-be. He suggested in his 1825 manual that planters should not stop building lying-in rooms, as they provided the best environment for childbirth, but that they should always allow slave women the choice of giving birth in their own hut or in the lying-in room. To combat the dangers that the hut posed for the newborn infant, he suggested that planters should give the midwife and nurse sufficient food, clothes and medicine and call upon the white estate doctor 'in difficult cases'.[63] That Hibbert displayed a less disconcerted attitude towards slave women's preference to deliver in their own hut than Mathison can perhaps be explained by the fact that the island faced an increased risk of slave resistance when he wrote his account. In August 1823, some 1,000 slaves rose up against their owners and local authorities in Demerara. This revolt, which lasted for four months and caused the death of 250 slaves, may have impressed upon Hibbert the idea that it was crucial for planters not to create conditions that could trigger slave resistance, including forcing or bribing slave women into giving birth in a place that was subject to white control.[64]

Thus while some proslavery writers saw the lying-in room or lying-hospital as a means to exert greater control over the enslaved labour force, others perceived it as an institution that undermined effective slave control. A similar tension can be detected in the proposals that aimed to make slave midwives more attentive to the needs of the slave mother and her newborn infant. In the late eighteenth century, it was suggested that a monetary or material reward for every successful birth and the planter's repeated insistence upon the midwife to ask for assistance 'if the presentation of the child is not according to nature', would go some way to achieve this goal.[65] After the turn of the century, it was increasingly argued that high slave infant mortality rates could only be counteracted if the old, African-born midwives were replaced by young, locally-born women who had been taught a 'judicious method of managing infants' by the white estate doctor or, as Mathison suggested, by local white women.[66] This proposal was not only informed by a concern about the traditional practices that the old midwives used and which increased the risk of mortal infant diseases, but also by the threat that these women posed to the white estate officers' control over the slave labour force. Former planter and manager Thomas Roughley captured this threat most clearly in his 1823 manual for planters: 'They impress, by the nature of their office and by such assertions, such an awe and reverence for them on the minds of all classes of slaves, that few practising doctors wish to encounter them, or be called in to assist at a birth or give relief to a female slave in travail, which those harpies attend.'[67] Gilbert Mathison's suggestion that planters should bribe the slave midwife in order to move childbirth within the orbit of the estate hospital also hints at the midwives' position of importance in the slave community. Historians have argued that midwives occupied a high status in the slave community because they: delivered babies; provided other forms of healthcare; used African methods which had been handed down from generation to generation; and acted as an intermediate between the secular and the sacred worlds, as the babies that they delivered were seen as gifts from the ancestors.[68] The power that the old, African-born midwife commanded in the slave community, then, made the replacement of the old midwife by a young, locally-born woman instructed in European knowledge of obstetrics an inefficient policy to enhance the management's control over the slaves.

Considering the more urgent need to achieve natural increase and also the increased risk of slave resistance (massive slave revolts occurred in Barbados in 1816, Demerara in 1823, and Jamaica in 1831–32), it is not surprising that the proposal to train young, locally-born slave girls as midwives was only articulated after the abolition of the slave trade. Another factor that helped to shape this proposal is the metropolitan debate at the time about midwifery. In the course of the eighteenth century, many young men embarked upon midwifery as a means of gaining entry into general practice.[69] The medical profession and society at large, however, did not regard midwifery as a male profession. By the late eighteenth century, therefore, man-midwives tried to raise their social and professional profile. They did this, amongst others, by severely criticizing the old midwives who had learned their skill from other women, usually their mothers or grandmothers. They pointed out, for instance, that these traditional midwives intervened too quickly and inappropriately in childbirth because they were not well-trained. Proslavery writers seemed to echo their words in their accounts of old African-born midwives. Thomas Roughley stated, for example, in his slave management manual that 'they are generally egregiously ignorant, yet most obstinately addicted to their own way; but still if they find danger fast approaching, most probably brought on by their own tampering, they will cunningly run to the overseer, tell him of the dangerous case and that he should send for the doctor.'[70] The medical profession was keen to keep midwifery a female profession because it thought obstetrics a defiling activity. It fiercely attacked the man-midwives accusing them, for example, of endangering the sexual purity of mothers-to-be. It did not deny, however, the man-midwives' accusation that traditional midwives practised in such a way that many mothers and children were put at great risk. In fact, it produced manuals for midwives and, more importantly, suggested that the elderly, married midwives should be replaced by young, single girls who should be given a basic training in midwifery skills.[71] Proslavery writers, then, drew not only upon the rhetoric of this metropolitan debate but also on its proposals to improve the skills of midwives.

The metropolitan idea that midwifery degraded male medical practitioners is one reason why only a few proslavery writers advocated increased participation of the white estate doctor in the delivery. Another and linked reason is the fact that if implemented, the proposal would have increased the costs of the plantations. Planters paid white estate doctors an annual fee for each slave on their plantation. If they wanted them to also take on midwifery cases, they had to pay a higher annual fee. Dr Collins was convinced that this was one way in which planters could counteract the old, African-born midwives' lack of skill. Collins was not averse to the use of these midwives, perhaps because he feared the power that they exerted within the slave community. He believed that 'a few lessons from any gentlemen of the faculty or even one from her own sex' could improve their skills. He believed, however, that in spite of these basic midwifery lessons, slave midwives were capable of 'neglect' and that it was therefore essential that planters pay the doctor an extra fee so that they could call upon him in 'cases pronounced of emergency by the midwife'.[72]

Gilbert Mathison wanted the white estate doctor not only to assist in cases of emergency but also to pay routine visits to the lying-in room or lying-in hospital in order to check upon the lying-in women, the midwife, and the nurse.[73] This suggestion contrasts with his idea that young, locally-born women could be taught proper methods of childcare management by local white women. As mentioned, this training scheme expressed the assumption that slave women could become like white women. His suggestion to increase the role of the white estate doctor as a check upon the slave midwife, on the other hand, conveyed the idea that slave women would never make as good midwives as white women. Such contradictions are typical of proslavery discourse and stemmed from the conflicting demands upon proslavery writers. On the one hand, they had to justify slavery to themselves and the outside world which, as mentioned, required an emphasis on slave women's difference, while on the other they had to guarantee the future of the plantation economy. The second demand implied that they had to provide not only suggestions to improve the lives of the slaves but also rose-coloured accounts of their conditions that had to counteract abolitionist attacks on the behaviour of white islanders, and more importantly, avert interference of the Imperial Government in the workings of the plantation system. As many suggestions drew upon metropolitan discourses, they usually relied, like the rose-coloured accounts, on images of slave women as similar to white women.

Various factors shaped the proposals to encourage slave women to give birth more often and enhance the survival rate of newborn slave infants, which were predominantly articulated by men who had plantation experience but did not own slaves themselves. First, there was a concern about the profitability of the estates, which was seldom directly articulated. Most of the proposals put forward had to keep costs low, sustain output levels, and also prevent forms of social upheaval that could cause productivity to decline. And second, the metropolitan discourses on gender and childbirth. Considering the economic concerns of the authors, their proposals were relatively modest. The following section tries to assess whether resident planters also regarded them as such.

FROM BEARERS OF CHILDREN TO ECONOMIC BURDENS

The primary sources available do not make it easy to trace the various changes that were adopted in childbirth practices on Jamaican estates from the late 1780s till 1834. The aim of this section, however, is not to provide a conclusive account of these changes but to determine whether the proposals examined in the previous section, which were supported by images of slave women as both different from and similar to white, metropolitan women, exerted any influence. It will mention the proposals that planters (wholly or partially) adopted on their estates and speculate about the motives underpinning their action. The section furthermore seeks to outline the main reactions of the planters to the 1833 Abolition Act by examining what happened to the implemented proposals after August 1834.

The only changes in childbirth practices that were legislated were those that aimed to encourage slave women to give birth more often.[74] In 1792, the Assembly enacted that mothers with six or more living children should be exempted from hard labour and their owners from paying taxes for them. It furthermore stipulated that owners of estates that showed natural increase should give overseers three pounds to be divided equally between the slave mother, the slave midwife, and the overseer.[75] These two pieces of legislation undermined the proslavery idea that natural decrease was caused not by the planters' and overseers' management of the slaves but by slave women's sexual promiscuity and ignorance of proper childbirth and child-rearing practices. The two acts echoed some of the proposals mentioned in the previous section. The second, for example, strongly resembled John Baker Holroyd's suggestion to give slave women a cash reward for every successful birth. It was more generous, however, than Holroyd's scheme as it offered slave women who had delivered a healthy child one pound rather than 20 shillings, which illustrates the importance that planters attached to this measure as a means to facilitate natural increase. Although the second act did not include Holroyd's suggestion not to give slave women the reward immediately upon birth, it seems that most planters did not give slave women the one pound until a month after the delivery, in order to prevent infanticide. The fact that slave women received the monetary reward alongside a material reward (usually a bottle of rum or a set of baby clothes), which was also commonly offered to poor women in metropolitan society at the time, demonstrates most clearly that planters did not fear but exploited slave women's desire for material, consumer goods.[76] Evidence suggests that some estates had already adopted the practice of offering slave women both a material and monetary reward for successful birth several years before the act was passed. A manager of absentee plantations told a committee of the House of Lords in 1792, for instance, that for the last three years it had been practice on the estates in his care that 'every Negro woman who should produce a child a month old, should have two dollars as a reward.'[77] The 1792 act to give slave women a small sum of money for every child delivered, then, built not only on proposals articulated by pro-slavery writers but also on existing plantation practices.

Not surprisingly, the monetary reward for successful births featured extensively in the rose-coloured accounts of childbirth practices.[78] To present themselves as 'men of sensibility', some planters emphasized that they offered slave women more than the one dollar stipulated by law. Robert Hibbert mentioned, for instance, in 1825 that he gave slave women a 'doubloon' and an 'ornament of dress' for every child delivered.[79] Monk Lewis mentioned in his journal that in addition to the one dollar, he provided each new slave mother with a 'scarlet girdle with a silver medal in the centre'. The medal entitled the slave woman to 'marks of peculiar respect and attention', such as being the first to be served breakfast in the field. It is possible that Lewis based his reward scheme on the one proposed by Philip Gibbes in 1788, as upon every additional child an additional medal was to be affixed to the belt, entitling the slave mother to even more privileges.[80] His and other planters' accounts of rewarding practices, however, did little to convince the abolitionists that planters were not insensitive to the needs of slave women. For the abolitionists, the practice of giving slave women money or material goods for giving birth was as much a degrading practice as the purchasing of slave women from Africa to keep up numbers.[81] It was not so much abolitionist criticism, however, that underpinned the repeal of the act in 1827 but a concern about declining profit rates of sugar, from 9.6 per cent in the period 1799–1810 to 5.3 per cent in 1820–34.[82] The repeal was one of several measures taken by planters (as individuals on their estates and as members of the Assembly) to cut their costs and thus enable them to keep their estates profitable.[83] The justification given for the repeal does not hint at this motive. It argues instead that a repeal had been necessary in order to create more stability on the estates:

> the premium for the birth is not continued, because it practically proved to be a source of jealousy and ill-will amongst the slaves on a property; the mother who had lost her child before the age when the premium was received, envying her more fortunate fellow servant.[84]

This justification, which shifted the blame for the lack of natural increase from the planters to the slave women, reinforced the idea that slave women lacked an intrinsic affection for their offspring and were driven by an innate desire to consume.

The 1792 act to exempt slave women with six or more living children from field labour drew upon some of the least generous schemes to reward exceptionally fertile slave women, although it did not include, like the one implemented in the Leeward Islands, the recommendation that such women should only be released from work if their youngest child was old enough to join the third gang.[85] Few slave women qualified for the reward because of the high slave infant mortality rate. On Mesopotamia Estate, for instance, only 1.4 per cent of all slave women aged 25–34 were exempted from field labour on account of the number of their living children.[86] Realizing that the act failed to function as an incentive for slave women to give birth more often, the Assembly amended it in 1816 to include both biological and adopted children.[87] It was common practice for slave women to adopt children whose mothers had died in childbirth, had been sold away, or who for other reasons were unable to take care of them. Adoption gave slave women who had children respect and recognition within the slave community, while it allowed childless slave women to achieve the social status associated in the slave community with motherhood. According to Lucille Mathurin, Jamaican slaves followed their African ancestors' tradition of regarding motherhood as the fulfilment of female adulthood. As a result, they not only treated childless women as objects of contempt, derision or compassion, but also made adoption an acceptable substitute for natural motherhood.[88] The amendment suggests, then, that planters were aware of the slaves' ideology of good mothering and that they used elements of it to reinforce their own ideas of slave mothering. Even by including adopted children, however, few slave women qualified for the release from labour. The fact that this incentive to childbirth did not have a major impact on productivity and profitability levels and could also easily be mobilized to convince the Imperial Government and abolitionists that planters elevated slave women explains, perhaps, why it was never repealed during slavery.

In order to enhance the survival rate of newborn slaves, most planters followed the suggestion to give pregnant slave women a lighter workload; that is, moving them from the first to the second gang when visibly pregnant and allowing them to join the third gang during the last stages of their pregnancy. Concerns about productivity led them to ignore the Duke of Portland's suggestion to exempt women from work six to eight weeks before and after the delivery.[89] Planter Robert Scott, for instance, told the 1832 Select Committee that pregnant women did the 'lightest work' until the very end, while Lady Nugent, the wife of the governor, mentioned in 1802 in her diary that slave women on Clifton Estate returned to work within 14 days after the delivery.[90] Several large estates added a lying-in room to the estate hospital or built a lying-in house. As most of them followed Robert Hibbert's suggestion to allow slave women the choice to give birth in their hut or in the lying-in room, few slave women made use of these new facilities.[91] Considering the debate about the slave midwife, it is surprising to find that planters did very little to counteract her alleged lack of skill. There is no evidence that they paid the estate doctor the extra fee for midwifery cases, replaced the old, African-born midwives by young, locally-born women, or provided slave midwives with a basic training. To make slave midwives more attentive to the needs of slave mother and child, planters gave them the legally required dollar for every successful birth; provided them with sufficient medicine, bed linen, and baby clothes; and exempted them from other work on the estate.[92] Although these measures did not come cheap, planters were more willing to adopt them than some of the other proposals to improve the midwives' skill because they did not entail the risk of social instability. And finally, many planters gave pregnant and lying-in women extra allowances of sugar, rice and flour.[93] It seems, then, that they had some idea that the diet of slave mothers before and after the delivery had an impact on the survival rate of newborn infants, although they saw its importance more in terms of quantity than quality.[94]

Jamaican planters were thus not averse to the various proposals to achieve natural increase but were highly selective in their implementation. That they regarded slave women first as producers and second as reproducers can be deduced from the fact that the proposals that they adopted were those that cost them very little, did not greatly affect the output levels of their estates, and could easily serve as evidence of their own sensibility. The extent to which they implemented the proposals was also determined by a concern about stability (especially in the case of the midwife and the lying-in room) and by practical concerns. The small number of doctors in the island, for instance, made it difficult to increase their role in childbirth, while the lack of resident white families practically ruled out Mathison's idea to provide young, locally-born women with training in proper midwifery skills by letting them live with white families.[95] If we look at slave birth rates for the period after the abolition of the slave trade, we have to conclude that the adopted changes in childbirth practices had very little effect. The birth rates fell from 29.1 per 1,000 in 1817–20 to 27.4 per 1,000 in 1826–29.[96] For a marked increase to occur, planters would have had to attach equal weight to the two identities of slave women (producers and reproducers) and also acknowledge blame for the lack of natural increase by shifting their attention away from incentives to give birth towards improvements in the condition of pregnant and lying-in women.

Although there are no accurate birth rates available for the period 1834–38 because slave registration came to an end in Jamaica in 1832, it is safe to assume that the birth rate further declined as the condition of pregnant and lying-in women significantly worsened after the onset of apprenticeship.[97] Most of the changes that had been brought about in childbirth practices since the late 1780s were reversed. Thus pregnant women were seldom given a lighter workload; full-time midwives were replaced by part-time midwives; the material reward upon successful delivery was discontinued;

mothers with six or more living children were no longer exempted from work; and women had to return to work sooner after the delivery. Abolitionists, several S.M.s, the governor and various members of the Colonial Office (hereafter, critics of apprenticeship) were convinced that the former indulgences for pregnant and lying-in women were essential for women to properly carry out their maternal duties and that their withdrawal was a violation (in letter or in spirit) of the 1833 Abolition Act. In other words, the critics thought that amongst the various rights bestowed on the ex-slaves under the 1833 Abolition Act was the right to mother. Some added that by withdrawing the indulgences, planters not just violated the Abolition Act but also severely endangered the aim of turning Jamaica into a stable and prosperous island upon full freedom. Former Governor Sligo mentioned, for instance, in 1837 that the withdrawal of the indulgences gave female apprentices a sense of having been 'defrauded of their rights', implying that it could make them distrustful of the law upon freedom.[98] And an article published in *The Edinburgh Review* in 1838 pointed out that the withdrawal would fail to endear the planters to the apprentices, and thus increase the chance that many apprentices would prefer independent production over plantation work after the termination of apprenticeship.[99]

Critics of apprenticeship were even more outraged about two 'new' childbirth practices, which further increased the burden of pregnant and lying-in apprentices. On many estates women were forced to 'pay' for the services of a midwife and for their lying-in period, by working extra hours for the plantation after they returned to work. In addition, pregnant female apprentices were as likely to be sent to the workhouse to dance the treadmill and/or work in the penal gang as other female apprentices.[100] Planters and planter-friendly S.M.s justified the first practice with the argument, which will be explained in more detail in the next chapter, that the indulgences for pregnant and lying-in women were 'luxuries' that had to be obtained by additional effort. The second practice was supported with the claim that pregnant women were troublemakers; they not only turned up late in the field but also refused to do any work 'three to four months' before the delivery.[101] Planters and their supporters, then, argued indirectly that sending pregnant apprentices to the workhouse was a means to teach female apprentices to carry out the duties associated with their apprenticeship.

It needs to be stressed that some critics of apprenticeship also presented pregnant and lying-in female apprentices as troublemakers. S.M. John Daughtrey, for instance, mentioned in several of his reports that the behaviour of pregnant women had improved less than that of other categories of apprentices. Contrary to the planters and planter-friendly S.M.s., he excused the women for their unruly behaviour by arguing that it was the sheer result of having lived under a system which for decades had indulged pregnant and lying-in women.[102] He and various other critics, however, were convinced that slavery compared favourably to apprenticeship. They pointed out, for instance, that the two new practices had led to an increase in the infant mortality rate. The practice of sending pregnant women to the workhouse had led to more miscarriages and stillbirths, while the extra labour that women had to pay for the 'luxury' of using the services of a midwife and not returning to work immediately upon birth had prevented apprenticed mothers from devoting sufficient attention to their newborn infants.

Some attempts were made to end the two new practices. Several S.M.s who had been faced with demands from planters and overseers to order women to work several Saturdays in order to repay the time lost during the delivery, asked Governor Sligo in 1835 how they should respond to such demands, especially considering the fact that the local Abolition Act, which had to give effect to the 1833 Abolition Act, only stipulated extra work as a punishment for 'wilful absence' from work.[103] Sligo issued a guideline for S.M.s in which he told them that they should regard pregnancy as any other illness and that they could thus not order female apprentices to repay time lost in labour.[104] As the 1833 Abolition Act did not have a particular clause upon this issue, however, he consulted Lord Glenelg, the colonial secretary. Glenelg's remark that 'I scarcely know how to argue in favour of the claim of women in childbirth to be exempted from all responsibility for their unavoidable absence from their duties', suggests that he regarded the female apprentices' right to mother not just as a legal but also as a natural right.[105]

Sligo's 1835 guideline for S.M.s did not put an end to the practice of demanding extra work for time lost in labour. The abolitionists Joseph Sturge and Thomas Harvey observed, for instance, during their visit to the island in 1837 that on many estates women had to work nine Saturdays to repay time lost in giving birth and lying-in.[106] Many S.M.s also ignored the circular that Sligo's successor Lionel Smith issued in December 1837, which equally presented maternity as a serious duty and responsibility. It instructed S.M.s not to send pregnant women to the workhouse but to order a form of punishment 'suited to their state of infirmity' and which they could carry out in their free time.[107] This circular followed the publication of the report of an inquiry into the workhouse of St. Ann's. In September 1837, Governor Smith had appointed the S.M.s Daughtrey and Gordon as head of a commission (hereafter, Daughtrey and Gordon Commission) to investigate accusations about abuses in this workhouse made in the abolitionist pamphlet *A Narrative of Events Since the First of August 1834 by James Williams, an Apprenticed Labourer in Jamaica* (1837).[108] The report concluded that many planters and overseers had sent women far advanced in pregnancy to the S.M. on account of minor offences resulting from their condition, knowing (and in many instances also hoping) that the women would be sentenced to time in the workhouse. The estate constable James Brown, for example, had told Daughtrey and Gordon that he had tried to prevent Elisabeth Bartley from being sent to the workhouse for not having turned up on time in the field and not keeping up with the gang, by telling both the overseer and S.M. Light that she 'was with child'. Neither the overseer nor the S.M., however, listened to his plea and Elisabeth was subsequently sent to the workhouse to 'dance the treadmill for four days'.[109]

The report of the Daughtrey and Gordon Commission also illustrated the loss of life that resulted from sentencing pregnant women to the workhouse. Various witnesses mentioned that pregnant women who had spent time in the workhouse often miscarried or gave birth to children who died shortly after the delivery.[110] This feature of apprenticeship was an excellent means for abolitionists to appeal to their audiences to fight for a premature end to the system. The popular pamphlet *A Statement of Facts Illustrating the Administration of the Abolition Law and the Sufferings of the Negro Apprentices* (1837) told its readers, for instance, about Harriet who had 'delivered of a dead child' after five weeks of hard labour in the workhouse. Even more harrowing was its account of Sarah Murdoch, who had been sentenced to two weeks of hard labour and the treadmill when she was seven months pregnant. On her fourth day in the workhouse, she 'suddenly gave birth to an infant, which fell to the ground dead.' To convince the audience that white men in the island had become even more insensitive after August 1834, the author emphasized that the workhouse supervisor had paid no attention to Sarah's request to bury her child.[111]

Planters and their friends, then, argued that pregnant and lying-in apprentices committed 'crimes' when they did not turn up on time in the field or when they failed to return to work by the time stipulated by the overseer. Critics, on the other hand, presented the women's failure to fulfil their legal obligations not as a crime but as a logical result of their condition which required, according to them, not punishment but protection. Some critics tried to explain why planters and overseers had begun to punish rather than indulge pregnant and lying-in women after August 1834. The coloured S.M. Richard Chamberlaine mentioned two reasons: a concern about profit levels and a desire to sustain as much of their former power as possible.[112] Sligo agreed with Chamberlaine that the way that they treated their pregnant and lying-in workers allowed planters to hold on to much of their former power because it reduced the rights accorded to female apprentices under the 1833 Abolition Act. He did not, however, accept Chamberlaine's idea that it was also triggered by concerns about profitability. In his *Jamaica under the Apprenticeship System* (1838), a pamphlet which he wrote after his resignation as governor and which acted as a weapon in the hands of the abolitionists, he argued that planters could easily have afforded to continue the indulgences for pregnant and lying-women because 'the years 1834, 1835, and 1836 were the most favourable years which have been known for a long time.'[113] For him, and also for the abolitionist Joseph Sturge, the withdrawal of the indulgences and the additional hardships that planters had placed upon pregnant and lying-in apprentices were nothing but spiteful acts because the children that the women gave birth to were free and thus of no value for the planters.[114]

Output and profit levels during apprenticeship confirm Sligo's opinion that economic motives were not the overriding factor in the worsening of the condition of pregnant and lying-in women after August 1834. During apprenticeship, output levels declined by 23 per cent, a drop which was expected because field apprentices could only work 40½ hours per week. Planters were nevertheless able to keep up their profit levels because of the compensation that they received for their slaves and the rise of the price of sugar on the London market by almost 40 per cent during apprenticeship.[115] Planters, then, could have afforded to continue the indulgences. The fact that such measures as sending elderly midwives back to the field and letting women work until far advanced in pregnancy would have led to only marginal increases in output levels, provides further support for Sligo's idea that it was a concern about the impact of the 1833 Abolition Act on their social rather than on their economic status that led planters to withdraw the indulgences and adopt additional practices that deteriorated the quality of childbirth.

During slavery, the planters' superior social position in the island had relied on the ownership and control of their labour force. By freeing children under six, extending the rights of their workers and, perhaps most importantly, by withdrawing their right to punish their workers, the 1833 Abolition Act severely compromised the planters' social status. In order to hold on to their former superior status, planters tried to exercise as much control over their workforce as possible, using both legal and extra-legal means. It is no surprise that in this attempt planters focussed more on female than male apprentices. The 1833 Abolition Act bestowed namely various rights upon female apprentices which reminded planters more of their former social status than the rights accorded to male apprentices. The 1833 Abolition Act not only gave women the right to 'own' the children they gave birth to but also the right not to be flogged. In chapter six, we shall see that planters used various means to undo the ban on female flogging, which symbolized for them more than anything else their loss of control over their workforce. It was mainly by withdrawing the reward for exceptionally fertile women and the indulgences for pregnant and lying-in women and by placing additional hardships on these categories of female apprentices, that planters tried to displace the anger that they felt about no longer being the legal owner of the bodies that toiled for them.

Planters and the S.M.s, workhouse officers, and Assembly members who supported them in their cause to uphold their former position of power (hereafter, opponents of apprenticeship) counteracted the critics' accusations not only by arguing that the withdrawal of the indulgences and the additional hardships placed on pregnant and lying-in women helped to facilitate the transformation of the ex-slaves into free wage labourers but also by pointing out that these childbirth practices were perfectly legal. They mentioned, for instance, that the withdrawal of the indulgences was in line with clause 16 of the local Abolition Act which stipulated that only allowances and indulgences that had had statutory basis prior to August 1834 were to be continued.[116] Lawyer and former public prosecutor of Mauritius, John Jeremie[117] questioned this argument in his analysis of the Jamaican Abolition Act, which he delivered before the Select Committee that was set up in April 1836 as a result of abolitionist campaigning and which aimed to 'enquire into the working of the apprenticeship in the colonies, condition of apprentices, laws and regulations affecting them' by limiting itself to the island of Jamaica (hereafter, 1836 Select Committee).[118] Jeremie argued, along with the Jamaican Attorney General, that clause 16 was a severe limitation of clause 11 of the 1833 Abolition Act, which stated that apprentices were entitled to the same allowances 'as by "any law" in force in the colony' when they were slaves. According to Jeremie, this meant that apprentices were not just entitled to those allowances which had been mentioned in the last Slave Law, including the provision that women with six or more children were allowed to withdraw from field work, but also to those which had been 'settled and reasonable customs' and had 'the force and operation of laws', such as extra allowances of food for pregnant and lying-in women.[119] That Jeremie saw clause 16 of the Jamaican Abolition Act as a deliberate attempt by Jamaican planters to counteract the change in their social status can be deduced from his remark that if the Imperial Government had realized that the Jamaican Assembly would have regarded the customary allowances and indulgences as 'mere matter of favour' rather than 'conveniences which ... proved indispensable to render the lot of the negro tolerable', it would 'certainly have made such an enactment' that would have guaranteed previous allowances and indulgences.[120]

To improve the condition of pregnant and lying-in apprentices, Jeremie did not suggest a circular to S.M.s instructing them to ensure that pregnant and lying-in women were to receive their former indulgences. He recommended instead that the Imperial Government issue an Order in Council that would clarify the meaning of the term 'any law' in clause 11 of the 1833 Abolition Act.[121] This proposal seems to stem from Jeremie's distrust of a large number of S.M.s. Some S.M.s read clause 11 in the same way as Jeremie and did their utmost to ensure that pregnant and lying-in women received their former indulgences. Former S.M. Robert Madden mentioned, for instance, in his statement before the 1836 Select Committee that he had ordered overseers not to let pregnant women 'work up till within two months of their parturition, except at very light work.'[122] Many S.M.s, however, did not regard clause 16 as a violation of the 1833 Abolition Act and made sure that pregnant and lying-in apprentices who defied authority by taking their former indulgences were sent to hard labour in the workhouse, such as S.M. Rawlinson who in 1837 sentenced Eliza Nathan to ten days in the workhouse for trying to 'sit down' a month before the delivery.[123] It took nearly two years before Jeremie's suggestion to improve the condition of pregnant and lying-in apprentices was adopted. The Act to Amend the Act for the Abolition of Slavery in the British Colonies (hereafter, the 1838 Amendment Act), which was proposed in March 1838 as a means to remedy the abuses of the workings of apprenticeship that had come to light in the report of the Daughtrey and Gordon Commission and other accounts of the system and which became law in April, contained a clause which stated that apprentices were entitled to all allowances and indulgences that they had been entitled to 'by law or custom, for at least three years before the abolition of slavery.'[124] Upon receipt of the Amendment Act, the Jamaican Council (the appointed Upper House of the Legislature) recommended that legislation be passed to end apprenticeship on 1 August 1838. Based on the assumption that if they passed such legislation they would thereafter be able 'to legislate for the benefits of all classes without any further Parliamentary interference', the Assembly approved the Act Abolishing the Apprenticeship of Praedial Labourers, which was signed by Governor Smith on 16 June 1838.[125] The next chapter will provide further examples of the Imperial Government's reluctance to force Jamaican planters to fulfil their duties under the 1833 Abolition Act and recognize the new status of their workers, and will furthermore mention some factors that may explain the Government's attitude.

We see, then, that Jamaican planters used at least two ways to counteract the change brought about in their socio-economic status by the 1833 Abolition Act. As members of the Assembly, they devised a local Abolition Act which interpreted the Imperial Act in such a narrow way that pregnant and lying-in women were no longer indulged. And, as hinted at by estate constable James Brown in his statement before the Daughtrey and Gordon Commission, they asked S.M.s to turn a blind eye to any treatment of pregnant and lying-in apprentices on their estates that violated the local Abolition Act and also had them do their bidding by persuading them to send recalcitrant pregnant and lying-in apprentices to the workhouse and force female apprentices to pay back time lost in labour. In case they faced a S.M. who tried to interpret the 1833 Abolition Act in both letter and spirit, planters often undertook action to have him replaced. Former S.M. Charles Brown, for example, told the 1836 Select Committee that in those cases in which he had interfered on behalf of pregnant women, their owners had complained to the governor and had threatened him with action for damages.[126] The two measures indicate, then, that while planters had deemed it essential during slavery to treat their female workers as both producers and reproducers in order to keep up their socio-economic status (even though they often failed to give equal weight to the two identities), they were convinced after August 1834 that to uphold their former status they had to if not completely annihilate than at least give a very low priority to the women's identity as childbearers.

CONCLUSIONS

The onset of a system that threatened the future of their economic enterprises and which posed a danger to their superior social status led planters to adopt a variety of measures to sustain as much of their former socio-economic status as possible. This chapter has mentioned some of the main methods used and has also suggested that planters and their friends justified attempts to keep the old race relations in the island intact with images of apprenticed women that placed them beyond the pale of womanhood. The following chapter will show that their justifications also relied on images of apprenticed women as incapable of exercising the duties and responsibilities associated with freedom.

This chapter has not only outlined the main strategies used by planters to uphold their socio-economic status after August 1834 but has also described the changes adopted on Jamaican plantations to achieve natural increase, which engaged to some extent with proposals put forward by proslavery writers since the late 1780s but failed to achieve a rise in birth rates and a decline in slave infant mortality rates. Some of the proposed and implemented changes in childbirth practices during slavery can be seen as a form of what Foucault has called 'disciplinary power'; that is, a modern mode of power organized around processes of normalization and surveillance, such as the proposals and attempts to move childbirth from the hut to the estate hospital and to increase the role of the white estate doctor in childbirth, and Rose Price's enquiry into the fertility of his slaves. Other examples of the planters' use of modern power to control their slave population that relate to childbirth practices are the clause in the 1816 Slave Law which stipulated that planters had to keep extensive records about the increase and decrease of their slave population and Dr William Sells' suggestion that planters should keep a detailed record of slave women's childbirth experiences.[127] According to Foucault, disciplinary power emerged during the Enlightenment and displaced 'sovereign power'; that is, a pre-modern form of power based on the subjection of bodies. In recent years, Foucault's account of modern power has been severely questioned, especially by colonial historians. Diana Paton, for example, has argued in her recent analysis of punishment practices in Jamaica between 1780 and 1870 that modern power works on both the body and the mind.[128] Chapters five and six will lend support to her claim that Jamaican planters not only tried to keep their slaves docile and hardworking by closely surveying their lives but also by inflicting pain on their bodies.[129]

The rhetoric that accompanied the changes in childbirth practices between the late 1780s and 1838 was highly contradictory. Childbirth practices within the enslaved and apprenticed community were predominantly described as a major deviation from those in metropolitan society, especially when the planters' socio-economic status was most at threat. At times, however, these practices were seen as similar to, or at least capable of becoming like, those in metropolitan society. As we have seen in the case of the planters Mathison and Hibbert, such contradictions could even occur within the space of one work. The proslavery discussion about childbirth, however, was not only contradictory but also changing. During slavery, planters argued that childbirth was an important duty and responsibility expected of African Jamaican women but ceased to articulate this after August 1834, when all children born were free.

Through such remarks that slave women were not naturally endowed with affection for their offspring and that they were not intelligent enough to know what was best for their unborn infants, proslavery writers helped to reinforce the assumption widely expressed in metropolitan society at the time that although childbirth was a natural phenomenon, women needed instruction in it. In the course of the eighteenth century, childbirth gained the attention of the medical establishment and numerous treatises were written, telling pregnant women and those who delivered them what they had to do in order to bring healthy babies into the world. These treatises were part of a wider metropolitan discourse about motherhood that constructed maternity as 'noble, strong, and self-sacrificial'.[130] The following chapter explores the ways in which proslavery writers engaged with this discourse and tries to show how their engagement differed from those who supported the abolition of the system of slavery.

2 Pickeniny mummas
Slave women's childrearing practices

In the course of the eighteenth century, motherhood in metropolitan society was increasingly presented as a woman's main identity. Novels, conduct books, medical treatises and magazine essays not only glorified this identity but also specified the main duties expected of mothers, as it was assumed that although motherhood was a natural thing it could be improved upon. A mother first of all had to raise healthy children. This duty implied, amongst others, that she had to provide her children with nutritious food and had to keep them clean. Second, she was expected to show a deep affection for her children by staying within the close proximity of a newborn infant, giving individual attention to each child, and by undertaking such activities as singing and talking to her children. Third, she had to turn her children into responsible citizens, which meant that she had nurture their morality through persuasion and example and inculcate in them general standards of behaviour by teaching them industry, regularity, correct speech, and discipline. And finally, she was supposed to put her children's needs before her own. Women who did their utmost to be a caring, loving, responsible and self-effacing mother were elevated to a higher status within society, while women who did not fully embrace this motherhood ideal were regarded as abnormal and also as unfeminine.[1]

This chapter explores the engagement of discourses of slavery and abolition with the metropolitan motherhood ideal. Pro- and antislavery writers and also critics and opponents of apprenticeship wanted African Jamaican women to live up to the ideal. We shall see that because of their different projects, they emphasized different attributes of the motherhood ideal, expressed different beliefs about enslaved and apprenticed women's ability to exercise all four attributes, and also proposed different measures to make the women better mothers. The chapter is not only concerned with the various factors that shaped the proposals to enable enslaved and apprenticed women to live up to all or some of the attributes of the metropolitan motherhood ideal and the extent to which they were implemented on the estates but also with the mother images used to justify them, which ranged from the selfish, ignorant, and indifferent mother to the affectionate and struggling mother. It will be shown that both sides in the debate about enslaved and apprenticed women's childrearing practices[2] used similar mother images to justify their divergent plans to make the women better mothers.

The first section examines the proslavery discussion about slave women's childrearing practices, which consisted of rose-coloured accounts to excuse the planters for the lack of natural increase and to counteract abolitionist attacks on their masculinity, and of appeals to planters to change the childrearing practices on their estates. Both the rose-coloured accounts and the appeals to the planters emphasized a mother's duty to raise healthy children. Antislavery writers were initially also concerned about this attribute of motherhood. By the mid-1820s, however, they were far more interested in a mother's obligation to show affection for her offspring. The second section examines this shift in antislavery writing and mentions the main rhetorical strategies used by antislavery writers to appeal to their audiences, some of which were also employed by proslavery authors. Pro- and antislavery writers did not devote much attention to a mother's task to turn her children into responsible citizens. This motherly duty played a considerable role, however, in accounts of childrearing practices produced by critics and opponents of apprenticeship. The third section explains the reasons for this and illustrates more clearly than the two other sections that motherhood in the discourses of slavery and abolition was a site of political and cultural contestation. It also pays considerable attention to the changes in childrearing practices after August 1834, which demonstrates once more that planters ceased their paternalistic attitude towards mothers when children born were no longer their property. The last section sums up the main differences in the ways in which the two sides in the debate about childrearing practices on Jamaican estates invoked the metropolitan motherhood ideal.

A DUTY OF LESSER CONCERN

The proslavery writers' initial interest in slave women's childrearing practices was triggered by a concern about the lack of natural increase. It was argued that the nursing practices in place on the estates led to the undernourishment of young infants, and hence high infant mortality rates. It was furthermore suggested that slave women's preference for late weaning prevented natural increase because it made young children more susceptible to mortal diseases and also affected slave women's reproductive ability, as breast-feeding could act as a natural form of contraception. Not all proslavery writers, however, were critical of slave women's childrearing practices. This section first explores the rose-coloured accounts of the childrearing practices on the estates. It then moves on to examine critical accounts of childrearing practices and the various suggestions put forward to improve them, which were informed by metropolitan medical texts and aimed to create a hardworking and docile future labour force without a major loss of output. It finishes with a section that assesses the extent to which the suggestions were adopted on the estates.

The first rose-coloured accounts of childrearing practices were a direct response to James Ramsay's claim in his *Essay on the Treatment and Conversion of African Slaves in the British Sugar Colonies* (1784) that planters did not offer nursing slave women a reduced workload, forced them to take their children to the field and leave them there unattended and exposed to extreme weather conditions, and seldom gave them extra allowances of food.[3] They, and also the rose-coloured accounts that were published in the 1820s and early 1830s in an attempt to present planters and white estate officers as civilized men and avert Imperial interference in the management of the plantations, tried to contradict Ramsay's claim by emphasizing that nursing women faced reduced labour demands and were given extra allowances of flour and other foodstuffs and by pointing out that the nursing arrangements in place on the estates ensured not only that nursing children were regularly fed but also protected against heath, rain and other factors that could endanger their health.[4] Some authors went even further and suggested that nursing women could choose from a variety of nursing arrangements. James McQueen, for example, mentioned in his *The West India Colonies* (1824) that slave women could take their children to the field and leave them there in the care of an attentive nurse who allowed them plenty of time to feed their children, or they could leave them with a similar attentive woman in the slave quarters and regularly leave the field in order to feed them.[5] As it was assumed that it was first and foremost the quality of breast-feeding and weaning that determined the chance of a slave infant to become a strong adult worker, it is not surprising that post-weaning childrearing practices did not feature extensively in the rose-coloured accounts. The only post-weaning childrearing practice mentioned in order to show that planters did everything to allow slave women to raise healthy children was the nursery for weaned children. In his *A Practical View of Slavery in the West Indies* (1827), written after a stay of more than 20 years in the island, planter Alexander Barclay presented the nursery not only as a place where young children received the utmost care from 'the best nurses' but also as a method used by planters to counteract slaves' lack of responsibility for their children: 'however able the parents may be to provide for them, they [the nursery children] are supported by the master with the food best adapted for their age'.[6] His remark covered the main reason underpinning the nursery, namely to get as much labour out of the weaned children's mothers as possible. The nursery also aimed to create docile and hardworking future estate labourers. The elderly slave woman in charge of the nursery, for example, had to keep weaned children employed in light work around the plantation. While Barclay masked this aim by stating that the children spent the entire day sleeping and playing, another contemporary observer covered it by pointing out that weaned children stayed in the nursery until they were 'old enough to be useful to their parents.'[7]

Like the rose-coloured accounts of childbirth practices, those describing childrearing practices also greatly exaggerated the truth. One of the indulgences bestowed upon nursing women from the late eighteenth century onwards was the right to turn up later in the field than other slaves. The time that the women laboured in the field as a result of such labour-reducing arrangements, however, was much closer to the ten hours suggested by Gilbert Francklyn in 1788 than the six hours mentioned by James McQueen in 1824.[8] Another strategy employed in these accounts to present the planters as sensitive to the needs of slave women with young children was the omission of features of the slave system that prevented slave women from living up to the metropolitan motherhood ideal, such as the practice of selling slave mothers away from their children. We see, then, that the rose-coloured accounts of childrearing practices defined motherhood first and foremost as looking after the physical needs of children, and that they suggested that without the indulgences slave women would not be able to properly exercise this duty, as they had a deficient maternal instinct.

The idea that raising healthy children was a mother's most important duty was also articulated in accounts that criticized the nursing practices and put forward proposals to change them. James Adair and William Beckford agreed with James Ramsay that many slave infants failed to become healthy adult labourers because planters did not offer nursing women a lighter workload, a nurse in the field to take care of their nurselings, or extra allowances of food. They pointed out, for instance, that the work demanded from nursing women not only affected the quality of their breast-feeding but also caused them to 'overlay their infants' at night.[9] According to Adair, the planters' lack of interest in their condition had led nursing slave women to regard their children as an 'incumbrance' and made them 'less solicitous' about their survival.[10] Beckford, on the other hand, did not believe that the planters' lack of attention to nursing women made slave women less affectionate mothers than white women. The sheer fact that there were many slave women who had managed to raise healthy children with so 'little encouragement', proved to him that slave mothers were generally 'tender of their children'.[11]

Although Beckford believed that maternal affection was an important precondition for the first duty expected of mothers (raising healthy children), he did not suggest that planters should adopt measures to make nursing slave women more affectionate mothers. Instead, he proposed that planters should give nursing women the means to improve the quality of their breast-feeding and protect their nurselings in the field: a reduced workload and the appointment of an elderly slave woman to look after the nurselings in the field. A reduce workload served not just to enhance the survival chances of newborn infants by improving a slave mother's milk but also, if not more, to protect the productive potential of slave women: 'for the more moderate the work [of a nursing woman] is, the longer will it endure, and the more likely will she be to continue to raise supplies for the plantation.'[12] Several other proslavery writers in the late eighteenth and early nineteenth centuries also advocated a lighter workload for nursing women. They not only suggested that nursing women should start work later than other slave women but also that they should be exempted from particular tasks. Dr Collins proposed, for instance, that nursing women start an hour later and that they be excused from picking grass.[13]

Thomas Roughley agreed with William Beckford that slave women needed a nurse to look after their nurselings while they were at work in the field. To shield the nurselings from severe weather conditions, he suggested in 1823 that planters should build a hut in the field where the nurse and the infants in her care could take shelter. He furthermore proposed that planters should offer nursing women extra allowances of flour and sugar in an attempt to encourage them to give their children additional food and thus gradually wean them, and also mentioned a nursing scheme that took into account the planters' desire for both short-term profits and a self-perpetuating labour force: 'one mother out of every four in the field should be allowed to go and suckle her child for a quarter of an hour, then succeeded by others'.[14] Roughley's nursing scheme differed considerably from that proposed by Dr Collins in 1803. Collins suggested that planters build a nursery in the slave quarters for all children under five and that they order slave women to bring their nurselings to the nursery early in the morning. The women were to be allowed one hour over breakfast to breastfeed their infants, while for the rest of the day the children's needs were to be met by pap made from flour, bread, and sugar. As the slave woman in charge of the nursery was likely to 'misappropriate' the foodstuff and neglect the children in other respects, Collins recommended that planters keep a 'strict eye' upon her.[15] In other words, Collins was as distrustful of the nurse as he was of the slave midwife, and was convinced that slave women would not care well for their own or for other children unless subject to some degree of white control. It is possible that Collins based his nursing scheme on the assumption that even with an elderly slave woman to look after nurselings, the field posed a tremendous threat to the health of young slave children. It is more likely, however, that it was based on a concern about the productivity of nursing slave women. Under his nursing scheme a planter would only lose one hour's work of a nursing woman, whereas under Roughley's scheme a planter would lose at least two hours' work of a nursing woman. Collins may also have feared that if nursing infants were kept within the close proximity of their mothers and thus develop a strong bond with them, they would become unsuitable for their future role as docile and hardworking labourers.

The regulated breast-feeding schemes proposed by Roughley and Collins are an example of what Foucault has called 'bio-power'; that is a set of disciplinary technologies specifically aimed to foster life and produce docile and hardworking bodies.[16] The schemes aimed to train the bodies of nursing slave women in such a way that they could be used to almost their full productive potential, while simultaneously allowing these bodies to produce a milk that would turn slave nurselings into strong and healthy labourers. They were informed by metropolitan medical texts about infant feeding, which not only recommended that women breastfeed their infants as soon as possible but also that they feed on supply rather than demand. Women were to breastfeed their children at regular intervals during the day but never more than four to six times in order to prevent overfeeding. The texts also suggested that from three months onwards, children should be given pap (flour or breadcrumbs cooked in water or milk) or panada (bread, broth or milk) three times a day until they were weaned.[17]

In his response to Ramsay's essay, James Tobin argued that the above-mentioned proposed indulgences for nursing women were already in place on the estates. He added, however, that some of these indulgences posed a risk to natural increase. The reduced labour demands and the additional allowances of food explained, according to him, why so many slave women preferred late weaning. Tobin was not the only proslavery writer who attributed late weaning to slave women's selfish desire for 'idle time' and material goods, and disapproved of it on the grounds that it endangered the health of mother and child.[18] Forty years later, Thomas Roughley argued that long breast-feeding, which he estimated at three years, made the slave mother weak and infertile, and reduced the quality of her milk so that her infant became susceptible to disease. It was, however, more the practice's impact on productivity that led him to suggest that planters encourage slave women to wean their children at the age of 12 to 14 months. He believed that long breast-feeding made slave women 'prone to idleness and disaffection to work' and exposed slave children to 'too much tenderness' and encouraged in them a 'fretful longing for the mother'.[19] In other words, early weaning would enable planters both to use the full productivity potential of slave mothers and to create docile and hardworking labourers.

Scholars have recently estimated that in the years following the abolition of the slave trade, slave women breastfed for up to 18 months.[20] Roughley and other writers exaggerated the period of breast-feeding in order to depict slave women as different from white women, which in turn had to justify their far-reaching proposals for early weaning. By the late eighteenth century, the average child in metropolitan society was weaned at 7.25 months. The medical establishment favoured early weaning but recommended 8.5 to 12 months as the most appropriate time for weaning.[21] It stressed that weaning was a dangerous process that could trigger mortal diseases and should therefore only be undertaken when the child was healthy enough. This recommendation could explain why proslavery writers suggested that slave children should be weaned at the age of 12 to 14 months.[22] Based on the assumption that slave women lacked an intrinsic desire to care well for their infants, they proposed that planters 'bribe' slave women into weaning their children at this age by continuing the extra allowances of food.[23] Both Philip Gibbes and Dr Collins suggested that slave mothers should continue to receive these allowances, which provided them with some relief, until their weaned children joined the third gang, that is until the planter's investment in them had paid off. Collins added that the nurse in charge of the nursery should wean the infants by keeping them from their mothers, day and night, for several days.[24] Metropolitan medical tracts on weaning mentioned sudden weaning but generally recommended gradual weaning; that is, breast-feeding children only at night and giving them meat broth in addition to milk and pap for several weeks.[25] Collins' preference for sudden weaning was, of course, triggered by a concern about the productive potential of slave mothers and the future role of the nurselings.

The proposal to continue a slave mother's extra allowances of food until her child was old enough to join the labour force shows that some proslavery writers believed that it was in the planters' best interest not to ignore the well-being of children after they were weaned. These authors, most of whom had plantation experience, also suggested that planters set up nurseries or 'rearing houses' for weaned children, run by a 'well-disposed and orderly' nurse who had to provide the children at regular intervals with 'wholesome and plentiful' food, make sure they were clean, check them for disease, and employ them in some light work around the plantation. The nurse, in other words, was allocated the important task of turning out not just healthy but also docile and efficient future labourers.[26] To counteract the nurse's propensity to neglect the children in her care, the authors proposed not only to give the nurse a reward for every child that moved from the nursery to the third gang but also a high degree of white control over the nursery. Philip Gibbes, for example, suggested that the nursery should be built 'near the manager's house'.[27] The various proposals to set up a nursery for weaned children expressed as much as the rose-coloured accounts of the institution, the idea that slave mothers were ignorant of proper childrearing methods and lacked maternal affection. Gilbert Mathison, for instance, described the nursery in 1811 as a 'check upon ignorant and neglectful' mothers.[28]

In their rose-coloured accounts of childrearing practices and proposals to change these practices, proslavery writers argued that motherhood was first and foremost about looking after the physical needs of children. They placed a lot of emphasis on the feeding practices of nurselings and weaned children and were also concerned about their safety and cleanliness. For several proslavery writers, the second attribute of the metropolitan motherhood ideal (showing a deep affection for one's children) was also an important one. Even though they expressed different beliefs about the extent to which nature had endowed slave women with affection for their offspring and also about the desirability to develop this attribute in slave women, they were convinced that a slave woman would only care well for her children if she loved them. As for a mother's duty to turn her children into responsible citizens, proslavery writers wanted slave women to raise not 'responsible citizens' but 'responsible workers'. They devoted the least attention to the fourth attribute of the metropolitan motherhood ideal (putting the children's needs first) and referred to it only in their explanations for slave women's preference for late weaning.

Planters were also convinced that a mother's most important duty was to ensure the survival of her infants. The following cursory examination of the changes that they brought about in nursing and weaning practices during slavery illustrates that like the proslavery writers, they also held a dual opinion about a mother's duty to show affection for her children; while some of the changes had the potential to strengthen a slave mother's bond with her children, others aimed to weaken it. The condition of nursing women prior to these changes was very much like that described by James Ramsay. As there was no nurse in the field to look after their infants, nursing women either had to work with them on their backs or leave them on their own at the side of the field. Not only did they have to turn up in the field at the same time as the other women, they were also not allowed much time to feed their infants. Captain Hall mentioned, for instance, in his statement before the Slave Trade Committee that drivers and overseers easily flogged women who stopped work to feed their infants.[29]

Planters implemented the suggestion to reduce the workloads of nursing women. Most seem to have put nursing women in the second gang and allowed them to turn up half an hour later in the field. The majority also appointed a nurse to look after nurselings in the field and built a hut where she could take shelter with the children in case of rain.[30] According to the planters Alexander Barclay and Henry De La Beche, there were in the mid-1820s estates that did not employ a nurse but allowed half of the nursing mothers to look after the nurselings, while the other half was at work, alternating regularly. Under this nursing scheme, nursing women were only allowed to feed their infants when it was their turn to look after them.[31] The nursing arrangements in place on the majority of the estates were far less regulated; if a child cried, the nurse called upon its mother to feed it. Unless the driver or overseer thought that the slave mother abused this indulgence, she was seldom refused to feed her child.[32] It seems, then, that planters did not like the feeding-on-supply schemes proposed by Roughley and Collins. Its disruptive potential — the women would be out of sight of the white estate officers when they travelled to and from the nursery — and also its reliance on supplement feeding, seem to explain why planters disapproved of Collins' scheme, while logistics and a loss of the nursing women's productive potential (which was higher than under a feeding-on-demand scheme) can account for their rejection of Roughley's scheme.

The feeding-on-demand schemes that were adopted from the late 1780s onwards provided slave women with a greater opportunity to develop a strong bond with their children, as did the practice adopted on many estates that women could take time off from work in case one of their children was ill.[33] The practice of offering women sugar and flour for their nursing children, on the other hand, aimed to weaken the bond between a nursing woman and her child, as it had to encourage women to wean their children earlier.[34] Monk Lewis offered to continue the food allowances for two months, if nursing women decided to send their children to the nursery when they were 15 months old.[35] Other planters also bribed slave women into early weaning. The absentee planter John Baillie, for instance, told the 1832 Select Committee that he had offered slave women two dollars if they weaned their children at the age of 12 months.[36] Some planters bribed nursing women into early weaning in a less direct way. They set up a nursery for weaned children and hoped that the cooked meals offered to the children and the excellent care bestowed upon them would persuade slave women to wean their children earlier.[37] There were, however, also planters who forced slave women to wean their infants earlier. In 1820, for instance, five slave women from Orchard Plantation complained to a magistrate that their manager had ordered their children, who were 12 months and older, to be weaned.[38] The realisation that slave women could not be bribed into early weaning may have led this manager to resort to force. John Baillie, for instance, had to admit that his reward scheme failed to achieve its goal; since 1807 none of his slave women had claimed the reward.[39] Slave women resisted early weaning not only because of the contraceptive effect of continued breast-feeding but also because they were aware that early weaning posed health risks for the infants. Thomas Roughley suggested as much when he stated in 1823 that slave women preferred long breast-feeding not only because it gave them 'loitering idle time to spend' but also with the 'view of making the child strong'.[40] According to Barry Higman, most planters were of the opinion, like metropolitan medical writers, that there was a link between early weaning and infant mortality rates, and that they therefore refrained from such draconian measures as Dr Collins' suggestion of separating the child from its mother for several days.[41] A concern about social stability also informed the planters' decision to either bribe women into early weaning or not to interfere in the practice at all. This comes most clearly to the fore in Monk Lewis' account of slave mothers from a neighbouring estate, who had complained to their attorney (a white male professional who looked after estates of absentee owners) that they had been forced to wean their children early. Upon the attorney's dismissal of the complaint, one of the slave women had exclaimed that if her child was to be put in the weaning house, the attorney 'would see it dead in less than a week'.[42] This account contrasts sharply with Lewis' description of his slave women's response to his own weaning plan: 'All who had children of that age immediately gave them up; the rest promised to do so, when they should be old enough; and they all thanked me for the continuance of their indulgences, which they considered as a boon newly granted to them.'[43] We see, then, that Lewis presented himself as a 'man of sensibility' not only by listing the various indulgences that he bestowed on his slave labour force but also by indirectly comparing his own slave management methods to those of other planters.

48 *Slave women in discourses on slavery and abolition, 1780–1838*

Few planters took on board the recommendation that they should be as concerned about the well-being of weaned children as about that of nurselings. Like Lewis, some planters set up nurseries for weaned children. Most, however, simply put weaned children in the care of an elderly slave woman who kept them employed around the plantation and made sure that they were given one cooked meal a day.[44] The changes, then, that planters brought about in nursing and weaning practices show that they regarded motherhood as an important duty expected of slave women but not as their main identity. They only recognized slave women as mothers until their children were weaned or until they were old enough to join the third gang. But even then, however, the women's identity as mothers was overshadowed by their identity as producers.

A NATURAL AND LEARNED DUTY

Several antislavery writers denied the changes in childrearing practices that had been adopted on estates since the late 1780s. One author claimed, for instance, in 1826 that nursing women performed 'the same labour, the hoe and mattock as the men'.[45] In other words, antislavery writers engaged as selectively with the realities of plantation life as proslavery authors. This section, however, will show more differences than similarities between pro- and antislavery accounts of childrearing practices. Because of their project of ameliorating or abolishing slavery, antislavery writers did not focus exclusively on nursing and weaning practices nor define motherhood primarily as looking after the physical needs of children. Their project also led them to devote more attention to similarities than to differences between slave and white mothers.

Few antislavery writers addressed slave women's childrearing practices in the late eighteenth and early nineteenth centuries, as they were more concerned at the time about the slave trade than slavery. Those early antislavery writers who did pay attention to childrearing practices painted a picture of the condition of nursing women that was very similar to James Ramsay's, and denounced it on the same grounds as some of the more critical proslavery writers, namely that it endangered the health of slave infants and lessened slave women's maternal affection. Dr Jackson, an antislavery witness for the Slave Trade Committee who had practised in the island in the 1770s, mentioned, for instance, that many nurselings died because of their mothers' heavy workload. He also argued that this and other hardships suffered by nursing women explained why slave women 'naturally become indifferent to the rearing of their children.'[46] To encourage their readers to undertake action on behalf of the slaves, some antislavery activists concentrated in particular on the practice of flogging slave women who had stopped work in order to nurse their infants. The author of the pamphlet *A Dialogue Between A Well-Wisher and a Friend of the Slaves in the*

British Colonies, for example, asked her female readers to put themselves in the place of a slave mother who would be given 'cruel stripes' on her 'bare body' in case she 'yielded to the cries of her hungry infant' without her overseer's consent.[47]

Early antislavery writings on nursing practices aimed, however, not only to change the views of metropolitan audiences about slavery but also to convince planters of the necessity to improve nursing practices. Thomas Clarkson, the well-known abolitionist and co-founder of the Committee for the Abolition of the Slave Trade, told planters in 1788 that indulgences for nursing women, such as a reduced workload, would not only allow them to achieve natural increase but also 'endear' them to slave mothers.[48] Although Clarkson criticized the fact that weaned children were 'left neglected at home' or in the care of an 'old, infirm woman', he did not recommend that planters build a nursery. The nursery for nursing and weaned children which James Ramsay recommended in 1784 was very similar to the one proposed by Dr Collins nearly twenty years later. The two nurses in charge of the institution had to keep the children clean and well-fed. To ensure that they would not neglect their important duty, Ramsay recommended that the nursery be built near the manager's house and that the manager's wife should regularly inspect the place. Contrary to Collins, Ramsay did not propose a strict nursing scheme. He merely suggested that for the first six months, nursing women should be kept at light work in the proximity of the nursery so that they could 'suckle their children from time to time.' He added that if planters put the women back to normal field work after the first six months, gave them extra allowances of food, and also offered them a material reward for every child weaned, they could achieve early weaning.[49] Thus although Ramsay fiercely attacked the planters' treatment of slave mothers in his work, he far from advocated the abolition of slavery. In fact, if planters had implemented his suggestions, the profitability of their estates would have been guaranteed in both the short and long term, and thus the continuation of the system of slavery. Ramsay's stance was not unusual amongst late eighteenth- and early nineteenth-century abolitionists. Most were convinced that the slaves were not yet 'fit for freedom'. The parliamentary abolitionist William Wilberforce mentioned, for instance, in 1791 that the slaves' 'state of civilization is very imperfect, their notions of morality extremely rude and the powers of their government ill-defined.'[50]

Accounts about slave women's childrearing practices that were mobilized in the campaign to abolish slavery in the 1820s and early 1830s differed considerably from those produced in the late eighteenth and early nineteenth centuries. Early accounts of childrearing practices focussed on the lack of indulgences for nursing women; were especially concerned about slave women's ability to raise healthy children; and tried to appease the planters. Later accounts of the practices concentrated on slave women's ability to be affectionate mothers. William Wilberforce mentioned, for instance, in 1823 that a slave woman's 'instincts of nature are too sure not to produce great affection for her children.[51] They also addressed various childrearing practices other than nursing and fiercely attacked the planters and their white officers. The emphasis that Wilberforce and other antislavery writers placed on slave women's (natural) maternal affection is not surprising, considering the important role that they allocated for slave women in their project of creating a free, stable, moral, and prosperous Jamaica; namely, teaching children the behaviour expected of free, responsible, healthy, and hardworking citizens. As we shall see in this section, committed abolitionists and various other writers who criticized the system of slavery believed that the development of a strong bond between slave mothers and their children was an essential precondition for this duty.

Another reason why antislavery writers concentrated on slave women's maternal affection is that it enabled them to convince their audiences of the humanity of the slaves and their suitability for freedom. It was especially in emotive accounts of affectionate slave mothers that the writers tried to convey similarities between slave mothers and white, middle-class mothers, and thus slave women's alleged humanity. The pamphlet *A General History of Negro Slavery* (1826) argued, for instance, that slave women tried to be affectionate mothers but that the lack of time afforded to them to feed their infants while at work in the field, did not make it easy for them to express love for their infants and develop a strong bond with them: 'No sooner is the tear of the infant grief chased away, and the smiling babe clings delighted to the throbbing bosom of its *anxious* mother than it is roughly torn away; she durst not attempt to prevent the act, or scarcely cast a look after her darling.'[52]

Emotive accounts of affectionate slave mothers mentioned not only the nursing practices in place on the estates as a factor impeding on slave women's ability to express and develop their maternal affection but also the risk of being separated from their infants. Until the Slave Law was changed in 1826, it was perfectly legal for a provost-marshal to sell members of a slave family taken in a levy to different planters.[53] To convince the public of slavery's destruction of family life, the *Memoirs of a West India Planter* (1827), edited by the Baptist Reverend John Riland, included a description of a levy that concentrated on the reaction of a mother whose youngest child had been seized by the provost-marshal's deputies, which was presented as similar to that of a white mother who had lost an infant through death: 'she wept aloud and very bitterly, saying, that she must give up herself if the child was not got back, for she could not live separated from it.'[54] As the 1826 Slave Law did not prohibit the separation of mothers from children by sale, gift or bequest, many slave women continued to experience the forceful separation of their children in the years leading up to apprenticeship.[55] The pamphlet *A Concise View of Colonial Slavery* (1830) conveyed the horrors of this practice through an account of a slave woman who killed her children and herself, after she had learned that her children were to be sold away from her. Contrary to late eighteenth- and early nineteenth-century antislavery writings that presented the suicide of slave women on board of the slave ships and the throwing overboard of babies born on the ships as evidence of the immorality of the slave trade, the pamphlet presented the slave woman's act as one 'of many proofs of maternal feeling cherished by the negro women towards their offspring'.[56]

Concentrating on practices that were in accordance with the Slave Law but which had a tremendous impact on a slave woman's ability to bond with her child, allowed antislavery writers to demonstrate that if the amelioration of the slaves was left to the local assemblies not much would happen. For some antislavery writers, it was not so much these practices or the nursing practices in place on individual estates that explained why slave women's maternal affection was not as ardent as that of white middle-class women but the fact that slave women did not own the children that they gave birth to. In his *Facts Illustrative of the Condition of the Negro Slaves in Jamaica* (1824), Thomas Cooper, a Unitarian minister who had lived and worked on Robert Hibbert's estate, argued that it was not surprising that slave women were 'generally careless' about the habits that their children formed because they did not have the same authority over their children as mothers 'in a free country'.[57] Cooper believed that only immediate abolition of slavery would allow African Jamaican women to fully develop their natural maternal affection. Former Wesleyan missionary Peter Duncan, on the other hand, was convinced that gradual emancipation could achieve this end. He supported the Anti-Slavery Society's idea to free all children born after a certain date because it would make slave women 'consider that the child was more their own' and develop 'a kind of tie which never existed before.'[58] The Society's scheme, which was proposed in 1823, was not only rejected by the Imperial Government but also by many supporters of gradual emancipation, who argued that a slave mother would still be a slave and thus subject to practices that did not give her the time and other means necessary to raise healthy children and be an affectionate mother. They also pointed out that planters would be unlikely to provide slave mothers with food, medical care, and other allowances for their free children and that the scheme would thus increase rather than reduce the hardships suffered by slave mothers.[59]

Not surprisingly, then, several gradual abolitionists proposed the freeing of slave mothers rather than slave children.[60] The most detailed of these proposals entitled *Plan for Effecting Emancipation by the Redemption of Female Slaves* (1824), suggested the compulsory manumission of all slave women under 45 with compensation for the slaveholders. As children followed the condition of the mother, children born after the scheme would take effect, would be free and firmly within 'the power of their mothers'. It was argued that this combined with the fact that under the scheme women would have all the time necessary to take care of their children, would allow African Caribbean women to fully develop their maternal feelings and 'promote the preservation both of health and life'.[61] The remark that like women in 'civilized countries', slave women ought to be 'principally engaged . . . in such domestic duties as have for their object the care and comfort of husbands and children', illustrates most clearly that contrary to proslavery writers and planters, the designers of this emancipation scheme saw motherhood not only as an important duty expected of women but also as a woman's main identity and one that required protection beyond the period of nursing and weaning.[62]

The plans launched in the 1820s to allow slave women to take better care of their children thus differed considerably from those presented in the late eighteenth century. They not only firmly put the onus on the Imperial Government rather than on the planters but were also informed by a different assumption about slave women's ability to mother. While Ramsay's plan for a nursery and early weaning articulated the idea that slave women would only mother well if they were rewarded for their efforts and closely monitored by white estate officers, the plan for the compulsory manumission of slave women assumed that nature had endowed slave women with enough maternal instinct to care well for their children without a carrot or stick. Following chapters will illustrate more clearly that by the mid-1820s antislavery writers were fully convinced of the humanity of the slaves and no longer trusted the planters and their friends in the Assembly to lift the slaves up from a less than human condition. It needs to be stressed, however, that the humanity which antislavery writers attributed to the slaves was a potential humanity. As we have seen, most antislavery writings from the 1820s and early 1830s depicted the slave mother as a suffering victim. The image of the suffering slave mother expressed the idea that slave women were not yet as good mothers as white, middle-class, metropolitan women, but could become so if certain obstacles to their most important and natural duty were removed. To convince their readers of the slaves' humanity, antislavery writers not only provided narratives of suffering but also accounts of resistance, such as that of the slave mother who killed her children and herself in order to avoid separation. We shall see that acts of slave women's resistance featured most prominently in antislavery accounts of the sexual and physical violence done to the slave woman's body and that they drew heavily on emotive language and asked readers to put themselves in the place of not just the slave woman but also her partner and children.

MOTHERING UNDER APPRENTICESHIP

The indulgences for nursing women adopted since the late eighteenth century came to an end in August 1834. As a result, nursing female apprentices had to turn out at the same time as other apprentices, were allowed little time to feed their infants while at work in the field, could not take shelter with their nursing infants in case of rain, and did not receive extra allowances of food. Most estates, however, continued to employ a nurse in the field and allowed women to take time off from work to look after a sick child but demanded that female apprentices pay for these two indulgences by working extra hours for the estate.[63] Apprenticed women who took their previous indulgences by, for instance, turning out late, were brought before a S.M., who either sent them to the workhouse or ordered them to work extra hours for the estate. In most instances, the extra hours stipulated far exceeded the 'crime'. A nursing woman who had turned up half an hour late, for example, was usually ordered to pay back one whole Saturday. As apprentices used Saturday to cultivate their provision grounds, this sentence severely impacted upon an apprenticed woman's ability to raise healthy children. The same can be argued about the other form of punishment; workhouse officers did not provide nursing women with food for their children nor did they allow them enough time to feed their nurselings while at work in the penal gang.[64]

Mothering became also harder after August 1834 because planters did not provide free children with food, clothing, and medical care. On many estates, free children were guaranteed access to the estate hospital, the white estate doctor, and medicine, if their mothers worked a specified number of hours for the estate on a weekly, monthly, or annual basis. On Cambridge estate, for instance, mothers had to pay four and a half hours per week for this indulgence.[65] Most estates, however, seem to have operated on a 'pay-as-you-go' basis; that is, women had to obtain permission from their planter or overseer to take their free child to the estate hospital or the white estate doctor and were shortly upon their return to work informed about the number of hours that they had to pay back for the time taken off. To provide their free children with sufficient food, female estate workers increased the number of hours that they worked on their provision grounds. They tried to raise money to buy clothes for their children not only by selling excess produce and hand-made materials in the market but also by hiring themselves out for wages to their own or a neighbouring planter during their free time. Apprenticed women, however, not only had to struggle to ensure the physical survival of their free children but also to guarantee their freedom. Clause 18 of the local Abolition Act allowed for the apprenticeship of free children till the age of 21, if there was evidence that they were 'unprovided with adequate maintenance'. In addition, many planters encouraged apprenticed women to apprentice their free children to them in return for which the children would receive not only free allowances of food, clothing, and medical care but also a basic education.[66]

The withdrawal of the indulgences for nursing women was addressed by the critics of apprenticeship not long after August 1834.[67] They explained it in the same way as the discontinuation of the indulgences for pregnant women; namely, that the children were free and that they thus compromised the planters' socio-economic status. Joseph Sturge told a Birmingham audience in June 1837, for instance, that planters did not find it profitable to indulge nursing women because they were no longer 'rearing young labourers to perpetuate the system', and that they regarded nursing children as 'a bar to their rights'.[68] The critics, however, were less concerned about the withdrawal of the indulgences for nursing women than about the other two obstacles that planters put in the way of apprenticed mothers: not providing free children with food, clothes and medical care and the voluntary apprenticeship of free children. Focussing on these obstacles enabled them to estimate the ability of planters and apprentices to develop a society upon full freedom that was both stable and prosperous. In their accounts of the two obstacles, critics posed the question whether upon full freedom planters would guarantee the rights of the nearly 300,000 men, women, and children over the age of six that were presently apprenticed and if African Jamaican women would do their utmost to raise docile and efficient labourers and responsible citizens. This section first examines the critics' attitudes towards the changes in childrearing practices and the solutions that they provided to enable apprenticed mothers to raise healthy children and turn them into responsible citizens. It then moves on to discuss how opponents of apprenticeship responded to the critics' claim that by preventing apprenticed women from exercising their natural duty, planters and their friends prevented apprenticeship from becoming a success.

The withdrawal of the indulgences for nursing women featured extensively in the pamphlets that were written in support of the abolition of apprenticeship because it was an excellent means to arouse the passion of the readers.[69] The pamphlets described the nursing practices that were in place on the estates after August 1834 in terms very similar to Ramsay's essay and other early abolitionist writings. One pamphlet, for instance, mentioned that nursing women were 'compelled to work with their children strapped to their backs' and that 'when rain came down in torrents, they were obliged to remain in the field with their infants exposed to it.'[70] And like early abolitionist writings, they also asked readers to put themselves in the place of nursing women. The readers of Sturge's *Horrors of the Negro Apprenticeship in the British Colonies* (1838), for instance, were asked to think of themselves as an apprenticed woman with four children under six, one of which a nursling; having to 'be at work in the field the same time as the rest of the negroes'; not having enough time to prepare food for the family; and taking the youngest child to the field, while leaving the rest of the children 'unprotected at home'.[71] But contrary to early abolitionist writings about nursing practices, the pamphlets did not call upon the goodwill of the planters. Instead, they accused planters and their white officers of lacking the sensitivity associated with the metropolitan ideal of masculinity. They did this not only by providing highly emotive accounts of nursing women who had been sentenced to the workhouse because their planter or overseer had accused them of turning up late or feeding their nurselings too long, but also by drawing comparisons between planters and men in the mother country. Sturge, for instance, was convinced that the 'people of England' would never subject to cruelty 'a woman who had committed no offence but having a large family' nor let their own interests be 'superseded by any claims of humanity or the natural ties between a parent and child.'[72]

Abolitionists also accused the planters and their white employees of criminalizing rather than protecting a woman's most important and natural duty (motherhood) in their accounts of free children's lack of access to medical care. Most of these accounts argued that the planters' refusal to give medical care to the free children resulted in a loss of human life. In 1837, the American abolitionists Thome and Kimball visited Jamaica and several other islands in order to assess the progress of emancipation. They mentioned in their travel account the death of a free child, which was also mentioned by Sturge and Harvey in their *The West Indies in 1837* (1838). A female apprentice whose employer (a doctor) resided in Spanish Town had hired her out to a planter in the country. When her child became sick, she had taken it to her employer, who was described in both travel accounts as a 'monster'. He, however, had refused to even look at the child and had ordered the woman to go back to the plantation. Rather than going back, she had gone to the freeborn coloured S.M. Richard Hill, hoping that he could change her employer's mind. Before he could do so, however, her child had died.[73] Accounts such as these which, like the abolitionist writings from the 1820 and early 1830s, presented the mother as a suffering victim clearly aimed to arouse the readers. They also tried to convince them that the planters' interpretation of the 1833 Abolition Act endangered the continuation of the plantation economy upon freedom. Planters who withheld medical care from free children on the grounds that under clause 11 of the 1833 Abolition Act only apprentices were legally entitled to medical care, obstructed the formation of a large and strong future labour force. The accounts, however, expressed no doubt about the ability of apprenticed women to do their bit to realize the abolitionist project of a prosperous, moral, and stable Jamaica upon freedom; the women not only tried to raise healthy future labourers by ensuring them access to medical care but also resorted to the law to defend their free children's interests rather than to alternatives to official justice.

The planters' demand that apprenticed women pay back time lost in looking after a sick child was not mentioned in either the Imperial or the local Abolition Act. This explains why S.M.s who criticized the workings of apprenticeship were more concerned about this practice than about the planters' refusal to grant free medical care for children under six, which was in accordance with the local Abolition Act.[74] In October 1835, they asked Governor Sligo how they should respond to such demands. Drawing upon an image of apprenticed women that was commonly used by opponents of apprenticeship — the selfish mother —, Sligo suggested that S.M.s should grant the planters' requests because he feared that if female apprentices did not pay this time back, they would soon come up with all sorts of excuses to 'evade the just proportion of labour which it is their duty to give the master.' He was, in other words, convinced that this practice would teach apprenticed women about contracts, which he deemed an important lesson as society would be governed by contract upon freedom.[75] The colonial secretary, on the other hand, did not see a difference between this planter demand and the one to ask women to pay back time lost in labour. Glenelg argued that in both cases an apprenticed woman fulfilled her natural duties. As these duties superseded those that she owed to her employer, he overruled Sligo's decision and ordered S.M.s to carefully assess the nature of a child's disease and the time that a woman had spent looking after it, and only make those women pay back time who had used their child's illness as 'an excuse for indolence'. This order, he believed, was in accordance with the spirit of the 1833 Abolition Act as 'no Act of Parliament could ever be meant to confer on any man the power of visiting by penal infliction a mother who had neglected her duties to him, in order to afford her child the aid and solace which in a state of disease it might require at her hands.'[76] While some S.M.s agreed with Glenelg that taking care of sick children was not an 'offence' but 'a natural obligation' and followed his guideline, many ignored it and in so doing, enabled planters to retain some of their former power.[77]

Critics of apprenticeship, then, argued that in spite of the numerous difficulties that they faced, apprenticed women saw taking care of their children's physical needs as their foremost duty. They portrayed the women, however, not only as caring but also as loving mothers. While some did this through case studies of mothers who went to considerable lengths to ensure their children's health, others did it by comparing them to mothers elsewhere. S.M. Patrick Dunne mentioned, for instance, in his report from June 1836 that 'the affection and care manifested by the women in attending to their 'pickaninnies' under the peculiar difficulties under which they labour ... are not surpassed by the women of any other country.'[78] They also conveyed the women's deep affection for their offspring in accounts of their stern opposition to the 'extra-hours-for-extra-allowances schemes' and the planters' demands to voluntarily apprentice their free children.[79] According to the critics, the women refused the schemes because they realized that they were 'dictated by motives of personal advantage'.[80] While most praised the women for not accepting the schemes, few acknowledged, like S.M. Bourne, that it was not only due to the efforts of fathers but also mothers that free children were 'well-fed' and did not suffer from 'neglect'.[81] By not mentioning the hard work that apprenticed women undertook to raise the money needed to feed and clothe their free children, critics helped to reinforce the metropolitan gender ideal of the husband-provider and the wife-carer. We shall see more clearly in chapter four that they envisioned this gender ideal as the bedrock of the future free society.

Critics bestowed even more praise on apprenticed mothers for opposing the voluntary apprenticeship of their free children, a practice which they described as having no other purpose than to increase output and create an abundant supply of cheap and docile labour upon full freedom.[82] Some opponents of apprenticeship interpreted the women's strong opposition to voluntary apprenticeship as evidence that they did not realize the importance of education.[83] Critics strongly denied this accusation. They pointed out that those women who refused to apprentice their free children did their utmost to secure an education for them. S.M. Cooper mentioned, for instance, in 1836 that they sought 'protectors who will impart to them the blessing of education'; that is, missionaries who ran free schools that were subsidized by the Imperial Government.[84] They argued furthermore that the women's desire to educate their children along with their rejection of the voluntary apprenticeship schemes demonstrated that apprentices had an innate drive for human betterment. Cooper, for example, suggested that 'their more fortunate neighbours' could learn from the apprentices' desire to provide their free children with a good future, by sternly refusing to condemn them 'to the thraldom they have themselves so long suffered under'.[85] Cooper suggested here that apprentices lived up to the script underpinning the 1833 Abolition Act. The various people who helped to draw up the Act had expressed the hope that apprenticeship would develop the desire for human betterment that lay dormant in the ex-slaves. Henry Taylor, whose elaborate plan for emancipation had helped to shape the Act, saw this desire as essential for the future prosperity of the island. Apprentices who wanted to improve their own or their children's lives would eagerly work for wages in their free time to obtain non-essential goods and services; and hence, were more likely to stay on the estates as wage labourers upon full freedom.[86]

In their accounts of the women's refusal to apprentice their free children, critics thus suggested that apprenticed women were capable of carrying out the weighty task of transforming their children into responsible citizens. They pointed out, however, that the women could not fully exercise this attribute of the metropolitan motherhood ideal because of the duties that they had to fulfil under the terms of the Abolition Act and also the additional demands made upon them by the planters, and suggested that schools be set up in order to help them raise responsible citizens.[87] Not all critics, however, welcomed the Colonial Office's plan to educate the free children. In November 1835, Governor Sligo asked the Assembly, on the request of the colonial secretary, to enact compulsory education.[88] S.M. Dunne believed that this education scheme would have little success as the children's parents would resist it because they associated coercion with slavery.[89] Compulsory education was not implemented during apprenticeship. The few improvements in education that took place during this four-year period were the result of Imperial rather than local action. In 1835 and 1836, for instance, the island received money to build new schools and support existing ones.[90]

Critics also proposed suggestions that had to enable apprenticed women to take better care of their children and develop a stronger bond with them. Like the designers of the 1824 *Plan for Effecting Emancipation by the*

Redemption of Female Slaves, some proposed that apprenticed women should become full-time mothers by removing them from field work. Sturge and Harvey concluded on the basis of their visit to Jamaica and other islands that apprenticed women should be withdrawn from the field gradually and voluntary; that is, the women's husbands should buy the remainder of their apprenticeship.[91] S.M. William Ramsay, on the other hand, deemed the condition of apprenticed mothers and their free children so urgent that he suggested in July 1837 that not only female domestics but also field women should be set free in August 1838.[92] Both proposals engaged with the two interlinked metropolitan ideas that motherhood was incompatible with paid work and that through the nurturing of their children's morality, women played a crucial role in improving society.[93] Sturge and Harvey argued, for instance, that the implementation of their scheme would lead to the 'improvement of the negroes' and 'the prosperity of the whole community'.[94]

Some critics were convinced that the gradual or immediate withdrawal of apprenticed women from the field would prevent the development of a sound economic basis for the future free society. As women made up the bulk of the field labour force, their withdrawal from the field would significantly reduce output levels. To ease the burden of apprenticed mothers, they proposed instead amendments to the local Abolition Act. They suggested first of all that the Assembly enact that free children would be entitled to the same allowances and medical care as apprentices. Second, that all issues relating to nursing women on the estates should be made the responsibility of the S.M.[95] And third, that the Assembly should bring clause 18 of the local Abolition Act, which provided for the apprenticeship of free children, in line with clause 13 of the Imperial Act, and that the procedure to decide upon the apprenticeship of free children should become more rigorous.

Clause 18 replaced the phrase 'absolute destitution' in clause 13 of the Imperial Abolition Act by 'inadequate maintenance'. It narrowed clause 13 further down by not incorporating the provision that planters should 'allow reasonable time for the education and religious instruction' of the free children apprenticed to them.[96] Clause 18, then, clearly stemmed from the planters' concern about their socio-economic status. It had to allow them to enlarge their labour force at no extra costs and thus counteract the decline in output levels, while simultaneously prevent an increase in educated and skilled blacks and coloureds after freedom. In his analysis of the Jamaican Abolition Act, John Jeremie not only criticized the Assembly's narrow interpretation of clause 13 but also clause 13 itself. He pointed out that free children apprenticed under clause 13 were to serve till they were 21 and not till the end of apprenticeship and that such a weighty decision was to be made by only one S.M. Jeremie, however, did not advocate the repeal of clause 13 but suggested instead that S.M.s should ascertain whether there were any relatives or another third party willing to guarantee the child's future maintenance and that they should keep a record of all the children that they apprenticed, clearly stating the reason for their decision.[97] This recommendation had to ensure that clause 13 would benefit planters as little as possible and also prevent S.M.s from doing their bidding. To understand why Jeremie did not propose the repeal of clause 13 in order to guarantee the freedom of free children, we have to know that at the time children in metropolitan society whose parents could not provide for them could also be apprenticed. Since the beginning of the seventeenth century, parish authorities had bound out children who were likely to become a burden on ratepayers.[98] The 1834 Poor Law Commission deemed this practice an appropriate method of poor relief. It only recommended that in the future an inquiry could be made into the workings of the laws governing the practice of apprenticeship.[99]

The 1838 Amendment Act restored some of the indulgences for nursing women. It did not, however, stipulate that free children were to receive the same allowances of food, clothing, and medical care as apprentices or that apprenticed women were to be withdrawn from the field on 1 August 1838, and it also firmly kept in place clause 13. The letter sent to S.M.s in July 1837, which instructed them to 'resist demands [from the planter] upon services of mothers which shall have the effect of depriving them of the time or the opportunities requisite for the discharge for their necessary maternal duties', went some way towards making nursing women the sole responsibility of S.M.s.[100] We see, then, once more the reluctance of the Imperial Government to force the planting class to acknowledge the new status of their workers and their children. One of the main aims of apprenticeship was to ensure the continuation of a profitable plantation economy after freedom. The Imperial Government supported this aim as much as the planting class because sugar duties constituted an important form of revenue. It was convinced that to achieve this goal, it was essential not to thwart the planting class. It was, however, not only its concern about plantation production after freedom that prevented the Imperial Government from ordering far-reaching changes in the condition of apprenticed mothers and their free children, but also what Demetrius Eudell has recently called the 'political languages' that the Imperial Government was surrounded by and worked with.[101] Ideas about poor relief at the time, such as that of self-help, clearly limited its ability to undertake action to ensure the provision of food for free children and to prevent them from being apprenticed. And we should also not forget that legal arrangements restricted the ability of the Imperial Government to counteract the limitations that the planters placed upon the freedom of the apprentices. As it was custom for colonial laws to follow rather than precede those in metropolitan society, the Imperial Government would, for instance, have been hard pressed to endorse a repeal of clause 13.

Opponents of apprenticeship also expressed the idea that a good mother was an affectionate and self-effacing mother who was as concerned about her children's physical development as about their moral and mental development. Contrary to the critics, they supported this idea with images of apprenticed mothers that emphasized their difference from white metropolitan mothers. These images were remarkably similar to those used by early proslavery writers in their accounts of childbirth and nursing practices. The image of the indifferent mother, for example, featured extensively in explanations of the women's refusal to work extra hours in return for medical care for their free children. S.M. Ralph Cocking stated, for instance, in his report from December 1836 that 'so every thing unlike *maternal feeling* do they display that humanity revolt at their barbarity: many of their children, when ill, are allowed to consume away from disease'.[102] He was not the only opponent who emphasized the women's (natural) lack of maternal affection by stating that many free children had died because their mothers had withheld medical care from them. In fact, some provided accounts of dying free children that were as emotional as those presented by the abolitionists Sturge and Harvey and Thome and Kimball. S.M. Odell described, for example, the case of an apprentice who had been allowed to take her sick child to the estate doctor but because she had waited too long to ask her planter to see the doctor, the child had died on the way to his practice.[103]

The apprenticed women's lack of maternal affection was not the only reason mentioned for the women's refusal to provide their free children with medical care. Another was their selfishness: 'when children are ill, the mothers will not take them to the estate's hospital . . . lest they should have to pay the estate the time occupied in attending them'.[104] Accounts such as this of apprenticed women who stubbornly refused to pay for the medical treatment afforded to their children, aimed not just to excuse the planters for the condition of the free children but also to question the progress that apprenticeship had made in terms of turning the ex-slaves into free wage labourers. According to the opponents, the women had thus far failed to comprehend one of the most important principles of a free wage economy; namely, that luxuries had to be paid for. They also indirectly suggested that the women had not yet realized the importance and workings of contracts. To further excuse the planters for the condition of the free children and also to counteract the critics' claim that white men on the plantations did not measure up to the metropolitan norm of masculinity, opponents argued that the 'extra-hours-for-medical-care schemes' emanated solely from the goodwill of the planters and that they were very 'liberal' and 'generous' schemes. S.M. Hawkins believed, for instance, that if it 'was not for the kindness of their former masters, in allowing them into the hot-houses and the medical gentlemen attending them', the mortality rate of the free children would have been much higher.[105]

It was also in their accounts of the women's refusal to apprentice their free children that opponents expressed a concern about the state of the island upon full freedom. It was argued that by not apprenticing their children, the women prevented them from becoming docile and industrious future labourers, and thus endangered the continuation of the plantation economy. One S.M. predicted in 1837 that 'having been all their life, idle', the children would 'be very much inclined to remain so', while planter Maurice Jones pointed out that as nobody corrected the free children's behaviour in the day time, they never learned the important lesson of obedience, failing even to obey their own parents.[106] Opponents suggested that in order to make apprenticeship a success, legislation would have to complement the apprenticed women's shortcomings as mothers. They proposed an act that would make 'extra indulgences', such as medical care and food for free children, only available in return for 'extra labour', as it was 'mistaken kindness to allow the apprentices benefits which were not given to paid workmen in other societies'.[107] As W. L. Burn has argued in his 1937 study of apprenticeship, the opponents' argument did not hold because apprentices were not paid for their 40½ hours a week and therefore lacked the means of wage labourers in the mother country to purchase such 'luxuries' as medical care for their infants.[108] Opponents furthermore recommended a local or an Imperial act that would keep the free children occupied during the day.[109] It is not surprising that planter Maurice Jones wanted this scheme to be a labour scheme that would teach the children industry. S.M. Edward D. Baynes, on the other hand, envisioned a scheme that would teach the children a wider range of habits and virtues. In 1835, he proposed not only the establishment of 'houses of industry', which would teach free children to become docile and hardworking labourers, but also compulsory Sunday and evening schools that would improve their moral behaviour. Baynes was convinced that only by removing them from 'contagion of example', free children could come to possess 'advantages not yet enjoyed by the negro race'. His 'houses of industry' were to be located at a considerable distance from the plantation and parents would only be allowed to visit their children on Sundays. Thus like the rearing houses, the 'houses of industry' had to provide a check upon ignorant and neglectful mothers.[110]

The opponents' proposals for legislative change were justified with the idea that if implemented, they would bring the ex-slaves to a higher level of civilization. S.M. J. Kennet Dawson argued, for instance, that if none of the schemes to keep free children occupied during the day was adopted, apprentices would continue to 'bring up their children as slaves to themselves'.[111] The lack of proposals that would give apprenticed women that which they needed most to raise healthy, strong and well-behaved individuals — time to mother —, suggests most clearly that not the apprentices but the planters were to benefit from the implementation of the proposals. Under the various schemes proposed, planters not only gained extra labour but also retrieved some of their former arbitrary and proprietary power.

We see, then, that motherhood was as much a vehicle for opponents of apprenticeship to express their views on the success of the system as for the critics. While critics argued that apprenticeship could only achieve its aims if the planters' behaviour was corrected by legislation, opponents singled out the apprentices as the main obstacle to the workings of the system. Like proslavery writers, opponents believed that the mothers on the plantations lacked the degree of maternal affection needed to raise healthy, hard-working and docile labourers, and they seemed to firmly agree with Dr Collins that 'policy should be made to supply the place of instinct, where that is deficient, and to co-operate with it when otherwise'.[112]

CONCLUSIONS

The participants in the debate about childrearing practices on the estates measured slave and apprenticed women against the metropolitan motherhood ideal. Their different projects led them to emphasize different attributes of this ideal. A concern to raise a supply of healthy future labourers explains why proslavery writers were especially concerned to see whether slave women measured up to the first attribute of the ideal (raise healthy children), while a need to demonstrate the slaves' suitability for freedom explains the antislavery writers' focus on the second attribute (show deep affection for offspring). The third attribute (raise responsible citizens) was only fully invoked during apprenticeship. As critics and opponents of apprenticeship wanted the island to become not only a prosperous but also a stable society upon full freedom, they concentrated on the efforts of apprenticed women to ensure the physical survival of their children and to inculcate in them general standards of behaviour. The fourth attribute (put a child's needs before anything else) was only indirectly addressed by proslavery writers and opponents of apprenticeship in an attempt to justify far-reaching changes in childrearing practices.

The two sides in the debate not only differed in their engagement with the metropolitan motherhood ideal in terms of the emphasis that they placed on the four attributes but also with regards to their belief in the ability of slave and apprenticed women to live up to the ideal. As the numerous images of selfish and indifferent mothers in their writings illustrate, proslavery writers and opponents of apprenticeship tried to persuade their audiences that slave and apprenticed women fell short of the metropolitan motherhood ideal. They argued that the women would never or only in a very distant future be capable of fully exercising the four attributes, and therefore proposed interventions in their childrearing practices. Antislavery writers and critics of apprenticeship agreed with them that the women were deficient in mothering skills. They believed, however, that nature had endowed the women with the same degree of maternal instinct as white, middle-class metropolitan women, and were convinced that if the various obstacles to their mothering skills were removed, the women would soon live up to the metropolitan motherhood ideal.

The sides differed furthermore in their ideas about the combination of motherhood and work. Their proposals to withdraw mothers from the field show most clearly that antislavery writers and critics of apprenticeship believed, like the authors of metropolitan motherhood manuals, that motherhood was such an important task because of its impact on wider society that it was incompatible with work outside the home. Proslavery writers and opponents of apprenticeship thought mothering an important duty expected of slave and apprenticed women but one that bestowed first and foremost advantages on the planter. As they were more concerned about his interests than those of wider society, they put forward various proposals to enable slave and apprenticed women to take better care of their nurselings but while remaining at work in the field. Thus like many feminists today, they did not present 'mother' and 'labourer' as oppositional and mutually exclusive constructs.[113]

This chapter has not only shown differences but also similarities between pro- and antislavery discourse. We have seen in the second section that antislavery discourse was also a changing discourse. Its discussion of childrearing practices in the late eighteenth and early nineteenth centuries differed only marginally from that of the proslavery writers. By the mid-1820s, however, it addressed themes and provided suggestions to enable slave women to become better mothers that were strikingly different from those presented several decades earlier and also proslavery suggestions at the time. And like proslavery discourse, antislavery discourse was not without its contradictions. Authors not only contradicted one another but also contradicted themselves, as we have seen in the case of Governor Sligo. The chapter has also mentioned some of the main rhetorical strategies employed in antislavery discourse. As antislavery writers and critics of apprenticeship appealed not only to audiences already convinced of the abolitionist cause, it is no surprise that some of the strategies used were similar to those employed by proslavery authors and opponents of apprenticeship. We have seen, for example, that antislavery writers and critics of apprenticeship also regularly turned a blind eye to the realities of plantation life. They not only ignored important changes that planters had brought about in the condition of slave mothers in order to portray white Jamaican society as an uncivilized society but they also failed to mention slave women's own notions of good mothering. This omission of plantation reality was to some extent a conscious decision because they could only convince their metropolitan audiences of slave women's humanity by presenting them as desirous of living up to the metropolitan motherhood ideal. It was also the result, however, of the naturalization of the metropolitan motherhood ideal. Most authors could simply not imagine that motherhood could be defined in any other way than that of their own society. Some critics of apprenticeship were for that reason surprised to find that most apprenticed men used the money that they had earned by hiring themselves out for wages or by working their provision grounds for purposes other than purchasing their wives' freedom so that they could become full-time mothers.[114] And finally, we have seen that antislavery discourse also used the slave woman as a vehicle to express wider concerns. The masculinity of white Jamaican men and the moral and economic state of the island upon full freedom were amongst the wider concerns raised in antislavery writings about childrearing practices.

By drawing upon the metropolitan ideal of motherhood, the participants in the debate about childrearing practices on the estates helped to reinforce the metropolitan idea that having children and caring for them was a woman's natural and necessary duty.[115] Metropolitan society, however, not only held up motherhood as an important pillar of women's identity but also wifehood. In the two following chapters, we will see that the discourses of slavery and abolition were divided over the question whether slave and apprenticed women should not just be caring, affectionate, and self-effacing mothers but also devoted and docile wives.

3 Deviant and dangerous
Slave women's sexuality

Slave women's sexual behaviour occupied a prominent role in pro- and antislavery writings. This role should first be seen within the light of the natural decrease of the slave population. It was argued by both defenders and opponents of slavery that slave women contracted venereal diseases in their sexual relations with white and slave men which made them incapable of conceiving or carrying a child full-term, and that they also easily aborted their offspring. And second, within a context of changing ideas about sexuality in metropolitan society. While permissible sex remained confined to the married, procreative couple, different norms of male and female sexual behaviour emerged, which were first directed at middle-class men and women.[1] In the eighteenth century, men were attributed with excessive sexual desires and manhood was defined primarily through sexual potency. After the turn of the century, it was still assumed that men were naturally endowed with a strong and potentially dangerous sex drive but it was no longer seen as a force beyond their control, and they were increasingly urged to control and ration their sexual passion. Advice literature directed at young men told them, for instance, to abstain from masturbation. Adultery was regarded as an inappropriate way for middle-class men to accommodate their sexual desires but was condoned if it was committed with either a woman without a family or a lower-class woman because this limited the risk of introducing illegitimate offspring into the middle-class family.[2]

The changes in the norm of female sexuality were even more pronounced. For centuries, it had been argued that women were 'highly sexed, closer to nature than men by virtue of their greater sexual drive, and sexually demanding'.[3] From the mid-eighteenth century onwards, women were urged to control their sexual passion both before and after marriage. By the early nineteenth century, it was generally argued that women did not have an innate sex drive and that their sexual feelings were only invoked through love in marriage. As a result women who displayed sexual agency, such as prostitutes, were seen as unnatural and unfeminine.[4] This change from an active to a passive model of female sexuality was largely achieved by defining women as maternal beings and aimed to facilitate the domestic ideology; that is, the set of ideas and practices that located women firmly in the home and defined them as mothers and wives.[5]

Antislavery writers addressed slave women's sexual behaviour from the late eighteenth century onwards. Partly as a result of an increased concern in the metropolitan society about the sexual purity of married women, their debate intensified in the mid-1820s when they discussed slave women's sexuality even more than before alongside various other forms of irregular sexual behaviour in the island. Proslavery writers also presented slave women's sexual behaviour as a marked deviation from the metropolitan ideal. And like antislavery advocates, they too were more concerned about slave women's sexual relationships with white men than with slave men.[6] For various reasons, however, they discussed slave women's sexuality more in the late eighteenth and the early nineteenth centuries than in the 1820s and early 1830s. This chapter therefore starts with an analysis of the proslavery debate about slave women's sexuality. As neither side devoted much attention to black female sexuality during apprenticeship, it covers only the late 1780s till 1834.[7]

The fact that slave women's sexuality occupied a prominent role in the discourses of slavery and abolition does not mean that these discourses regarded slave men's sexuality as unproblematic. Various antislavery writers, especially (former) missionaries, criticized the ways in which slave men tried to satisfy their sexual needs, in particular their preference for multiple partners, on the grounds that they were seen to corrupt slave women.[8] Antislavery writers concentrated on slave women's sexuality not only because it was a better means to arouse the public than slave men's but also because it enabled them to articulate both their belief in and fear about the success of their project of turning Jamaica into a free and moral society. Proslavery writers also presented slave men as uncontrollably lusty and polygamous. The planters amongst them were especially concerned about the fact that slave men took as wives not women from their own estates but rather those who lived on nearby plantations. This practice not only meant that slave men were for longer spells of time beyond the control of the planter and his staff but also that offspring of such abroad unions did not belong to the slave man's owner but to that of the slave woman.[9] That slave men's sexuality did not feature as extensively in proslavery writings as slave women's is because it was seen to constitute less of a threat to the social order. Especially the growth of the free and enslaved coloured population was presented as a danger to the social stability in the island. Because of the paucity of white women in the island, this growth was not the result of slave men's sexual relations with white women but of slave women's sexual encounters with white men. We shall see in the following that proslavery writers articulated through their images of slave women's sexuality various other fears besides a concern about social stability.

This chapter tries to advance existing scholarship on Caribbean slave women's sexuality. It was not until the 1980s that scholars of Caribbean slavery developed an interest in slave women's sexuality.[10] Like their American counterparts, they focussed primarily on slave women's relations with white men and tried to do away with the myth presented by proslavery writers that slave women were scheming Jezebels (immoral and evil temptresses) and took readily to the prostitution of their bodies, by providing evidence that slave women's sex with white men was based more on force than consent. Using, amongst others, Foucault's argument that the 'deployment of sexuality . . . engenders a continual extension of areas and forms of control' and drawing upon antislavery writings, they argued that the sexual exploitation of slave women by white men was as much, if not more, a means of control as the whip and that it made female bondage worse than male bondage.[11] In recent years, scholars have moved away from the idea that slave women were nothing but victims of white men's sexual lust. They now argue that there were also consensual sexual relationships between white men and slave women and that many slave women, especially those who were light-skinned, aimed for such a relation in order to gain advantages for themselves and their children, including a better job and the chance of freedom.[12] And as mentioned in the introduction to this book, scholars of Caribbean slavery have also more recently begun to explore images of slave women's sexuality in contemporary writings, in particular the image of the scheming Jezebel in late eighteenth- and early nineteenth-century proslavery writings.[13]

The first section of this chapter confirms the conclusion of previous studies on the imagery of Caribbean slave women's sexuality that proslavery writers invoked the scheming Jezebel to justify white men's forced and consensual sexual relations with slave women. It adds to this body of work, however, by pointing out that this image also served various other purposes and that it jostled for power, especially after the abolition of the slave trade, with the image of the potentially virtuous slave woman. The second section illustrates that two images of slave women also dominated the antislavery debate about slave women's sexuality: the potentially virtuous slave woman and the naturally chaste slave woman. It furthermore demonstrates that these images competed with those of the sexually unrestrained white Jamaican male and the sexually aggressive free(d) woman. The various images of slave women, white men, and free(d)women in the debate about Jamaican slave women's sexuality engaged not only with the reality of Jamaican slave society and the projects pursued by the participants in the debate but also with metropolitan discourses about sexuality, gender, and race. The last section argues that the images also helped to shape these discourses and mentions some of their other profound effects.

DEVIANT AND DANGEROUS

Proslavery writers constructed slave women as threatening deviants from the metropolitan model of passive female sexuality in their discussion of slave women's sexual relations with both white and slave men. First, they argued that slave women began sexual activity at an early age. Second, they claimed that they changed partners frequently. Third, they believed that the women preferred to have multiple partners. Planter and historian Bryan Edwards mentioned, for instance, in 1793 that slave women 'would consider it as the greatest exertion of tyranny, and the most cruel of all hardships to be compelled to confine themselves to a single connection with the other sex.'[14] The argument that lent most support to the construction of slave women as deviant from the metropolitan model, however, was that they took readily to the prostitution of their bodies. The overseer in the proslavery novel *Marly* (1828), for instance, was surprised at the readiness with which slave women offered themselves or their daughters to white estate officers: 'He was incessantly importuned by the pickeniny mothers, to take a wife; and there was not an individual among them, who had not some one of their young female friends to recommend for that purpose.'[15]

Two theories were put forward to explain why slave women deviated from the metropolitan norm of female sexuality. The first, adhered to primarily by those who (had) resided in the island (hereafter, Jamaican writers), was that slave women were naturally promiscuous. Bryan Edwards, for example, was convinced that slave women's sexual desire was nothing but 'a mere animal desire'.[16] The second theory, which was put forward less often, attributed slave women's lack of sexual purity to various external pressures on them. Resident Anthony Davis, for instance, blamed it in 1832 on nonconformist missionaries, the most prominent symbols of humanitarianism and abolition in the island. He mentioned that a missionary in Spanish Town was alleged to have told the slave women in his congregation to raise money to build a chapel in New Zealand by 'the prostitution of their bodies'.[17] Only a few proslavery writers suggested that the brutalities of slavery might have contributed to slave women's promiscuity. Former bookkeeper J. B. Moreton expressed this possibility in his guide to prospective estate personnel, entitled *West India Customs and Manners* (1793):

> I say if the most virtuous woman now in England had been tutored like blacks, a slave in like manner, she would be as lascivious and as common as any; and again, I say if blacks were tutored from their infancy in England, they would be as virtuous as white women.[18]

Moreton, then, was of the opinion that although slave women were less rational, more emotional and in other ways different from white, middle-class women in metropolitan society, they could become as virtuous.

Considering these two diametrically opposed theories of slave women's sexual deviance, it is not surprising that the proslavery debate about slave women's sexuality contained competing dominant representations of slave women: the *scheming black Jezebel* and the *potentially virtuous slave woman*. These representations both characterized slave women in terms of their sexual relations with white men, distinguishing two types of inter-

Deviant and dangerous 69

racial sexual relations. First, short-term relationships initiated by a black, or as was more common, a coloured[19] slave woman, who was generally referred to as a 'prostitute'. It was argued that she initiated the relationship solely to obtain material favours and that she did everything possible to hurt her white partner as soon after she had received the money or gifts. Second, long-term relationships initiated by white men but with the consent of the slave woman, who was referred to as a 'housekeeper'. Like the prostitute, the housekeeper's innate appetite for material goods was provided as the main reason why she entered such a relationship. Monk Lewis mentioned, for instance, that his slave Psyche had left her enslaved husband for an estate officer because he 'had a good salary, and could afford to give her more presents than a slave could'.[20]

While all proslavery writers in the late eighteenth and early nineteenth centuries presented both the prostitute and the housekeeper as scheming Jezebels, they regarded the latter as more of a threat to Jamaican society than the former. They raised four objections against housekeeper relationships.[21] First, such relationships threatened the social order because they led to 'spurious offspring'. By this they meant that owners set a large percentage of coloured slaves free in recognition of their white paternity or special and personal services, and that these free coloureds upset the delicate balance of power in the island, which was increasingly based on skin colour.[22] During slavery, a small number of whites occupied the highest rung of the social ladder, although they were internally divided on the basis of wealth, education, ethnicity, and occupation. The large number of slaves was at the bottom of the ladder, while freemen — black and coloured — occupied the middle rung, even though many had an economic position similar to or even exceeding that of the whites.[23] Second, 'spurious offspring' posed a threat to the productivity of the estates, as coloured slaves were generally exempted from heavy labour in the fields and were employed around the house.[24] Third, slave housekeepers endangered the stability of the estates because they managed to obtain 'complete ascendancy and sway' over their white men and, as Moreton argued, became 'intolerably insolent to subordinate white men'.[25] This objection should be seen in light of the tendency of Jamaican slaveholders to bequeath property and wealth to their free coloured offspring. The legitimate sons and daughters and other relatives of these men generally argued that the slave mistress had persuaded the deceased to include his coloured offspring in his will, and hence was to blame for their own limited inheritances.[26] And finally, the housekeeper was alleged to retard natural increase, since she, like the prostitute, developed venereal diseases that made her infertile and, as James Adair and others argued, aborted offspring in order to retain her white partner's favours.[27]

Even though the last objection was hard to sustain in the face of a reality of large numbers of coloured slaves on the plantations, it was articulated often. This obsession with infertility is not surprising, however, considering the extensive public debate about the natural decrease of the Jamaican slave population. As mentioned in the first chapter, planters took part in this debate not only because of the accusation that the way they treated their slaves caused natural decrease but also because they feared that abolitionists might succeed in banning the international slave trade. A ban on the trade would lead to a decrease in the slave labour force, which in turn would cause a decline in output and profit levels. It could be argued, then, that the image of the housekeeper as a scheming Jezebel served to contain this interlinked fear of natural decrease and declining productivity.

From the 1820s onwards, Jamaican writers no longer focused on the prostitute and presented the housekeeper less as a scheming Jezebel and more as a potentially virtuous slave woman. This shift was a direct response to the attacks of antislavery writers on the loose sexual mores of white Jamaican men. Antislavery writers contended that most interracial sexual relations were the result of force. To further portray the planters and the estate officers as a marked deviation from the metropolitan norm of male sexual restraint, they mentioned that these white men gratified their sex drive outside of marriage and often took married slave women as their sexual partners. Several Jamaican writers tried to deny these accusations. They pointed out that no force was involved, as slave women were keen to become housekeepers because of the benefits bestowed upon them, and that the relations did not 'trespass on the connubial rights of the slaves' because the slave women who engaged in sex with white men were young and single.[28] Their strongest argument in favour of housekeeper relations, however, was that they mirrored the monogamous, stable and affectionate relationships of English, middle-class men and women. One local resident, for example, wrote in 1827 that housekeepers were 'faithful and attached, and, in hours of sickness, evidenced all the kindness and affection of wives'.[29] To emphasize that love rather than lust underpinned housekeeper relations, Anthony Davis mentioned that most estate officers did their utmost to have their housekeeper accompany them to new places of employment; they often had to pay a great sum of money to compensate a planter for his loss of labour.[30] Thus in the late 1820s and early 1830s, some proslavery writers argued that both slave women and white Jamaican men lived up to, rather than deviated from, gendered metropolitan norms of sexuality.

The greater prominence of the potentially virtuous slave woman in the proslavery debate about interracial sexual relations by the mid-1820s was accompanied by a stronger denunciation of more casual sexual relations across the colour line. This discussion no longer warned of natural decrease but focussed solely on the fact that offspring of interracial unions led to social and political instability. The Anglican Reverend G. W. Bridges, one of the leading Jamaican defenders of slavery described interracial sexual relations in 1826, for instance, as an 'evil' because it 'bequeathed some of the largest proportion of coloured children'.[31] The discussion also differed from the earlier one in that it called upon slave women and white men not to cross the colour line in satisfying their sexual desires. Cynric Williams, who had visited the island in 1823, suggested, for example, that white estate officers should bring 'a white wife from England' and that slave women should marry 'black men rather than commit adultery with white ones'.[32]

The stronger denunciation of interracial sex was a direct response to the growth of the free population, which consisted mainly of coloured men and women. In 1810 the free population comprised 7.4 per cent of the total population of the island. Largely as a result of natural increase, it constituted 10.6 per cent of the total population in 1830.[33] This growth, which stood in sharp contrast with the decline of the white population from 6.9 to 5.0 per cent of the total population, was accompanied by a greater assertiveness of free(d)men.[34] From 1815 onwards, free(d)men held regular meetings in Kingston and petitioned the Assembly to extend their social and political rights. Their political assertiveness reached a climax in 1830 with the establishment of the first freedman newspaper *The Watchman*, which became the major organ to attack the racial discrimination in the island.[35]

The growth and increasing assertiveness of the free population threatened not only the social but also the economic status of the white islanders, especially that of the non-slaveholders because free(d)men were usually highly skilled and thus competed with white tradesmen on the labour market. Several proslavery writers suggested a legal ban on sex between white men and slave women to contain the threat posed by the growing free population. Some writers argued, however, that such a ban would do little to stop the growth of the free population, as existing Slave Law stipulated that anyone who was four or more generations removed from black ancestors was free.[36] They advocated instead endogamy within each of the six races that made up Jamaican society: white, mulatto (white and black), mustee (white and quadroon), quadroon (white and mulatto), sambo (mulatto and black), and black.[37]

Endogamy was most clearly advocated in the anonymously published novel *Hamel, the Obeah Man* (1827), which appears to have been written by Cynric Williams.[38] The highly derogatory representations of slave women in this novel demonstrate not only that black female bodies were simultaneously despised and desired but also the extent to which race, sex and gender were interwoven in the proslavery debate about slave women's sexuality. The main character in *Hamel, the Obeah Man* is Roland, a white missionary. While he tries to incite the slaves of a plantation to plan a rebellion and establish a black king, he falls in love with Joanna, the white daughter of the plantation owner. Roland's assistant Sebastian, a free mulatto man, is in love with Joanna's personal servant, a quadroon slave woman called Michal. Michal, however, has set her heart on the missionary, Roland. It is especially the inset story of Sebastian's futile attempts to court Michal that conveys the novel's message not to blur the colour line.

Sebastian realizes, shortly after his first meeting with Michal, that because of his skin colour his hopes to win this slave woman's heart are in vain:

> Quadroon damsels do not look for beauty in the youth of their own colour; their first ideas of admiration or love are devoted to the genuine white breed, either native or imported, to which they are themselves indebted, as they think, for the charms of their own persons, and all the favour they find in the eyes of those who sigh for their affections.[39]

The author presents Michal's sexuality as a deviation from the metropolitan norm of female sexuality, mainly by comparing her with her white mistress, Joanna. Whereas Joanna does not even entertain Roland's advances, Michal actively tries to woo him so as to become his housekeeper. Like earlier proslavery writers, the author presents her move as devoid of the love that metropolitan, middle-class girls were supposed to entertain towards their suitors: 'this young girl is in love with some white gentleman — for they always aspire: *ambition* goes hand in hand with love'.[40] This negative image of Michal as an immoral temptress coexists, however, with very positive descriptions of her physical appearance:

> Her skin was nearly as white as that of any European, of a clear and animated hue, the roses glowing upon her cheeks — ... and her forehead was shaded by some of the prettiest brown curls that ever graced the brows of a Quadroon damsel ... the long black eyelashes which like portcullises, guarded those portals of her heart, or mind, or genius, ... had been designed by nature with such attention to symmetry, and to what we have learned from our ancestors to consider beautiful.[41]

Michal is here not only presented as physically similar to white women but is also eroticised. It can be argued that the author eroticised Michal in order to ease his guilt of being sexually attracted to a coloured woman. Coloured women, especially the most light-skinned, were far more the objects of white men's sexual desire than black women, not only because they were seen as more aesthetically pleasing but also because they were considered more 'refined', as they were generally employed around the house rather than in the field. As a result of the growth of the free population, and to a lesser extent also the shift toward containment in the metropolitan norm of male sexuality, sexual attraction to coloured slave women had become a less accepted desire by the mid-1820s. The author could thus give vent to his sexual fantasies about light-skinned slave women by providing elaborate accounts of their beauty. It is, however, also possible to read the author's eroticisation of Michal as a means through which he expressed his anxieties about the status of white Jamaicans. Quadroon women posed far more of a threat to Jamaica's social structure than other coloured women because they were so similar to white women that they could easily pass among strangers as white and also because the children that resulted from their relations with white men added to the growth of the free population, as they were four generations removed from black ancestors.

One could argue, however, that Michal's eroticisation undermined rather than enhanced the author's assumption that coloured slave women, especially quadroons, were given over to sexual excess. At the time, feminine beauty was strongly linked to virtue, and it was assumed that a woman's virtue was visible on her face. The eyes of a virtuous woman, for instance, were seen to be clear and transparent like water.[42] A woman with irregular features, on the other hand, was believed to be capable of irregular conduct. Various other defenders of slavery also combined representations of coloured slave women as evil temptresses with favourable descriptions of their physical appearance, describing their faces as 'soft', 'sweet', and 'fine', their eyes as 'bright', 'brilliant' and 'sparkling' and their teeth as having a 'regular shape'.[43] Thus by giving coloured slave women the transparent and regular faces associated with virtuous metropolitan women, these proslavery writers presented slave women simultaneously as scheming Jezebels and as potentially virtuous women.

Hamel, the Obeah Man's discussion of slave women's sexuality supports Patricia Mohamed's contention that by the early part of the nineteenth century 'black women's centrality in production and reproduction may have very well been shared or superseded by [that of] mulatto women'.[44] In this novel, black women feature only secondarily in the account of Roland's attempt to stir some slaves up into rebellion, which is averted by the obeah man Hamel, and representations of them compare unfavourably to those of coloured slave women. Not only does the author omit references to black women's physical appearance, but he also rarely gives them names and refers to them mainly in derogatory terms:

> The missionary was no sooner left alone with the *black dame* than the latter asked him if he was hungry or thirsty, and offered him all she had to offer in the shape of refreshments. 'Black *woman*', said he, '*mistress Hamel*, or by what other name shall I address you? *Negress! sister in the spirit*! ... Tell me *mistress — mammy*, I should say — are you the only wife of Hamel?'[45]

Thus while black slave women in the novel, like their coloured counterparts, are presented as dangers to the social order, their danger is not linked to their sexuality but rather to their submissiveness to black men; they docilely obey their male partners' orders to help overthrow the plantation regime. In fact, the last line of the quote seems to suggest that the author regarded black men's sexuality as a greater threat to plantation society than black women's. Early proslavery verse and fiction lends further support to the idea that by the mid-1820s, proslavery writers had come to displace their main fears more onto coloured than black slave women. This literature presents both black and coloured slave women's sexuality as a deviation from the metropolitan norm of female sexuality. The song 'Me Know No Law, Me Know No Sin', which is included in Moreton's guide, demonstrates the lack of sexual restraint attributed in the late eighteenth century to black slave women:

> Alth'o a slave me is born and bred,
> my skin is black, not yellow:
> I often sold my maidenhead
> To many handsome fellow.[46]

The treatment of slave women's sexuality in *Hamel, the Obeah Man* suggests, then, that by the 1820s proslavery writers contrasted not only slaves to English middle-class men and women but also distinguished behaviours among the six races in Jamaica. They attributed to each racial category a set of defining internal characteristics, such as laziness or strength, which were used together with the visible signs, such as skin colour and hair texture, to rank them in a hierarchy. We have seen, for instance, in the first chapter that some proslavery writers ranked mulatto slave women higher than black slave women because the latter bred faster and recovered sooner after childbirth than mulatto slave women, whom they saw as more similar to white women in this respect. Such basic and dogmatic ideas about the racial hierarchy informed plantation practices, most notably the allocation of jobs. As Barry Higman has shown in his *Slave Populations of the British Caribbean, 1787–1834* (1984), coloured women predominated amongst the female domestics because planters regarded them as weak and not suitable for hard field labour.[47] In other words, by the 1820s skin colour had become a primary signifier of human difference for white Jamaicans.[48]

We have seen, then, that two images of slave women jostled for power in the proslavery debate about slave women's sexual relations with white men. These images served to express and thereby control fears that troubled the writers and which were exacerbated by abolitionist campaigning: natural decrease; declining profits; the growth of the free population; and slave revolts, as suggested in *Hamel, the Obeah Man*. They also aimed to justify forced and consensual interracial sexual relations. An estimate of the extent of these relations can be gained from the percentage of coloured slaves in the island.[49] In 1817, there were about 30,000 whites in the island and 300,000 slaves, including 36,000 coloureds.[50] A population of 24,000 adult white men, then, leads to a coloured slave (descendant)/white adult male (paternity) ratio of 1.5. This was considerably higher than that on the North American mainland at the time. An adult white male population of 2.8 million and 150,000 coloured slaves led there to a ratio of 0.05 coloured slaves per one white male.[51] At a rough guesstimate, then, the incidence of mixed offspring per available white father in Jamaica was 30 times that in North America. By presenting the slave woman as a scheming Jezebel, white men in the island could deny responsibility for their casual relations with slave women (and possible offspring), as she was inherently wanton and lured white men in order to fulfil her insatiable sexual appetite.[52] The potentially virtuous slave woman, on the other hand, was used in the 1820s and 1830s to justify housekeeper relationships in the island which were, according to the resident John Stewart, a common and accepted feature of Jamaican society: 'Every unmarried man, of every class, has his black or his brown mistress, with whom he lives openly; and of so little consequence is this thought, that his white female friends and relations think it no breach of decorum to visit his house'.[53]

As slave women's sexuality was regarded not only as deviant but also as potentially dangerous, several proslavery writers put forward proposals to regulate slave women's alleged excessive sexuality. The remainder of this section will examine these proposals and assess the extent to which they were adopted. Suggestions to contain slave women's sexuality were put forward throughout the period but they were especially prominent in the late eighteenth and early nineteenth centuries. They aimed to encourage monogamous sexual relations among slaves and discourage cross-plantation unions. In 1831, James Simpson, a manager of several plantations owned by absentee planters, expressed the opinion that both objectives could best be achieved by 'locking up and securing the female sex from all intercourse with the male sex at night'.[54] His proposal was clearly based on the idea that slave women were naturally promiscuous. Another and more often articulated suggestion was to offer female slaves a reward, such as a small sum of money or a furnished cabin, upon a marriage solemnised by an Anglican minister (hereafter, formal slave marriage).[55] It was not the representation of the scheming Jezebel or the potentially virtuous slave woman that underlay this proposal, however, but that of the maternal Jezebel; that is, a slave woman who would remain sexually pure but only if she was generously compensated for the exchange of her trade in sexual favours for a life of childbearing and childrearing.

Several proslavery writers were of the opinion that these schemes to make slave women cohabit with slave men from their own estates would not succeed unless accompanied by measures to curtail the interracial sexual relations of white estate officers. One measure proposed towards this end and which clearly built on the metropolitan idea that marriage would tame men's sexual passions, was to employ only married white men as estate officers. By the late eighteenth century, most planters employed only single men on their estates. This was largely a means by which they tried to counteract the declining profits on sugar, from 8.9 to 3 per cent between 1763 and 1782, which was caused mainly by the loss of trade resulting from the American War of Independence.[56] Employing married estate officers significantly increased a planter's expenses. He not only had to build houses and other facilities to accommodate the wives and children of his married employees but also pay family wages. Edward Long, who advocated the employment of married men as early as 1774 argued that this method to reduce interracial relationships would only succeed if the few white, single women in the island would become 'more agreeable companions, more frugal, trusty and faithful friends' than slave women, who willingly offered themselves to become housekeepers.[57] The scheming Jezebel who underlay Long's proposal also supported James Adair's suggestion to punish slave women who engaged in sex with white men.[58] Moreton, on the other hand, supported his proposal to curb interracial sex with a representation of slave women generally presented by antislavery writers, namely that of the naturally chaste slave woman. He proposed to protect slave women's 'virtue and chastity' through a law that would fine white men for having sex with them.[59]

There is no evidence that planters adopted Simpson's scheme. While some encouraged their slaves to marry, the majority did not because, as the following chapter will explain, formal marriage posed a threat to their enterprises. The proposals to employ only married estate officers and punish those who had sex with slave women were also not implemented on the estates. As white estate officers were in short supply as a result of high white mortality rates and many white men who came over to work on the estates were not well-suited to be overseers or book-keepers, planters may have tried to hold on to their officers by imposing as few limits on their behaviour as possible.[60] The Jamaican Assembly never discussed Moreton's proposal, which seems to have been based on a law that was adopted in the Leeward Islands in 1789 and which fined white men who had sex with married slave women, and also on some early North American anti-miscegenation laws.[61] The only act inhibiting interracial sexual relations that was passed was an 1826 measure that introduced the death sentence for the rape of female slaves: 'If any person or persons shall at any time after the commencement of this act commit a rape on any female slave, then and in every such case every person being therefore lawfully convicted shall be deemed guilty of felony, and suffer death without benefit of the clergy'.[62] This was a radical prohibition as none of the other slave societies in the Americas at the time allowed adult slave women legal recourse in case of alleged rape.[63] Not a single white man appeared in court after 1826 under the terms of this act. This should not be seen, however, as an indication that it succeeded in discouraging interracial sex. Rather the absence of complaints reflects the complicated process that the act imposed on slave women to have a white man convicted of rape. As chapter five will show, whites accused of physically abusing slave women in other ways were usually acquitted in the courts, and slave women ran the risk of corporal punishment if their allegations of abuse were not proven.[64]

It needs to be stressed that the 1826 rape act was not a response to calls to criminalize interracial sex in order to limit the growth of the free population. Instead, it was a means to please the abolitionists and the government at home. In May 1823, largely as a result of abolitionist campaigning, the House of Commons adopted a set of resolutions intended to ameliorate the condition of the slaves in the West Indies in preparation to abolish slavery at as early a date as might be compatible with the welfare and safety of the colonies. These included a proposal to admit slave testimony in courts of law; a programme to encourage religious instruction and marriage; and a ban on the flogging of female slaves.[65] In July, Colonial Secretary Lord Bathurst, asked the governor to encourage the Assembly to enact the ameliorative proposals for local implementation. The Assembly declined to do so, however, because it saw them as a step towards immediate emancipation.[66] Instead it passed the 1826 rape act to convince the Imperial Government that Jamaican planters were not unwilling to improve the condition of the slaves, and thus ward off future interference in their affairs. The act also had to deny the abolitionist accusation that planters treated their slave women inhumanely.[67]

Two reasons seem to explain why in spite of the various fears that interracial sex posed for the socio-economic status of white islanders, planters and the Assembly were so reluctant to undertake action to curb it. First, the demographics of Jamaican slave society. Throughout the period under discussion, there were four men to every one white woman in Jamaica.[68] This low ratio of white women provided, along with the significant (c. 40% and more) numbers of females among the huge slave majorities, the demographic convenience for interracial unions. It furthermore worked against the development of cultural mores against interracial sex, a task deemed most suitable for women because of their supposed moral superiority. Recent studies on the development of anti-miscegenation legislation on the North American mainland have shown, for instance, that this process was accompanied by an evening-out of the sex ratios of the white population and an increase in the status of women in society and family. More even sex ratios enabled women to refuse to accept their husband's offspring into the family, which was a strong disincentive against interracial sex.[69] The paucity of white women also left most white men in the island without one of the most powerful cultural constraints on their alleged powerful sexual energy: marriage.

Another and more important reason for the planters' inaction to tackle interracial sex is that it brought short-term economic benefits to their estates. It not only enabled them to keep white estate officers on their estate but also allowed them to increase their labour force at no extra costs through their own or their employees' offspring of sexual unions with slave women because children in Jamaican society took the status of the mother. This became an important reason for not acting against interracial sex between 1807 and 1834 when, as a result of the abolition of the slave trade and failure to achieve natural increase, the slave population drastically declined.[70] Interracial sex also helped planters to control their enslaved labour force since forced interracial sex demonstrated to slave women that the planter's (and his officers') power was absolute, even more so than flogging. Consensual sex with housekeepers, on the other hand, enhanced the stability of the estates as the jobs, clothing, housing and other gifts bestowed upon these women and their coloured children enlarged the divisions within the slave community, by setting them apart from the rest of the slave community.

VIRTUOUS AND VICTIMIZED

By the late eighteenth century, sexuality was seen as a polluting power and sexual restraint was used as one of the main indicators of civilization. It is therefore not surprising that antislavery writers supported their demand for a complete transformation of the slave societies in the Caribbean with accounts of sexual excess. Early antislavery writers focussed almost solely on the planters' and white estate officers' abuse of slave women. Later writers continued to centralize forced interracial sex but discussed it alongside instances of sexual excess in interslave relations and consensual relations between free coloured women and white men. In this way, they tried to demonstrate that slavery demoralized each of the three groups that made up the slave societies in the Caribbean: whites, free(d)men, and slaves. Or, as one writer argued in 1828:

> The dreadful effects of slavery are not more visible in the physical sufferings of its victims, than in the moral darkness and degradation by which it is inseparably attended. The unbounded licentiousness existing among the blacks, extending its baneful influence over the white population, paralyzing every feeling of morality, and permitting practices abhorrent to humanity, and unknown in civilized society.[71]

The three groups were thus seen as interlocking groups whose sexual behaviour deviated from the metropolitan norm of sexuality because of the existence of slavery. This section first explores what antislavery writers said about the sexual behaviour of slave women in interslave relations. It then goes on to examine their remarks about white men's sexual abuse of slave women, which centred on the idea that slave women were naturally chaste. This idea was challenged by the few accounts of the sexual behaviour of free coloured women. The section concludes with an examination of these accounts and the proposals that antislavery writers put forward to make slave women's sexuality conform to the metropolitan norm of female sexuality, some of which were remarkably similar to those presented by proslavery writers.

Antislavery writers argued that slave women lacked as much restraint as slave men in interslave sexual relations. Echoing almost the words of some proslavery writers, former missionary Thomas Cooper argued, for instance, that slave women had sex at an early age, usually had multiple sexual partners, and easily broke off sexual relationships and started new ones.[72] One explanation given for the women's deviation from the metropolitan ideal of passive female sexuality was their owners' disregard of slave marriage. Planters not only failed to encourage their slaves to marry but also obstructed the development of a proper legal slave marriage; that is, a marriage that gave slaves the same rights and duties as married couples in metropolitan society.[73] According to the M.P. George Henry Rose, slaves had as a result lost the knowledge of and the respect for the institution of marriage that they had carried with them upon the slave ships, and had quickly fallen into a state of 'perfect licentiousness'.[74] Another explanation for slave women's deviation from the metropolitan ideal of female sexuality was the bad example that planters and their white estate officers set for slave men. It was argued that slave men did not give slave women the 'respect which they ought to receive' because white men indecently exposed the women's bodies when they flogged them and they also sexually abused them. The lack of respect that slave men bestowed on their womenfolk, it was suggested, had led slave women to place little value on their sexual virtue.[75] In other words, white Jamaican men corrupted slave women's sexual mores not only directly but also indirectly.

By attributing slave women's deviation from metropolitan norms of female sexuality to factors external of them, antislavery writers presented slave women in their debate about interslave sexual relations as *potentially virtuous slave women*. Only a few voices in this debate suggested that slave women were not *potentially* but *naturally* chaste women. The author of *Considerations on the Expediency of an Improved Mode of Treatment of Slaves in the West India Colonies* (1820) mentioned, for instance, that although 'extremely rare', there were known cases of slave women who had abstained from sex before 'union', which was evidence, according to him, of slave women's 'natural modesty . . . which no abuse is able so entirely to eradicate'.[76] The idea that slave women were naturally chaste was more convincingly articulated in the numerous accounts of forced interracial sexual relations, which were presented as a common feature of Jamaican slave society. Antislavery writers explained the extent of the sexual abuse that slave women suffered at the hands of white men in terms of the planters' 'unlimited power' over the bodies of their female slaves and the lack of legal protection offered to slave women against sexual abuse.[77] Even after the Assembly had adopted the afore-mentioned rape act, antislavery writers continued to argue that slave women were not legally protected against sexual abuse. In one of the lectures that he gave in Yorkshire in 1830, the Reverend Benjamin Godwin told his audience that the government protected 'their persons and . . . property' but gave to 'another . . . the negro's wife'.[78] By ignoring the 1826 rape act, antislavery writers were able to sustain their claim that slaves were helpless victims and that it required the positive action of virtuous men and women in metropolitan society to transform their negative condition.

Godwin's remark suggests that in their accounts of forced interracial sex, antislavery writers were not only concerned about the planters' licentious power but also about slave women's status as a commodity. Several writers, in fact, mentioned that planters offered their slave women to white men who visited their estates and that they also encouraged estate officers and even their own sons to have sex with their slave women because any offspring resulting from these unions would add to their labour force.[79] Some writers went even further and suggested that slaveholders, both male and female, hired slave women out for sex in order to supplement the profits derived from their estates.[80] The idea that planters 'prostituted' their slave women was a most powerful argument because in metropolitan society at the time prostitution had become a metaphor for moral decay in general.[81] Two images of prostitutes dominated the debate about prostitution in the late eighteenth and early nineteenth centuries: the agent of destruction and the fallen woman.[82] As we have seen, proslavery writers presented both the 'prostitute' and the 'housekeeper' as an agent of destruction; that is, as a vicious woman who had chosen her calling and who caused through her actions physical damage. Antislavery writers, on the other hand, presented the slave woman who had sex with white men as a fallen woman; that is, a woman who had entered into vice against her wishes but who had preserved her virtue. The radical Robert Wedderburn, who was the illegitimate son of a slave woman and a white planter, articulated this most clearly in his autobiographical pamphlet *The Horrors of Slavery* (1824).[83] He mentioned that his slave mother had been 'chaste and virtuous' before his white father had made her 'the object of his brutal lust', and that when she became his housekeeper, she had remained 'a woman virtuous in principle'.[84]

Few antislavery writers articulated as directly as Wedderburn that slave women were naturally chaste. They provided instead accounts of slave women's attempts to resist their sexual abuse to demonstrate their innate virtue. Mark Cook, who had spent several years on Jamaican plantations, told the Slave Trade Committee about a slave woman who had run away with her husband and children in order to escape the overseer's sexual abuse.[85] Former estate doctor John Williamson described a similar case in 1817 but without a happy ending. When her overseer insisted that she should become his housekeeper, a married slave woman convinced her husband to poison the overseer by putting arsenic in his lemonade. Unfortunately, the overseer detected a metallic taste and did not finish the drink.[86] Both men argued, then, that slave women tried to live up to the metropolitan ideal of sexuality, as they did their utmost to be faithful to their husbands.

Most accounts of slave women's resistance against their white abusers ended, as in Williamson's case, in failure. Former bookkeeper Benjamin M'Mahon, for example, narrated the case of an attorney who tried to submit an 11-year-old slave girl to his sexual wishes. The girl struggled so fiercely that the attorney hit her repeatedly with his walking stick. Even though the girl passed out as a result of the strokes inflicted upon her, the attorney managed to finish 'his horrible purpose'. To further emphasize the power that white men in the island had over the bodies of slave women,

M'Mahon added that the girl's mother 'dare not even give utterance to a murmur' about her daughter's rape.[87] Accounts of unsuccessful resistance enabled antislavery writers to persuade their audiences that the slaves needed their support to overthrow slavery and that their project of a free, stable and moral Jamaica would succeed. They in particular conveyed the idea that upon full freedom, African Jamaican women would exercise one of the most important requisites for their role as the moral guardian of the family: chastity. The accounts furthermore allowed the authors to portray white Jamaican men as a marked deviation from the metropolitan ideal of masculine restraint and thus lend support to their claim that emancipation involved more than the freeing the slaves; it also implied a complete reformation of all sectors of Jamaican society.

Forced interracial sex was also a prominent theme in antislavery fiction, which expressed slave women's natural chastity not only through accounts of unsuccessful resistance but also by depicting abused slave women as asexual. Edward Rushton, who had worked on slave ships and had become an outspoken opponent of the slave trade in the early 1780s, mentioned, for instance, in one of the verses in his *West Indian Eclogues* (1787) that Quama had endured the overseer's rape but had not enjoyed it, while the mulatto girl Jenny in Elizabeth Helme's novel *The Farmer of Inglewood Forest* (1824) failed to feel any sexual feelings for her master because he had poisoned her in order to commit his horrendous act.[88] As in Quama's and Jenny's case, the sexual feelings of the slave girl Flowney in Robert Bage's novel *Man as He Is* (1792) are not aroused by the forced sexual encounter. Bage, however, went much further than other fiction writers to convince his readers of slave women's natural chastity. He presented Flowney as a young slave girl, who tries hard to live up to the metropolitan norm of female sexuality. The reader is told that she was a Christian girl, who thought it 'a great sin' for slave women to offer their sexual services to white men and had always 'refused to gratify Master Benfield'. After she has been raped by Benfield and his white male servant, she feels so tainted that she decides that she cannot marry her fiancé, the black slave man Fidel Benihango. As she cannot bear the thought of living without him, however, she drowns herself in the estate's pond.[89]

The licentious power, then, that slavery invested in planters and white estate officers was seen as a force that corrupted naturally chaste women. The fact that estate officers play a more prominent role in antislavery accounts of forced interracial sex than planters is largely a reflection of the reality of Jamaican slave society. As more than half of the slaves belonged to absentee owners by 1832, most of the sexual abuse was committed by white overseers and bookkeepers.[90] The antislavery writers' focus on this category of white Jamaican men, however, was also a rhetorical strategy. It allowed them to show how much of a corrupting force slavery really was, as even those who did not legally own the bodies of slave women thought it no less of a sin or crime to abuse them than those who were their legal owners. As we have seen, resident proslavery writers also suggested that it was mainly estate officers who engaged in interracial sex, especially in their proposals to control slave women's alleged excessive sexuality. Their focus on estate officers served a rather different purpose, however. It had to shift the antislavery accusation of uncontrolled white male sexuality away from the planting elite and onto the estate officers, and thereby sustain the class hierarchy within the white Jamaican population, which placed planters far above estate officers. It also had to enable planters to displace their anger about the fact that they were at the mercy of what Trevor Burnard has called, 'a motley crew' of white estate officers. Because white officers were in short supply, planters had to take whatever was on offer and pay them high wages. Many of the men that they hired, used excessive violence towards their slaves, turned up to work drunk, or did not do any work at all.[91]

It was argued that because estate officers did not own slave women, they had to use or threaten to use, physical force to make the women submit to their sexual wishes. Mark Cook mentioned, for example, that if an overseer sends for a girl 'she is obliged to come or else be flogged'.[92] Even more damaging was the accusation that these men used predominantly married slave women and young slave girls to satisfy their sexual needs; that is, women who in metropolitan society were seen as 'off limits' for men to satisfy their sexual needs.[93] It is not surprising that this accusation was more often articulated in later than early antislavery writings, as after the turn of the century, middle-class metropolitan society increasingly came to see children less as little adults and more as innocent and innately virtuous beings in need of protection, and it also began to place more emphasis on marriage as the only legitimate avenue for sex. Antislavery writers seldom argued that planters used violence in their interracial sexual encounters. Their deviation from the metropolitan norm of masculine restraint was seen to lie primarily in their deviant sexual acts, which included incest. Benjamin M'Mahon, for instance, mentioned a planter who had not only sexually abused his own mulatto daughter but also his quadroon granddaughter.[94] The planters' deviation from metropolitan norms of sexuality was also located in their lack of action to control the sexual behaviour of lower-class, white men in the island. Thomas Cooper, for instance, argued that by adopting a policy of employing only single men as estate officers, planters had actively encouraged the sexual excess of lower-class, white men.[95]

White men in the island, then, were seen to fall short of the metropolitan norm of masculine sexual restraint because they did not try to control their sexual urges or discharge them through the legitimate avenues, and also did not take their fatherly duties seriously. As for the last point, antislavery writers not only provided accounts of incest committed by planters but also mentioned various other ways in which planters, officers and other white men abused their mixed offspring. The *Memoirs of a West India Planter* cited, for example, a slave man, stating that 'many children of black women, whose fathers are attorneys, overseers and masters ... work like the rest and their fathers treat them as bad'.[96] Robert Wedderburn added that many planters sold their mixed children away from their enslaved mothers, without scruples.[97] As Christer Petley has shown in his study of Jamaican slaveholder wills, not all planters abused their mixed offspring. There were planters who gave their mixed offspring an education, set them free, or bequeathed them property upon their death.[98] The previous section has shown that it was well-known in the island that there were planters who acknowledged their mixed-race children and treated them favourably and that this caused some defenders of slavery great concern. The antislavery writers' suppression of this knowledge in the 1820s and early 1830s should be seen within the light of the emerging discourse of fatherhood. After the turn of the century, fathers in metropolitan society were not only expected to exert authority over their children but also take a loving and caring interest in their lives.[99] As Paul Langford has recently shown, many foreign visitors were surprised to find that Englishmen took this expectation so seriously and singled it out as an important marker of Englishness.[100] Suppressing information about planters who treated their mixed offspring well, then, was as much a means to construct white Jamaican society as a marked deviation from the norm of Englishness as the provision of detailed descriptions of white Jamaican men's transgressive sexual practices.[101]

Forced interracial sex posed several problems for antislavery writers. First, it did not allow slave women to develop and retain the purity which they needed for their future role as moral guardians. This problem, however, was seldom directly articulated. The *Memoirs of a West India Planter* hinted at it, for instance, by posing the question how offspring of forced interracial unions could 'manage to honour their parents'.[102] Second, it caused natural decrease. It was argued, not only during the campaign to end the slave trade but also in the 1820s and early 1830s, that slave women contracted venereal diseases from forced interracial sex, which in turn made them infertile or caused them to die prematurely.[103] Third, it had a negative impact on the welfare of the slave family. Benjamin M'Mahon, for example, pointed out that slave girls who became pregnant as a result of forced sex were unable to work on the provision ground so that the members of their families 'were either literally starving, or were dependent upon their black relations for support'.[104] And finally, it did not allow slave men to properly exercise their role as the protector of the family.

The large number of references to the last problem suggests that many antislavery writers regarded forced interracial sex more as a problem for slave men than for slave women. They invited their readers to empathize with the male slave who could not prevent his partner's or daughter's abuse. Thomas Clarkson, for instance, asked in 1824 what an Englishman would do if his wife or daughter was 'torn from him, with a knowledge that they are going to be compelled to submit to the lust of an overseer! and no redress!'.[105] Most authors tried, like Clarkson, to arouse their readers by presenting the male slave as an emasculated man; he silently acquiesced in his loved one's abuse because he would risk at least a severe flogging if he tried to defend her honour.[106] While some fictive accounts of forced interracial sex contain images of emasculated slave men,[107] most portray the wronged slave man as an angry man, bent on avenging his partner's abuse. The man whose wife had been taken away by the overseer in one of Edward Rushton's poems, for instance, acts out his desire to make his 'thirsty knife' drink the white man's 'streaming gore', while the wronged slave men in *Man as He Is* and *The Farmer of Inglewood Forest* shoot their partner's abuser.[108] Such acts of resistance served to convince the readers that slave men placed a high value on female sexual purity and that they had the ability to act as proper household heads. In other words, upon full freedom African Jamaican men would exercise their proper gender roles, and as such contribute to the transformation of the island. These fictive accounts, however, also had the potential to undermine the abolitionist project. Abolitionists favoured a scheme of emancipation that would prevent rather than encourage direct and violent slave action, as is conveyed most clearly in the device of the kneeling, shackled slave with the words 'Am I not a man and a brother?'. Accounts of slave men who killed white men, however, could make readers seriously question the abolitionists' commitment to non-violence.[109]

That only a few antislavery writers addressed consensual interracial sex is not surprising of course, as their project of a future free, stable and moral society depended on passive and not active female sexuality.[110] Those who did, focussed mainly on relations between white men and free coloured women. They presented the women as prostitutes by using phrases such as 'illicit commerce,' to describe their relations with white men. The women, however, were not seen as agents of destruction and beyond redemption but, like the slave women who were forced by their owner to have sex with white visitors, as fallen women who had not lost all of their virtue. The former Wesleyan missionary John Barry mentioned, for instance, that he had noticed during his stay in the island in the late 1820s that free coloured women who had been exposed to religious teaching, had given up their trade in sexual favours in spite of the 'greatest inducements offered by their former keepers to return to it'.[111] Free coloured women were not only described as prostitutes but also as madams. It was mentioned that the women encouraged their daughters to become mistresses of white men rather than marry free or slave men of their own colour because a relationship with a white man would enhance their material status.[112] Both images of free coloured women served to convey the idea that slavery corrupted free men and women as much as whites and slaves. They suggested that free coloured women had internalized one of the main ideas on which the institution of slavery was based; namely, that bodies were for sale.[113] It is interesting to note that none of the writers presented free coloured women's desire to have a relationship with a white man as evidence of a major effect of slavery: the premium placed on white skin. The emphasis that they placed on the fact that free coloured women did not marry men of their own colour seems to suggest, in fact, that they did not want to see an overhaul of the existing colour hierarchy of Jamaican society after full freedom. It could be argued, then, that antislavery writers were not, as they themselves suggested, outside of power as they indirectly supported a system of power relations based on skin colour.[114]

The accounts of free coloured women's relationships with white men could have made some readers question the assumption that with full freedom slave women would become sexually pure because these ex-slave women had moved further away from rather than closer to the metropolitan norm of passive female sexuality. Robert Wedderburn's account of his mother's long-term relationship with her white owner also challenged this assumption. As we have seen, he presented his mother as a virtuous woman prior to being sexually assaulted by her owner and becoming his housekeeper. Wedderburn contradicted his claim that his mother was a sheer victim of white man's sexual lust and had remained 'virtuous in principle', however, by suggesting that she had enjoyed her status as housekeeper and had used her sexuality in order to obtain favours from her owner. When her owner had told her, for instance, that he was going to replace her with a new housekeeper, she had shown such a strong resistance that he had agreed not only to sell her back to her former owner but also to set free the child (Wedderburn) that she was carrying at the time.[115]

Various proposals were put forward to make slave women's sexuality conform to the metropolitan model of passive female sexuality, especially after the turn of the century. The suggestion to encourage and legalize formal slave marriage, which was mainly proposed in the 1820s and early 1830s, will be discussed in the next chapter. It suffices here to state that those who proposed this solution saw it more as a means to regulate interslave sexual behaviour than as a means to curb interracial sex because they did not think that white Jamaican men would internalize the metropolitan idea that men should not use married women to satisfy their sexual needs.[116] One of the earliest measures proposed was the criminalization of interracial sex. The agriculturalist and political economist James Anderson suggested in 1789 that the Assembly should enact that a slave woman who was pregnant with a child from her owner or overseer should be relieved from work for one year after the delivery and that planters had the right to force overseers to pay for such a loss of labour.[117] Three years later, the well-known politician Edmund Burke proposed that 'any white person' who had 'committed adultery with any Negro woman' or had abused 'any Negro woman under sixteen years of age' had to pay a fine and could never again serve as overseer or attorney.[118] Both men suggested, then, that the best way to safeguard slave women's purity was through the pocket of white Jamaican men. That none of the antislavery writers suggested the life imprisonment or the death penalty for white men who had sexually abused slave women seems to stem from their assumption that such an act was already in place in the island. As many metropolitan laws made their way to the colonies, they probably assumed that the same had happened to the 1576 act which made the rape of a girl under ten a capital crime and stipulated that anyone convicted of such a rape forwent the benefit of the clergy, and also believed that this act applied equally to white and black women.[119]

Two other proposals singled out estate officers as the main obstacle to slave women's sexual purity. Richard Bickell suggested that planters provide slave girls with more decent clothing than the 'long shirt or shift' so that they would not gain the unwanted attention of white estate officers, while William Wilberforce and Thomas Cooper agreed with Edward Long that planters should employ only married estate officers.[120] It could be argued that these proposals, like those by Anderson and Burke, helped to reinforce the proslavery idea that planters deviated less from the metropolitan ideal of masculine sexual restraint than lower-class white men in the slave colonies. While these proposals were based on the idea that slave women were naturally chaste, the one put forward by John Barry in his statement before the 1832 Select Committee drew upon the idea that slave women were not naturally but potentially virtuous. Using the earlier-mentioned example of free coloured women, Barry suggested that the best way to make slave women live up to the metropolitan model of passive female sexuality was to provide them with religious instruction.

Another proposal which presented slave women as naturally chaste and as innocent victims of white men's sexual desires was the one put forward by the Reverend George Whitfield in 1830. Whitfield proposed a change in manumission practices which had to make it easier for slave men to purchase their wife's or their children's freedom.[121] He, in other words, believed that the best way to protect slave women's chastity was not to disarm white men but to empower slave men. As we shall see in the next chapter, antislavery writers were convinced that slave men could only properly exercise their role as the protector of their dependants if they had full authority over them; that is, if they were no longer the planter's property. Whitfield's proposal, however, was not only based on the assumption that slave men had to be given the autonomy to act as household heads but also on the metropolitan idea that female purity was best safeguarded through 'the shelter and protection of the domestic sanctuary'.[122]

The following chapter will indicate the outcome of the proposals to encourage slave marriage and to change manumission laws. As for the other proposals, it has already been indicated that the Assembly did not criminalize interracial sex apart from the 1826 rape act. The 1826 Slave Law put more pressure on planters to provide their slaves with decent clothing. Whereas the 1816 Slave Law had simply stated that they had to provide their slaves with 'proper and sufficient' clothing, the 1826 Law stipulated that they had to make an annual account of the quality and quantity of the clothes handed out to the slaves and that the justice and vestry could fine them five pounds for each slave found with insufficient clothing.[123] The Assembly made little attempt, however, to expose slaves to religious instruction because it regarded this as a destabilising factor, especially after the 1831–32 rebellion. In January 1832, for instance, the Colonial Church Union was set up which not only persecuted nonconformist missionaries, who were seen as the instigators of the rebellion, but also tried to put the established clergy under the control of the vestries. This planter bulwark, in other words, also questioned whether the established clergy could be trusted to act in the interests of the planters.[124]

Two images, then, also dominated the antislavery debate about slave women's sexuality: the *potentially virtuous slave woman* and the *naturally chaste slave woman*. The coexistence of these two images had the potential to challenge the antislavery project because the potentially virtuous woman seemed to question the ability of slave women to live up to the metropolitan norm of passive female sexuality upon freedom. The antislavery project, however, depended on both images. While the naturally chaste woman had to convince the audience of slave women's ability to become moral regenerators, the potentially virtuous woman had to arouse the public into action by convincing them of slavery's morally corrupting power. Thus whereas proslavery images of slave women's sexuality served to justify action and control fears, antislavery images aimed to encourage action and remove fears.

CONCLUSION

All the participants in the debate about slavery and abolition depicted slave women's sexuality as a marked deviation from the metropolitan ideal of passive female sexuality. For proslavery writers, this deviant sexuality threatened the socio-economic standing of the planters and others whose livelihoods were closely tied up with the plantation economy because it caused natural decrease and social instability and negatively impacted on productivity levels. Antislavery writers singled out various immediate problems associated with slave women's deviant sexuality including natural decrease but were far more concerned with its long-term impact; namely, the postponement of the creation of a more moral society. According to them, slave women could only act as the moral guardians of their families and thus lay the groundwork for a future free and moral society, if their sexuality conformed to the metropolitan norm of passive female sexuality. Contrary to proslavery writers, they did not see slave women's deviant sexuality as a problem in itself. Instead, they presented it as one of several problematic sexualities in the island, each of which demonstrated the powerful corrupting influences of slavery.

Three images of slave women dominated in the debate: the scheming Jezebel, the potentially virtuous slave woman, and the naturally chaste slave woman. The coexistence of the first two, diametrically opposed images in the proslavery debate, illustrates most clearly the contradictory nature of proslavery discourse. Proslavery writers located in metropolitan society were more inclined to invoke the potentially virtuous slave woman than resident writers, not only because they were more influenced by metropolitan ideas about feminine virtue but also because they held different ideas about the best way to avert abolitionist attacks on the plantation system. They preferred grandscale amelioration, whereas resident writers proposed a limitation of the slaves' autonomy through physical punishment and other drastic forms of coercion. As the justification of extreme measures to restrict slave autonomy required images of slaves as 'different', it is not surprising that resident writers resorted primarily to the scheming Jezebel. The images of the potentially virtuous and the naturally chaste slave woman were articulated alongside each other in the antislavery debate on slave women's sexuality, sometimes even within the space of one work, such as Robert Wedderburn's autobiographical account. Although not as diametrically opposed as the two images of slave women's sexuality in the proslavery debate, their coexistence also had the potential to confuse the audience.

Both sides in the debate addressed similar themes, such as the prostitution of slave women's bodies, while ignoring others, including slave women's sexual enjoyment. This illustrates that what pro- and antislavery writers said and did not say, was as much determined by their projects as by the public debates of the time, most notably that on sexuality. Both sides measured not only the sexual behaviour of slave women against metropolitan gendered norms of sexuality but also that of the white men in the island. As we have seen most clearly in their remarks about slave women as prostitutes, the two sides were highly selective in their engagement with the metropolitan discourse on sexuality. Both sides, however, drew not only upon this discourse but also helped to shape it. Some of the proposals that were put forward to change slave women's sexual behaviour reinforced, for instance, the idea that marriage was the only legitimate place for sexuality.

Both sides in the debate about slave women's sexuality furthermore helped to racialize the metropolitan discourse on sexuality. The construction of the naturally passionless white woman in the late eighteenth century required the displacement of female sexual agency onto various groups of women defined as 'other'. According to Sander Gilman, by the turn of the century not only the white prostitute was used for this purpose but also the scheming Jezebel.[125] Although the potentially virtuous slave woman in both the pro- and antislavery debate was not as sexually aggressive as the scheming Jezebel, she was also overtly sexual and as such helped to construct and sustain the ideal of the passionless white woman. Pro- and antislavery writers simultaneously helped to sexualize the discourse on race. By depicting slave women as different from white, metropolitan women because of their sexual practices, they helped to make sexual behaviour one of the key characteristics defining the inferiority of people of African descent.[126] Both processes — the racialization of sex and the sexualization of race — have thus far relinquished few of their powers. Various studies have pointed out, for instance, that black women in Africa and the Diaspora are still regarded as naturally promiscuous and immoral and that as a result, they suffer rape and other forms of sexual abuse by white and black men.[127] Accounts of the spread of HIV in Africa, furthermore, link sexual excess and racial inferiority in the minds of contemporary politicians, journalists, and even scientists as firmly as they did in the minds of the pro-slavery writers.[128] Finally, and linked to the foregoing, the debate about slave women's sexuality also supported the metropolitan idea that men were naturally endowed with a greater sex drive than women. It did this, amongst others, by concentrating on slave women's deviant sexual behaviour while largely ignoring that of slave men, and also by putting forward proposals that aimed to encourage white men to control their natural sexual urges.

The debate about slave women's sexuality also engaged with the metropolitan discourse on gender. It not only mentioned — mostly indirectly — roles expected of women, such as their duties to obey their partner and guard the morals of the family, but also that of men. In their attacks on white men's loose sexual mores, antislavery writers presented restraint as a key attribute of masculinity, which proslavery writers acknowledged in their response to these attacks and also in some of their proposals to contain slave women's deviant sexuality. Antislavery writers also articulated ideas about masculinity in their accounts of slave men who were incapable of defending the virtue of their partner. A proper man, these accounts suggested, was an independent householder. Various scholars working on New World slavery have reiterated the antislavery idea that slavery emasculated slave men. Orlando Patterson, for instance, stated in his seminal work *The Sociology of Slavery* (1967) that white men's sexual abuse of slave women and slave women's ability to use sexuality to their own advantage 'resulted in the complete demoralization of the negro male' who 'could not exert his authority as husband or father'.[129] Patterson's and similar ideas about the emasculization of slave men and its long-term impact have increasingly come under scrutiny. The American feminist bell hooks, for instance, has argued that slave men's inability to resist the sexual abuse of their loved ones shows that slavery stripped them of their patriarchal status but that it had not taken away other essential attributes of masculinity, such as virility and strength.[130] Hilary Beckles has reached a similar conclusion in a recent article entitled 'Black Masculinity in Caribbean Slavery' in which he accepts Patterson's conclusion that slavery marginalized black fatherhood, while adding that slave men did their utmost to assert a masculinity which shared many tenets of white Jamaican men's ideology of masculinity. Using amongst others the diary of the Jamaican slaveholder Thomas Thistlewood, he points out that slave men tried to assert their authority over their enslaved partners, protested their loved ones' sexual abuse, and used violence to resist their enslaved condition.[131]

90 *Slave women in discourses on slavery and abolition, 1780–1838*

As a result of various factors, including an increased presence of free blacks in the metropolis and new methods of scientific inquiry, differences in skin colour came to occupy a prominent place in the late eighteenth- and early nineteenth-century metropolitan discussion about human differences, as is evidenced most clearly by the publication of some basic racial classifications that attributed a set of defining characteristics to groups with a distinctive complexion.[132] *Hamel, the Obeah Man* and other calls for the endogamy of the six races in Jamaican society illustrate most clearly the proslavery writers' engagement with this metropolitan discourse of race. The antislavery writers' engagement with this discourse is rather more complex. They tried to challenge the discourse's associations between complexions and their internal characteristics. We have seen, for instance, that they suggested that both black and coloured women could be as virtuous as white women. At the same time, however, they reinforced the hierarchization of people based on their skin colour, as we have seen in their account of free coloured women's relationships with white men. The following chapter will provide more evidence to support the conclusion that the antislavery writers' belief in the equality of human kind did not prevent them from articulating ideas of black inferiority. This contradiction in antislavery discourse should not surprise us, however, as antislavery writers were as steeped in the discourse of racial hierarchy as proslavery advocates.[133]

The pro- and antislavery representations of slave women's sexuality thus shaped in various and lasting ways the metropolitan discourses on sexuality, gender and race. More intense, however, was their negative impact on the lives of slave women. The proslavery representations justified the planters' and estate officers' sexual abuse of slave women (and till 1826 also their lack of protection against it) which led both slave women and slave men to perceive the power of the planter as absolute. The antislavery representations also limited slave women's sexual lives but in a less direct way. They informed, amongst others, the nonconformist missionaries' close scrutiny of the sexual lives of the female members of their congregations. Women who were not 'virtuous' because they had sex before marriage, or worse 'lived in sin' with white men, were either severely reprimanded or expelled from church.[134]

4 Till death do us part
Slave wives and slave husbands

Lord Hardwicke's Marriage Act of 1753 specified that in order to be valid, a marriage had to be performed in a church or public chapel with banns or licence and parental permission for minors, in the presence of two or more credible witnesses besides the ordained minister of the Church of England, and had to be entered into a parish register signed by the couple and the minister.[1] The 1753 Marriage Act has generally been considered as a first step in the struggle of the rising middle classes in Britain to end the general contempt for marriage and impose their particular norm of marriage on the rest of society. The middle classes favoured a marriage that was legal, indissoluble, monogamous, co-resident, and based on affection and personal compatibility. They expected husbands and wives to occupy separate spheres and carry out distinct tasks. The husband had to spend his day outside the house earning money in order to provide for his wife and children and he also had to protect his dependants. In return for his financial support and protection, the wife had to run the household, take care of the children's physical and spiritual development, and contribute to her husband's moral welfare.[2] Although these gendered tasks were presented as reciprocal and complementary, they were firmly based on the assumption that the husband was the head of the household and that the wife had to obey her husband's wishes.[3]

By the end of the eighteenth century, the upper classes had come to accept the middle classes' norm of marriage. Thereafter, the middle classes tried to impose their marriage norm on the lower orders of society. This effort was largely determined by economic self-interest. The industrial middle class, for instance, hoped that a rise in the marriage rate of the lower orders would lead to an increase in the population, which was seen as essential for the future of their economic enterprises as it guaranteed them a large supply of labour and also an increased demand for their products. The lower middle class, on the other hand, thought that a rise in the lower classes' marriage rate would make them less of a drain on parish resources. Parishes, for example, were responsible for the costs of maintaining illegitimate children whose reputed fathers had absconded or who were too poor to pay the weekly maintenance sum set by the magistrate. All middle-class men and women, however, agreed that if the lower orders made their unions legal and adopted the other attributes of the middle-class marriage ideal, in particular monogamy and gendered roles and gendered spheres of activity, society would become more stable because lower-class wives would persuade their husbands not to drink too much, stay out too late, or engage in other forms of vice. In other words, the middle classes regarded the adoption of their marriage ideal by their social and economic inferiors as a means to create a more stable and prosperous society.[4]

Pro- and antislavery writers posed the question whether it would be worthwhile to offer the metropolitan, middle-class marriage ideal to the slaves in the Caribbean colonies. Antislavery writers were convinced that if slave marriage conformed to the ideal and if more slaves married, a foundation would be laid for a stable and moral society. Although they wanted slave marriage to include all the attributes of the metropolitan marriage ideal, they emphasized in particular co-residence, legality, gendered roles and gendered spheres of activity. Proslavery writers were more divided over this question. Some were completely opposed to the idea, while others were convinced that planters could benefit economically from offering their slaves a limited version of the metropolitan marriage ideal; that is, a monogamous and long-lasting but not an indissoluble and co-resident marriage.

Both sides posed another and linked question: Are slaves able to live up to the metropolitan marriage ideal? Antislavery writers answered this question more positively than proslavery writers, although not all were convinced that slaves would be willing and capable of properly exercising all the attributes associated with the ideal. It was not until the mid-1820s that some proslavery writers admitted that in the distant future slaves could exercise some but never all the attributes of the marriage ideal. During apprenticeship the same questions were asked but slightly different answers were given. Critics of apprenticeship reiterated the antislavery idea that the promotion of the metropolitan marriage ideal amongst the African Jamaican population would help to lay the foundation for a moral society after freedom, while adding that it was also crucial for the economic future of the island. Although opponents, especially the planter-friendly S.M.s, expressed severe doubts about the apprentices' ability to live up to their marriage vows because of their ingrained customs, they put forward legislation that aimed to enable apprentices to live up to far more attributes of the metropolitan marriage ideal than those favoured by proslavery writers in the 1820s and early 1830s.

This chapter examines the debate about slave and apprenticed marriage. Although most participants expected slave and apprenticed women to become wives, they did not explore in great detail the roles expected of slave and apprenticed wives. It was not only the fact that they worked with and within a language of marriage that attributed a greater role to husbands than wives but also the socio-economic conditions of the island that led them to focus more on slave and apprenticed husbands than on slave and apprenticed wives. This chapter will nevertheless try to unravel the various roles that the participants in the debate about marriage directly and indirectly ascribed to slave and apprenticed wives. These will be discussed alongside the roles that they allocated to slave and apprenticed husbands in order to draw a picture of the gender order that the participants envisioned for the island upon full freedom. The first section sketches the relational lives of the African Jamaican population during slavery. It provides a context for the three following sections, which examine the answers given to the question as to whether slaves and apprentices could and should model their relationships on the metropolitan marriage ideal. The last section summarises the roles ascribed to wives and husbands in the debate about slave and apprenticed marriage and argues that this debate reinforced various metropolitan ideas about marriage.

SLAVE MARRIAGE[5]

Contrary to slaves on the North American mainland, Jamaican slaves could legally marry. Only a marriage performed by an Anglican minister (hereafter, formal slave marriage), however, was regarded as legal. The formal marriage rate remained low in the decades leading up to abolition. Between 1808 and 1822, the Anglican Church performed only 3,600 slave marriages on a slave population of about 330,000.[6] The fact that slaves needed permission from their owner or overseer, had to pay a small fee and undergo a detailed examination by the minister, explains why so few slaves opted for formal slave marriage. Most slaves preferred instead a marriage performed by a nonconformist minister or an informal slave marriage. As a nonconformist slave marriage required usually no more than proof of having been baptized, it is no surprise that their numbers far exceeded those of formal marriages.[7] An informal marriage consisted of a brief ceremony in which slaves who had lived together for some time promised to support one another in face of a large congregation of friends and family.[8] This type of slave marriage was very popular amongst the slave population because it allowed for divorce, which was an African carry-over.[9]

Slaves who opted for a formal or a nonconformist marriage were usually locally-born slaves who had lived together for some time and had children, which means that the marriage age must have been considerably higher than the 25.3 for men and 23.4 for women in metropolitan society at the time.[10] One reason why some slaves preferred a church-sanctioned over an informal marriage is that it enabled them to improve their status within the slave community. Former missionary Reverend Trew mentioned, for instance, that slaves who had married in church were held 'in greater respect' by their 'fellow servants over those who still continue in their heathenish state'.[11] Some slaves may also have regarded a church-sanctioned marriage as a precondition for freedom. They thought that if their lives mirrored those of respectable whites, including their intimate relationships, their chances of freedom would be enhanced.[12] It has also been suggested by some scholars that slaves opted for a church-sanctioned marriage because they thought that planters would be more reluctant to separate church-married than informally-married slave couples and that a church-sanctioned marriage would protect them against some of the other strains that planters put on slave relationships, most notably the sexual abuse of slave women.[13]

Barry Higman has estimated that 30 to 50 per cent of all church-married slave couples resided on different estates (hereafter, abroad marriages).[14] Plantation practices explain to some extent this high rate of abroad marriages. Planters 'actively' separated slave husbands from wives by sale, gift or bequest or by hiring them out to other plantations, and till 1827 'passively' separated married couples when levies were made on their property. Planters also facilitated abroad marriages through their practice of buying more male than female slaves. By the time the slave trade was abolished, a plantation sex ratio of 118 slave men to 100 slave women was not uncommon.[15] Slave customs and preferences also account for the high rate of abroad marriages. For example, a ban on sibling and cousin-mating in the slave community forced many slaves to look for a partner elsewhere.[16] And finally, the numerous occasions that slaves had to fall in love with slaves from surrounding plantations also explain the high incidence of abroad marriages, such as market day when slaves from various plantations sold and bought excess produce.

Most abroad slave couples lived no more than two miles apart and tried to see each other as much as possible. To do so, however, they needed written permission from their owner or overseer. That owners and overseers gave easily permission suggests that they were aware of the importance that slaves attached to their families and that they realized that withholding permission could trigger fierce resistance. Evidence suggests that slaves in an abroad marriage asked for a ticket to visit their spouse during the weekend but that they visited them often clandestinely during the week, and also that abroad wives did as much of the visiting as abroad husbands.[17]

Some slaves were married to a free black or coloured person (hereafter, mixed marriage). As this type of marriage had the same legal status as that of two slaves, it could at any time be broken up by the enslaved partner's owner, through such actions as hiring the enslaved partner out to a distant plantation. This, however, was not the only difficulty faced by mixed-married couples. They also found it hard to live under the same roof because the enslaved partner's owner forbade the free partner to live on the estate or demanded a very high rent. It is not surprising, then, that most mixed marriages were abroad marriages.[18]

As suggested in the previous chapter, it was not only planters and white estate officers who exerted pressure on slave couples but also missionaries.

In 1833, there were 16 Methodist missionaries in the island, along with 14 Baptists, 8 Moravians and 5 Presbyterians. Their main activities consisted of holding Sunday services, running Sunday schools, and visiting the estates in their vicinity.[19] The marital lives of the slaves played a central role in each activity. The Moravians, for example, tried to encourage slaves to marry by holding 'love feasts' (services only for married couples) and conveyed in their services and Sunday school meetings such important lessons as 'thou shall not commit adultery' or have sex before marriage. They also closely monitored the lives of their married members. Couples who did not live up to the norm of a Christian marriage were called in for questioning and were, if necessary, punished for their deviant behaviour. It has been estimated that some 3 to 4 per cent of their members were expelled annually on account of adultery.[20]

Missionaries also encouraged slaves to adopt distinct gender roles upon marriage. It is difficult to say, however, whether the distinct roles displayed by married slaves were the result of these teachings or, as Barbara Bush has suggested, a carry-over from Africa.[21] Married slave men tended to cultivate the garden surrounding the hut, while their partner sold excess produce that they had raised together on their combined provision grounds. Even couples who lived on separate estates tried hard to carry out distinct and complementary roles. When they visited each other over the weekend, husbands gave their wives provisions, such as fish or yams, while their wives cooked them a nice dinner and mended their clothing.[22]

A MORAL INSTITUTION

Like slave motherhood, slave marriage did not occupy a major role in early antislavery writings because it was of little use in the campaign to abolish the slave trade. The centrality of the institution in later antislavery writings was first of all the result of an increased discussion in metropolitan society about marriage. From the late 1810s onwards, various groups called for an amendment to the 1753 Marriage Act. Nonconformists pointed to the oppressive nature of enforced Anglican marriage, while others mentioned that the Act had done little to reduce cohabitation because many people could not afford to marry or did not like the publicity given to an Anglican marriage. The pressure exerted by these groups was instrumental in bringing about the 1836 Marriage Act, which ended the monopoly of the Anglican Church over legal marriage.[23] The prominent place of marriage in later antislavery writings was also a response to changes in the status of slave marriage. Although marriages performed by an Anglican minister had been regarded as legal since the turn of the century, the 1826 Slave Law was the first to recognize such marriages as 'valid in law'. Clause 4 stipulated that:

> It shall and may be lawful for any slave or slaves, who has or have been baptised, who may be desirous of entering into the holy state of matrimony, to apply to any clergyman of the established church to solemnise such marriage, who is hereby required to perform the same without any fee or reward, if such clergyman shall, upon examination of such slaves consider them to have a proper and adequate knowledge of the nature and obligation of such a contract: provided always, that such a slave shall produce to the clergy a permission in writing from his owner or from the legal representative of his owner for that purpose.[24]

This clause was the result of several years of pressure exerted by the Imperial Government on the Assembly to encourage slave marriage. In May 1823, it asked the Assembly, as part of its series of ameliorative proposals, to recognize both Anglican and nonconformist slave marriage as legal, and enact that slave women who had given birth to a certain number of children born in wedlock were to be exempted from field work.[25] As mentioned, the Jamaican Assembly did not seriously consider the ameliorative proposals. It also did not pay much attention to the Order in Council for Trinidad, a slave code which incorporated most of the 1823 ameliorative proposals and which it was asked to consider for local implementation in March 1824. The Order included the 'Bill for Regulating the Celebration of Marriages among Slaves', which tried to increase the slave marriage rate by legalizing nonconformist marriages and abolishing the marriage fee. Because the Assembly sternly refused to adopt this and most other bills in the Order in Council, it was dissolved by the governor in March 1826. The newly elected Assembly was ordered to consider a number of ameliorative bills drawn up by law officers of the Crown. This led in December 1826 to a revised Slave Law which included the earlier-mentioned rape act.[26] The passing of the Slave Law did not put an end, however, to practices that made it difficult for slaves to obtain a formal marriage or for formally married couples to live up to their marriage vows, such as withholding written permission for marriage and the flogging of slave women. This is not surprising as in the late 1820s and early 1830s, the planters' arbitrary and proprietary power over their labour force was fiercely attacked by various forces within and outside of the island.

Throughout the period 1780–1834, antislavery writers based their discussion about slave marriage on the assumption that marriage improved people's moral condition, and provided arguments in support of slave marriage that were identical to those used in the metropolitan discussion about the relational lives of the lower classes. James Ramsay mentioned, for instance, in 1784 that it was crucial to encourage slave marriage because 'marriage, or a family, is the embryo of society; it contains the principles, and seeds of every social virtue', while William Wilberforce referred some forty years later to slave marriage as 'the source of all domestic comfort and social improvement — the moral cement of civilized society'.[27] Antislavery writers suggested, in other words, that if slaves married in greater numbers and if their marriages mirrored those in metropolitan society, a foundation would be created for a moral and stable society upon freedom. It needs to be stressed that a few early antislavery writers also mentioned some economic benefits associated with slave marriage. In order to convince planters to encourage their slaves to marry, Ramsay pointed out, for instance, that marriage made slave men more 'industrious'.[28] Edmund Burke mentioned in his *Sketch of the Negro Code* (1792) a different economic benefit of slave marriage: a rise in the slave birth rate. This benefit was not directed at planters, however, but at abolitionists. Burke hoped that it would convince abolitionists of their folly to press for immediate abolition of the slave trade. He believed that if slaves married more and reproduced more, slave imports would decline and the slave trade would gradually cease to exist.[29]

Considering that they saw marriage primarily as a moral institution and the fact that the home was increasingly presented in metropolitan society as a 'nursery of virtue', it is no surprise that in their discussion about slave marriage antislavery writers placed a good deal of emphasis on co-residence.[30] This attribute and that of legality received little attention in early antislavery writings about slave marriage.[31] Another striking difference between early and later antislavery writings about slave marriage is the belief in the slaves' ability to live up to the metropolitan marriage ideal and the depiction of the planters' attitudes towards slave marriage. Some early antislavery writers presented their readers with stories that had to convince them that slaves were capable of living up to the metropolitan marriage ideal. Captain Marjoribanks, who had been stationed in the island in the 1780s, included in his *Slavery: An Essay in Verse* (1802) a highly sentimental poem that aimed to show that slave relationships were based on affection and that slave couples did their best to support one another:

> By various masters families are bought amidsts
> Their unregarded *sighs* and *tears,*
> The wife and husband fall to different shares;
> Their clinging offspring from their arms are tore,
> And hurried from them, ne'er to meet them more![32]

There were, however, also some early antislavery writers who severely questioned the slaves' ability to exercise the various attributes of the metropolitan marriage ideal. James Ramsay and Edmund Burke, for instance, doubted whether nature had endowed slaves with the ability to stay faithful and not desert their partner. Ramsay suggested that planters adopt means to prevent married slaves from breaking 'the yoke at their caprice', while Burke deemed it the task of Anglican ministers to ensure the monogamy and indissolubility of slave marriage and proposed that they should be given the 'full power and authority to punish all acts of adultery, unlawful concubinage, and fornication'.[33]

Little or no doubt about the slaves' ability to live up to the metropolitan ideal was expressed after 1807. Not only in their accounts of the hardships suffered by married slave couples at the hands of their owner but also in their fiction, did later antislavery writers try to demonstrate both the slaves' desire to marry and their ability to conform to the metropolitan marriage ideal. The couple Afiba and Quante in the novel *The Koromantyn Slaves* (1823), for example, had to convince readers that slaves could live up to the rules of fidelity, indissolubility, and companionship: 'They had formed the *natural* attachment of two young hearts possessed of warm affections; their religious instruction, and the genuine reception of its principles had preserved the constancy of each.'[34] The idea that religious instruction was needed to ignite or perfect the slaves' natural ability to carry out the attributes of the metropolitan marriage ideal was, of course, most directly expressed by missionaries. Their accounts about slave marriage demonstrate what Catherine Hall has called, the missionaries' struggle between the languages of equality and hierarchy.[35] Reflecting on his sermon about the commandment 'thou shalt not commit adultery', one Moravian missionary remarked, for instance, that 'the universal vice of the West Indies' had so 'blunted the feelings of the negroes as to make it very difficult to convince them of the exceeding sinfulness of this sin'.[36] Thus while he believed, like other missionaries, that slaves were naturally endowed with the ability to live up to the metropolitan marriage ideal, he undercut his belief in the equality of the slaves by arguing that they needed his help to learn to be faithful and fully exercise the other attributes of the ideal.

The stronger belief in the ability of the slaves to exercise the attributes of the metropolitan marriage ideal in the 1820s and early 1830s was accompanied by a more fervent denunciation of the planters and their white officers. While most early antislavery writers argued that planters were relatively 'indifferent' towards slave marriage, that is they provided little or no encouragement to slave marriage or adopted measures to ensure that married slaves lived up to their vows, later writers suggested that planters and estate officers actively prevented slaves from marrying each other and modelling their relationships on the metropolitan ideal. This is not to say, however, that early antislavery writers completely excused planters for slave marriage's deviation from the metropolitan marriage model. In fact, they mentioned some obstacles that planters put in the way of married slaves to exercise their conjugal roles, which were also mentioned by later antislavery writers, including the wilful separation of married couples and the sexual and physical abuse of married slave women. Before we look at these obstacles and the proposals that antislavery writers put forward to undo them, we need to examine how the authors explained the low incidence of formal slave marriage.

Later antislavery writers regarded the planters' refusal to grant their slaves permission to marry as the most important reason for the low formal marriage rate. To illustrate how difficult it was for slaves to obtain permission to marry, former missionary Peter Duncan told the 1832 Select Committee about two 'respectable' members of his congregation who shortly after they had made their vows before him, had tried to marry in an Anglican church in order to give their marriage civil standing. Their master, however, had refused to grant them permission, even after Duncan had written a letter in which he had argued that the two slaves had always led exemplary lives. Duncan suggested that the planter's refusal was, like that of other planters, driven by sexual needs. He told the Select Committee that slaves who asked their planter or overseer for permission to marry were generally told that they 'may live as I am living myself'; that is, promiscuously.[37] The Reverend Trew articulated more directly that sexual needs underpinned the planters' decision to withhold permission: 'a master might from the most unworthy motives, resist the marriage of his female slave . . . in order to gratify his mere caprice'.[38] It was, however, not only their sexual but also their economic needs that led planters to refuse slaves permission to marry. A planter was especially reluctant to grant a slave man permission to marry, if the object of his choice was either a slave woman from another estate or a free woman because offspring of such unions would not belong to him. That only a few antislavery writers mentioned this economic motive is a clear indication that antislavery writers regarded slave marriage first and foremost as a moral institution.[39]

The practice of voluntary manumission was also mentioned as an obstacle to a rise in the marriage rate. The marriage rate referred to, however, was not that of formal slave marriage but of normal marriage; that is, the voluntary and binding contract between two free people in which third parties had no claim and which offered the couple the same protection as legally married couples in metropolitan society. In order to marry under the normal rather than the Slave Law, free men and women wanted to purchase their enslaved partner's freedom before marrying her or him. This was not always easy after 1807, as planters faced with an increasing free population and a declining slave labour force set very high prices for purchase, especially for slave women as they would lose not just their productive but also their reproductive potential. In order to illustrate that slavery affected not just the slaves and their owners but also the free population, antislavery writers included in their writings on slave marriage accounts of free men who had tried but failed to manumit their partners in order to marry them.[40] Implicit in these accounts is the assumption that existing manumission procedures prevented free men from acting as proper householders. Because his wife and children did not belong to him but to the planter, a free man could not assert his authority over his family nor protect them. He also could not act as the sole provider of his family because the planter provided his wife and children with allowances and a provision ground. And until 1827, he could also not pass property on to his children upon his death.

In the 1820s and early 1830s, accounts of free men desirous to purchase their enslaved partner's freedom were usually discussed alongside stories of slave men who had tried to purchase their wives' freedom so as to relieve them from heavy work in the field.[41] Antislavery writers wanted these men to succeed in obtaining their enslaved partners' freedom because future offspring would be free. They therefore proposed compulsory manumission; that is, manumission against the wishes of the owner.[42] As they wanted not just free but also legitimate children, they suggested that free and enslaved men who had succeeded in obtaining their partner's release from slavery should marry them as soon as possible in an Anglican church. Former missionary Richard Bickell suggested this in his 1825 account of a free tradesman who had failed to buy his enslaved partner because her mistress had asked for 'so great a sum for her'. Bickell argued that if the mistress had demanded a more 'moderate and equitable sum', the tradesman's partner would have been emancipated and his 'children (now being slaves and bastards) would have been free and legitimate'.[43] Bickell's remark should be seen within the light of both his religious training and the discussion in metropolitan society at the time about women who gave birth to illegitimate children. Attacks on 'bastard bearers' became, as Lisa Forman Cody has noted, more common in the 1820s and were triggered by growing numbers of illegitimate births and various cultural changes, such as the spread of Evangelism. Poor Law officers were at the forefront of these attacks. In the early 1820s, they expressed concern about the costs of illegitimacy and demanded a change in the Poor Law's bastardy clauses. The attacks increased in the early 1830s when plans for a new Poor Law were proposed and discussed.[44] Not surprising, then, illegitimacy occupies a more prominent role in the debate about apprenticed than about slave marriage.

It was especially in their discussion about plantation practices that separated married slave couples that antislavery writers conveyed the idea that co-residence was an essential precondition for the exercise of conjugal duties. Early antislavery writers addressed not the separation of married slaves who resided on the same estate but that of recently imported slaves. This type of separation, however, was not very prevalent as few slaves made the Atlantic crossing with a partner. The reason why early writers, such as Captain Marjoribanks, concentrated on this marginal phenomenon is that it was a most effective means to arouse the readers. It enabled Dr Harrison, on the other hand, to portray himself as a 'man of sensibility'. When asked by the Slave Trade Committee whether families were sold apart upon arrival, he replied that he had once 'bought a negro woman and child out of *compassion* that she might not be taken from her husband'.[45]

Later antislavery writers used the separation of married slave couples primarily as a means to allow their audiences to empathize with the slaves. The fact that slaves faced more of a risk of being separated from their partner after the abolition of the slave trade also explains why this aspect of plantation life features so prominently in their writings. As James Ward and other scholars have demonstrated, the depression of the 1820s and early 1830s, caused by falling sugar prices and increasing sugar duties, brought many planters into heavy debt. Some tried to pay off their debts by selling their slaves, usually without taking into consideration their marital status. In case they failed to pay off their debts, a levy was made which also posed the threat of separation. Planters with sufficient resources tried to sustain their output levels by hiring slaves from struggling plantations or if they owned more than one estate, by moving their most productive slaves to the estate that most needed manpower. These two methods led to the temporary or long-lasting separation of many slave couples.[46]

Antislavery writers were mostly concerned about the first threat of separation: sale. James Losh, for example, told a Newcastle audience in 1824 that the proslavery lobby was wrong to argue that 'English peasants [were] more to be pitied than slave men' because enslaved men could be 'sold and separated from their wives and children, at the caprice or for debts of their masters'.[47] Most writers were less concerned about the planters' sheer power to separate married couples than about the ways in which separation affected a married couple's ability to exercise their conjugal duties. One Moravian missionary mentioned, for instance, that separation by sale made it very difficult for married slave men to do their 'duty to God'.[48] The fact that many slaves who lived on separate but nearby estates eagerly opted for a church-sanctioned marriage suggests that slaves themselves did not regard co-residence as an essential precondition for their conjugal duties. There is evidence which suggests that many slaves may have preferred to reside separately from their spouse. Some witnesses before the 1832 Select Committee, for example, pointed out that many slave men married slave women from nearby estates so that they would not have to witness their daily floggings and other forms of abuse.[49] We should also not rule out that like their American counterparts, Jamaican slave women preferred to live some distance away from their partner in order to retain some degree of independence.[50]

Antislavery writers failed to see that residence on nearby estates could be conducive to the quality of slave marriage. They were especially concerned about the impact that non-residence had on the husband's role as his wife's protector and comforter, as comes clearly to the fore in a lecture given before the Edinburgh Abolitionist Society in October 1830, which centred on a runaway advert of a slave woman suspected of being harboured by her abroad husband. According to the lecturer, by placing the advert in the paper, the slave woman's owner had condemned her act as a 'crime'. For him, however, the woman had not committed a crime but had merely sought 'shelter under the roof of her husband', while he had done his proper duty by offering 'protection to his toil-worn and suffering wife'.[51] He suggested, in other words, that co-residence was not only a natural right of married couples but also an important prerequisite for the exercise of conjugal duties.

According to early antislavery writers, the sexual and physical abuse suffered by slave women made it difficult for slave men to conform to the metropolitan ideal of the husband-protector. Henry Coor, for instance, told the Slave Trade Committee that a slave who knew that his wife had been sexually abused by a white estate officer or her owner 'dared not resent it ... for if he did, he would be sure of having a very smart flogging for it'.[52] Later writers reiterated his point but added that the abuse also acted as an important impediment to a church-sanctioned marriage. The Wesleyan missionary John Jenkins, for example, pointed out that many slave men did not want to marry in church because their wife could at any time be flogged in a naked state before a large congregation of slaves and estate officers: 'with whatever indifference they may regard the degradation of a concubine, we know that they look with horror on the degradation of a wife'.[53] His remark, then, served not only to explain the low rate of formal and nonconformist marriage but also to demonstrate that slave men understood the importance of marriage and realized that amongst the various duties expected of married men was the protection of their wife's sexual purity.

Thus far we have seen that in their discussion about the ways in which planters prevented slaves to marry and model their marriages on the metropolitan marriage ideal, antislavery writers focussed primarily on the slave husband. That they concentrated more on his protector than provider role is another indication that they regarded marriage more as a moral than an economic institution. The slave husband's role as the provider of the family was more directly addressed, however, in late eighteenth-century proposals that planters should allow slave husbands time to work for themselves. As a means to increase both the slave marriage rate and the slave birth rate, Edmund Burke suggested that planters should give slave men who were 30 years and older and had at least 'two children born of any marriage', one or two days a week to work for themselves. Burke assumed that their desire to protect their wife and children and to exercise full authority over them would lead slave husbands to use their free days to raise produce on their provision grounds and use the money earned from selling excess produce to purchase their wife's and children's freedom.[54] Burke, then, presented the practice of allowing slave husbands time to work for themselves as a means to teach slave husbands the habits and skills required of the husband-provider. In a speech that advocated gradual emancipation through easier manumission laws, James Anderson was concerned to show that slave men had already internalized most of these habits and skills and that upon freedom they would not forsake their duty as the provider of the family so that ex-slaves would not become a drain on public resources. According to him, manumitted men would 'be glad to hire a small spot of ground' and cultivate it 'with utmost care for the sustenance of themselves and families'.[55]

In their remarks about slave men's inability to act as their wife's protector, antislavery writers implicitly mentioned two roles expected of married slave women: to stay faithful within marriage and to care for their husband and children. Their role as carer of the family was more directly addressed in three proposals to exempt married slave women from field work. The least progressive was James Anderson's suggestion that planters should offer slave men the option to work extra hours so that their wives could take time off when pregnant or when one of the children was ill. His plan was as much, if not more, concerned with the conjugal duties of slave men than those of slave women, as is illustrated by his question why 'the poor slave [should] be debarred the satisfaction of cherishing and relieving the woman he loves — when the interest of the owner is not to suffer by it'.[56] Captain George Young's plan, which was mentioned in his statement before the Slave Trade Committee and presented as a means to increase the birth rate and thus gradually end the slave trade, went a step further than Anderson's. It suggested that a married slave woman should be taken away from the field and put 'to such labour as she is capable of as a woman bearing children'.[57]

The most far-reaching proposal to relieve married slave women from the field was the earlier-mentioned 1824 plan to withdraw by Imperial act all women under 45 from field labour. Like the other two, this one suggested that withdrawal from field work would allow married slave women to take better care of their children's needs. Contrary to the others, it also argued that it enabled the women to devote themselves more to the needs of their husbands. It was stated that if put in place, the plan would allow slave husbands to look forward to a proper meal at the end of their working day and that they would also see their chances of manumission increase. The authors of this plan namely assumed that upon their manumission, married women would spend their days not just looking after their family's needs but also undertaking efforts to raise money to purchase their husband's freedom, such as raising excess produce on their provision grounds and selling it in the market or hiring themselves out to their former master or neighbouring planter. The designers of the plan did not think that this additional but temporary role of married women would temper with a slave husband's authority over his wife: 'The husband, as head of the family, would possess the requisite authority to secure due subordination, and to restrain improper licentious conduct.'[58] They thus clearly assumed that slave women were naturally endowed with the ability to submit within marriage.

A married slave woman's main duty — taking care of her husband's and children's needs — was also mentioned in several accounts written by (former) missionaries in the 1820s and early 1830s that examined the legality of formal slave marriage. They pointed out that contrary to an Anglican marriage in metropolitan society, a formal slave marriage was not a *voluntary* and *binding* contract between *two* parties. It involved a third party — the planter —, who had to give permission to marry and who also adopted practices that made it difficult for couples to live up to their vow to 'stay together till death'. In addition, it was argued that for a marriage to be 'valid in law' it had to be protected by law. Formally-married slave couples had no legal protection against separation by sale, gift or bequest and levies, and were also not protected against desertion or against a spouse's evasion of his or her domestic responsibilities.[59] In his attack on the Reverend Bridges' account of slave marriage, Thomas Cooper mentioned, for instance, that the wife of a slave man who had ignored his family's well-being by not working on his provision ground could expect nothing more than to get her husband 'a good flogging, and perhaps not even that'.[60] Cooper concentrated in his attack especially on the 'natural duties' expected of slave husbands and wives but which they could not exercise because of the presence of the third party and the lack of legal protection. A slave wife could neither 'promote the comfort of her household' nor 'obey the wishes of her husband' because her 'body, strength and time' belonged to her owner and not her husband. And because his wife and children were another man's property, the slave husband could not 'exercise absolute authority over his family', protect them, and make 'his cottage the scene of domestic love and happiness'.[61] Cooper, then, clearly portrayed the slave husband as an emasculated man because he was unable to exercise one of the most important attributes of adult masculinity: full economic, legal and moral responsibility for and absolute authority over dependants.[62]

If we compare Cooper's account of the slaves' ability to exercise their conjugal duties with that of Maria Edgeworth in her 1804 novel *The Grateful Negro*, we see that by the mid-1820s antislavery writers had given up hope that planters would voluntarily ameliorate the condition of the slaves. The novel centres around the couple Caesar and Clara, who had successfully averted their separation by having persuaded a neighbouring planter to buy them both but whose relationship is put under severe pressure from slaves from their old plantation who try to stage a revolt. It argues that if the third party in a formal slave marriage was a paternalistic planter, his presence did not prevent slaves from exercising their conjugal duties. Contrary to Cooper, Edgeworth does not focus on the slaves' field work and its negative impact on their conjugal duties but concentrates instead on the slaves' free time. She depicts Caesar and Clara as occupying their proper spheres and exercising their gendered roles. The first time the reader meets Caesar, he is on his provision ground, cultivating bananas and other products 'to a degree of perfection nowhere else to be seen on this estate', while Clara, the woman with whom he lived and was about to marry, is located in the hut that Caesar had built for them. Caesar, however, takes not only his role as the provider seriously but also his role as his wife's protector, by asking their neighbouring planter to buy them both. This planter provides his new slaves with a provision ground and orders a carpenter to renovate their cottage. He also tells Caesar that 'you may work for yourself, without fear that what you earn may be taken from you; or that you should ever be sold, to pay your master's debts'. Trusting his new employer's promise, Caesar quickly becomes 'indefatigable in his exertions to cultivate and embellish the ground near his cottage in hopes of making it an agreeable habitation' for Clara. Although Clara does not feature prominently in the novel, she is throughout presented as a subservient and loving wife. When she is, for instance, told that Caesar is about to be sold and that her owner will provide her with 'another husband', she not only weeps but also says that she will never have another husband than Caesar. And she also obeys Caesar when he tells her to firmly reject any proposals from the neighbouring slaves to join their planned revolt.[63]

Although Thomas Cooper severely criticized the legality of formal slave marriage, he did not propose legislation to make it conform to metropolitan marriage because he believed that the slaves had not yet reached the degree of civilization needed to exercise all the attributes of a fully legal marriage. As we have seen in his account about interslave sexual relations, he was especially concerned about their ability to be sexually faithful.[64] Although many antislavery writers agreed with Cooper that formal slave marriage was 'a mock marriage', they were keen to see its numbers increase and legislation adopted to make it mirror more closely to that in metropolitan society. Their desire was triggered by the strong links between marriage and freedom. Although any church-sanctioned marriage was regarded as a means to civilize the slaves and thus prepare them for freedom, formal marriage was more strongly linked to freedom than nonconformist marriage because it was the only legal contract that slaves could engage in. As Amy Dru Stanley has shown in her study of marriage in the American South in the years immediately preceding and following emancipation, legal contracts signified freedom because they assumed 'self-ownership', 'consent' and 'exchange'.[65] Even though the 'self-ownership' and the 'consent' of the slave couple was compromised because they needed permission from their owner to marry, signing a marriage contract and exchanging promises of obedience and protection in front of a state representative enabled them to assert their individuality and humanity; and hence, temporarily assume the status of free men. Formal slave marriage was also linked to freedom in the sense that it was one of the few methods available for slaves to establish a bond with the law.[66] Previous chapters have suggested that antislavery writers wanted the future free society to be based on the rule of law; that is, a state in which citizens obey the rules and use the law to advance their conditions, while their fundamental liberties and civil rights are protected indiscriminately. A formal slave marriage, then, may have been regarded by some antislavery writers as a means to train slaves for a future in which they would have full legal rights and duties.

Most of the proposals put forward to achieve an increase in the formal marriage rate tried to persuade slaves to marry by making formal marriage a more attractive option. Some writers who questioned, like Cooper, the slaves' ability to fully understand the importance of marriage because of their lack of exposure to religious instruction, were convinced that a 'stick' was needed as much as a 'carrot' to make slaves marry in an Anglican church. Edmund Burke suggested, for instance, that planters should provide single slave men with a woman of childbearing age and marry them 'publickly in the face of the Church,' and added that slave men who refused their master's choice and did not propose another woman were to be punished by increased workloads and lessened allowances.[67] Considering the strong denunciation of planters in later antislavery writings, it is not surprising that it was argued in the 1820s and 1830s that it was planters and not slaves who needed a 'stick'. *A Plan for the Abolition of Slavery Consistently with the Interests of all Parties Concerned* (1828) proposed, for example, that a 'tax be imposed on all single persons in the colonies', including slaves.[68] The 'carrot' proposals include besides the earlier-mentioned proposals for the withdrawal of married women from the field and compulsory manumission, plans to facilitate the co-residence of married couples. Edmund Burke suggested legislation that would prohibit the sale of married couples belonging to the same planter and prevent married slaves owned by different planters from being sold 'at such a distance to prevent mutual help and cohabitation'.[69] Contrary to Burke, later antislavery writers saw co-residence as an essential precondition for the exercise of conjugal duties and suggested that planters be forced by means of an 'agreement between masters' to facilitate the co-residence of abroad couples.[70] We shall see in the next section that some of these 'carrot' proposals found their way into the 1833 Abolition Act.

In 1788 Thomas Clarkson envisioned a freedom in which the ex-slaves were 'legally [engaged] in the bands of connubial happiness', while occupying different spheres and carrying out distinct roles.[71] To convince their audiences of the viability of this notion of freedom, antislavery writers not only had to provide accounts of slave couples who lived up to the metropolitan marriage ideal but also ignore some of the realities of the slaves' marital lives. They did not mention, for instance, that non-residence was as much the result of slave preferences and courtship customs as plantation practices; that most slaves preferred an informal over a church-sanctioned marriage; and that many slave marriages were not harmonious and were even voluntarily broken up.[72] This blocking-out of the less wholesome features of the slaves' relational lives explains to some extent why many abolitionists were surprised to find that so few apprentices opted for a formal marriage after August 1834, when various obstacles to formal marriage were removed.

A MORAL AND ECONOMIC INSTITUTION

The 1833 Abolition Act abolished one of the main obstacles to formal marriage— planter permission — and also held out the promise of indissolubility and co-residence, by forbidding the separation of married couples by 'bargain or sale, writ, deed, conveyance, will or descent' and by making manumission compulsory.[73] Each of these provisions was included in the local Abolition Act. As I have demonstrated elsewhere, because planters interpreted this Act very narrowly and did not include in the local Act provisions that had to enable married apprentices to live up to the metropolitan marriage ideal, apprenticed marriage did not differ much from slave marriage.[74] We shall see in this section that critics of apprenticeship also saw little difference between apprenticed and slave marriage. They were particularly concerned to show that apprenticed marriage also suffered from the presence of a third party, who prevented couples from living up to the attributes of the metropolitan ideal, especially co-residence, and thereby endangered the creation of a stable, moral, and prosperous society upon freedom.[75]

During the first year of apprenticeship, some 1,724 formal marriages were performed in the island.[76] Critics displayed an ambivalent attitude towards this rise in the formal marriage rate. On the one hand, they presented it as evidence that the moral order had rapidly improved after August 1834 and that apprentices were thus fitted for full freedom. To add weight to their argument, they emphasized that it was not only young apprentices who had married but also apprentices who had long lived together and had several children.[77] On the other hand, they expressed their disappointment that there were still many apprentices who favoured cohabitation over marriage. They excused the apprentices for their preference, however, by attributing it not only to plantation practices that made a 'mock marriage' of formal marriage but also to the apprentices' past of slavery. S.M. Arthur Welsh, for instance, mentioned that 'marriage was never promoted or encouraged among them'.[78]

Welsh and other critics proposed a variety of methods that planters could adopt to increase the formal marriage rate, including schemes to prevent white officers from sexually abusing female apprentices and more lenient visiting arrangements for abroad couples.[79] Considering the planters' concern about the continuation of the plantation economy upon freedom, it is hardly surprising that critics used mainly economic arguments to convince planters to implement their proposals. S.M. John Daughtrey suggested, for instance, that if planters ensured that the huts of married couples were 'their homes, secure of intrusion of mere authority', the 'social bond' between them and their apprentices would be 'drawn closer' and they would thus increase their chances of having an abundant supply of wage labour upon full freedom.[80] That Daughtrey saw a close link between the marriage contract and the wage contract comes even more clearly to the fore in his remark that a married apprentice 'who aspires to a good house will be ambitious to see it a little furnished' and that his ambition would act as 'a stimulus to labour'.[81] Daughtrey thus suggested that because of their provider role, married male apprentices were more likely than single male apprentices to follow the script of the designers of the Abolition Act and hire themselves out for wages.

As planters were unwilling to adopt the proposed schemes, some critics turned to the Imperial Government for help.[82] In February 1836, the Secretary of the Wesleyan Society, Mr Beecham, asked the colonial secretary to extend the metropolitan marriage bill which allowed for nonconformist marriage to the West Indian colonies, but with the addition that past nonconformist marriages should also be declared legal.[83] Mr Beecham mentioned two reasons why it was so important that nonconformist missionaries should be given the right to solemnize marriages. First, there were too few Anglican ministers in the islands to make formal marriage a viable option for many apprentices. And second, that it was an essential means to turn the islands into more moral and stable societies. Beecham emphasized that under the Abolition Act, marriages performed by nonconformist missionaries prior to or following the commencement of apprenticeship were defined as 'concubinage'. He objected to this definition not only on the grounds that concubinage was 'opposed to the spirit and precepts of Christianity' but also because it implied that apprentices married by nonconformist missionaries lacked legal protection against desertion and could not demand that their spouse properly exercised his or her conjugal duties.[84]

Beecham, however, saw the recognition of past and future nonconformist marriages also as a means to develop a sound economic foundation for the islands in the Caribbean. He supported his proposal that past nonconformist marriages should be declared legal with instances of male apprentices who, realising that their nonconformist marriages were not legally binding, had left their wives and children and married somebody else in an Anglican church. He suggested that the recognition of past nonconformist marriages would prevent a rise in deserted wives, so that with full freedom the parishes would not have to spend large sums of money on the support of deserted wives and their illegitimate children.[85] And like the barrister Richard Matthews, who reviewed the marriage laws in the islands for the 1836 Select Committee, Beecham argued that the legalization of past and future nonconformist marriage would legitimate offspring and thereby making them capable of inheriting their parents' property. Both men deemed it essential that the generation that would come of age after the termination of apprenticeship would have the material basis from which to support their families so as not to become a burden on the parish, and also to expand their material aspirations.[86] Matthews, in fact, regarded this so important that he suggested that even the nonconformist marriages of those who had died since the onset of apprenticeship should be recognized as valid in law and that the children born in these marriages should be given certificates to prove that they were legitimate.[87]

In March 1836, Colonial Secretary Glenelg forwarded Beecham's letter to Governor Sligo and asked him to persuade the Assembly to come up with a 'liberal and comprehensive law' that would legalize past and future nonconformist marriages.[88] Sligo's subsequent request and the report of the 1836 Select Committee which recommended the legalization of future nonconformist marriages were instrumental in the Assembly's passing of Glenelg's desired act in December 1836.[89] Considering their distrust of nonconformist missionaries, it is doubtful whether the Assembly members were persuaded by the moral and economic arguments that Glenelg, Sligo and the Select Committee used in support of their recommendations. It is more likely that they passed the act to legalize past and future nonconformist marriages in order to avert drastic interventions by the Imperial Government in the area that enabled them more than any other to regain some of their former power: the punishment of female apprentices in the workhouses. We shall see in chapter six that by the time the marriage act was passed, this issue had begun to cause a major rift between the Assembly and the Colonial Office.[90]

Critics not only held up the rise in the formal marriage rate as evidence of the moral progress of the ex-slaves but also of the apprentices' desire to conform to metropolitan gender ideals. They gave the highest praise to male apprentices who bought their wife's discharge from apprenticeship.[91] The fact that wives thus freed did not devote themselves solely to the concerns of their husbands and children did not greatly disturb the critics. They saw the women's higgling and other activities to earn money as a temporary deviation from their proper role, which served only to purchase the remainder of their husband's term or to save money to buy a small plot of land upon full freedom.[92] They also did not think that the women's income-generating activities made them less submissive wives. Thome and Kimball, for instance, included in their travel account a conversation with a woman freed by her husband, who stated that she gave all the money that she earned as a higgler to her husband because 'what for him, for me'.[93]

A complicated valuation procedure that aimed to enable planters to hold on to their labour force and thus keep up their output levels explains why so few male apprentices were able to release their wives from apprenticeship.[94] The discharge price of an apprentice was decided by three valuators: one appointed by the claimant (the S.M.), one named by the planter (a local magistrate), and a third, who was not to have an interest in either party (another local magistrate). As their interests were closely bound up with the continuation of the plantation economy, the two local magistrates usually joined forces to overrule the low price demanded by the S.M. and thereby prevented the discharge. Several S.M.s called upon the governor in spring 1836 to change the composition of the valuation committees or to insist that every valuation be ratified by an official with the power to reject those that were seen to be too excessive.[95] In October 1835, however, Sligo had already asked Glenelg what method he should adopt to counteract over-valuation cases. Glenelg had replied that local magistrates who had clearly acted improperly in valuation cases were to be dismissed and threatened with prosecution.[96] This remained policy until the 1838 Amendment Act, which contained the provision that field apprentices were to be valued according to the gang in which they worked. This stipulation did not bring the dream of domesticity nearer for apprenticed women employed around the house, as they were to be valued as before.[97]

Because of the unfair valuation process, many male apprentices saved the money that they had earned by hiring themselves out or by working their provision grounds in order to buy land. From 1836 onwards, S.M.s regularly reported that male apprentices were buying small plots of land.[98] Critics were divided over this development. Some held these men up as evidence that apprentices were following the script written by the designers of the Abolition Act. They not only pointed out that the men took their duty as the provider of the family seriously but also argued that because they used their free time productively, they would work very hard upon full freedom. The coloured S.M. Edward Lyon mentioned, for example, that male apprentices who had purchased land had conveyances drawn up so that in case they died before the end of apprenticeship, their wife and children would be provided for.[99] As they saw the preservation of the plantation system upon freedom as the main aim of apprenticeship, most critics expressed a concern about the development, which became more pronounced as apprenticeship progressed. They feared that if too many ex-slaves managed to buy land and become small peasants upon freedom, plantations would face a severe shortage of wage labour and thus become unprofitable.[100] They were keen to see that male apprentices based their future role as the main provider of the family on wage labour. This idea comes most clearly to the fore in a speech given by S.M. Richard Chamberlaine on the day that apprenticeship ended and which aimed to encourage the men in the audience to stay on the estates as wage labourers:

> your wives and your daughters will require their fine clothes for their chapels, churches and holidays. You will visit your friends with your coat and your shoes, and you will require your dinners prepared for you with some respect to comfort and cleanliness; your soup will be seasoned with beef and port; and in order to obtain these, the comforts and necessaries of civilized life, you will have to labour industriously.[101]

Some critics masked the economic motives underpinning their disapproval of the land purchasing activities of the apprentices by arguing that wage labour on the plantations exercised a civilising influence. Glenelg argued, for instance, in 1836 that ex-slaves who stayed on the plantations after freedom would be 'more open to civilizing influences' and that if the majority did so, there would emerge a 'sounder state, morally, politically and economically' than if the 'population were to spread over the surface of the country'.[102] Thus although the critics differed about the financial basis from which married African Jamaican men were to exercise their provider role upon freedom, they all agreed that this was the main role expected of them because it would cultivate 'artificial wants', which in turn would stimulate economic growth and prevent the ex-slaves from becoming a burden on public resources.

Thus far we have looked at those features of the apprentices' marital lives which critics presented as evidence that the ex-slaves had morally progressed since August 1834. They devoted far more attention, however, to two obstacles which made it difficult for married couples to live under the same roof and carry out their distinct gender roles: sexual and physical abuse and visiting rights. As will be discussed in detail in chapter six, female apprentices who were sent to the workhouse could be flogged and also ran the risk of sexual abuse. Married female apprentices were also not free from sexual and physical abuse on the estates. Planters refused to adopt measures to prevent their white employees from having sex with their female labourers and they themselves often issued 'illegal' punishments, such as putting female apprentices in the estate dungeon for a period of up to 24 hours.[103]

Most critics portrayed abused married female apprentices as passive victims. A notable exception is S.M. William Ramsay. In his report from October 1836, he discussed the increase in rape trials since the onset of apprenticeship. According to Ramsay, the increase did not reflect an increase in rape per se and should be seen as evidence of rising rather than declining moral standards. He argued that the growing number of rape cases signified that apprenticed women had begun to place more emphasis on one of the most important feminine virtues — chastity — and also that apprentices had started to develop, as envisioned by the designers of the Abolition Act, a positive relationship with the law. Rather than accepting their sexual abuse or seeking an alternative form of justice, the abused women had used the law to seek redress; or, in Ramsay's words, the women had assumed 'the dignity of the citizen'.[104] Ramsay was not only unusual in portraying abused women as active victims but also by presenting them as evidence of the apprentices' ability to become law-abiding citizens. We shall see below that most critics conveyed this message mainly through male apprentices who sought the help of a S.M. to improve the quality of their lives. This strategy is not surprising because it was assumed that upon freedom, wives would withdraw to the private sphere of the home and husbands to the public world of work. As it was the public world where crimes were committed and injustices carried out, critics were obviously more concerned to show that male apprentices had the potential to become law-abiding citizens than female apprentices.[105]

Critics were generally more concerned about the impact of the abuse on the women's husbands than on the women themselves. They depicted the husbands as passive victims of the 'third party'. Thome and Kimball, for example, mentioned that husbands who had to see their wives dragged off to the workhouse 'suffered a great deal of misery from that; but they could not help it', while Captain Studholme Hodgson, who was based in the island from 1833 till 1836, pointed out that 'no husband dare refuse

112 *Slave women in discourses on slavery and abolition, 1780–1838*

him [the planter] his wife'.[106] It was argued that the abuse prevented husbands not only from exercising their protector role but also their role as their wife's comforter. The pamphlet *A Statement of Facts* (1837), for example, mentioned a husband whose wife had been unlawfully put in the estate's dungeon. The husband had tried to bring her some supper and talk to her but was apprehended by the overseer and also put in the dungeon.[107] Like the non-fictive accounts of partners of sexually abused slave women discussed in chapter three, such accounts of 'emasculated' male apprentices served merely to arouse the audience and convince them to undertake action.

The extensive number of remarks about the difficulties that apprenticed couples experienced to visit or live with one another indicates that critics deemed this a more important obstacle for apprentices to live up to the metropolitan marriage ideal than the sexual and physical abuse of female apprentices. A number of legal and extralegal practices, which illustrate once more the planters' unwillingness to accept the change in their socio-economic status, made it very difficult for abroad apprenticed and free-apprenticed couples to enjoy, what one critic called 'a proper interchange of matrimonial rites'.[108] The local Abolition Act stipulated that three months before receiving his or her freedom, an apprentice would be given notice to leave the estate in order to arrange for alternative accommodation, and that failure to do so would lead to ejection from the estate followed by a fine or imprisonment. Not all planters, however, strictly implemented this clause and allowed the free spouse to remain on the estate in return for a high rent. To visit their abroad free or apprenticed spouse, an apprentice had to obtain written permission to leave the estate. An apprentice caught without written permission was under clause 27 of the local Abolition Act liable to be punished as a vagabond and sent to the workhouse for a period of up to four weeks. Planters furthermore implemented clause 13 of the third Jamaican Abolition Act which was passed in November 1834 but disallowed by the Colonial Office. This meant that they refused free or apprenticed spouses who were not formally married to their partner or whom they deemed to be of 'not good character', entry to their estates.[109]

In his report from September 1836, S.M. Lyon argued that these various practices 'augmented the influence of a pernicious state of public opinion, and the habits and feelings of the labouring population are left unsettled or exposed to very false views of happiness and utility'.[110] In other words, they did not allow for the development of the 'social bond' that was essential for the preservation of the plantation economy and also endangered the project of turning apprentices into law-abiding citizens. To convince the governor, however, that in spite of these practices many apprentices had managed to develop a positive bond with the law, he included in his report the case of Robert Graham, a man who had recently purchased the remainder of his term. Graham had visited his apprenticed spouse but as her owner had implemented clause 13 of the third and disallowed Abolition

Act, he had been apprehended and put in the estate dungeon. Shortly after his escape from the dungeon, Graham had appealed to Lyon, who was his wife's S.M. After a visit to the estate, Lyon had managed to secure Graham 'his domestic rights'. Lyon also used the Graham case to convince the governor that upon freedom the ex-slaves would do their utmost to exercise the attributes of the metropolitan marriage ideal. He mentioned, for instance, that Graham's visit to his wife was motivated by his promise 'at the altar of his God . . . that forsaking all others, he would cleave unto her until God did them part'.[111]

Accounts of free men who, like Graham, clandestinely visited their apprenticed partner featured also in some pamphlets published in support of the campaign to abolish apprenticeship. As these and other accounts of the difficulties faced by free-apprenticed couples to visit one another had to encourage the readers to undertake action, they ended less happily than Lyon's report of Graham's attempts to be with his wife. *A Statement of Facts*, for instance, mentioned a free husband who was brought before two local magistrates on account of the 'crime of being found in his wife's house' and subsequently sentenced to one month of hard labour in the workhouse.[112] The accounts conveyed primarily the idea that planters were unlikely to protect the civil rights and liberties of the ex-slaves upon freedom, as they already and extensively violated the rights of free(d)men. *A Statement of Fact* asked its readers, for instance, 'what can we expect for the liberated apprentices after the year 1840 if free men are severely punished for merely exercising their conjugal duties'.[113]

Critics tried hard to deny the local magistrates' claim that attempts by free men and women or by abroad spouses to visit their loved ones were crimes. While some argued that married partners had a 'natural right' to be together, most mentioned that the 1833 Abolition Act had bestowed upon apprentices the right to visit or be visited by their loved ones.[114] John Jeremie, for example, pointed out that the planters' practice of granting only formally married apprentices the right to receive their free or apprenticed partner was 'an invasion of the rights of the apprentice' because the third Jamaica Abolition Act had been disallowed,[115] while Glenelg was convinced that a married male apprentice had '*a strict legal right* to receive whoever into his hut' because the law regarded him as 'a tenant paying rent for his occupation in the form of manual labour'.[116] Jeremie and Glenelg presented the issue of visiting rights solely as a problem for male apprentices: they could not receive their wives into their huts. The Robert Graham case and other evidence suggest, however, that both spouses in abroad couples travelled to visit one another. It could be argued, then, that by portraying the male apprentice as the main victim of the planters' visiting rights policy, both men drew upon and helped to reinforce the metropolitan idea that masculinity was essentially about being 'master of one's own house'.[117]

It is interesting to compare Glenelg's remarks about visiting rights with his response to Mr Beecham's letter. In the latter, Glenelg articulated an 'idealized' version of apprenticed marriage. He was convinced that apprenticed marriage could only bestow its beneficial effects on society if it displayed the attribute of legality. In his discussion of visiting rights, on the other hand, Glenelg conveyed a 'realistic' version of apprenticed marriage. According to planters, clause 13 of the third Jamaican Abolition Act was an encouragement to formal marriage and did much to 'promote the interests of morality'. Glenelg firmly dismissed this argument in June 1835. He argued that because of various factors that had been common during slavery and had continued after August 1834, most notably the lack of religious education, few apprentices were married by either an Anglican or a nonconformist minister, and that by not allowing nonconformist married couples or those in a long-term, loving relationship to visit one another, clause 13 prevented rather than promoted morality. As Glenelg assumed that the factors that prevented an increase in church-sanctioned marriage would remain in place until the end of apprenticeship, he told the Assembly that planters should treat all long-term, stable relations as formal marriages and that thus a male apprentice should be able to admit to his hut not only his wife but also 'his concubine'.[118] In his discussion about visiting rights, then, Glenelg argued that legality was a less important attribute of marriage than gendered spheres of activity and authority.

Glenelg's call upon the Assembly had little effect, as is illustrated by the Robert Graham case. Critics therefore proposed various solutions to secure the domestic rights of apprentices. They suggested first of all an amendment to the Jamaican Abolition Act that would make it compulsory for owners to sell 'at a fair valuation' a female apprentice to her husband's owner or vice versa, in order to facilitate the co-residence of abroad apprenticed couples.[119] In addition, they proposed that the Assembly pass a law that would fix the rent that planters could charge from free men and women so that free-apprenticed couples could reside together.[120] And, they also suggested a repeal of clause 27 of the Jamaican Abolition Act in order to make it easier for apprentices to visit their free and apprenticed spouses.[121]

The Colonial Office's response to these proposals illustrates once more that it was more inclined to remedy abuses associated with apprenticeship by giving S.M.s orders on how to interpret certain provisions in the local Abolition Act than by ordering the Assembly to amend the local Act. It did not entertain the first proposal, probably because it realized that the Assembly was never going to pass a law that would increase the planters' costs at a time of declining output. As for a law that would fix the rent that planters could ask from free men and women residing on their estates, the Colonial Office agreed that the practice of charging high rents was 'to be regretted', but stated that it was '*of course* impossible to interfere' with this legal right of the planters.[122] The Colonial Office also accepted the critics' claim that clause 27 was a clear violation of the apprentices' domestic rights. Rather than asking the Assembly to repeal it, however, it issued a circular to S.M.s which declared that it was 'quite illegal' for planters not to allow free and apprenticed spouses access to their apprenticed partner's hut, and that when faced with visiting rights cases they should always rule in favour of the couple, whether formally married or not.[123] This directive, however, did little to safeguard the apprentices' domestic rights. Not only because S.M.s could easily ignore it, but also because it applied only to apprentices. Free men and women relied for the protection of their domestic rights on local magistrates. Considering that magistrates were keen to limit the rights of the free population in order to sustain their superior position in the island, they were usually unwilling to help free men and women secure their rights to visit their apprenticed partner. This led some S.M.s to argue that it was better if those African Jamaican men and women who had purchased their discharge from apprenticeship remained the concern of the S.M.s until full freedom.[124]

Thus like those who advocated marriage amongst the lower classes in metropolitan society, critics of apprenticeship saw marriage as a building block for a sound moral and economic order. The socio-economic context within which the critics operated implied, however, that they stressed rather different attributes of the metropolitan marriage ideal. They placed most emphasis on gendered spheres of activity and authority, closely followed by co-residence. That co-residence received so much emphasis was not only because it was seen as an essential precondition for the exercise of conjugal roles but also because the obstacles that the planters put in the way of apprentices to live up to this attribute enabled critics to demonstrate the planters' determination to hold on to as much of their former power as possible. Legality was emphasized by some critics because it provided couples with protection against desertion and ensured the legitimacy of offspring, each of which was seen to facilitate the moral and economic development of the island. Contrary to the advocates of marriage amongst the lower classes in metropolitan society, critics of apprenticeship did not regard affection as an important attribute of marriage. This and the fact that their discussion was largely framed in terms of legal rights suggest, then, that they saw marriage first as a civil contract, and second as a relationship between two human beings.

AN ECONOMIC INSTITUTION

Proslavery writers addressed slave marriage as much before as after the abolition of the slave trade. They discussed it in the late eighteenth and early nineteenth centuries mainly in response to the problem of natural decrease. It is therefore not surprising that the early proslavery discussion about slave marriage was dominated by writers of slave manuals and planters. This section will first examine their discussion and then move on to look at the later proslavery discussion about slave marriage, which aimed to dispel the abolitionist claim that planters did not encourage their slaves to marry in church or in other ways enable them to model their relationships on the metropolitan marriage ideal. It finishes with an examination of the views on apprenticed marriage by planter friendly S.M.s and other opponents of apprenticeship. Each of these three discussions presented marriage as an economic institution; that is, an institution which either benefited or harmed the planters' financial interests. This comes not only to the fore in the reasons that the writers put forward to encourage or discourage slave or apprenticed marriage but also in their remarks about the gendered roles expected of married couples. The husband's role as the provider of the family received, for instance, far more emphasis than his protector role. As they operated with and within a language that described marriage not solely as an economic institution, the authors discussed at times slave and apprenticed marriage also in moral terms.

Early proslavery writers held wide-ranging opinions about the desirability and practicability of slave marriage. There were first of all those, mainly former residents, who advocated slave marriage as a means to facilitate natural increase. In addition, there were resident writers with a direct interest in the plantation economy who argued that it was impossible for planters to encourage church-sanctioned slave marriage because slaves were not 'calculated for this state'.[125] And finally, there were writers who were convinced that planters did their utmost to allow slaves to mirror their marriages on the metropolitan ideal. The first group of proslavery writers did not think that slave marriage had to display all the attributes of the metropolitan ideal to bring about an increase in the birth rate. Monogamy was one attribute, however, that they felt very strong about. As we have seen, most early proslavery writers doubted whether slaves, especially slave women, could be monogamous. Some nevertheless put forward proposals to teach the slaves monogamy. Jesse Foot suggested, for instance, in 1792 that planters should provide slave girls with lessons in the importance of 'chastity'.[126] Others proposed that planters should 'severely punish' adulterous slaves, set slaves an example by staying faithful themselves, and allow their slaves access to religious instruction.[127] As mentioned some estates adopted some basic forms of pronatalism in the late eighteenth century. When it appeared that these had little impact on the birth rate, some authors began to argue that nature had not predisposed the slaves to monogamy. Foot, for instance, concluded in 1805 that his proposed lessons would yield little success because polygamy was 'the natural passion of the Negroes'.[128]

As natural increase depended as much on an increase in births as a decrease in deaths, the first group of early proslavery writers deemed it also essential that planters adopt measures to make it easier for married slave women to look after the needs of their young children. Although their concern about natural increase led them to focus more on the duties expected of married slave women, they did not completely ignore the roles required of slave husbands. They suggested that planters could encourage slave marriage by giving newly-weds a furnished cabin and some land to cultivate. By stipulating that the reward was to be handed out to the slave husband, they expressed the idea that his role was to be that of the master of the house and the (additional) provider.[129] Jesse Foot was the only writer who suggested that married slaves should not only exercise distinct roles but also occupy distinct spheres. Similar to the 1824 abolitionist *Plan for Effecting Emancipation by the Redemption of Female Slaves*, Foot suggested that 'the negroe wife should be left to the care of her family and employed in domestic pursuits'.[130] As it was highly inimical to the economic interests of the estates, it is hardly surprising that no other early proslavery writer presented such a far-reaching proposal to increase the slave marriage rate.

The early proslavery writers who saw slave marriage as a means to promote natural increase all favoured co-resident over abroad slave marriage. Jesse Foot saw co-residence as a means to facilitate monogamy and suggested that planters adopt mutual arrangements to facilitate co-residence. His insistence that slave women and not slave men should move residences as a result of these mutual arrangements suggests that he envisioned the slave husband's role as that of the head of the slave household.[131] For James Adair, co-residence was a means to assist slave wives in their duty to take good care of their children. He argued that women who travelled to see their husbands failed to properly carry out their motherly duties, as they took their nursing infants with them but left their other children 'at home, neglected'.[132]

A co-resident and monogamous slave marriage in which a wife concentrated on her motherly duties and the husband acted as the head of the household was promoted by the first group of early proslavery writers not only as a means to achieve natural increase but also as a way to enhance the stability of the estates. Lady Nugent, for instance, accepted the view of the owner of Plumstead that marriage made slaves more 'sober, quiet and well-behaved'.[133] Their suggestion that slave marriage should centre round the home, an idea which antislavery writers did not fully articulate until the 1820s, clearly indicates that they were in tune with the metropolitan marriage ideal.[134] Their engagement with this ideal, however, was highly selective. They omitted those attributes which were not seen to have a direct impact on natural increase or which could enhance slave autonomy: legality, indissolubility and affection.

Affection featured prominently in the discussion about slave marriage by the second group of early proslavery writers. These writers argued that the love that slaves felt for one another was qualitatively different from that which underpinned metropolitan marriage. Bryan Edwards, for instance, referred to it as 'a mere animal desire' and believed that it was so strong that slaves could never live up to the attributes of monogamy and indissolubility.[135] John Stewart, who described the slaves' affection for one another as 'savage and selfish', on the other hand, believed that the affection was capable of change. He had noticed, for instance, that baptized slave men seemed to 'lay aside all thoughts of other women than the one to whom they are united'.[136] He nevertheless questioned whether large-scale encouragement of church-sanctioned slave marriage through religious instruction would yield lasting effects, not only because the slaves' minds were 'imbued . . . with strong passions' but also because slaves were exposed to the 'licentiousness of their more enlightened rulers'.[137] Stewart, then, invoked not only the slaves' nature but also the society in which they lived in his explanation as to why it was so difficult to encourage slaves to marry, which brings him nearer to those proslavery writers who advocated slave marriage as a means to facilitate natural increase than to Bryan Edwards, Edward Long and others who were firmly convinced that it was naturally impossible for slaves to live up to the ideal of a monogamous and indissoluble, church-sanctioned marriage.

Like the second group of early proslavery writers, the third did not want to see an increase in church-sanctioned slave marriage because it undermined the planters' absolute authority over the slave household. To counteract the abolitionist claim that planters did not do enough to encourage slave marriage, they argued that planters did not have to adopt methods to encourage church-sanctioned slave marriage because informal slave marriage already displayed most of the attributes of the metropolitan marriage ideal. It was, according to them, 'long-lasting', companionate, based on 'real inclination', and marked by a gendered division of labour.[138] Former bookkeeper J. B. Moreton mentioned, for example, that informally married slave men 'build their huts and assist to work their grounds' while their wives 'prog for food, boil their pots at noon and night, louse their heads, extract chiggers from their toes, and wash their socks and trousers'.[139] To further steal a march on the abolitionists, they also argued that it was because of practices adopted by the planters that informal slave marriage largely mirrored the metropolitan ideal. It was mentioned, for instance, that married slave women were allowed to take time off from work to look after a sick husband or child; that the weekly allowances of food handed out to slave husbands allowed slave wives to cook 'the most nourishing meals' for their family; and that slave wives were protected against 'insecurity'.[140] This group of proslavery writers suggested, in other words, that informally married slave women were better placed than married lower-class metropolitan women to exercise their main duty (to take care of the needs of husband and children) because planters alleviated their husbands from their duty as the provider and protector of the family.

Early proslavery writers, then, disagreed about the question whether slaves were capable of exercising the attributes associated with the metropolitan marriage ideal. While some argued that the slaves were naturally incapable of exercising all the attributes, others suggested that they could exercise a few attributes but only within a supportive environment. Later proslavery writers were also selective in their engagement with the metropolitan marriage ideal. The looming of freedom, however, meant that they paid more attention to the role of the slave husband than early proslavery writers. Although many also questioned the slaves' natural ability to model their relationships on the metropolitan marriage ideal, increased abolitionist attacks as well as a stronger emphasis in metropolitan society on marriage as a natural and ideal institution meant that they were more inclined than early writers to acknowledge the slaves' potential to live up to the ideal. This comes most clearly to the fore in their explanations as to why church-sanctioned slave marriage showed no signs of increase. Not surprisingly, they all blamed the slaves and not the planters for the low marriage rate. Many reiterated Bryan Edwards' claim that nature had not equipped slaves for a church-sanctioned marriage, but articulated this alongside the argument that slaves had not yet reached the level of civilization needed to live up to the attributes of a church-sanctioned marriage. James McQueen, for example, told his readers that the slaves' African past made it 'impracticable and idle' to even attempt to teach them 'the restraint of being bound to each other', but only to confuse them later with the remark that 'knowledge and intelligence must first be diffused' before the slaves 'can or will be bound by the marriage tie'.[141] He suggested, in other words, that the slaves had not yet been sufficiently exposed to religious instruction to fully understand the importance of marriage.

By attributing the low rate of church-sanctioned slave marriage not just to the slaves' nature but also to the society in which they lived, later proslavery writers acknowledged the virtuous potential of the slaves. As this undermined their project of sustaining the plantation economy, they usually followed their explanation of the low marriage rate not with concrete proposals to bring the slave population to a higher level of civilization but with examples of slave marriages that had failed in spite of planter support. Planter Alexander Barclay, for example, narrated his attempts to help a slave man be reunited with his wife and the mother of his five children. Although Barclay had 'admonished, threatened and ultimately punished' the married slave woman, she had not returned to her husband. Barclay argued that this and the other cases of slave marital discord in which he had interfered, had convinced him that no matter how much 'well-meant' advice a planter could give, it would always 'produce an opposite effect' because a slave 'boldly disclaims [the planter's] right to control or interfere with his inclination and free will in matrimonial connections'.[142]

Later proslavery writers were concerned not only to disprove the antislavery claim that planters did not encourage slave marriage but also the argument that planters actively obstructed slave marriage by, for example, withholding written permission. Their strategy consisted of denying that such practices occurred; explaining them in terms of slave customs; and arguing that plantation practices allowed slave couples to exercise many attributes of the metropolitan marriage ideal. Proslavery writers admitted that planters often refused slave women to marry free men but argued that this was not driven by the planters' sexual urges but by their concern about the women's well-being. They argued that marriage to a free man made it difficult for a slave woman to take care of her children because free men did not take their role as the provider of the family seriously. In fact, they suggested that a free man's motive for marrying a slave woman was not affection but a desire 'to avoid the trouble and burden of providing', as living of his enslaved wife's allowance and provision ground and sharing her rent-free hut enabled him to shirk work.[143] This argument clearly aimed to counteract the abolitionist claim that upon full freedom slave men would willingly and properly exercise their provider role.

When abolitionists stepped up their campaign in the late 1820s and demanded immediate emancipation, it became even more important for proslavery writers to emphasize slave men's inability to provide. In his 1827 travel account, Cynric Williams painted a picture of conjugal roles after freedom which was a complete reversal of that presented by antislavery advocates: 'A few hours work daily, for only a few weeks in the year, would enable a negro to bring up a family, though blacky would rather his wife, or wives, should work for him, while he smokes his pipe.'[144] Anthony Davis agreed with him that abolitionists were wrong in assuming that slave men would work for wages upon freedom, though he freely admitted that it was the planters and not slave wives who suffered as a result. In his *The West Indies*, which was published around the same time as the 1832 Select Committee's report, Davis furthermore rejected the abolitionist demand for easier manumission. He predicted that most manumitted men would not, as abolitionists alleged, purchase their enslaved wife's freedom but instead leave their wife and children because they knew that they would be provided for.[145] Slave men, then, were not only seen as inadequate providers and protectors but also as incapable of living up to the vow 'till death do us part'.

The abolitionist demand for a law that would prevent the separation of married couples upon sale was equally dismissed. There was no need for such a law, it was argued, because most planters only sold couples together. To present the planters even more as 'men of sensibility', it was added that they also sternly refused to buy slaves if they knew that the sale would separate them from their spouses.[146] That there were married slaves who resided on different estates was not denied nor the fact that church-sanctioned slave marriages were dissolved. Both features of the slaves' marital lives were attributed to ingrained slave customs and were severely criticized. It was argued, for instance, that if it was not for the planters, children born in abroad marriages would suffer tremendously because abroad couples did not make 'fit parents'.[147]

Later proslavery writers, then, also saw co-residence as an important attribute of slave marriage. Not only their remark that married couples were not separated upon sale but also their descriptions of the slave huts had to convince their readers that planters did their utmost to facilitate co-residence. The huts were presented as a paragon of domestic comfort. They contained a kitchen, a store-room, and a bed-room divided into two compartments: one for the parents and one for the children.[148] The kitchen was presented as the slave wife's domain, while the store-room was the place where the slave husband kept 'his tools and little things'.[149] The descriptions, then, also tried to convince readers that the home around which slave marriage was based, enabled couples to exercise their gendered activities.

The antislavery argument that work, especially that of slave women, made it difficult for married couples to carry out their gendered roles was swept aside by accounts of married couples undertaking their distinct roles during their free time. Alexander Barclay, for instance, argued in his 1827 response to Thomas Cooper's account of slave marriage that slave women spent their two-hour lunch break taking care of domestic chores, such as washing, cleaning and mending clothes, while their husbands used that time to cultivate the vegetable garden surrounding their hut.[150] This and the fact that nursing women were given a light workload led Barclay to conclude that field work did not hinder a married slave woman's ability to take care of her husband's and children's needs; and hence, that there was no need for the Imperial act envisioned in the 1824 *Plan for Effecting Emancipation by the Redemption of Female Slaves,* unless the 'same kindness' was extended to rural women in the mother country.[151] Barclay, then, presented a limited version of the metropolitan marriage ideal to some extent as a 'natural right'.

Later proslavery writers did thus not deny that there was a third party involved in a slave marriage but presented this party as a facilitating rather than an obstructing party. That only two writers mentioned a scheme to increase the marriage rate illustrates most clearly that the numerous remarks about planters having 'the wish and interest' to see their slaves marry and live up to the metropolitan marriage ideal were empty phrases that served no other purpose than to avert abolitionist criticism.[152] Former resident Captain Henderson and estate manager William Taylor believed that slave marriage facilitated the stability and profitability of the plantations because it made slave men more docile and hardworking. Henderson, however, doubted the ability of the slaves to live up to their vows and therefore suggested that planters closely monitor the marital lives of their slaves and offer, in addition to a marriage reward, 'occasional allowances' to couples who showed 'correct deportment' and were 'observant of the obligations of this rite'.[153] William Taylor was more optimistic about the ability of the slaves to exercise some attributes of the metropolitan marriage ideal. He was convinced that the sheer control over their partner and children upon marriage made slave men more industrious and content. Not only this assumption but also his proposal to increase the marriage rate echoed antislavery sentiments. Having observed, like some antislavery writers, that slave men were averse to marriage because their wives could be flogged in a naked state, he suggested that planters follow the example of the owner of Savannah estate and exempt all slave women from flogging.[154]

Neither Henderson's nor Taylor's scheme to increase the marriage rate was discussed by the Jamaican Assembly. The Assembly also did not seriously consider the one proposed in April 1823 by the West India Committee (a permanent association of West India merchants and absentee planters based in London): turning the customary right of allowing slaves to own personal property into a statutory right for formally married slaves only and giving legitimate slave children the right to receive bequests.[155] The fact that the 1826 Slave Law gave all slaves and not just formally married slaves the right to own personal property and receive bequests is one indication that the Assembly did not want to see a drastic rise in the formal marriage rate.[156] Another is the earlier-mentioned clause 4 of the 1826 Slave Law, which was modelled on the 'Bill for Regulating the Celebration of Marriages among Slaves in Trinidad'. Clause 4 did not contain the Bill's provision that slaves could appeal against their owner's refusal to give written permission and that marriages performed by nonconformist ministers and Catholic priests should be recognized as legal. It did, however, include the provision that slaves who desired to marry had to undergo an examination by the minister. The only encouragement that clause 4 gave to slave marriage was the proviso that marriages were to be performed free of charge.[157] Clause 4, then, clearly aimed to keep formal marriage within limits and served, like the rape act, no other purpose than to convince the government and abolitionists at home that Jamaican planters were committed to slave amelioration, in order to ward off future Imperial interference in local affairs.

Clause 4 poses the question why the Jamaican planting class was so opposed to formal slave marriage. It could be argued that because of its connotation with freedom and equality, formal slave marriage undermined the planters' project of increasing their wealth, which was based on the idea that slaves were nothing but chattel and fully under their control. A note added to clause 4 supports the idea that planters regarded formal marriage as a threat to the control over their labour force: 'Marriages of slaves shall not invest the parties with any rights inconsistent with the duties they owe to their proprietors.'[158] The Assembly's rejection of the provision in the Trinidadian marriage bill to legalize nonconformist marriages indicates that it was also distrustful of nonconformist slave marriage. Their distrust of this type of slave marriage stemmed also from a fear of losing control over the slave population, which can be deduced from planter Henry Shirley's explanation for the Assembly's rejection of his 1834 bill to legalize nonconformist marriage: 'It was considered to be one which would give the missionaries too much power over the negroes.'[159] Nonconformist missionaries undermined the planters' control over their slaves because they introduced slaves to new activities, skills, and organizational forms that not only acknowledged the slaves' individuality and humanity but also encouraged them to claim new rights and privileges on the plantation.[160]

The Assembly did little besides rejecting proposals to legalize nonconformist marriage and passing laws that made it difficult for missionaries to preach, in order to keep the nonconformist slave marriage rate low. It could be argued that its inactivity stemmed from the fact that for many planters the benefits of nonconformist slave marriage outweighed its disadvantages. As mentioned, nonconformist missionaries were very concerned to see that their married members were monogamous and lived up to the ideals of the husband-protector/provider and the wife-carer. Various planters must therefore have agreed with the owner of Plumstead and with manager William Taylor that nonconformist slave marriage was conducive to natural increase, stability, and profitability. They probably also preferred a nonconformist over a formal slave marriage because it made it easier for them to separate a couple by sale or hire in case of debt because nonconformist marriage was not a legal contract performed in the Established Church.[161]

Later proslavery writers, as we have seen, were as concerned as Assembly members about the threat that a church-sanctioned slave marriage posed to planter control. The fact that they did not mention protection as an important role expected of slave husbands is only one indication that they believed that slave marriage had the potential to reduce the slaves' loyalty to their owner and thus undermine his control. The slave marriage that they encouraged or pretended to encourage in their writings was, therefore, a long-lasting contract between three parties. It was furthermore a monogamous marriage in which the partners ideally lived on the same estate (so as to be within close vicinity of the planter and his officers) and exercised a limited number of gendered roles but not within gendered spheres. This slave marriage was presented through idealized accounts of slave marriage on the one hand, and accounts of unhappy slave wives on the other. As these accounts provided rather contradictory messages about the slaves' ability to live up to the metropolitan marriage ideal, they were not an effective means to counteract the specific antislavery claim that planters did not do enough to bring marriage within the reach of the slave population nor the more general antislavery assertion that the slaves were capable of freedom.

When formal marriage became a *voluntary* and *binding* contract between *two* parties after August 1834, the Jamaican planting class became even more determined to prevent a rise in the formal marriage rate. This is illustrated, for instance, by the Assembly's rejection of Henry Shirley's 1834 bill to legalize nonconformist marriage. We have seen, however, that in 1836 it agreed to legalize nonconformist marriage in order to avoid more drastic Imperial intervention in other areas. By extending the rights of the apprentices, the change in formal marriage after August 1834 further eroded the power of the planters over their labour force. Planters averted their anger about their declining power by adopting legal and illegal practices that made it difficult for apprentices to fulfil their conjugal duties. Some of these have already been mentioned, such as charging free men and women a high rent to live in their apprenticed spouse's hut. The remainder of this section explores how opponents of apprenticeship responded to the critics' accusation that planters failed to acknowledge the conjugal rights of apprentices and that they did little to increase the formal marriage rate. It needs to be stressed, however, that opponents did not reflect as extensively as critics on the apprentices' marital relations, and that they were mainly concerned to show the apprentices' inability to live up to the attributes of monogamy, indissolubility, and gendered roles in order to support their claim that apprenticeship had been put into operation too early to achieve its aim of transforming the slaves into wage labourers.[162]

Opponents dismissed the proposals to increase the formal marriage rate with the same argument as that used by some later proslavery writers; namely, that apprentices were not yet capable of exercising the various duties associated with formal marriage. Their argument centred round the apprentices' inability to be faithful in marriage. The *Kingston Chronicle*, a paper which openly expressed its opposition to apprenticeship, included an article in September 1835 which argued that 'almost every black and brown man has a plurality of wives . . . even the married Methodists are anything but true to their vows'.[163] S.M. Baynes also suggested that religious instruction had failed to instil in the apprentices a sufficient understanding of monogamy: 'It does not appear that the efforts of religious instruction of any sect have succeeded in preventing the indulging in polygamy.'[164] By emphasizing the low success-rate of religious instruction, opponents tried to argue that the apprentices' failure to be monogamous should not be attributed to slavery, as S.M. Welsh and other critics had argued, but to the apprentices' nature. Remarks such as Baynes' lend support, then, to Demetrius Eudell's argument that 'a belief in genetic inheritance was beginning to take shape as the emancipation process unfolded'.[165]

Opponents were also concerned to show that apprenticed couples failed to carry out their gendered roles. Chapter two has demonstrated that they argued that married women failed to mother properly because they refused the planters' 'liberal assistance'. Some opponents attributed the women's failure also to the fact that apprenticed husbands did not fully exercise their role as the provider of the family.[166] S.M. Dillon did so in his report from June 1836, in which he discussed abroad marriages. According to Dillon, the abroad husband, whom he referred to as 'the seducer or reputed husband', tended to shirk his responsibility as the provider of his children so that his wife was forced to work extra hours on her provision ground or otherwise raise money to clothe and feed her free children. This exhausted her so much that she was not only unable to take proper care of her children but also turned out late in the morning and thereby performed 'deficient labour'. Dillon argued, in other words, that the planter sustained a considerable loss because abroad husbands did not exercise their provider role properly.[167]

To make apprenticed husbands take their provider role more seriously, Dillon asked Governor Sligo whether it was not possible to implement locally 'the English law . . . which compels a father to support his offspring'.[168] He referred here to the bastardy clauses in the 1834 Poor Law. These clauses stipulated that a putative father had to make weekly payments for the upkeep of his child until it was seven, and that poor law officers could take proceedings against him if he failed to do so.[169] Dillon tried to convince the governor of the need to adopt a similar act by suggesting that it would make apprentices more trustful of the law. According to him, apprenticed women would receive it 'as an act of humanity' towards themselves and their children.[170] Dillon, thus, supported his demand for an act that aimed to make apprenticed men more thoughtful providers with an image of African Jamaican women that also underpinned some of the later proslavery writings on slave marriage; namely, that of the victim of her husband's selfish and material desires. By invoking this image, he not only tried to mask the real motive underpinning the proposal — the short-term economic interests of the planter — but also tried to divert the governor's attention away from the planters' visiting rights policy.[171]

S.M. Gregg presented married female apprentices also as victims of their selfish and sexually uncontrolled husbands. He argued that many male apprentices left their wives and children soon after they had paid off the remainder of their term and quickly moved in with another woman, or worse, remarried by special licence. As a result of the 'barbarity' of these 'unnatural fathers', 'innocent offspring' was, according to Gregg, threatened with starvation because their support relied wholly (if free) or partially (if apprenticed) on their mothers.[172] Gregg, then, confirmed Anthony Davis' prediction about manumitted men. To ensure that free and also other children would be provided for, he suggested, contrary to most opponents of apprenticeship, the encouragement of formal marriage. Like Mr Beecham and Richard Matthews, he justified his proposal with the argument that children born in a formal marriage were legitimate and could thus inherit 'part of the father's estate'. Gregg, however, did not favour an unrestricted rise in the formal marriage rate. He suggested that couples who already had children should not be allowed to marry unless they could demonstrate that 'ample provision is made for, not only the offspring, but also the female'. Gregg feared that if this was not done, 'many poor mothers will be left to provide for a young family and which must ultimately become paupers on the parish'.[173] Gregg echoed here the metropolitan concern about improvident marriages. One of the witnesses before the 1832 Poor Law Commission suggested, for example, that to prevent children from becoming a drain on parish resources, it was not only essential to discourage bastardy but also to forbid people below a certain income level to marry.[174] Thus contrary to Dillon's account of male apprentices who failed to exercise their provider role, Gregg's was not only concerned with the short-term economic interests of the planters but also with the long-term economic interests of all white islanders.

We see, then, that to safeguard the socio-economic status of the planters and other white islanders during and after apprenticeship, some opponents supported existing and even proposed further legislation to enable apprentices to live up to some attributes of the metropolitan marriage ideal. Their ideal apprenticed marriage was a contract between a man and a woman in which the former promised to maintain his family. There were, however, also opponents who strongly disapproved of existing marriage legislation and who wanted apprenticed marriage to be like slave marriage; that is, a long-lasting contract between three parties. Opponents of apprenticeship were thus as divided as proslavery writers about the ability of African Jamaican men and women to live up to the metropolitan marriage ideal and also about the importance of the various attributes of this ideal.

CONCLUSIONS

The discussion about marriage during slavery and apprenticeship was inextricably intertwined with the metropolitan marriage debate. Both sides measured husbands and wives against the metropolitan marriage norm and found them lacking. Antislavery writers were especially concerned about slave husbands' inability to act as independent householders; that is, to assume full responsibility for their wife and children and exercise absolute authority over them. They attributed this inability to the fact that slave men were not the lawful owners of their wives and children. Early proslavery writers who advocated slave marriage as a means to achieve natural increase and later proslavery writers who welcomed slave amelioration, were keen to see slave husbands assume a degree of financial and moral responsibility for their wife and children and assert some authority over them. Most proslavery writers, however, wanted slave men to take on only a very small degree of responsibility for their wife and children (mainly financial) and were also most opposed to the idea of allowing slave husbands to exert control over their dependents. They wanted slave husbands not to be independent but secondary householders; that is, act as second-in-command to the planter and his white estate officers.

A husband's duty to assume financial responsibility for his dependents received even more attention after August 1834. Critics of apprenticeship wanted apprenticed husbands to assume some degree of financial responsibility for their family because it made them more likely to hire themselves out for wages, which in turn would increase the chances of a sufficient supply of wage labour upon freedom. Some opponents of apprenticeship proposed legislation to make apprenticed husbands exercise their provider role; however, not with the aim of ensuring the continuation of the plantation economy upon freedom but to prevent a short-term decline in the planters' profits and a long-term decline in the economic status of the white non-planting class.

Whereas pro- and antislavery writers depicted slave husbands as men who actively tried to live up to or avoid their conjugal duties, they generally portrayed slave wives as passive victims of either their owner or their irresponsible husband. Antislavery writers depicted slave wives not only as passive victims by emphasizing the horrible things done to them but also by ignoring some of the realities of the slaves' marital lives. They, for example, did not support their demand for easier manumission laws with cases of free women who had unsuccessfully tried to purchase their enslaved partner's freedom.[175] The passivity that they ascribed to slave wives reflects the role that they wanted them to assume upon full freedom: the subservient wife. They did not believe, like past and present feminists, that a woman's submission within marriage is akin to slavery.[176] According to them, the fact that a husband could protect his wife and that she had recourse to the law in case he failed to properly exercise his conjugal duties, meant that a slave woman gained rather than lost freedom when she substituted upon emancipation submission to her owner for submission to her husband.

Because the moral foundation of the future free society depended on it, antislavery writers were even more concerned about another role expected of slave wives: carer of the family. To exercise this and the other wifely duty properly, antislavery writers suggested that slave wives should occupy a different sphere from their husbands, namely the home. Proslavery writers also wanted slave wives to be submissive wives and excellent carers of their families. Their rose-coloured pictures of slave marital life stressed the need of slave wives to put their husband's needs before their own, while their accounts of irresponsible slave husbands emphasized a slave wife's role to take care of her children. As slave women made up the majority of the field labour force and were thus crucial for the profitability of the plantations, proslavery writers did not suggest that slave wives could only sufficiently exercise their wifely duties if they withdrew from the field.

The place and roles of wives received even less attention after August 1834. Critics of apprenticeship presented the home as the proper and even natural sphere of a wife, both during and after apprenticeship.[177] Within this sphere, she had to first of all devote herself to the 'domestic comfort' of her family. The afore-mentioned speech by S.M. Richard Chamberlaine, directed at male apprentices on the day that apprenticeship came to an end, suggests that this duty implied that she had to turn the hut into a place where the husband could recover from a hard day of labour and where the morals of husband and children were improved. She furthermore had to submit to her husband. As S.M. Ramsay's discussion of rape trials suggests, this included sexual submission. Opponents of apprenticeship, on the other hand, did not suggest that wives occupy a sphere separate from their husbands. They also mentioned a narrower range of duties expected of wives. They did not, for instance, mention that a wife was to take care of her husband's needs and did not stipulate that in return for her husband's financial support, she had to obey his wishes.

The various participants in the debate about slave and apprenticed marriage thus measured existing slave and apprenticed marriages against the metropolitan marriage norm and used this norm to devise their ideal versions of these marriages, which differed considerably in terms of the place that they allocated to wives. In doing so, they helped to reinforce several metropolitan ideas about marriage. First, that marriage was a relationship based on male domination and female submission. Second, that marriage was an important precondition for the social and economic order and that it could exert more beneficial influences if it centred around the home. And third, that marriage was the proper place to have and raise children.

It could be argued that the participants contributed to the naturalization and idealization of marriage; that is, the process which took place in the early nineteenth century whereby marriage was presented as Man's natural condition and expectations of marriage were raised.[178] We have seen, for instance, that many antislavery writers presented the slaves' right to marry as a natural right and that they idealized the married state by including in their writings accounts of slaves who found personal fulfilment through marriage, while simultaneously excluding remarks about non-harmonious slave marriages. Proslavery writers also contributed to these two processes. They naturalized marriage by advocating slave marriage or by suggesting that planters were supportive of it. Their rose-coloured pictures of married couples living in well-equipped huts and exercising different roles, on the other hand, idealized the institution of marriage.

5 The indecency of the lash

The system of production on Jamaican plantations depended on the successful subjugation of the slave body. The first two chapters have shown that a variety of methods were in place to train slave women's reproductive bodies in such a way that they would produce strong and docile future labourers for the estates, while the third chapter has suggested that the sexual violation of slave women's bodies was largely a means to assert control over the slave labour force. It was, however, not only slave women's reproductive and sexual bodies that planters and their officers tried to control but also, and more importantly, their productive bodies. They did this largely through the use or threat of physical punishment, especially flogging.

Under the 1788 Slave Law, a slave woman could be given no more than 10 lashes if the owner or overseer was absent, but in the presence of an owner or overseer, she could get 39 lashes maximum. No exceptions were made for pregnant, old, or infirm women. The usual mode of flogging was to have a woman held down by several fellow slaves, while a slave driver, overseer, or her owner flogged bare parts of her body with a cart whip, ebony brushes or another instrument of torture. On most estates, flogging was a public event that took place in front of a large gathering of slaves and estate officers.[1]

Realizing that excessive flogging could destroy the slaves' capacity to produce and reproduce and also breed resentment amongst them, the Jamaican planting class not only passed a bill that laid down the maximum number of lashes but also one that gave slaves the right to obtain legal redress in case they were excessively flogged. From 1788 onwards, slaves could launch a complaint with a local magistrate against their owner, an estate officer or any other person in the island for exceeding the legally allowed number of lashes or for other forms of gross physical abuse. The process of achieving redress was lengthy and complicated. If three or more local justices were of the opinion, after an examination of the complainant's body, that the complaint was grounded, a so-called Council of Protection was formed, consisting of the vestry and local justices. If the complaint was found to be 'frivolous or unfounded', the justices could order confinement to hard labour, whipping, or both. The main duty of a Council of Protection was to investigate the complaint by examining several witnesses and if necessary, file a suit against the offender. If an assize or quarter sessions court found the accused guilty, he could be ordered to pay a fine of 100 pounds or sent to prison for 12 months.[2]

In the 1820s, several planters changed their attitude towards female flogging. Some modified the practice by replacing the whip by a switch or by flogging women only in private, while others exempted certain categories of women from flogging or substituted the practice by solitary confinement.[3] The majority of the planters, however, remained firmly convinced that only the threat and use of flogging could keep slave women under control. The Assembly was the major line of defence in their battle to uphold their right to punish slave women as they pleased. The Assembly dismissed not only recommendations from the Colonial Office to regulate or abolish female flogging, but also those proposed by the West India Committee and by some of its own members. As a result, Jamaican slave women continued to be subjected to the lash until August 1834.

Of all the indecencies tied up with slavery, antislavery writers were most enraged about the flogging of slave women. They regarded this as more horrific than the flogging of slave men not only because slave women were physically weaker than slave men and thus less able to bear it, but also because flogging led to the exposure of their bodies. The first section of this chapter shows that for antislavery writers, the flogging of slave women symbolized above all the moral degradation of the slaves. They concentrated in particular on the naked exposure of the women's bodies; contrasted this feature of Jamaican slave society with the value placed in metropolitan society on female purity; and argued that it prevented the moral development of the slave community because it did not allow slave women to exercise their role as guardians of morality and enraged their partners and children. Or, as the Methodist missionary Robert Young put it in 1832: 'It is much calculated to sour and brutalise the minds of all concerned.'[4] Antislavery writers provided not only moral and legal objections to the practice of female flogging, which depicted the slave woman as an innocent and suffering victim, but also proposals to ameliorate or end it. The proposals demonstrate once more that for antislavery writers, the creation of a moral, stable and prosperous society upon freedom required not only the moral development of the slaves but also a change in the behaviour of the planters and their white employees. We shall see, however, that in their discussion about female flogging they also sharply criticized the behaviour of the few white women in the island. They were, in other words, convinced that unless accompanied by a complete transformation of white Jamaican society, the abolition of slavery would not lead to a free, moral, stable and prosperous society.

Considering that they contained attacks on their masculinity and also proposals which, if implemented, could drastically affect their socio-economic status, it is not surprising that resident proslavery writers fiercely responded to antislavery accounts of female flogging. Their responses contrast markedly with those presented by proslavery writers based in metropolitan society. Because of their location and also their ideas about the best way to defend the institution of slavery against abolitionist attacks, metropolitan-based proslavery writers articulated views on female flogging that were not that dissimilar from antislavery writers. The second section examines the responses of proslavery writers to antislavery accounts of female flogging and also the arguments used by the Assembly to defend the planters' right to flog slave women. These engaged as much as the antislavery accounts of female flogging with metropolitan discourses about punishment and human suffering. From the 1770s onwards, the public flogging of soldiers, sailors, children, convicts, servants and others was increasingly denounced in the metropolitan society as a barbaric practice that had such pernicious effects on the victim, the practitioner and the spectators that it failed to achieve its aim of deterrence, and suggestions were put forward to replace public flogging by punishments that were private and aimed to reform offenders by concentrating on their soul rather than body.[5] The last section sets out some of the links between the debate about female flogging and metropolitan discourses of suffering and punishment and illustrates that the lacerated slave woman's body in the debate about female flogging was a site where notions of Englishness were contested.

AN INDECENT PRACTICE

Female flogging played a marginal role in writings that were mobilized in the abolitionist campaign to abolish the slave trade. A few (former) residents mentioned it in their testimonies before the Slave Trade Committee and expressed their disapproval of the practice in verse. It featured more prominently in antislavery writings produced in the 1820s and early 1830s, especially in those advocating immediate emancipation.[6] The accounts of lacerated female bodies, which were largely based on missionary accounts, official documents and local newspapers, served first and foremost as a means of arousing compassion and encouraging action on behalf of the sufferer. Antislavery writers tried to achieve this by asking their readers to identify themselves with the suffering slave woman and/or her partner. Contrary to their accounts of suffering mothers and sexually violated slave women, they did this more through case studies of real than imagined slave women. The pamphlet *A Letter to Sir Robert Peel on the Subject of British Colonial Slavery* (1830) mentioned, for instance, the case of Eleanor Mead, a mother of nine, who had been given 58 lashes and had been confined 'in her naked and exposed state' in the stocks.[7] Antislavery writers provided in their case studies rich layers of detail that focussed on the lash's interaction with the body and aimed to make the pain of the women seem real. Captain Studholme Hodgson, for example, described the following scene:

Imagine a woman brought out before the whole assembled gang, then stripped of her covering, and thrown upon the earth, her legs and arms tightly held by four men. These appalling preparations concluded, executioners, armed with knotted cords, proceed to inflict stripe after stripe until nature almost sinks under the murderous punishment.[8]

Some antislavery writers refrained from giving such vivid descriptions. They conveyed the atrocious nature of female flogging by informing their readers that they had been unable to watch the event, a strategy which enabled them to present themselves as 'men of sensibility'. In his 1825 account of a court case investigating the physical abuse of several slave women, Richard Bickell mentioned that they 'were in such a state that I could not bear to look at them after the first sight, but turned my face away while the examination went on'.[9]

The scenes of female flogging in antislavery writings expressed the general theme that slavery reduced the slaves to a less than fully human condition; or, in the words of the Reverend Trew: 'Every stroke inflicted upon her sinks her lower in the scale of being.'[10] By focussing more on the fact that during the flogging parts of the woman's body were exposed (either because she was forced to bare parts of her body or because the lash tore the clothes from her back) than on the severity of the lash, antislavery writers articulated more particularly a concern about slave women's ability to sustain and improve the moral qualities of their husbands and children.[11] The 'indecent' nudity prevented, according to them, slave women from attaining the level of purity needed to act as moral regenerators. Colonial Secretary Lord Goderich remarked in 1831, for instance, that the usual mode of flogging repressed the 'growth of the appropriate virtues of the female character'.[12] As the authors lived in a society that placed a very high value on female sexual purity, they had but little choice to concentrate on the exposure of the female body during flogging. The value attached to female sexual purity meant of course that accounts of the exposure of the naked female slave body were a powerful tool to convince readers not just of the immorality of the system of slavery but also of the lack of civilization of white Jamaican society. The anonymous author of *The Death Warrant of Negro Slavery* (1829) suggested, for example, that the usual mode of female flogging served to satisfy the sexual appetites of the white men in the island: 'What we pay a poll-tax for, is simply, that the West Indians may have the luxury of the whip. We pay for the pleasurable titillation excited in colonial men by the exercise of the constitutional right of the flogging of women.'[13]

To convey the immorality of flogging slave women in a naked state, some antislavery writers gave very vivid descriptions, in an almost voyeuristic way, of the exposed body parts. Former bookkeeper Benjamin M'Mahon mentioned that the 'velvet skin' of the young girl was 'covered with blood — her body from the shoulder to the thighs, was one frightful mass of mangled flesh'.[14] Others, however, avoided any direct references to the women's nudity, mainly in an attempt to demonstrate their own sensibility. Richard Bickell wrote, for example, that slave women were flogged 'on those parts which shall be nameless for me, but which in women, for decency's sake, ought never to be exposed'.[15] Another strategy used to express the immorality of the practice was to compare slave women to women in their own society. *The Negro's Memorial* (1825) declared, for instance, that 'the females accustomed to the exposure of their persons, can have none of that attractive modesty which forms a part of their character in Europe'.[16]

Through the use of a variety of rhetorical strategies, then, antislavery writers articulated an important attribute of the metropolitan ideal of womanhood — purity — which they offered slave women on the assumption that they were full and equal human beings.[17] Examples of slave women who resisted their indecent exposure were provided to demonstrate slave women's ability to be pure. Former resident Henry Bleby, for example, presented the case of a married slave woman and mother of several children, who had asked her tormentor that 'her nakedness might not be indecently exposed', as an example of 'matronly modesty'.[18] Considering their aim to incite passion and action, it is no surprise that all examples of resistance ended in failure. The saddest tale of resistance is without doubt that of Cato, a slave woman who felt so 'indignant at being thus degraded' that she 'tore her dress, and hung herself with it'.[19]

Like slave women's sexual abuse, antislavery writers presented flogging more as a problem for the partners and children of slave women than for the women themselves. They often described scenes where a woman was held down by one of her own children or where her children were among the spectators of the event.[20] They argued that the flogging had a detrimental impact on the children; it gave them an incorrect understanding of right and wrong in society. According to the Reverend Trew, the only lesson that children learned from watching their mother being flogged was 'a wish to desecrate the wretch that made their mother weep'.[21] And it furthermore 'weakened', if not completely 'destroyed', the children's already less than ardent affection for their mother.[22]

As to slave women's partners, it was generally argued that the flogging blunted their feelings and aroused a negative taste for cruelty.[23] As mentioned in previous chapters, it was also suggested that the practice of female flogging prevented slave men from respecting slave women's sexual purity and made them hesitant to marry a long-term partner. Some antislavery writers were furthermore of the opinion that female flogging caused slave men to be unfaithful.[24] And finally, female flogging was seen, like slave women's sexual abuse, as an obstacle for slave men to exercise their role as the protector of the home. Captain Majoribanks conveyed this idea in verse:

> No sex, no age, you ever learn'd to spare,
> but female limbs indecently lay bare;
> see the poor mother lay her babe aside!

nor midst her pangs, her tears, her horrid cries,
dare the sad husband turn his pitying eyes.[25]

It was most often, however, expressed in direct appeals to the readers' sympathy. The pamphlet *A Letter to John Bull* (1823), for instance, asked: 'What would thou have said John, if, . . . thy wife, or perhaps thy grown-up daughter were stretched naked, with face downwards on the floor . . . and lacerated with a whip.'[26]

Antislavery writers, then, assumed that a ban on female flogging would not only turn the slave man into a dutiful husband and a devotee of hearth and family but also into a 'man of sensibility', whose self-control and compassion were marks of his virtuous nature. Their idea that a proper man was a 'man of sensibility' was most clearly conveyed in their remarks about the slave drivers that applied the whip.[27] These slave men were generally described as having a positive taste for cruelty. Captain Studholme Hodgson mentioned a driver who 'directed the lash, with unerring aim, at the same precise spot, until he has worked deep into the flesh, and well established what he facetiously called a raw'.[28] The drivers were also accused of lacking compassion. The well-sold pamphlet *Excessive Cruelty to Slaves* (1833), written by the Methodist missionary Henry Whiteley and based on a seven-week stay in the island, mentioned a driver who had given a woman who had tried to leave work early in order to visit her child in the estate hospital, such a severe flogging that she had 'screamed out violently'.[29] Accounts of sadistic slave drivers served to show that slavery corrupted everyone involved. In 1823, William Wilberforce articulated most directly the idea that the institution of slavery taught not only the planters and their white employees a wrong relationship to power, but also the slaves:

> they [the drivers] are forbidden to give more than a few lashes at a time, as the immediate chastisement of faults committed at their work, yet the power over the slaves which they thus possess *unavoidably invests them with a truly formidable tyranny*, the consequences of which, to the unfortunate subjects of it, are often in the highest degree oppressive and pernicious.[30]

As remarks such as these had the potential to convince readers that slave men were incapable of becoming 'men of sensibility', some authors provided examples of drivers who did their utmost to spare slave women. Henry Bleby mentioned, for instance, a driver who not only showed compassion but also took his duty to protect his family seriously, by sternly refusing to flog his own wife for having stolen a piece of sugar cane.[31]

Bleby's and the other reactions to female flogging clearly show that the humanity that antislavery writers bestowed on the slaves was a potential humanity. They not only described slave women's degrading condition in terms of what their bodies felt rather than what they thought or said about it but also defined slave women and men on the basis of what they lacked. Slave women were seen to lack the feminine virtue of purity, while slave men did not possess such male virtues as compassion, courage, and determination and also lacked a proper attitude towards power. The women's white tormentors were also accused of lacking these gendered virtues. We shall see below that although antislavery writers attributed this lack also to the system of slavery, they were far less convinced of the white islanders' ability to exercise gendered virtues upon freedom than of that of the slaves.

As in their accounts of slave women's sexual abuse, antislavery writers concentrated upon the most vulnerable slave women in order to make their readers question the supposed civilization of the planters and their white male employees. Various examples were given of women who were flogged for no other 'crime' than exercising their most essential duty: motherhood.[32] The writers were even more enraged about the 'barbarous' and 'revolting' practice of flogging pregnant women, which was presented as the main reason for the lack of natural increase.[33] Considering their potential to arouse compassion, it is unsurprising that antislavery writers used accounts of flogged pregnant women to support their demand for a ban on female flogging. The *Anti-Slavery Reporter* stated, for instance, in February 1831:

> Nay, the pregnant female is not by law exempted. One would have thought that our legislators, moved by the common feelings of our common nature, would have interposed, the protecting arm of the law to shield the female, when thus situated, from the brutal power of ferocious men. But no — even she can be laid down, exposed, and flogged in the presence of the assembled population of the estate![34]

Another and perhaps more powerful method used by antislavery writers to convey the idea that white men in the island did little to elevate slave women was to give examples of female flogging that exceeded the legally allowed number of lashes. Most of these examples concentrated on white overseers because they were the ones who ordered most of the flogging and often inflicted it themselves. Like the slave drivers, these men were presented as sadists whose feelings had been blunted as a result of the regular infliction of pain. Henry Whiteley mentioned, for instance, that an overseer had told him, after excessively flogging two young girls for not having done their work sufficiently, that it was the 'best cracking, by G-!'.[35]

Antislavery writers used far more condemning language for planters who exceeded the allowed number of lashes. Reverend Benjamin Godwin, for example, referred to one such planter as a 'monster of cruelty'.[36] In his discussion of the 1829 court case relating to the flogging of the slave woman Kitty Hylton by the Reverend G. W. Bridges, Goderich pointed out that the punishment had been out of all proportion: 'For a trifling mistake in the execution of her master's orders, this female slave appears to have been first violently struck and kicked by her master, and then, by his directions, flogged with such severity as to have excited the commiseration of every person who bore witness to her appearance after the punishment.'[37] Goderich furthermore concluded that Bridges' conduct had been 'unmanly and disgraceful' and could not be excused as a 'momentary ebullition of anger' because the cruelty had been 'repeated and persevering'.[38] He also referred to the conduct of the planter Mr Jackson, who in 1831 had physically abused the mother and daughter Kate and Ann Whitfield, as 'unmanly'.[39] Goderich clearly measured these planters against the metropolitan masculinity ideal which, as mentioned, encouraged men to control their natural propensity to aggression.[40] Other contemporary accounts of the Kitty Hylton case also emphasized Bridges' lack of self-control. Because the tormentor was a clergyman of 'talent and respectability', the case provided antislavery writers with an excellent means to demonstrate that slavery corrupted not just large slaveholders and the lower-class white men employed by them but all white men in the island. Henry Bleby, for instance, regarded Bridges as an incarnation of all the 'evils inherent in human slavery'.[41]

It was not only through accounts of brutal men such as Bridges that antislavery writers conveyed the idea that white Jamaican men deviated as much, if not more, from the metropolitan ideal of manhood than slave men but also through direct comparisons between white men in the island and men in metropolitan society. The Baptist missionary William Knibb, for instance, asked an audience at Exeter Hall in 1832: 'What Englishman could stand by, what Englishman could even contemplate the flogging of a female without a flush of indignation?'[42] The various accounts of white Jamaican women who superintended the whipping of slave women or even flogged slave women themselves supported Knibb's suggestion that white Jamaican society fell beyond the pale of Englishness because it failed to conform to metropolitan gender ideals.[43] Dr Jackson told the Slave Trade Committee that he had been shocked to find 'a lady of some consequence in the island, superintending the punishment of her slaves, male and female, ordering the number of lashes, and with her own hands flogging the negro driver, if he did not punish the slaves properly'.[44] His shock stemmed from the fact that the mistress violated the metropolitan gender norms even more than her male counterpart. Antislavery writers were less concerned about the fact that she was not confined to her 'proper sphere' (the home) than about her lack of tenderness and delicacy caused by the regular infliction of pain. As these were virtues that women needed in order to exercise their role as guardians of morality, it was argued that the white mistress was incapable of correcting the sexually and otherwise excessive behaviour of white men in the island.[45]

Like the planter and overseer, the white mistress was presented as having a positive taste for excessive cruelty and lacking compassion for her victims. The pamphlet *A Word from the Bible* (1829) described one mistress as a 'monster in the shape of a woman' because she had ordered a domestic slave woman to be severely flogged for having burnt some clothes 'which were not worth five shillings', while Lieutenant Baker-Davison mentioned in his statement before the Slave Trade Committee that his attempts to stop a neighbouring mistress from 'flogging her slaves too cruelly' had been in vain.[46] In the 1820s and early 1830s, it was especially the mistress's lack of action to prevent the naked flogging of her slave women that was presented as evidence of her lack of compassion.[47] Some antislavery writers suggested that mistresses refrained from action because they were sexually aroused by the spectacle of watching their female victims in a state of nudity. Richard Bickell referred, for instance, to a mistress who would only flog her slave women when they were washing themselves in a pond.[48]

Thus like the slave woman, the slave mistress was seen to lack sexual purity. As she did not possess most of the virtues associated in metropolitan society with femininity, it was argued that the mistress failed to set slave women an example of female virtue and thereby prevented the moral development of the slave community. Goderich expressed this most clearly in his discussion of Mrs Jackson's abuse of Kate and Ann Whitfield which, according to him, had been even more horrific than Mr Jackson's: 'With such a domestic example, what decorum could be expected from an ignorant negress?'[49] The white slave mistress, then, was seen as the complete opposite of the middle-class, metropolitan mistress who tried to control her female servants by means of rewards rather than punishments; treated them with respect; and taught them important moral values.[50]

Thus far we have seen that antislavery writers used a variety of ways other than directly contrasting the behaviour of white Jamaicans with that of men and women in metropolitan society in order to present themselves as men who lived up to the metropolitan ideal of masculinity, which was an important marker of Englishness. They were convinced that Jamaica could become a more moral and civilized society if black and white Jamaican men followed their example and learned to control their aggression, became more sensitive to the suffering of others, and protected the purity of their womenfolk, and if black and white Jamaican women developed those sensibilities that were the hallmark of women in their own society, such as tenderness. In the 1820s and early 1830s, they argued that a ban on rather than the regulation of female flogging was an essential step to conform the gender roles in the island to those in metropolitan society. James Losh and the Reverend Trew, for instance, did not see the point of only forbidding the flogging of slave women in a naked state or of replacing the whip by a less harsh instrument of torture.[51] After the Assembly's stern refusal to implement the ameliorative proposals put forward by the Canning government in 1823, which included a ban on female flogging, antislavery writers decided that only direct Imperial action could end the indecent practice.[52]

Calls for a ban on female flogging were often supported with remarks about the insufficiency of the criminal justice system[53] in the island, which largely echoed the sentiments expressed about the planter and his white employees. It was argued that white men who exceeded the legally allowed number of lashes were seldom punished for their transgression because biased magistrates dismissed slave women's complaints of excessive flogging. Henry Bleby mentioned, for instance, that it was not surprising that the Council of Protection that investigated the case of Kitty Hylton had not issued a lawsuit against Bridges, because it was 'composed entirely of persons who were slave owners and the personal friends of Mr. Bridges'.[54] According to some antislavery writers, the magistrates' biases explained as much as the risk of being punished in case the complaint proved unfounded, why so few slave women sought legal redress in the case of excessive flogging.[55]

That so few white men were punished for excessively flogging female slaves was also attributed to the fact that local magistrates obstructed the course of justice. Goderich mentioned, for example, that magistrate McLeod had forsaken his duty in the case of Eleanor James, a slave woman who had been excessively abused by a neighbouring planter in December 1829 and whose case was dismissed by a Council of Protection several months later. Because of some 'urgent business', McLeod had sent Eleanor to the clerk of peace, who lived 30 miles away. This led Goderich to conclude that McLeod lacked 'the active feelings and natural charities to be expected in a man whose dispositions are just and humane'.[56] Goderich also complained about the fact that it had taken McLeod nearly two months to set up a Council of Protection and that its meetings were regularly postponed because members had failed to turn up.[57]

Until 1831 slave evidence was not admitted in courts that tried white people.[58] This was also seen as an important reason why only a few white men in the island were tried and convicted of exceeding the number of allowed lashes. Grand juries usually acquitted white men accused of excessively flogging slave women on the grounds that there was no evidence that they had surpassed the legally allowed number of lashes.[59] Like most antislavery writers, Goderich argued that such verdicts reflected badly on the whole of white Jamaican society. In his account of the Reverend Bridges' acquittal, he called the grand jury's decision 'an error of judgement, which, for every consideration of what is due to the ends of public justice, to their own good repute, and to the credit of the Colonial Society, is deeply to be deplored'.[60]

Antislavery writers, then, argued that the island deviated from civilized English society not just in terms of its gendered behaviour but also in its attitudes towards the law. The Slave Law did not fully protect slave women against physical harm, while the machinery designed for their protection defended not their interests but those of their owners. Accounts of slave women who had refrained from seeking redress because of the bias of the criminal justice system had to convince the readers that if the abolition of slavery was accompanied by an overhaul of this system and if laws were drawn up that protected the fundamental liberties and rights of all the inhabitants, African Jamaican men and women would eagerly submit themselves to the constraints of the law. The idea that freedom implied the rule of law featured also in the antislavery debate about male flogging. More prominent in this debate, however, was the idea that freedom was about self-ownership and self-discipline; that is, a free labourer belonged to nobody and did not require physical coercion to make him work because he had an innate desire for self-improvement.[61] The fact that antislavery writers envisioned a future in which the ex-slave husband provided for his family while his wife took care of the family's needs, explains why the idea of freedom as self-ownership and self-discipline was not articulated in the debate about female flogging. In fact, the emphasis that the writers placed on the impact of flogging on slave women's ability to be pure conveys most clearly that they envisioned the future role of slave women to be that of moral regenerators and not free wage labourers.

This section has illustrated once more that antislavery writers drew upon a wide range of methods to appeal to their audiences. A prominent method was to compare the slaves and white islanders to men and women in metropolitan society. In doing so, the authors articulated a notion of Englishness of which an abhorrence of cruelty was an important attribute.[62] In recent years, scholars have explored how white colonial society responded to the antislavery claim that they fell beyond the pale of Englishness. The following section will lend support to their conclusion that white colonial society both asserted and contested the antislavery norm of Englishness.[63]

A DIVIDING PRACTICE

Proslavery writers did not address female flogging until the government and abolitionists at home began to attack the practice in the early 1820s. While they all agreed with absentee planter Henry De La Beche that slave women were 'more troublesome to manage than the men', they differed as to whether flogging was the best means to control them.[64] There were those who strongly disapproved of the practice and wanted it to be replaced by more 'decent' forms of punishment, while others argued that without it, plantation discipline would be destroyed. Considering their immediate exposure to metropolitan debates about feminine virtue and punishment, it is not surprising that the demand for more civilized means of female punishment was predominantly expressed by metropolitan-based proslavery writers. Their ideas about female flogging were also shaped by their conviction that the plantations in the island would benefit from a more civilized slave population. For them, the public flogging of slave women in a (semi) naked state was an impediment to slave civilization:

> But we concur with Mr Canning in thinking, that, "one of the first principles of improvement in civilization, is the observance paid to the difference of the sexes"; and we cannot but consider "the shocking and

unseemly practice of the chastisement of females by the whip," as a bar to their moral improvement and civilization, which is absolute necessary to remove.[65]

Thus as in their accounts about the sexual abuse of slave women, metropolitan proslavery writers depicted slave women as potentially virtuous women. To enable them to develop virtues such as 'delicacy or sensibility' that distinguished moral from immoral women, they recommended that the flogging of slave women in a naked stated be replaced by solitary confinement, confinement in the stocks, or a light switching in private.[66] Metropolitan proslavery writers, however, echoed not only the antislavery writers' abhorrence of the practice of flogging women in a state of undress but also their conviction that the practice had the potential to foster 'unmanly dispositions' in the planters. They created a hierarchy of planters that placed those who refused to exempt women from the lash firmly at the bottom. They portrayed these men as insensitive to the suffering of their victims. The novel *Marly* mentioned, for instance, that they 'possessed feelings very different indeed from the generality of mankind'.[67] The middle rank of the hierarchy consisted of planters who modified the practice or exempted certain categories of women from the lash, while the top was formed by the few planters who had 'voluntarily and successfully' abolished female flogging.[68] Drawing up such a hierarchy of planters enabled absentee proprietors to present themselves as men who embraced the metropolitan norm of Englishness. Monk Lewis mentioned, for instance, that 'one must be an absolute brute not to feel unwilling to leave them subject to the lash.'[69]

Metropolitan proslavery writers, then, agreed with the antislavery writers that female flogging had a morally corrupting influence. For them, however, this influence did not stretch beyond the victim and her white male perpetrator. None of them described, for example, how the practice affected the women's partners or the slave drivers who performed the flogging. The omission of such information reflects the authors' concern to prevent slave men from exercising their proper gender roles. The institution of slavery, which benefited them directly or indirectly, would cease to exist if slave men adhered to the metropolitan ideal of responsible and independent masculinity. As the metropolitan ideal of femininity stressed dependence, however, they were less reluctant to advocate the idea that slave women should be encouraged to exercise at least some crucial attributes of the metropolitan ideal of womanhood.

The opinion of the metropolitan proslavery writers found its expression in the request of the West India Committee in June 1823 to the local legislatures to enact a ban on female flogging.[70] This had as much impact on the Jamaican Assembly as the request of Colonial Secretary Lord Bathurst, a month later, to adopt 'legislative measures for preventing the punishment of flogging in every case where the offender is a woman', which was rejected on the grounds that it 'violated the constitution of the colony'.[71] During the two following years, the colonial secretary regularly ordered the governor to address the Assembly on the issue of female flogging, which was largely the result of pressure exerted by the West India Committee.[72] The Assembly, however, remained deaf to calls to replace female flogging by more decent forms of punishment. As mentioned, in March 1824, the Assembly refused to adopt for local implementation the Order in Council for Trinidad. In its rejection of the Order's clause to replace female flogging by solitary confinement and punishment by stocks, the Assembly firmly expressed the opinion that female flogging in a state of undress should be allowed.[73]

Although the Assembly eventually included in the 1826 Slave Law, albeit in a reduced form, the Order in Council's clause to encourage slave marriage, it did not include the Order's ban on female flogging.[74] After various attempts to change the Assembly's attitude towards female flogging, the governor informed the colonial secretary in 1828 that the Assembly would never adopt a ban on female flogging because it was of the opinion that there was no other punishment for women that promised the 'same salutary dread'. He mentioned furthermore that the Assembly did not even consider a clause that would forbid the flogging in a naked state because it was convinced that slave women did not have 'the sense of shame that distinguishes European females'.[75] Similar arguments were used by the Assembly to dismiss the 1833 bill on female flogging that was put forward by its member August Beaumont, then a newspaper proprietor.[76] It was eventually Imperial action in the form of the 1833 Abolition Act that put an end to the practice of female flogging. The fact that the Assembly did adopt some of the ameliorative proposals put forward by the House of Commons in May 1823 but never issued a ban on female flogging, illustrates most clearly that planters and other members of the Assembly believed that their socio-economic status depended on the physical control of the enslaved population.[77]

Most of the resident proslavery writers and also some former residents agreed with the Assembly that a ban on female flogging would lead to the destruction of plantation discipline because slave women were natural troublemakers.[78] The remainder of this section will examine how these authors responded to the antislavery writers' claim that female flogging was a brutal and degrading practice, and illustrate that in their accounts of female flogging, they tried to present Jamaica as an English society. Like antislavery writers, this group of proslavery writers used the flogged slave woman's body to reveal the 'truth' about female flogging.[79] Cynric Williams, for instance, denied the accusation that female flogging was severe by pointing out that the bodies of slave women he had seen bathing in Turtle Crawl had not had 'a mark' or a 'scratch'.[80] He also refuted the claim that the practice degraded slave women because it exposed their bodies, by arguing that they were usually flogged over their clothes.[81] The same was argued by an anonymous planter in his refutation of Thomas Cooper's pamphlet *Facts*

Illustrative of the Condition of Negro Slaves (1824): 'The body ... is not exposed ... it is always partly covered, and not left naked as a statue.'[82] Some writers did not deny that slave women were flogged in a naked state but tried, like the Assembly, to justify this practice on the grounds that slave women had not yet developed the decency to feel degraded by being flogged in a state of undress.[83] Anthony Davis went a step further and argued that flogging in a naked state was a means to bring slave women to higher level of civilization because it helped to 'correct the vices and abuses practised by the slaves among themselves, to the injury of others'.[84] This illustrates, like his remarks about slave marriage, that Davis tried to avert the threat of emancipation not only by emphasizing the slaves' lack of civilization but also by presenting the planters as paternalistic slaveholders.

In his account of the 1818 court case in which the planter Joseph Boyden was sentenced to six months' imprisonment for having excessively abused one of his slave women, Alexander Barclay articulated most directly the idea that Jamaican society was an English society:

> If those who had been led to believe that there is no proper feeling in the colonies, witnessed the indignation at the conduct of the criminal, which prevailed in the court-house of Kingston that day, it would have satisfied them that Englishmen in Jamaica *are not so different* from Englishmen at home, or so callous to the ill-treatment of the negroes, as some persons are anxious to believe.[85]

It was, however, more often indirectly expressed in refutations of the antislavery accusation that white islanders did not measure up to metropolitan gender ideals and that their conduct was not based on the rule of law. Although it was acknowledged that there were exceptions such as Boyden, it was generally argued that planters and their white employees possessed self-control and felt compassion for the most vulnerable slaves. Cynric Williams mentioned, for example, a planter who had refused to give a girl extra lashes for the various rude remarks that she had made towards him during a flogging, while Robert Scott told the 1832 Select Committee that no planter or estate officer 'would flog a pregnant woman, knowing her to be pregnant'.[86] As to the mistress, she was presented as the epitome of femininity. According to John Stewart, she was an 'affectionate wife', 'tender mother', 'dear friend', and 'agreeable companion'.[87] Her recourse to the whip in the superintendence of female domestic slaves did not make her, in their opinion, less of a domestic manager than the middle-class mistress in metropolitan society. In fact, it was argued that she treated her female domestics with the utmost care and respect. Dr William Sells mentioned, for instance, that she did not flog without scruple.[88] And in the Council of Protection investigation into the abuse of Kate and Ann Whitfield, it was argued that Mrs Jackson had acted like a mother towards the women. She had, for instance, offered Kate medicine and had regularly turned the women's stocks around so that they would not hurt their legs.[89]

The Boyden case was not only used by Barclay to show that most white men in the island were 'men of sensibility' but also to demonstrate that the criminal justice system in the island protected slave women against excessive abuse.[90] Accounts such as these, however, could easily lead to the conclusion that slave women were capable of submitting themselves to the constraints of the law; and hence, that the abolitionist demand for an extension of the slaves' rights could be safely granted. Some opponents of a ban on female flogging therefore provided accounts to show that slave women were prone to abuse their legal rights. Anthony Davis included in his 1832 warning against gradual abolition, a conversation between a slave mother, an overseer, and an attorney. The mother claimed that the overseer had punished her daughter, showing the attorney the 'whale across the back of the girl's neck'. The overseer, however, claimed that it was the result of 'a blow of switch' she had received while playing with a boy. Their arguments led the attorney to address the whole slave congregation: 'The laws, which were intended for your protection, are converted to this infamous purpose! The children mothers, and old people among you, are put forward as the leaders of this conspiracy, knowing that they are protected! shame, shame upon you.'[91] Various other writers agreed with Davis that if freedom was granted too soon, the law would not become the rule of civil conduct in the island because the ex-slaves would not submit to the constraints of the law but try to find the loopholes within it. Admiral Flemming, who had been stationed in the island in the late 1820s, mentioned in 1832, for instance, that slave women were aware of the rape act and that they tried to avoid punishment for work-related offences by accusing their overseer of sexual abuse.[92]

Thus like antislavery writers, proslavery writers also defined themselves in their accounts of female flogging. Largely by comparing themselves to resident planters, metropolitan-based proslavery authors tried to present themselves as 'men as sensibility'. Resident writers were also concerned to depict themselves as such, in an attempt to refute the accusation that they and their womenfolk fell beyond the pale of Englishness. The Assembly's attitude towards the demands from the Imperial government and the West India Committee to issue a ban on female flogging suggests that white men and women in the island asserted not only an English but also a Jamaican identity. Its members defended a practice which metropolitan society regarded as backward and not English, on the grounds that the specific circumstances of the island required its retention. The local residents' rhetoric of sameness and difference with metropolitan society lends support, then, to David Lambert's claim that during the height of the abolitionist campaign, the West Indies were 'a site in which Britishnesses and Englishnesses were produced, deployed, contested and rejected'.[93]

144 *Slave women in discourses on slavery and abolition, 1780–1838*

CONCLUSIONS

Humanitarian reform was the name given to a large number of middle-class movements in the eighteenth and nineteenth centuries that aimed to achieve the individuality and autonomy of various groups of people as well as a general reform of the manners and morals of the nation. It identified a range of formerly unquestioned social practices as unacceptable cruelties, such as blood sports and public executions. The antislavery movement was part of this larger movement for humanitarian reform. Its campaigns centred, like those of other reform movements, upon pain and suffering. It provided, as we have seen, vivid descriptions of the floggings and the wounded female body that concentrated upon three actors: the victim, the practitioner, and the spectator. These descriptions conveyed the idea that the infliction of pain on the slave woman's body deadened the feelings of the practitioner and the spectator and aroused in them a taste for cruelty, while it destroyed the victim's self-respect.[94]

The antislavery narratives of female suffering were first and foremost a means to arouse popular opposition to slavery. They also served to teach the readers virtue by softening their hearts and eliciting tears of sympathy.[95] To avoid the charge that they were not proper Englishmen because their own sensibilities had been blunted or because the spectatorship had generated in them a taste for cruelty, antislavery writers often included descriptions of their emotional response to the scenes of suffering that they described. Some mentioned that they had been unable to watch the spectacle, while others demonstrated their sensibility by omitting some features of the flogging or discussing them only in covert terms.

Metropolitan-based proslavery writers engaged more selectively than antislavery writers with the humanitarian reformers' discourse of suffering. They did not, for instance, discuss the impact of female flogging on the spectators nor did they provide detailed accounts of the cruelty inflicted on the body of the female slave. Their proposal to replace female flogging by solitary confinement or confinement in the stocks drew as much as the antislavery demand for a complete ban on female flogging on the metropolitan campaign for penal reform. This campaign, in which some leading abolitionists played a central role, advocated secluded punishment because it did not legitimize the open expression of dangerous passions nor inflict needless pain. By the late 1820s, it had succeeded in replacing the traditional penalties that had made up the arsenal of Georgian criminal sentences (the pillory, the whipping post, the gallows and the convict ship) by more private and measured forms of punishment that calmed and reformed rather than inflamed the offender.[96] Although resident proslavery writers did not engage with the penal reform campaign, they were not left untouched by the discourse of human suffering. They tried to refute the accusation made by both antislavery writers and metropolitan defenders of slavery that flogging slave women in a naked state had blunted their feelings. And they also did their best to demonstrate that the practice which they believed was the only mode to control female slaves, caused the victim little or no suffering and did not debase her.

As in previous chapters, we have seen that the slave woman's body was a site of cultural contestation. Around the lacerated slave woman's body ideas were articulated about Englishness. According to antislavery writers, a proper Englishman not only abhorred cruelty, showed restraint, and felt compassion for the suffering of others, but also exercised a disinterested power that protected the body, fostered sexual morality, and revered the law. The attribute of a just and disinterested power was articulated in their accounts of slave women's white tormentors and also in their remarks about the impact of female flogging on the slave drivers and the workings of the criminal justice system in the island.[97] Proslavery writers contested the antislavery notion of Englishness. In their responses to antislavery accusations about the severity and indecency of female flogging, they also expressed the idea that self-control, compassion, and commitment to the rule of law were the hallmarks of Englishness. They, however, did not to think that a person who exercised a power that aimed at the body and served his own interests was less English than one who exercised a benevolent power aimed at the soul. Even those metropolitan defenders of slavery who presented female flogging in a naked state as an indecent practice did not object, as we have seen, to flogging per se or to other forms of physical punishment. And like resident proslavery writers, they believed that without recourse to a wide range of punishment practices, planters were unable to sufficiently safeguard plantation discipline; and hence, their livelihoods.

6 Slavery by another name

The 1833 Abolition Act put an end to female flogging. Clause 17 stated that no other person than the S.M. had the right to punish apprentices and that they nor 'any court, judge or justice [could] punish any female apprentice by whipping or beating her person'.[1] Female apprentices who had not done their work properly or had committed other offences against their employer were sent to a S.M. who usually sentenced them to time and labour in the workhouse.[2] The workhouses were under the control of the custos (the chief magistrate) and the justices of the parish. They had the power to appoint the supervisor and other officers and to devise the rules and regulations of the institution. To ensure that the officers adhered to the regulations, workhouse committees appointed Visiting Local Magistrates (hereafter, V.L.M.s). These men inspected the workhouse on a regular basis and ordered the punishment of inmates who had disobeyed the institution's rules.[3]

As existing workhouses could not deal with the influx of so many apprentices, new workhouses were built from January 1835 onwards and existing workhouses enlarged. Around the same time, most workhouses had purchased a treadmill; that is, a giant wheel with a series of steps propelled by the inmates' climbing motion. From the beginning of 1835, then, most female apprentices were sentenced to a combination of hard labour in the penal gang and the treadmill.[4] Around six o'clock in the morning, they were taken out of their dormitories and put on the treadmill for a period of 15 minutes. Women who failed to keep step were given a severe flogging. Thereafter they were chained 'two in two' and taken to the field or street, where they were employed by local planters or local government in such works as cutting cane and building new roads. The women returned to the workhouse around five o'clock in the afternoon, when they did another session on the treadmill.[5]

It was from the workhouse that the most horrible stories of apprenticeship came. The pamphlets that were written in support of the campaign to abolish apprenticeship illustrate that the workhouse, and in particular the flogging of women within it, symbolized for the abolitionists more than anything the planters' deliberate violation of the 1833 Abolition Act. In his

Jamaica under the Apprenticeship (1838), former Governor Sligo referred, for instance, to the flogging of female workhouse inmates as 'the most palpable and barefaced violation of the abolition law'.[6] The first section of this chapter analyzes the numerous moral and legal objections that abolitionists[7] and other critics of apprenticeship put forward against flogging and several other disciplinary practices that female workhouse inmates were subjected to. We shall see that this group was especially concerned to show that since August 1834 planters and other white men in the island had failed to develop the benevolent and disinterested power that was the hallmark of Englishness, and that as a result apprenticeship was nothing but 'a first cousin' to slavery.[8]

The governor and the colonial secretary were also outraged about the flogging of female apprentices in the workhouses. They had assumed that apprenticeship would replace the arbitrary discipline of the driver's whip with a rational, impersonal, and rule-bound mode of discipline. The second section outlines the strategies that they adopted to combat the practice, ranging from persuading workhouse committees to amend their rules to demands for Imperial intervention, which illustrate once more the reluctance of the Imperial government to curb Jamaican legislative autonomy. The section also examines the responses of resident planters and their supporters to the action undertaken by the governor and the colonial secretary, which can be found in reports produced by the Assembly, workhouse committees, and the 1836 Select Committee, and also in published investigations into alleged abuses in the workhouses of St. Ann, St. Andrews, St. Catherine and St. John. These sources provide a good insight into the various and ingenious ways in which planters tried to sustain the old power relations in the island and also tell us much about how planters envisioned the period after the termination of apprenticeship. The last section summarizes the role that they wanted apprenticed women to carry out upon full freedom and compares this with the role articulated by critics of apprenticeship. It also sets out some of the main differences between the ways in which the two sides in the debate about the physical abuse of female apprentices engaged with metropolitan penal theories.

'REPUGNANT TO EVERY FEELING OF HUMANITY'[9]

It was not until August 1836 that abolitionists seriously began to address the abuse of female apprentices in the workhouses. Their concern was largely triggered by the publication of the report of the 1836 Select Committee, which listed the use of physical punishment on female apprentices as one of seven major objections against the workings of apprenticeship in Jamaica. The report mentioned that at least 24 cases of female flogging had taken place in Jamaican workhouses since August 1834 and that female apprentices in the workhouses were also subjected to chaining and the cutting off of hair. The report sharply criticized these three practices and suggested that a 'strict inquiry' should be carried out into all alleged cases of abuse. It did not propose more far-reaching measures because it was convinced that the Assembly would do its best to prevent 'the possibility of the continuance of a practice at once contrary to Law and abhorrent to the best feelings of our Nature'. It pointed out, for instance, that the Assembly had already taken some 'measures to prevent the recurrence of the violation'.[10] Thus by the summer of 1836, the Imperial government still believed that voluntary local action was enough to remedy abuses associated with apprenticeship.

Another factor that led abolitionists to address the physical abuse of female workhouse inmates were the reports that were sent to them by missionaries and residents in the island from mid-1835 onwards, which stated that female apprentices were flogged during their stay in the workhouse and also suffered major injuries from the treadmill. One of the most active reporters of these abuses was the outspoken Baptist missionary William Knibb. In one of his letters to the secretary of the Baptist Missionary Society, Mr Dyer, he mentioned that a female member of his congregation had been 'tied on the wheel and severely flogged', whilst pregnant. Knibb not only related such instances of female suffering but also asked Dyer and others to undertake action on behalf of apprenticed women. He asked Dyer, for instance, to find out whether it was legal to work female workhouse inmates in chains.[11]

The abolitionist accounts of female suffering that were published from 1836 onwards concentrated upon four disciplinary practices in the workhouse that aimed at the body of female apprentices: the treadmill, flogging for not keeping step, chaining, and the cutting off of hair. The report of the Daughtrey and Gordon Commission, which includes statements by former workhouse inmates, workhouse officers, and V.L.M.s, indicates that female workhouse inmates were also exposed to practices that aimed at their soul. They faced a comprehensive set of rules similar to those of English penal institutions at the time, including the rule that inmates could not speak to one another while at work in the gang or on the mill.[12] By concentrating on the disciplinary practices that aimed at the women's bodies while ignoring the more modern ones that targeted their soul, abolitionists tried not only to arouse their audiences and encourage them to undertake action but also to convince them of the backwardness of white Jamaican society, and hence the need to reform the whole of Jamaican society. While most abolitionists provided detailed accounts of the four forms of physical abuse and told their readers that they symbolized white society's determination to prevent the workings of apprenticeship, few spelled out the motives underpinning them. Although planters did not commit the physical abuse suffered by female apprentices in the workhouse, it allowed them, according to Sligo, to 'make up for the other annoyances, which, owing to the Abolition Law, it is no longer in their power to inflict on their apprentices'.[13] For

Sligo, then, the physical abuse of female workhouse inmates was as much as the withdrawal of the indulgences for pregnant and nursing women, a means through which planters expressed their anger about the loss of their arbitrary and proprietary power.

The change in the women's legal status after August 1834 from 'property' to 'human beings with legal rights' forced abolitionists to adopt some changes in the way they discussed female physical abuse. As we shall see, it led them to focus more on the illegality of the abuse. There was, however, also much continuity in the abolitionist debate about female physical abuse, especially in the way it tried to arouse the audiences' sympathy. Most abolitionists, for instance, focussed on vulnerable women (in particular pregnant and nursing women) and provided rich layers of detail. One of the most gruesome descriptions of female physical abuse can be found in Henry Sterne's *A Statement of Facts Submitted to the Right Hon. Lord Glenelg* (1837) which relates, amongst others, the author's experiences as a member of the jury investigating the death of Anna Maria Thompson in the St. George workhouse in August 1835. Sterne mentioned that at first sight the body had not shown signs of physical abuse but that it was only after the body was turned over and the clothes were removed, that he had noticed that 'her neck, back and shoulders down to her spine, were most dreadfully lacerated from flogging.'[14] And as much as before 1834, abolitionists directly addressed their audiences. Sturge and Harvey asked them, for instance, to 'balance the severity and degradation of the treadmill and the chain gang with the punishments by which the unrequisited labour of females was formerly extorted'.[15]

By not mentioning incidences of female resistance and by providing detailed descriptions of the wounded bodies and the infliction of pain, accounts of physically abused female apprentices in the workhouses relied as much as those of flogged slave women on images of African Jamaican women as suffering victims.[16] These accounts, however, did not silence the abused women. Sturge and Harvey's travel account, for instance, contains an appendix with statements made by female apprentices who had spent time in the workhouse. This new rhetorical strategy did not undermine the image of the suffering victim because the women whose voices were included, emphasized the dehumanizing nature of the workhouse regime. Abolitionists used this new strategy mainly to affirm the change in the women's legal status. Individual cases of female physical abuse, such as that of Sarah Murdoch mentioned in the first chapter, served the same purpose. It could be argued, then, that abolitionists attributed apprenticed women with a humanity that was less potential and slightly more real than that which they had ascribed to slave women.

Accounts of female physical abuse in the workhouse concentrated also on three sets of actors. The actors differed, however, from those in accounts of flogged slave women. Besides victims (apprenticed women) and perpetrators (workhouse officers), there were furthermore facilitators: S.M.s, Assembly members, and local magistrates, who in various and complicated ways allowed for the physical abuse of female apprentices in the workhouse.[17] As to the victims, abolitionists continued to argue that physical abuse prevented the women from developing the feminine virtues that they needed to carry out their future role as moral regenerators, such as chastity, modesty, and self-respect.[18] In 1837, women from the Sheffield Association for the Universal Abolition of Slavery mentioned that female workhouse inmates were 'scorned, polluted, ruined, both for time and eternity'.[19] Remarks such as this, which expressed the contention that amongst the various rights bestowed on the former slave women under the Abolition Act was the right to human dignity, were largely based on the fact that when the women were on the mill, they were partly naked. They wore a 'coarse Osnaburgh shift with short sleeves, half high in front and coming no lower than the waist' on top of a petticoat, so that whenever a weight was lifted, their skin appeared between the shift and the petticoat.[20] Although the nudity was not a conscious workhouse policy, it led many abolitionists and other critics of apprenticeship to agree with the female abolitionists from Sheffield that the mill in the Jamaican workhouse did not function, like that in prisons in metropolitan society, as a non-degrading form of punishment.[21] Sturge and Harvey mentioned, for instance, that the mill destroyed the women's 'decency' and suggested that it would be a less degrading experience for female workhouse inmates if they were supplied with 'a suitable dress'.[22]

S.M. William Oldrey provided another solution to the indecency of the mill. He suggested that female apprentices should only be put on the mill in the presence of a 'matron'.[23] Because most female prisoners in metropolitan society at the time were supervised by women, Oldrey's proposal indirectly criticized the gender disorder of the Jamaican workhouse. For abolitionists, the lack of gender order in the Jamaican workhouse symbolized the backwardness of Jamaican society as much as the punishments that aimed at the bodies of the inmates. They strongly disapproved of the fact that male and female inmates were put on the mill together, worked alongside each other in the penal gang, and were often chained together.[24] The supervisor of the workhouse in Oldrey's district rejected his proposal on the grounds that S.M.s could not amend workhouse rules.[25] It is likely that he was not keen to employ matrons to supervize female inmates because the exposure of the women's bodies to the gaze of male officers acted as a very effective means to control female inmates and prevent them from re-offending.[26]

Chaining was also seen to debase female apprentices. Female workhouse inmates wore a collar that was put around their neck, to which a chain was attached that went around their waist. It was only taken off when the women were put on the mill and on Sundays when they were employed in the workhouse yard. The 1836 Select Committee argued that this practice had an 'injurious influence on the characters and feelings' of the women because it lessened their 'self-respect'. Its remark that this female virtue was 'of the highest importance to maintain, or when it does not exist, to create', clearly illustrates the Committee's conviction that bringing apprentices in line with metropolitan gender ideals was one of the main aims of apprenticeship.[27] For Sligo, it was not the wearing of the horrific collar and the chains in themselves that prevented female apprentices from developing important feminine virtues but the inmates to which they were chained:

> If she has been heretofore pure in her conduct, the chances are strongly in favour of her being *corrupted by the vices of her companions*. Once seen among the criminals in the streets, disgrace attaches to her name, though she has really been guilty of no offence, except one of the most trifling nature ... yet, for this cause, she is made to associate with the vilest criminals of the chain gang.[28]

Apprentices sentenced by S.M.s were not the only workhouse inmates. The institution also housed whites, and free African Jamaicans who had been sentenced at petty sessions, quarter sessions and assizes courts, including lifers who were usually appointed as workhouse drivers.[29] In his *Jamaica under the Apprenticeship*, Sligo also fiercely attacked the practice of the cutting off of the hair of female apprentices upon entering the institution. He refused to accept the argument put forward by workhouse committees that it was for the 'sake of cleanliness'. As none of the estates had used this practice during slavery when it was more important for planters to ensure the health of their labourers, he concluded that it stemmed from 'no other motive than a wish to annoy these poor women'.[30]

For most abolitionists, however, the degrading impact of the four disciplinary practices lay less in the exposure of the women's bodies and their potential to corrupt the women's morals than in the sheer physical suffering that they caused. Oldrey argued, for instance, that because of the island's hot climate, the cutting off of female workhouse inmates' hair was most 'injurious' to their health, while Augustus Beaumont was convinced that chaining 'must be very torturing'.[31] The mill and flogging were especially presented as torturing experiences for apprenticed women. Flogging was extremely painful because it was practically inflicted on bare skin, whereas the mill injured many women as the construction was such that those who could not keep step hung with their hands in the straps while the keen side of the steps revolved against their bodies, knees and legs.[32] The pamphlet *Statements and Observations on the Workings of the Laws for the Abolition of Slavery throughout the British Colonies* (1836) conveyed the impact of the mill on the health of the women most clearly in its account of an apprentice who was sentenced to the mill, even though she was far advanced in pregnancy. After a spell on the mill, she had miscarried and not long after she had returned home, with her 'legs dreadfully bruised, and her whole frame bespeaking the utmost wretchedness', she had died.[33]

The four disciplinary practices were not only referred to as 'degrading' but also as 'inhuman'. This term emphasized even more white Jamaican society's lack of civilization and captured not just the severity of the practices but also the change in the women's legal status. As chains were the ultimate symbol of enslavement, it is not surprising that for some critics of apprenticeship, chaining symbolized more than the other practices the planters' denial of the women's new status. One S.M. described it, for instance, as a 'savage and disgusting custom'.[34] Sligo regularly invoked the term 'inhuman' in his accounts of female flogging. While the term referred mostly to the fact that the floggings were extremely painful, he also used it to point out that the floggings undermined the transformation of the former slave society into a free labour economy. As the floggings violated one of their recently acquired rights, Sligo feared that they would, like the withdrawal of the customary indulgences for pregnant and nursing women, fail to instil in female apprentices a commitment to the rule of law.[35]

It is important to note that although Sligo condemned the physical abuse suffered by apprenticed women in the workhouse on the grounds that it was illegal and debased both the victims and their perpetrators, he did not criticize the treadmill and hard labour as a form of female punishment per se. In fact, he called the treadmill a 'salutary mode' of female punishment because, compared to flogging, it was non-degrading.[36] In October 1834, Sligo encouraged the Assembly to adopt this 'salutary mode' of female punishment in Jamaican workhouses. He supported his call with the same images of African Jamaican women used by resident proslavery writers in the 1820s and early 1830s to dismiss calls for a ban on female flogging: the troublesome worker and the lawbreaker. He told the Assembly, for instance, that female apprentices were 'the most troublesome' apprentices on the estates because they 'have refused to come into terms', and predicted that the women would not soon become more docile labourers because there were 'no treadmills or other places of confinement yet in existence' for them that had the same deterrent effect as flogging.[37] This remark illustrates, like his response to the planters' demand that apprenticed women pay back time for looking after sick children, that in the beginning of his governorship, Sligo's vision of Jamaican society upon full freedom did not include the withdrawal of African Jamaican women from field labour and that his concerns at the time were first and foremost with the continuation of the plantation economy.[38]

As to the perpetrators of the abuse of female workhouse inmates, abolitionists and other critics of apprenticeship argued that the regular infliction of pain on helpless women had in them, like in the estate officers who had administered the flogging of slave women, instilled a positive taste for cruelty, which morally degraded them. An article in the free-coloured newspaper *The Watchman* mentioned, for instance, that 'the supervisor is in some cases so accustomed to his work and *hardened* in it, that not only can he stand it with the utmost torpidity but appears to *enjoy a fiend-like gratification* in adding to the distress of the afflicted.'[39] Abolitionists used accounts of the perpetrators especially to convey their view of the proper relationship to power. The convict workhouse driver symbolized more than the other perpetrators, the antithesis of a disinterested power. He not only willingly flogged the women, but also did it in most cases without having the authority to do so. Considering that abolitionists deemed sexual purity a precondition for apprenticed women's future role as moral regenerators, it is not surprising that they concentrated in particular on the fact that drivers forced female workhouse inmates to have sex with them. Captain Studholme Hodgson mentioned, for instance, that many young female workhouse inmates had been corrupted by the drivers' power and had submitted to their 'brutal passions' in the hope of receiving better treatment. To convince his readers of the women's ability to be chaste, however, he quickly added that most women did not entertain the drivers' immoral offers but 'preferred torture' instead.[40]

The power exercised by the higher-rank workhouse officers was also described as unjust and corrupt. Although such officers also often exceeded their authority, abolitionists and other critics of apprenticeship concentrated far more upon the fact that they served as 'subordinates of the magistracy'.[41] In his letters to the colonial secretary, Sligo regularly mentioned that these officers carried out a regime that aimed to please the local planters. In June 1836, he informed Glenelg, for instance, that many workhouse supervisors had adopted the rule to put inmates on the mill who had only been sentenced to hard labour. This punishment was, according to him, not only 'illegal' because workhouse officers did not have the authority to make rules but also 'additional', in that it 'very materially increases what has been ordered by the special justice'.[42] Henry Sterne articulated more directly that higher-rank workhouse officers used their power to realize the interests of the planters. He mentioned that one of the officers of the St. George workhouse had honoured the wish of planter John Bell to flog his female workers severely. Like many abolitionists before him, Sterne invoked the female body to support his argument. He mentioned that he had seen Bell's female apprentices at work in the penal gang with their 'backs bare, and blood running from some, with marks of severe flogging'.[43]

Even more implicated than the workhouse officers in the planters' attempts to regain some of the power that they had lost under the 1833 Abolition Act were, according to the abolitionists, large numbers of S.M.s and workhouse committee members. Only a few abolitionists directly accused S.M.s of carrying out the disciplinary wishes of local planters. Sterne mentioned, for instance, that John Bell had managed to persuade S.M. Fishbourne to commit 13 of his female apprentices to the workhouse.[44] Most abolitionists merely hinted at the S.M.s' implication in the planters' project of retaining their former power. They pointed out that many S.M.s gave apprenticed women sentences that far exceeded the offence committed and that they failed to take the women's physical condition into consideration when sentencing them. Sturge and Harvey, for instance, supported their idea that many S.M.s were 'Buckra Magistrates' with the case of Mary

Saunders. Shortly after Mary had bought the remainder of her apprenticeship, her employer had appealed to the governor and she had not received a 'free paper'. Her own appeal to the governor a year later had triggered a warrant by the S.M., and she had been committed to the workhouse as a runaway whilst heavily pregnant. Sturge and Harvey, who met her in the workhouse only two days after she had delivered her tenth child, concluded that 'the supervisor appeared to have done all he could to palliate, by kind treatment, the inhumanity of the magistrate'.[45]

Two methods were mentioned by which workhouse committee members enabled planters to hold on to much of their former power. First, they denied female workhouse inmates full legal protection against abuse. They not only made it difficult for S.M.s to visit the workhouse and thus notice instances of abuse, but also rejected the governor's repeated requests to amend the workhouse rules.[46] And second, they adopted rules that subjected female workhouse inmates to a disciplinary regime that was similar to the one administered on the estates during slavery. *The Edinburgh Review* mentioned, for instance, in its analysis of the report of the 1836 Select Committee that 'under that name [the workhouse regulations] lie cart-whips, chains, collars, and solitary cells'.[47] Far more concern, however, caused those workhouse rules that offered 'gratuitous oppression'; that is, punishments that increased the sentence issued by the S.M. and which were seen to serve no other purpose than to humiliate and thereby control the women, such as the cutting off of hair and chaining within the institution.[48]

Abolitionists tried to demonstrate that higher-rank workhouse officers, planter-friendly S.M.s, and workhouse committee members fell short of the metropolitan norm of masculinity not only by pointing out that they ordered excessive punishments and failed to display compassion for the women, but also by directly comparing them to men in their own society. At a public meeting in November 1837, which led to the establishment in London of the headquarters of the campaign to abolish apprenticeship, for example, one speaker emphasized that 'no man in this country is brutal enough to place any female upon the treadmill (cheers), it is a punishment reserved for ruffians of the male sex.'[49] Abolitionists and other critics of apprenticeship, then, were convinced that the four forms of physical abuse that female apprentices were subjected to in the workhouse degraded the perpetrators and the facilitators as much as the victims because they prevented these men from living up to a norm of masculinity that emphasized an abhorrence of cruelty, compassion for the suffering of others, and the use of power in a disinterested way. Or, in the words of Glenelg, these forms of abuse were 'intimately connected with the moral elevation of both sexes'.[50] To convince their audiences that white society had made little progress towards becoming a truly civilized and English society since the onset of apprenticeship, they emphasized its marked deviation from metropolitan gender ideals and preference for ineffective and outmoded forms of punishments as well as its lack of commitment to the rule of law.

Critics of apprenticeship presented not just the flogging but also the chaining and the cutting off of hair of female apprentices in the workhouse as illegal practices. As the last two practices were not specifically prohibited by the 1833 Abolition Act, they concentrated in particular on the illegality of flogging to demonstrate that planters grossly violated their contract with the Imperial government.[51] The Irish nationalist leader Daniel O'Connell, who was instrumental in setting up the campaign's headquarters in London in November 1837, told an audience, for instance, that 'females are not ordered to be flogged, they are sent to the treadmill but there is a man who flogs them there if they do not dance, as they call it, according to his pleasure.'[52] While most critics regarded the flogging of female workhouse inmates as a breach of the letter of the Abolition Act, lawyer John Jeremie argued that it was also a 'breach of the spirit of the Abolition Act'. He mentioned in his statement before the 1836 Select Committee that clause 17 contained the crucial proviso: 'excepting any law or police regulation in force against all other persons of free condition'. He pointed out that rule 20 of the Jamaica Gaols Act of July 1834 covered just such an exception, as it gave 'any ordinary justice' the power to correct inmates by 'corporal punishment' and allowed him to delegate such power to the supervisor, mill overseer and drivers.[53]

Critics argued that planters violated the spirit and letter of the 1833 Abolition Act not just in their capacity as lawmakers by passing the Gaols Act that allowed for the circumvention of clause 17 but also as members of the island's judiciary.[54] The fact that apprenticeship had not been accompanied by a change in the make-up and workings of the courts explained, in their opinion, why apprenticed women were only partially protected against physical abuse in the workhouse and also against other violations of their recently acquired rights. Amateur justices drawn from the planting class had continued to make up the courts and exercised their duties in the same way as described by Goderich in his analysis of the Kitty Hylton and the Kate and Ann Whitfield cases.[55] Henry Sterne conveyed most clearly in his account of the jury investigating the death of Anna Maria Thompson that the amateur justices obstructed the course of justice and dismissed incriminating evidence against members of their own community. When the trial started, there were only 11 jurors. And in spite of the marks of flogging on the woman's body and a witness statement that female workhouse inmates were regularly flogged, the jury had decided that Anna Maria Thompson had died of 'an inflammation of the bowels'.[56] To further emphasize the white islanders' lack of commitment to the rule of law, Sterne mentioned that he had asked for another juror because he knew that it was 'against the Abolition Act' and that he had also refused to sign the verdict.[57] Thus like the antislavery writers who emphasized their intervention in the flogging of slave women, Sterne used his account of female flogging as a means to present himself as a proper Englishman.

A more detailed analysis of the ways in which the criminal justice system failed to protect female apprentices against physical abuse in the workhouse can be found in Sligo's *Jamaica under the Apprenticeship*. Sligo argued that it was largely because of obstacles that planters put in the way of their apprentices to launch a complaint against a workhouse officer and provide incriminating evidence against them, that so few cases of female abuse went to trial. Planters, for instance, refused to give apprentices permission to leave the estate to give an affidavit.[58] Another important reason was the bias displayed by the juries. He mentioned, for example, that Mr Anderson had prepared bills relating to the flogging of two women in the Kingston workhouse but had torn them up when he had learned that a case supported by similar evidence had been dismissed by a grand jury.[59] According to Sligo, biased juries also explained the high number of acquittals and the fact that those who were found guilty of physically abusing female workhouse inmates were mostly lower-rank workhouse officers. Sligo mentioned, for instance, that driver Phillips of the St. Andrew workhouse had been found guilty of flogging a female inmate for not submitting to his sexual wishes, while his supervisor who had known about the incident had been acquitted because the president of the workhouse committee had led the trial against Phillips and had also persuaded the parish to pay the expenses of the supervisor's prosecution.[60] To convince his readers that it was not just lower-class men like Phillips who failed to exercise a benevolent power but also elite white men, Sligo focussed in particular on the workings of the grand juries. He mentioned various cases in which grand juries had thrown out bills and furthermore included in an appendix, notes relating to the unfound bill filed against Whiteman, a workhouse overseer accused of flogging Jane Rentford on the mill.[61] It was especially the workings of the grand juries that led Sligo to call for:

> a change in the judicial system of the colony . . . for the purpose of devising some means to prevent the recurrence of such abuses, not only during the continuance of the apprenticeship, but after the year 1840; when with all the prejudices felt against the blacks, more watchfulness, even than at present, will be requisite to protect their liberties.[62]

This remark demonstrates most clearly that during the second half of apprenticeship, Sligo had shifted his concern about the future of the island away from the continuation of the plantation economy and towards the civil rights of the African Jamaican population. It also shows that like most abolitionists at the time, he was fully convinced that unless full freedom was accompanied by drastic reforms at all levels of Jamaican society, Jamaica would never become the society envisioned by the architects of the 1833 Abolition Act.

To ensure that clause 17 of the 1833 Abolition Act was fully adhered to in the island, critics of apprenticeship suggested the repeal of rule 20 of the

Gaols Act, which made female flogging in the workhouse possible. Initially, they believed that this could be achieved by appealing to the Assembly. They soon realized, however, that the Assembly was as unwilling as before August 1834 to yield any of its legislative power and therefore pressed for Imperial action that would unequivocally declare illegal the flogging and chaining of female apprentices in the workhouse and also the cutting off of their hair upon entering the institution.[63] In January 1838, for instance, Sligo called for the following Imperial act that would remove the proviso to clause 17: 'no local law or regulations can interfere with the Abolition Act; and that the flogging of a female, no matter in what place, or under what circumstances, is a high misdemeanour'. To ensure that such an act would be observed, Sligo proposed that workhouses should be subjected to 'strict examination'. In his opinion, these two measures together would instil in apprentices respect for the law so that upon full freedom they would use the law to settle their disputes.[64] The 1838 Amendment Act largely incorporated Sligo's suggestions. It included the provision that 'no female apprentice could be punished by beating, placing on the treadmill or in penal gang or any offence against the abolition code or prison or other regulations' and also stipulated that S.M.s had the right to 'enter and examine all jails and workhouses' and that the governor had 'the power to make regulations covering the treatment of apprentices in such places'.[65]

For some critics, the 1838 Amendment Act did not go far enough to remedy the physical abuses committed against female apprentices in the island's workhouses. The liberal radical and abolitionist George Thompson mentioned, for instance, in one of his speeches that the Amendment Act lacked 'justice and compassion' and left corrupt white power intact. He therefore agreed with S.M. William Ramsay that only the immediate termination of their apprenticeship would allow apprenticed women to develop the feminine virtues that they needed to carry out their role as moral regenerators.[66] The following section tries to asses whether Thompson and other abolitionists were correct in claiming that since August 1834, the power exercised by white men in the island had moved not further towards but further away from the ideal of a benevolent power. It will first, however, examine how the perpetrators and facilitators responded to the fierce attack on their identity as Englishmen.

'I DID NOT SEE ANY CRUELTY PRACTISED'[67]

The assumption that apprenticed women were natural troublemakers underpinned the various attempts to justify the practices of putting female apprentices on the mill, flogging them for not keeping step, chaining them within as well as outside the workhouse, and the cutting off of their hair upon entering the institution. William Miller, a former property manager, told the 1836 Select Committee, for instance, that chaining was not, as critics suggested, an additional punishment but a means to deal with unruly female apprentices: 'They are frequently employed on the roads, there is only one or two people to look after them; it is to prevent escape.'[68] The image of the natural troublemaker was most frequently invoked in defences of female flogging. John Nethersole, a member of the Kingston workhouse committee, explained that the committee had adopted the rule to flog female inmates because so many had thrown themselves off the treadmill 'under the impression that they could not be flogged', while another committee member accounted for the flogging of Janet Williams on the grounds that she had been most violent and obstinate.[69] Opponents of apprenticeship, suggested, then, that like the 'extra-labour-for-extra-allowances schemes', flogging in the workhouse was not an additional hardship bestowed on apprenticed women but an essential means to ensure that the women would become the responsible and law-abiding citizens envisioned by the architects of the Abolition Act.

Various other disciplinary practices in the workhouse were justified on the grounds that they aimed to realize the interests of the apprenticed women. These justifications served mainly to undo the claim that planters and other white men in the island did not employ power benevolently. Not only the cutting off of hair but also the practice of strapping women to the treadmill, which made it an especially tormenting experience, was presented as benefiting the women's health. According to Robert Cadenhead, the deputy supervisor of the Falmouth workhouse, female inmates 'would bruise their legs severely', if they were not strapped on.[70] And the supervisor of the St. Ann workhouse, Alexander Levi, argued that chaining women within the walls of the workhouse was a means to protect their purity because the institution was very 'insecure at night'. To further deny the abolitionist charge that white Jamaican men failed to live up to the metropolitan masculinity ideal and also to counteract the claim that there was no proper gender order in Jamaican workhouses, Levi stated that he had ordered convict workhouse drivers to hand in their keys to the women's department in order to prevent sexual abuse and that he had stipulated that female and male inmates were to bathe in different rivers.[71]

Planters and their friends in the workhouse committees, the Assembly, and the courts used several other strategies to justify the physical abuse of female workhouse inmates, which simultaneously served to deny the accusation that they were 'men of hardened and brutal character'.[72] They, first of all, dismissed the abolitionist contention that female workhouse inmates were abused on a large scale as sheer myth. William Burge, the agent for Jamaica in London, pointed out in March 1836 that the cutting off of hair was not practised, as Governor Sligo had argued, on a large scale; only one case had taken place and that had been 'entirely in error'.[73] They furthermore shifted the blame for instances of female physical abuse away from themselves to either the female inmates or particular workhouse officers. Robert Cadenhead argued that women only got injured on the mill because 'they attempted to jump off' in order to avoid their sentence.[74] V.L.M. Richard Heming, on the other hand, tried to excuse himself for the injuries that the female inmates of the St. Ann workhouse sustained on the mill by blaming supervisor Drake. He pointed out that Drake had regularly changed the weights in order to 'favour those towards whom he is friendly disposed, or injure those against whom he entertains any ill-will'.[75] They also tried to present themselves as 'men of sensibility' by mentioning the action that they had undertaken to ameliorate the condition of female inmates. Supervisor George Deverell of the Mandeville workhouse mentioned that he had refused to give his assistants orders to flog women on the mill.[76] Not surprisingly, they emphasized in particular the changes that they had brought about in the treatment of pregnant and nursing inmates. Israel Lemon, the president of the St. Ann workhouse committee, mentioned that he had forbidden supervisor Levi to put pregnant and nursing women on the mill, whereas Levi himself stated that he had not only followed Lemon's order but had also ensured that nursing women were given a light workload and were exempted from chaining.[77]

The argument that the punishments inflicted on female inmates were moderate also aimed to deny the accusation that workhouse officers and members of the workhouse committees were brutal men. This strategy was more often used than those mentioned above, especially with regards to the mill and flogging for not keeping step.[78] It was generally argued that the mill was so carefully constructed that the women seldom suffered major injuries. Supervisor Liddel of the St. Andrew workhouse mentioned that it had a regulator, which ensured that it could only go to a certain speed.[79] The claim that the floggings were severe was furthermore denied by stating that the women were given only a few lashes. The supervisor of the Kingston workhouse, George Aitcheson, told an Assembly committee that he had ordered the driver to give Janet Williams 'only two or three stripes over her clothes'.[80] Some opponents of apprenticeship also denied the severity of the punishments inflicted, by invoking the women's bodies. V.L.M. John Kelly informed a committee investigating the flogging of Jane Reid in the Falmouth workhouse, that he had seen only a 'few marks on her back' and which did not look very 'severe'.[81]

The above-mentioned strategies, which were similar to those employed by resident proslavery writers in their attempts to prevent a ban on female flogging, were usually used in combination with the argument that the four disciplinary practices were legal and that apprenticed women could seek redress in case they had suffered excessive abuse in the workhouse. It was argued that chaining and the cutting off of hair were legal practices because they were mentioned in the rules and regulations of the individual workhouses, which in turn were in accordance with the 1834 Gaols Act. The supervisor of the St. John workhouse, for instance, denied that he had 'illegally' put collars and chains on several female workhouse inmates, by stating that he had acted 'in pursuance with the rules and regulations of the institution'.[82] We shall see further on that a similar argument was used with regards to female flogging. It was more difficult for planters and their friends, however, to counteract the claim that biased juries left apprenticed women only partially protected against abuse. They emphasized that the courts dealt mercilessly with workhouse officers who had violated the workhouse rules regarding the infliction of corporal punishment.[83] And they furthermore mentioned that the grand juries' verdicts depended on thorough and unbiased research. The president of the grand jury investigating a bill against several officers of the Kingston workhouse, which was dismissed on the grounds that the workhouse rules allowed for female flogging told an Assembly committee, for instance, that: 'A more *anxious, patient and deliberate* investigation was never bestowed by 23 gentlemen. The grand jury were occupied in the inquiry the greater part of two consecutive days; we even applied to the Court for *further evidence*, and the mayor of Kingston was sworn and sent before us.'[84] By emphasizing the modernity and the efficiency of the criminal justice system, planters and their friends not only tried to show that apprenticed women were protected against abuse but also that white society was fully committed to the rule of law; and hence, that the fear that the fundamental liberties and civil rights of the ex-slaves would not be protected upon full freedom, as articulated most clearly by Sligo, was completely ungrounded.

The workhouse enabled Jamaican planters to regain, albeit in an indirect way, some of the power that they had lost under the 1833 Abolition Act. As members of the workhouse committees, they devised rules which subjected female workhouse inmates to punishment practices similar to those used on the estates during slavery and which, alongside several others, ensured the subjugation of female apprentices, and appointed workhouse officers whom they knew would not hesitate to carry out their specific disciplinary wishes.[85] The disciplinary regime that female workhouse inmates were subjected to served the planters in other ways as well. It first of all allowed them to counteract their alleged decline in output levels because they could hire, at a relatively low cost, a penal gang to cut cane or do other chores around the estate.[86] It also helped them, in the absence of the whip on the estate, to keep their female labourers under control. Planter John Wallace's statement before the Daughtrey and Gordon Commission suggests that there were planters who regarded time in the workhouse as a deterrent that was as effective as flogging during slavery: 'I told her [his apprentice Mary James] that I would endeavour to obtain her release [from the workhouse], if she would promise to behave better in the future; she made the promise and then I went to Mr. Drake the supervisor.'[87] Based on the assumption that the future role of female apprentices was that of paid plantation workers, it was furthermore argued by some planters that time in the workhouse, especially on the treadmill, instilled in female apprentices such habits as regularity and industry, which would benefit their enterprises upon full freedom.[88] Considering the various direct and indirect benefits that the treatment of female apprentices in the workhouse bestowed upon the planters, it is no surprise that they fiercely combated attempts to improve the condition of female apprentices in the workhouse.

As flogging symbolized their former power more than the other three disciplinary practices, planters fought especially hard to uphold this practice. The first obstacle that they encountered in their struggle was the S.M.s. Following a change in legislation in metropolitan society that led to the establishment of a prison inspectorate, S.M.s were in July 1835 given the right to enter and inspect the workhouses as well as the right to ask the governor to investigate instances of noticed abuse.[89] Several S.M.s reported instances of 'illegal' flogging (that is flogging not specified in the workhouse rules), and were subsequently ordered by the governor to investigate the matter.[90] Workhouse officers were usually reluctant to co-operate with such investigations as they could lead to prosecutions.[91] The supervisor of the Kingston workhouse, for instance, refused S.M. Moresby in the 'most peremptory and insolent manner' to interview the head driver.[92] Evidence suggests that some S.M.s violated the July 1835 order by trying to influence the discipline in the workhouse. Upon their visits to the workhouse, they would give workhouse officers orders not to flog the female apprentices that they had committed to the institution. Workhouse committees obviously did not appreciate such interference in the management of the institution and told their officers to ignore orders given by S.M.s. In case this failed to have an effect, they asked the governor to penalize the S.M. concerned.[93]

The governor and colonial secretary formed the second obstacle in the struggle. Sligo and his successor Lionel Smith held different ideas about who should assume responsibility for the apprentices in the workhouses. Sligo was convinced that 'the punishment of all apprentices in these establishments should be exclusively under the jurisdiction of the special justice.'[94] Smith, on the other hand, was content to leave it in the hands of local magistrates, provided that the discretionary power that workhouse supervisors and their subordinates had enjoyed was withdrawn.[95] Both men nevertheless agreed with the colonial secretary that the flogging of female apprentices in the workhouse violated, if not so much the letter than certainly the spirit of the 1833 Abolition Act, and was a most immoral and inhuman practice.[96] Their campaign to end it, which took place between April 1835 and April 1838, consisted of three steps. First, they asked workhouse committees to abolish the rule that allowed for female flogging. When this failed to have an impact, they encouraged the Assembly to pass an act that would unequivocally prohibit the flogging of female apprentices in all places. And finally, they called for Imperial intervention in the form of an amendment to the 1833 Abolition Act. In earlier chapters, it has been demonstrated that the Imperial government was very conciliatory towards the Assembly until the beginning of 1838.[97] The following examination of the three steps illustrates that while the Assembly faced little intervention from the Imperial government until the last stages of apprenticeship, it had to deal throughout the period 1834–38 with considerable opposition from the governor.[98]

In April 1835, Sligo asked the Kingston workhouse committee why Janet Williams and Aglaia Ceffay had been flogged. The committee replied that they had 'considered themselves justified by the clause in the Gaols Act, in passing a rule that females should be flogged'.[99] In July, the governor sent a circular to the workhouse committees informing them that 'all corporal punishment was illegal without the order of a superior court'.[100] A month later, he was informed about the death of Anna Maria Thompson. This and two similar cases made him realize that a direct appeal to the workhouse committees was insufficient to combat the practice of female flogging. He therefore wrote a letter to the Assembly in November 1835 stating:

> A much more serious breach, not only of the spirit but even in the letter of the law, has been committed under the supposed authority of the Act in question. His Excellency alludes to the rule permitting the use of the whip upon women by the superintendents of treadmills. This is a direct infringement of the 21st section of the Abolition Act, which expressly forbids the whipping of the women under any circumstances.[101]

The Assembly did not respond to his letter. In February 1836, Sligo addressed them again on the issue, this time in a direct speech, in which he severely criticized their unwillingness to combat the practice:

> So far from passing an Act to prevent the recurrence of such cruelty, you have in no way responded your disapprobation of it; you have not even denied the truth of my assertion, and therefore must have credited it, notwithstanding you have taken no steps to put an end to it.[102]

The Assembly used various strategies to deny Sligo's claim that female flogging was practised on a large scale. First, they pointed out that the practice did not prevail, by stating that they were aware of only two cases: Eliza Carr in the Kingston workhouse and Jane Reid in the Falmouth workhouse. Second, they argued that these 'solitary cases of error' were 'illegal' because the workhouse officers had violated the rules of the institution. Eliza Carr's flogging, for instance, was 'illegal' because the rules of the Kingston workhouse stated that 'no corporal punishment is to be inflicted unless ordered by a special or visiting justice, and only when every other mode of punishment has been tried and failed.'[103] Third, they argued along the lines of the Kingston workhouse committee that although the Reid and Carr cases were 'illegal', the practice of flogging female apprentices in the workhouse in itself was in accordance with the law. By 'law' however, they did not mean the 1833 Abolition Act but the 1834 Gaols Act. And finally, they rejected Sligo's suggestion to pass an act to undo female flogging. They not only assumed that it was beyond their 'duty and power' to pass such an act but also that the 1834 Gaols Act was 'quite abundant' to prevent future instances of female flogging. Another argument used to reject Sligo's proposal was that those committed of such 'solitary cases of error' were subject to severe penalties. They mentioned, for example, that the supervisor who had ordered Jane Reid's flogging had been dismissed for his offence.[104]

In June 1836, Sligo sent another letter to the Assembly in which he listed 24 cases of female flogging that had taken place in seven workhouses since August 1834, which were mentioned by George Grey, the under-colonial secretary, in his statement before the 1836 Select Committee.[105] The Assembly conducted a quick inquiry into four of the mentioned cases. It used similar strategies as in February to 'refute the calumny contemplated by them'. It pointed out that these were 'solitary cases of error' and that the law was 'amply sufficient' because some of the accused workhouse officers had been fined or even indicted and found guilty.[106] Contrary to the February response, however, it blamed the 'solitary cases of error' not only on workhouse officers but also on S.M.s. The report concluded that in some cases 'blame must rest solely with those officers of the Crown whose peculiar duty it is to see that the laws are carried into effect'.[107] This argument served, like that which presented flogging as a means to teach apprenticed women to fulfil their apprenticeship duties, to excuse the planters and other members of the local elite for the failure of apprenticeship to change the ex-slaves into the docile and responsible citizens envisioned by the architects of the 1833 Abolition Act.

The report of the Daughtrey and Gordon Commission, which was completed in October 1837, and various abolitionist publications that addressed the condition of the workhouse, such as Sturge and Harvey's travel account, convinced the colonial secretary that more drastic action was needed to protect female workhouse inmates against flogging.[108] Like Sligo, Glenelg believed that the abuse suffered by the women stemmed from the fact that their protectors — the S.M.s — had no effective control over the discipline exercised in the workhouses. He therefore asked the Assembly in February 1838 to consider an act that would put the workhouses firmly under the control of the governor and the S.M.s, but told them that if they refused to do so, he would ask Parliament to interfere.[109] As the Assembly remained as unwilling as before to surrender the hold of the planting class on the workhouses, Parliament included in the 1838 Amendment Act the two earlier-discussed provisions.[110]

As we have seen, Sligo did not object to the treadmill as a mode of female punishment per se, neither did his successor nor the colonial secretary. Glenelg, in fact, argued that because female apprentices were used to hard labour, a punishment of only hard labour in the penal gang would not act as a sufficient deterrent.[111] The governors and colonial secretary were convinced, however, that the cutting off of hair and chaining were as illegal and oppressive as flogging and fought a similar struggle with the Assembly to end these two practices.[112] This struggle also demonstrates that the

Assembly was the best means of the planters to uphold the disciplinary practices that benefited them in various ways. The Assembly refused to undertake action against them because it considered them 'legal' (that is in accordance with the 1834 Gaols Act), and swept allegations of female physical abuse aside by blaming individual officers and S.M.s.[113]

The Assembly's struggle with the governors and the Colonial Office over the disciplinary practices that female apprentices were subjected to in the workhouse was less about the practices per se than about the question of who should control the workhouse. In their insistence that the workhouse should remain firmly under the control of local magistrates and that the Assembly should retain the right to draw up the rules for the institution, Assembly members articulated, as in their opposition to a ban on female flogging during slavery, a Jamaican identity. The provision in the 1838 Amendment Act that the governor was to be given the right to devise the rules for the treatment of apprentices in the workhouse, illustrates that the Imperial government was keen to prevent the development of this identity. It went even further in July 1838, when it issued a bill entitled 'Act for the Better Government of Prisons in the West Indies' (West India Prisons Act). The bill, which became law around the time that apprenticeship was abolished, placed the control of the prisons and the workhouses in the hands of the governor.[114] The rules which Governor Smith devised for the penal institutions in November 1838 demonstrate most clearly that it was not only abolitionists at home who were keen to see the island assert an English as opposed to a Jamaican identity. The rules aimed to bring the penal institutions in Jamaica in line with those in metropolitan society, in particular by imposing a gender order upon them.[115]

CONCLUSIONS

Although this chapter has been less concerned with the actual practice of female physical abuse in the workhouse than with the debate surrounding it, it has confirmed the conclusion of earlier chapters that planters displaced their anger about the loss of their power under the 1833 Abolition Act largely onto apprenticed women. They not only used Assembly members and S.M.s in their attempts to regain some of their former power but also workhouse officers and local magistrates. With their help, they succeeded in creating a system of discipline in the workhouse that was in many ways not markedly different from that employed on the estates during slavery. It could thus be argued that apprenticeship was slavery by another name. Considering that the workhouses adopted disciplinary practices that were not practised during slavery, such as the cutting off of hair and the treadmill, we could go even further and argue along the lines of the abolitionist Henry Sterne that apprenticeship was 'equally bad, if not worse' than slavery.[116]

That planters were so successful in their attempts to sustain the old power relations in the island (they did not face real opposition from the Imperial government until early 1838) is not only because apprenticeship relied upon existing penal institutions and an unchanged criminal justice system, but also because of the imperfectability and ambiguity of the 1833 Abolition Act. In previous chapters, we have seen that S.M.s often did not know how to deal with certain planter demands because the Act did not address them. This chapter has furthermore illustrated that some of the most crucial provisions in the Act were formulated in such a way that they could gave rise to interpretations that undermined the main idea underpinning the Act: the transformation from a slave to a free society.

The four disciplinary practices that Sterne and other critics of apprenticeship held up as evidence that planters aimed to prevent the island from becoming a truly free society (the treadmill, flogging for not keeping step, chaining, and the cutting off of hair) and the debate surrounding them, engaged with the metropolitan campaign, mentioned in the previous chapter, that aimed to transform prisons and other penal institutions into places that both punished and reformed offenders. Quakers played a leading role in this campaign. They set up the Society for the Improvement of Prison Discipline (SIPD), of which the well-known parliamentary abolitionist Thomas Buxton was a founding member. Based on the assumption that flogging was a practice that degraded the offender as well as the person administering the punishment and those who watched the event and did little to transform the offender into a responsible and self-disciplined citizen, the SIPD undertook great efforts in the 1820s to introduce the treadmill in British prisons. The treadmill was seen to fulfil the dual purpose of reform and punishment, as it taught prisoners regularity but also deprived them of all independence in regulating their own labour. The SIPD campaign proved very successful; by 1824 some 54 prisons had already adopted the treadmill.[117] As a result of this success, the SIPD recommended that the colonies also install treadmills in their penal institutions. By 1828, treadmills were in use in Trinidad, Berbice, and also in the Kingston workhouse.[118]

The strong disapproval that the abolitionists and other critics of apprenticeship expressed about the four disciplinary practices and their attempts to end them illustrates most clearly their engagement with the metropolitan penal reform campaign. They used similar terms as penal reformers to describe these practices as backward and inefficient modes punishment, such as 'savage', 'degrading', and 'inhuman' and like them, they accused the men in charge of the penal institutions of not being impersonal, impartial and professional.[119] Critics of apprenticeship furthermore accepted the penal reformers' premise that the treadmill was a rational, civilized, and efficient mode of punishment. This can be clearly deduced from the fact that in spite of the pernicious effects of the mill on apprenticed women's bodies and minds, they did not call for the removal of the machines from the workhouses. Instead, they put forward suggestions to make the mill operate more as it did in prisons in metropolitan society, such as providing female inmates with proper uniforms, employing matrons, and, most importantly, banning the use of the whip by mill drivers.[120]

Jamaican planters were also keen to keep the treadmill as a mode of punishment for female apprentices. It could be argued that they supported the installation of the mill in the workhouses between 1834 and 1835 not just because they thought the mill would help to instil in their apprentices habits which would benefit them in the short or long term, but also because the mill reflected well on them as it was held up in metropolitan society as the peak of civilized punishment. For Jamaican planters, however, this new mode of punishment could easily coexist with old modes of punishment. We have seen, in fact, that most were convinced that the mill could not exert its beneficial influences on female apprentices without the recourse to flogging.

Both sides not only differed with regards to the question whether female apprentices in the workhouse should be subjected to outdated and inefficient forms of punishment but also in the way they described the present and future status of the women. In the first two chapters, we have seen that planters and planter-friendly S.M.s regarded female apprentices who had committed offences against their employer, such as turning up late, as criminals. Once female apprentices entered the workhouse they were not only regarded but also treated as criminals, as from that moment onwards they fell under the 1834 Gaols Act. Abolitionists and other critics of apprenticeship strongly disapproved of this ingenious method to circumvent clause 17.[121] They argued that by being treated as criminals rather than apprentices upon entering the workhouse, the women failed to develop not only the feminine virtues that they needed to act as future moral regenerators, such as purity, but also a firm commitment to the rule of law. This, but even more so the fact that they did not object to the abuse suffered by female apprentices in the workhouse on the grounds that it failed to instil in them such habits as regularity and industry, illustrates that critics, with the notable exception of Sligo in the first half of the apprenticeship period, expected apprenticed women not to become wage labourers upon full freedom but to withdraw from the field and devote themselves to the concerns of their family. Planters and their friends, on the other hand, expected apprenticed women to remain plantation workers upon full freedom, as can be deduced from their argument that female apprentices who were committed to the workhouse would only learn the hard way about the workings of contract.

As in the debate about motherhood and marriage, critics and opponents of apprenticeship clashed over the question as to who formed the main obstacle to the transformation of the island. The main obstacle for the critics was the planters and their friends in the Assembly, the workhouses, and the courts. These men were especially accused of preventing the island from becoming a more moral, just, and stable society upon freedom. For the opponents, the apprentices formed the main obstacle. They were seen to impede the future economic development of the island by not developing the skills and habits of free wage labourers. Each side supported its answer with an image of African Jamaican women that had also dominated the debate about the flogging of slave women: the suffering victim (critics) and the natural troublemaker (opponents). It was thus not only the practice of but also the debate about female physical abuse, that showed a marked continuation after August 1834.

Conclusion

The discourses of slavery and abolition measured the African Jamaican female plantation worker against a metropolitan, middle-class norm of womanhood that defined women primarily as devoted wives and caring mothers and presented the home as their proper sphere. Although the contributors to the discourses argued that she did not live up to the whole norm, they did at times suggest that she effectively exercised some of its attributes. We have seen, for example, in chapter two that in his attempts to encourage planters to take better care of nursing slave women, former planter and historian William Beckford argued that slave women were generally 'tender of their children'.[1]

It was especially in their rose-coloured accounts, which increased in the 1820s and early 1830s, that proslavery writers presented images of slave women's alleged similarity with white metropolitan women. While this similarity was in most instances assumed, it was sometimes directly articulated by comparing slave women to rural and other lower-class English women. Planter Alexander Barclay, for instance, dismissed abolitionist calls to exempt slave mothers from field work with the argument that there was no 'good reason why the black women should all be made ladies, while so many of our white kindswomen must earn their bread by field labour'.[2] Proslavery images of slave women's similarity with white metropolitan women were usually wrapped in the argument that slave women were only able to live up to particular attributes of the metropolitan womanhood ideal because of practices that planters had adopted on their estates. The main purpose of these images was to avert Imperial legislation that would force planters to adopt far-reaching methods to ameliorate the condition of their slave labour force or worse, to abolish the system of slavery. The proslavery images of slave women's similarity also acted as a means to counteract the antislavery attack on white Jamaican society; at the time, the treatment of women was used more than anything else to determine a society's level of civilization.

Antislavery discourse also constructed slave women as similar to middle-class, English women. It did this, however, less by directly comparing slave women to English women than by arguing that nature had endowed slave women with the ability to exercise certain attributes of the metropolitan womanhood ideal. Antislavery writers argued, for instance, that slave women were 'naturally modest' and that they were 'naturally affectionate' mothers. Such images of similarity had to convince their audiences of the slaves' full humanity and their ability to live up to the cultural standards of metropolitan society, and thereby take away fears that freedom would lead, as predicted by many defenders of slavery, to disorder and savagery.

Images that stressed the similarity of African Jamaican female plantation workers with white metropolitan women coexisted in pro- and antislavery discourse, which is defined here more broadly than in foregoing chapters and includes also statements by opponents and critics of apprenticeship, with images that emphasized their difference. The natural or cultural difference that each discourse attributed to slave and apprenticed women served different purposes. In proslavery discourse, images of difference served first of all to justify proposed or implemented changes in the lives of slave and apprenticed women. Most of the changes that were proposed and implemented during apprenticeship aimed to enable planters to regain some of the power that they had lost under the 1833 Abolition Act, such as sending full-time midwives back to the field and withholding medical care from free children unless their mothers agreed to work extra hours for the estate. The images of difference that underpinned these changes, such as the 'unruly worker', thus exerted a controlling effect on apprenticed women's lives. Not all proposed and implemented changes, however, exercised a negative effect. In fact, many changes that were implemented during slavery enhanced the quality of life of African Jamaican female plantation workers, such as the employment of an elderly slave woman in the field to look after nurselings. As such 'positive' changes limited slave women's identity to that of producers and reproducers, it can be argued that the images of difference that supported them, such as the 'indifferent mother', exerted a controlling effect, albeit more indirectly than the images that supported the changes that took place after 1834.

The difference attributed to African Jamaican female plantation workers in proslavery discourse served furthermore to excuse the planters for some of the factors that affected the viability of their plantations, and to convince the government and abolitionists at home that slaves were not ready for freedom or that abolition had come too soon. We should also not forget that many local residents emphasized the difference of slave and apprenticed women in order to justify their sexual and physical abuse and thereby convince themselves that they were not, as antislavery writers suggested, beyond the pale of Englishness.

The suffering, innocent, and passive woman was a dominant image of difference in antislavery discourse. It was especially prominent, as we have seen in chapters three and five, in abolitionist verse and fiction. The image aimed to encourage readers to undertake action that would enable slave and apprenticed women to become as good mothers and wives as middle-class, English women and occupy their proper sphere. It undermined the antislavery writers' and the critics' professed belief in the full humanity of the slaves and apprentices not only because it kept in place a differential status between black and white but also because it withheld from the women one of the main markers of humanity: a voice. The authors silenced the slave and apprenticed woman mainly by concentrating on the harm that planters and their white officers did to her body. The humanity that antislavery writers and critics bestowed on slave and apprenticed women was thus more potential than real. The image of the 'passive female victim' informed various calls by antislavery writers and critics of apprenticeship for legislation that would allow slave and apprenticed women to withdraw from the field or to make them in other ways more caring mothers and devoted wives. As these proposals held up the metropolitan ideal of womanhood as the proper and even natural way to live for slave and apprenticed women, the image of the 'passive female victim' was more a controlling than a liberating image.

That pro- and antislavery discourse invoked the metropolitan, middle-class ideal of womanhood stems not only from the fact that the contributors to these discourses, especially those residing in metropolitan society, were steeped in a language that defined women as wives, mothers and domestic beings but also because their aims relied on the partial or complete realization of the metropolitan womanhood ideal in Jamaica. Antislavery writers and critics of apprenticeship wanted not only black but also white Jamaican women to live up to the metropolitan womanhood ideal because they assumed that this would facilitate the moral and economic development of the island upon full freedom. Proslavery writers and opponents of apprenticeship, on the other hand, believed that the financial interests of not just plantation owners but of all white islanders were served by turning slave and apprenticed women into caring mothers. They did not pressure for measures that would transform the women into devoted wives and domestic beings because these roles were seen to have a detrimental effect on the stability and profitability of the estates.

Whether they wanted slave and apprenticed women to live up to the whole or only part of the metropolitan womanhood norm, by measuring the women against this norm all participants in the discourses of slavery and abolition helped to reinforce and, as chapter four has suggested, even naturalize the metropolitan womanhood ideal. This suggests that if scholars want to gain a fuller understanding of the late eighteenth- and early nineteenth-century process that defined women as primarily relating to the home and family, they should not only explore how middle-class, metropolitan women were defined in opposition to their social superiors and inferiors but also how both black and white women in the colonies were described in relation to middle-class women in metropolitan society.[3]

The difference of slave and apprenticed women was especially read on their bodies.[4] Antislavery advocates and critics of apprenticeship presented the women's bodies as *degraded bodies*. They did this not only to arouse their audiences but also to convince them that abolition had to be part of a large-scale transformation of the West Indian colonies because the white men and women who allowed the degradation of the women's bodies — planters, mistresses, estate officers, workhouse officers, and local magistrates — failed as much as the slaves and apprentices to live up to metropolitan gender ideals. To counteract attacks on the gendered identity of white islanders and to justify practices that aimed to sustain their socio-economic status, defenders of slavery and opponents of apprenticeship depicted the bodies of slave and apprenticed women as *malfunctioning, overtly sexual, and undisciplined bodies*.

The 'different body' of the African Jamaican woman in the discourses of slavery and abolition was a site of cultural and political contestation. It was first of all used to debate attributes of femininity and masculinity. Although the participants in the discourses did not invoke the same 'different female body', they mentioned strikingly similar attributes of femininity and masculinity. They mentioned, among others, submissiveness, purity, and delicacy as attributes of femininity, and emphasized authority, restraint, compassion, and protection as the main markers of masculinity.

The participants in the discourses of slavery and abolition were more divided, however, over another identity that was discussed through the 'different body' of the African Jamaican woman: Englishness. Antislavery writers and critics of apprenticeship argued that an adherence to metropolitan gender norms, commitment to the rule of law, and the exercise of a disinterested power were the hallmarks of Englishness. In their attempts to avert antislavery attacks, defenders of slavery articulated the same notion of Englishness. Locally-based proslavery writers, however, articulated simultaneously another notion of Englishness, which was most prevalent in their attempts in the 1820s and early 1830s to prevent a ban on female flogging. This notion of Englishness, which was also mentioned by opponents of apprenticeship in their justification for the physical abuse of female workhouse inmates, did not include the attribute of a just and benevolent power and was more or less interchangeable with 'Jamaicaness'.

The 'different body' of the slave and apprenticed woman was also a site where ideas about freedom were articulated and contested. While the *malfunctioning, overtly sexual, and undisciplined body* in proslavery discourse defined freedom as a state in which the black body performed hard labour and was afforded limited legal protection so as not to threaten the superior socio-economic position of white islanders, the *degraded body* in antislavery discourse defined freedom as self-ownership, the absence of physical coercion, a proper gender order, and the indiscriminate protection of legal rights.

The 1833 Abolition Act contained elements of both the pro- and antislavery notion of freedom. It put in place a form of labour relations that aimed to ensure that upon full freedom the plantations would continue to be profitable and that a social order was kept intact that placed the mass of African Jamaican men and women at the bottom of the social ladder. Like Thomas Holt's *The Problem of Freedom* (1992) and Sheena Boa's recent article on female apprentices in St. Vincent, this study has argued that there were many continuities between this new system of labour relations and slavery, such as the reliance on physical force. It has, however, also suggested that abolitionists were not completely untruthful when they argued that apprenticeship was worse than slavery. Chapters one and two have shown that it was harder for apprenticed than enslaved women to mother well because they were afforded little or no special treatment when pregnant or nursing, had to provide completely for some of their children, and were given little time to look after sick children, while chapter four had demonstrated that many female plantation workers found it more difficult during apprenticeship than slavery to carry out their conjugal duties because of the various obstacles that planters put in their way to visit or live with their partner. In other words, the condition of apprenticed women was similar to but also different from that of slave women.

Several critics of apprenticeship explained the negative changes in the lives of African Jamaican female plantation workers after August 1834 in terms of the planters' fear that the proviso in the local Abolition Act that limited the field labourers' working hours to 40½ a week would lead to a steep decline in output levels. S.M. Madden mentioned, for instance, that planters had discontinued the practice of having a woman in the field to look after nurselings in order 'to get an additional quantity of time from the Negro'.[5] This study has not denied the impact of this and other provisos in the local and the Imperial Abolition Act that affected the economic status of the planters but has suggested that the negative changes in the lives of the women were mostly shaped by the planters' fear of a marked deterioration in their social status; that is, they were above-all an expression of the planters' anger at the decline in their arbitrary and proprietary power brought about by the 1833 Abolition Act. Although planters and their friends continued after 1834 to rely on old images of African Jamaican women in order to justify changes in the women's lives, most notably the 'indifferent mother' and the 'troublesome worker', they no longer regarded female plantation workers as both producers and reproducers but as producers only. Thus not only the lives of but also the discourse about African Jamaican female plantation workers was marked by continuity and discontinuity in the period 1834–38.

In their capacity as assembly men, planters tried to regain some of their former power by drawing up a local Abolition Act and other acts, such as the Jamaica Gaols Act, that denied many of the rights afforded to the ex-slaves under the 1833 Abolition Act, and by sternly refusing to adopt legislation proposed by the governor, the Colonial Office, and local residents that would diminish the planters' control over their labour force. They furthermore tried to prevent a decrease in their social status by discontinuing most of the customary rights granted to their labour force during slavery; refusing to interpret the local Abolition Act to the letter on their estates; befriending S.M.s and workhouse officers and asking them to do their bidding; and by demanding the dismissal of S.M.s who were seen to be too friendly with the apprentices. This study has lend support to the claim made by some historians that planters managed to regain much of their former power because the designers of the Abolition Act had failed to legislate for two different criminal justice systems in the islands: one dealing with free people and one with apprentices.[6] Apprenticeship depended on the existing criminal justice system; that is, the workhouses remained firmly under the control of the chief magistrate and five justices, while the courts continued to be manned by amateur justices, mostly planters and other members of the white elite, who ruled in favour of planters and other white men. Chapter six has illustrated that the implementation of apprenticeship without an overhaul in the criminal justice system paved the way for the violation of one of the most important provisions of the 1833 Abolition Ac: the ban on female flogging.

The conciliatory policy of the Imperial government also explains why practices were continued or put in place that enabled planters to resume some of their former power. As the Colonial Office believed that it needed the cooperation of the planters to ensure the survival of the plantation economy, it passed the local Abolition Act even though it deemed it 'extremely deficient', and it generally preferred issuing S.M.s with specific instructions to giving the Assembly orders to pass legislation to safeguard the rights of the apprentices.[7] It was not until March 1838 that the Colonial Office realized the fruitlessness of its conciliatory policy, when it asked Parliament for legislation to remedy abuses in the administration of apprenticeship in Jamaica. Its request, which resulted in the 1838 Amendment Act, was largely informed by reports of S.M.s and critics of apprenticeship which supported calls for amendments to the local and Imperial Abolition Act with images of planters and other white men in the island as sharp deviations from metropolitan standards of masculinity and Englishness. It was thus not only images of slave and apprenticed women's difference that exerted controlling effects but also images of white Jamaican men's difference.

This study has not only been interested, however, in the controlling effects of images that ascribed difference but also with the intellectual work done by such images. It has not only demonstrated that race, gender, and sexuality acted together to construct images of difference but also that these categories of difference were mutually constitutive. Chapter three, for example, has argued that those contemporaries who described slave women as scheming Jezebels helped both to racialize sexuality and to sexualize race. Another prominent image in chapter three and following chapters was that of the emasculated African Jamaican male, which was primarily presented by antislavery writers and critics of apprenticeship. This image of difference clearly illustrates that race acts as what Evelyn Brooks Higginbotham has called, a 'metalanguage'; race 'tends to subsume other sets of social relations, namely, gender and class, but it blurs and disguises, suppresses and negates its own complex interplay with the very social relations it envelops'.[8] Even though antislavery writers and critics of apprenticeship presented white Jamaican men as savages and brutes, they suggested that they were more 'masculine' than slave and apprenticed men because they exercised authority and were independent. Thus like proslavery writers and opponents of apprenticeship, they argued that the only real male was a white male. The antislavery writers' insistence that slaves and apprentices should live up to the cultural standards of white, middle-class metropolitan society also suggests that race superseded other categories of difference in the debate about slave and apprenticed women. The various articulations of white superiority in antislavery discourse, such as the doubts expressed by early antislavery writers about the slaves' ability to be faithful husbands and wives, and also the distinctions made in proslavery discourse between slave and apprenticed women of different skin colours, confirm Roxann Wheeler's argument that the during the late eighteenth and early nineteenth centuries, race became firmly established in British culture as 'the primary signifier of human difference'.[9]

This study has not aimed to provide a comprehensive account of the interplay between race, gender and sexuality in the debate about slave and apprenticed women in Jamaica. It has merely tried to suggest that these categories of difference intersected in various and complicated ways. Future research will have to examine the interplay in more detail and also the extent to which the debate affected metropolitan discourses. Chapter four, for instance, has argued that the debate helped to reinforce metropolitan ideas about marriage, while chapter three has suggested that it not only reinforced but also changed existing metropolitan discourses. To further support the idea that the debate about slave and apprenticed women exerted far-reaching effects on metropolitan discourses, a study is required that explores the circulation of the various images of difference presented in this study in contemporary metropolitan debates other than those on slavery and abolition, such as the debate on protective labour legislation.

In the decades leading up to the Morant Bay rebellion of 1865, Jamaican planters adopted a variety of practices to ensure a large supply of wage labourers on their estates. Some of these directly affected the lives of African Jamaican women, such as the practice of charging a rent from every family member on an estate. Baptist missionaries helped the ex-slaves in the wage-rent struggle by offering them loans to obtain land in so-called free villages. In return for their generous offer, however, the missionaries expected the ex-slaves to conform to metropolitan gender ideals. Several studies have been published in recent years that argue that African Jamaican women fiercely resisted the planters' practices to obtain their labour and also the missionaries' attempts to impose the metropolitan womanhood ideal upon them.[10] They have, in other words, suggested that during the immediate post-emancipation period, African Jamaican women rejected the dual representation of themselves as 'workhorses' and 'angels in the house'. Thus far, however, no study has posed the question how central African Jamaican women were to the 1840s and 1850s debate about the progress of emancipation in the British Caribbean, or has explored the extent to which images of African Jamaican women in this debate resonated with those in the debates about slavery and abolition.[11] This question needs to be answered, however, before we can argue, as previous studies on proslavery representations of Jamaican slave women have done, that the discourses of slavery and abolition exerted long-lasting and controlling effects on African Jamaican women.

Although this study has left many questions unanswered, it has demonstrated the centrality of gender to the discourses of slavery and abolition. Women of African descent played a central role in the discourses and their images articulated ideas about both appropriate female and male behaviour. It has also in other ways added to existing studies on the discourses of slavery and abolition. Detailed analyses of some writings, such as those of *Hamel, the Obeah Man* and Maria Edgeworth's *The Grateful Negro*, have demonstrated the contradictory and inconsistent nature of the discourses, while comparisons between texts have showed their varied and changing nature as well as their complex interplay and engagement with metropolitan discourses.

Notes

INTRODUCTION

1. *The Speech of James Losh, esq., in the Guildhall, Newcastle-upon-Tyne on the 31st March 1824*, Newcastle: T. and J. Hodgson, 1824, p. 10.
2. This summary of British abolitionism between 1787 and 1838 is based on W. L. Burn, *Emancipation and Apprenticeship in the British West Indies*, London: Jonathan Cape, 1937; R. Blackburn, *The Overthrow of Colonial Slavery, 1776–1848*, London: Verso, 1988; and D. Turley, *The Culture of English Antislavery, 1780–1860*, London: Routledge, 1991.
3. The term 'metropolitan society' refers in this study not to the capital of the mother country but to the mother country as a whole.
4. J. McQueen, *The West India Colonies: the calumnies and misrepresentations circulated against them by the Edinburgh Review, Mr. Clarkson, Mr. Cropper, etc.*, London: Baldwin, Cardock and Joy, 1824, p. 259.
5. C. Hall, *Civilising Subjects: metropole and colony in the English imagination, 1830–1867*, Oxford: Polity Press, 2002, pp. 107–15.
6. The term 'representation' has taken on a variety of meanings in historical studies. Here it refers to textual images of a social group. For more information on the varied uses of the term, see H. White, *The Content of Form: narrative discourse and historical representation*, Baltimore: Johns Hopkins University Press, 1987, chap. 1; and R. Chartier, *Cultural History*, Oxford: Polity Press, 1988, chap. 1. These were not the only contexts in which slave women were discussed. Another important context was that of leisure time, see my 'More than producers and reproducers', in S. Courtman (ed.), *Beyond the Blood, The Beach and the Banana: new perspectives in Caribbean studies*, Kingston: Ian Randle, 2004, pp. 71–90.
7. The term 'discourse' is understood in this study as a set of rule-governed and internally-structured groupings of utterings, sentences, and statements that act together to structure reality and inform notions of reality. See S. Mill, *Discourse*, London: Routledge, 1997, chap. 3.
8. The only sources that contain, albeit indirectly, the voices of slave women are songs, testimonies of four slave women before a Council of Protection, and statements made by female apprentices about the conditions in the workhouse of St. Ann.
9. See in particular bell hooks, *Ain't I a Woman: black women and feminism*, Boston: South End Press, 1981; A. Davis, *Women, Race and Class*, New York: Random House, 1981; D. Gray White, *Ar'n't I a Woman?: female slaves in the plantation South*, New York: W.W. Norton and Company, 1985; and P. Hill-Collins, *Black Feminist Thought: knowledge, consciousness and*

the politics of empowerment, New York: Routledge, 1990. Rupert Simms' article, 'Controlling images and the gender ideologies of enslaved African women', *Gender and Society* 15, no. 6, 2001, pp. 879–97 also explores the stereotypes of the scheming Jezebel and the Mammy but is less concerned to explore how they informed contemporary images of black women than to unravel their political significance at the time.

10. B. Bush, 'History, memory, myth?: reconstructing the history (or histories) of black women in the African diaspora', in S. Newell (ed.), *Images of African and Caribbean Women: migration, displacement, diaspora*, Stirling: Centre of Commonwealth Studies, 1996, pp. 3–28; H. McD. Beckles, 'Female enslavement and gender ideologies in the Caribbean', in P. Lovejoy (ed.), *Identity in the Shadow of Slavery*, London: Continuum, 2000, pp. 163–200; B. Bush, ' "Sable venus", "she devil" or "drudge"?: British slavery and the "fabulous fiction" of black women's identities, c. 1650–1838', *Women's History Review* 9, 2000, pp. 761–89; V. A. Shepherd, 'Gender and representation in European accounts of pre-emancipation Jamaica', in V. A. Shepherd and H. McD. Beckles (eds.), *Caribbean Slavery in the Atlantic World: a student reader*, Oxford: James Currey, 2000, pp. 702–12; and B. Bush, 'From slavery to freedom: black women, cultural resistance and identity in Caribbean plantation society', in T. Bremer and U. Fleishmann (eds.), *History and Histories in the Caribbean*, Frankfurt am Main: Vervuert, 2001, pp. 115–59. That only a few studies have thus far examined representations of slave women in the British Caribbean reflects the cautious appreciation of Caribbean historians of poststructuralist theories, which are read as negating the primacy of human agency in anti-establishment struggles by attributing too much power to language. See, H. Beckles, 'Sex and gender in the historiography of Caribbean slavery', in V. Shepherd, B. Brereton, and B. Bailey (eds.), *Engendering History: Caribbean women in historical perspective*, New York: St. Martin's Press, 1995, pp. 125–40.

11. The antislavery images of slave women in the studies mentioned in footnote 10 are usually presented as 'real' rather than 'fabled' images of slave women. This study will demonstrate that these images were no more real than those presented by proslavery advocates. American scholars have also been reluctant to subject antislavery images of slave woman to close scrutiny. Amy Dru Stanley, however, has opened up this field of study in her *From Bondage to Contract: wage labor, marriage, and the market in the age of slave emancipation*, Cambridge: Cambridge University Press, 1998.

12. The articles mentioned in footnote 10 are largely based on writings by authors who had experience of plantation life but resided in metropolitan society, including Edward Long, *History of Jamaica, or General Survey of the Antient and Modern State of that Island: with reflections on its situations, settlements, inhabitants, climate, products, commerce, laws, and government* [1774], London: Frank Cass, 1970; William Beckford, *A Descriptive Account of the Island of Jamaica*, London: T. and J. Egerton, 1790; and Bryan Edwards, *The History, Civil and Commercial, of the British Colonies in the West Indies*, London: John Stockdale, 1793. These texts have been extensively studied not only by historians of Caribbean slavery but also by literary scholars. See, for example, K. A. Sandiford, *The Cultural Politics of Sugar: Caribbean slavery and narratives of colonialism*, Cambridge: Cambridge University Press, 2000; and M. Harkin, 'Matthew Lewis's *Journal of a West India Proprietor*: surveillance and space on the plantation', *Nineteenth-Century Contexts* 24, no. 2, 2002, pp. 139–50. They have also frequently been used in studies that explore the development of racial ideologies in late eighteenth-century Britain. See, R. Wheeler *The Complexion of Race:*

categories of difference in eighteenth-century British culture, Philadelphia: University of Pennsylvania Press, 2000; and F. Nussbaum, *The Limits of the Human: fictions of anomaly, race, and gender in the long eighteenth century*, Cambridge: Cambridge University Press, 2003.

13. According to Catherine Hall, by studying the discourses in isolation scholars have highlighted the differences between the two but have masked their similarities. See her *Civilising Subjects*, p. 107. This study will not only demonstrate the extent to which the discourses influenced one another but also the similar strategies that they used to appeal to their audiences and their similarities in the way they depicted African Jamaican women.

14. N. Thomas, *Colonialism's Culture: anthropology, travel and government*, Oxford: Polity Press, 1994, p. 2. For a good introduction into 'colonial discourse', see A. Loomba, *Colonialism-Postcolonialism*, London: Routledge, 1998.

15. It follows in this respect Frederick Cooper and Ann Laura Stoler's call to attend 'to dissonant voices rather than assuming coherence' in order to see 'beyond an omniscient colonial apparatus to one shot through with conflict'. See their *Tensions of Empire: colonial cultures in a bourgeois world*, Berkeley: University of California Press, 1997, p. 20.

16. The first approach has been adopted by Bush, Beckles, and Shepherd in their articles on the imagery of slave women.

17. One of the first to explore the local residents' defence of slavery was M. J. Steel in his 'A philosophy of fear: the world view of the Jamaican plantocracy in a comparative perspective', *Journal of Caribbean History* 7, no. spring, 1993, pp. 1–20. For more recent works on local defences of slavery, see J. P. Greene, 'Liberty, slavery and the transformation of British identity in the eighteenth-century West Indies', *Slavery and Abolition* 21, no. 1, 2000, pp. 10–31; A. J. O'Shaughenessy, *An Empire Divided: the American revolution and the British Caribbean*, Philadelphia: University of Pennsylvania Press, 2000; S. Swaminathan, 'Developing the West Indian proslavery position after the Somerset decision', *Slavery and Abolition* 24, no. 3, 2003, pp. 40–60; D. Lambert, 'Producing/contesting whiteness: rebellion, antislavery and enslavement in Barbados, 1816', *Geoforum* 36, 2005, pp. 29–43; D. Lambert, *White Creole Culture, Politics and Identity during the Age of Abolition*, Cambridge: Cambridge University Press, 2005; and C. Petley, 'Slavery, emancipation and the creole world view of Jamaican colonists, 1800–1834', *Slavery and Abolition* 26, no. 1, 2005, pp. 93–114. Some of these scholars, in particular Lambert, have tried to explore the varied nature of proslavery arguments.

18. See, for instance, D. B. Davis, *The Problem of Slavery in the Age of Revolution*, Ithaca: Cornell University Press, 1975; Blackburn, *The Overthrow of Colonial Slavery*; Turley, *The Culture of British Antislavery*; J. R. Oldfield, *Popular Politics and British Anti-Slavery: the mobilisation of public opinion against the slave trade, 1787–1807*, Manchester: Manchester University Press, 1995; J. Jennings, *The Business of Abolishing the British Slave Trade*, London: Frank Cass, 1997; and A. Hochschild, *Bury the Chains: the British struggle to abolish slavery*, London: MacMillan, 2005. Since the 1990s much research has been done on female abolitionists, see, for example, C. Midgeley, *Women against Slavery: the British campaigns, 1780–1870*, London: Routledge, 1992; and K. L. Halbersleben, *Women's Participation in the British Antislavery Movement, 1824–65*, Lewiston/Queenston/Lampeter: The Edwin Mellon Press, 1993.

19. The most recent printed collections are P. J. Kitson and D. J. Lee (eds.), *Slavery, Abolition and Emancipation: writings in the British romantic period* 8 vols, London: Pickering and Chatto, 1999; and J. R. Oldfield (ed.), *The British Atlantic Slave Trade vol. 3: The Abolitionist Struggle*, London: Pickering and Chatto, 2003. Adam Matthew Publications has in recent years produced microfilm collections of some antislavery materials, including: *Wilberforce: slavery, religion and politics*; and *Abolition and Emancipation*.
20. For some recent analyses of antislavery writings by literary scholars, see K. Davies, 'A moral purchase: femininity, commerce and abolition, 1788–1792', in E. Eger, C. Grant, C. O. Gallchoir and P. Warburton (eds.), *Women, Writing and the Public Sphere 1700–1830*, Cambridge: Cambridge University Press, 2001, pp. 133–59; P. Gould, *Barbaric Traffic: commerce and antislavery in the eighteenth-century Atlantic world*, Cambridge, Mass.: Harvard University Press, 2003; B. Carey, M. Ellis and S. Salih (eds.), *Discourses of Slavery and Abolition: Britain and its colonies, 1760–1838*, Basingstoke: Palgrave Macmillan, 2004; and D. Coleman, *Romantic Colonization and British Anti-Slavery*, Cambridge: Cambridge University Press, 2005. For some historical studies that have analyzed antislavery writings, see R. McGowen, 'Power and humanity, or Foucault among the historians', in C. Jones and R. Porter (eds.), *Reassessing Foucault: power, medicine and the body*, London; Routledge, 1994, pp. 91–112; D. Paton, 'Decency, dependence and the lash: gender and the British debate over slave emancipation, 1830–34', *Slavery and Abolition* 17, no. 3, 1996, pp. 63–84; G. Matthews, 'The other side of slave revolts', in Courtman (ed.), *Beyond the Blood*, pp. 49–70. Visual materials produced by antislavery activists have also been subject of study in recent years, see M. Wood, *Blind Memory: visual representations of slavery in England and America, 1780–1865*, Manchester: Manchester University Press, 2000.
21. It is for this reason that this study uses the term 'antislavery advocates' rather than abolitionists.
22. L. Mathurin Mair, *Rebel Women in the British West Indies during slavery*, Kingston: IOJ, 1975; and *Women Field Workers in Jamaica during Slavery*, Mona, Jamaica: Department of History, 1987.
23. B. W. Higman, *Slave Population and Economy in Jamaica, 1807–1834*, Cambridge: Cambridge University Press, 1976; K. Kiple, *The Caribbean Slave: a biological history*, Cambridge: Cambridge University Press, 1984; R B. Sheridan, *Doctors and Slaves*, Cambridge: Cambridge University Press, 1985; and B.W. Higman, *Slave Populations of the British Caribbean, 1807–1834*, Baltimore: Johns Hopkins University Press, 1985. In addition to these monographs, various articles were published on the demographic features of Caribbean slaves, focussing in particular on family formation, including M. Craton's 'Changing patterns of slave families in the British West Indies', *Journal of Interdisciplinary History* 10, no. 1, 1979, pp. 1–35; and O. Patterson's 'Persistence, continuity, and change in the Jamaican working-class family', *Journal of Family History* summer, 1982, pp. 135–61.
24. Since the publication of these monographs, only a few works have been published on slave women's lives which have also largely ignored apprenticeship. See, for example, M. Turner, 'The 11 o'clock flog: women, work and labour law in the British Caribbean', *Slavery and Abolition* 20, no. 1, 1999, pp. 38–58.
25. P. D. Curtin, *Two Jamaicas: the role of ideas in a tropical colony, 1830–65*, Cambridge, Mass.: Harvard University Press, 1955, chap. 5; W. A. Green, *British Slave Emancipation: the sugar colonies and the great experiment*,

1830–1865, Oxford: Clarendon Press, 1976, pp. 132–3; and Blackburn, *Overthrow of Colonial Slavery*, pp. 451–8.
26. For early work that stresses the discontinuities between slavery and apprenticeship, see W. L. Mathieson, *British Slavery and Its Abolition, 1823–1838*, London: Longman Green and co., 1926; Burn, *Emancipation and Apprenticeship*; Curtin, *Two Jamaicas*; and Green, *British Slave Emancipation*. For studies that have emphasized the continuities, see S. Wilmot, 'Not "full free": the ex-slaves and the apprenticeship system in Jamaica, 1834–38', *Jamaica Journal* 17, 1984, pp. 2–10; T. C. Holt, *The Problem of Freedom: race, labor, and politics in Jamaica and Britain 1832–1938*, Baltimore: Johns Hopkins University Press, 1992; M. Sheller, *Democracy after Slavery*, Miami: University Press of Florida, 2000; S. Boa, 'Experiences of women estate workers during the apprenticeship period in St. Vincent, 1834–38: the transition from slavery to freedom', *Women's History Review* 10, no. 3, 2001, pp. 381–407. I have also stressed the continuities of apprenticeship in my 'Slavery by another name: apprenticed women in Jamaican workhouses in the period 1834–8', *Social History* 26, no. 1, 2001, pp. 40–59 and in '" To wed or not to wed?": the struggle to define African Jamaican relationships, 1834–1838', *Journal of Social History* 38, no. 1, 2004, pp. 81–111.
27. As advanced by Diana Paton in her *No Bond but the Law: punishment, race, and gender in Jamaican state formation, 1780–1870*, Durham, N.C.: Duke University Press, 2004.
28. This is not to say that no defences of slavery were written before this crucial decade. For an analysis of early defences of slavery, see Swaminathan, 'Developing the West Indian', pp. 41–50.
29. This study makes use of some material that is not specifically related to Jamaica, including several slave management manuals. This material has been included, however, as it exerted a substantial influence on Jamaican and metropolitan defenders of slavery.
30. Higman, *Slave Populations*, p. 74.
31. Ibid., p. 72.
32. Ibid., p. 77.
33. About 21 per cent of the slaves were engaged in the production of coffee, pimento and other minor crops; 13 per cent were employed on livestock pens; 6 per cent belonged to mobile jobbing gangs; and 8 per cent were employed by town people in various positions. See Higman, *Slave Populations*, p. 55.
34. Sheridan, *Doctors and Slaves*, p. 241. Not all slave women who lived on sugar plantations, however, worked in the field. About 15 per cent was employed as domestics, 5 per cent as field nurses, midwives and doctresses, and 6 per cent looked after the estate's garden and livestock. Nearly 12 per cent of the slave women was inactive. See V. A. Shepherd, *Women in Caribbean History*, London: James Currey, 1999, pp. 52–7.
35. Higman, *Slave Populations*, pp. 162–7 and 187.
36. The increased competition came amongst others from the newer British colonies in the Caribbean, such as Trinidad and Demerara, which produced sugar at a cheaper rate than Jamaica. On the economic depression of the 1820s, see J. R. Ward, 'The profitability of sugar planting in the British West Indies, 1650–1834', *Economic History Review* 31, no. 2, 1978, pp. 197–213.
37. For other factors that played a role, see Blackburn, *Overthrow of Colonial Slavery*, chap. 11. For more information on the rebellion, see M. Turner, *Slaves and Missionaries: the disintegration of Jamaican slave society 1787–1834*, Urbana: University of Illinois Press, 1982.
38. Blackburn, *Overthrow over Colonial Slavery*, pp. 451–7.

182 Notes

39. The term 'critics' refers in following chapters to a diverse group of abolitionists, governors, and S.M.s who accepted apprenticeship as a step towards full freedom but were highly critical of the way the system was implemented in the island. The term 'opponents' denotes a group of planters, S.M.s, workhouse officers, and Assembly members who were either opposed to the whole idea of apprenticeship or to the major provisions of the Abolition Act, and who made little efforts to make apprenticeship a success.
40. On the complicated relationship between various categories of difference, see E. Borris and A. Janssens, 'Complicating categories: an introduction', *International Review of Social History* 44, 1999, pp. 1–13. There is a large body of studies on the process whereby certain social groups are marked as the Other. For an introduction to this literature, see S. Hall and P. Du Gay (eds.), *Questions of Cultural Identity*, London: Sage, 1996, chap. 1.

CHAPTER 1

1. E. Long, *History of Jamaica, or General Survey of the Antient and Modern State of that Island: with reflections on its situations, settlements, inhabitants, climate, products, commerce, laws, and government* [1774], London: Frank Cass, 1970, pp. 436–7.
2. J. Ramsay, *Essay on the Treatment and Conversion of African Slaves in the British Sugar Colonies*, Dublin: T. Walker, C. Jenking, 1784, pp. 75–6. For a similar account by an abolitionist, see T. Clarkson, *An Essay on the Impolicy of the African Slave Trade in Two Parts*, London: J. Phillips, 1788, pp. 91–2.
3. [Tobin], *Cursory Remarks upon the Reverend Mr. Ramsay's Essay on the Treatment and Conversion of African Slaves in the Sugar Colonies: by a friend to the West India colonies and their inhabitants*, London: G. and T. Wilkie, 1785, p. 78.
4. For more information on the so-called 'cult of sensibility', see G. J. Barker-Benfield, *The Culture of Sensibility: sex and society in eighteenth-century Britain*, Chicago: University of Chicago Press, 1992.
5. On the construction of women as maternal beings in the eighteenth century, see R. Perry, 'Colonizing the breast: sexuality and maternity in eighteenth-century England', *Journal of the History of Sexuality* 2, no. 2, 1991, pp. 204–34. For a good overview of the 'invention of childhood', see H. Cunningham, *Children and Childhood in Western Society since 1500*, London: Longman, 1995.
6. They concentrated mainly on the flogging of pregnant woman. Their remarks will be discussed in chap. 5.
7. J. R. Ward, *British West Indian Slavery 1750–1834: the process of amelioration*, Oxford: Clarendon Press, 1988, pp. 121–2. Ward has calculated that Jamaican estates showed a depletion rate (excess of deaths over births) of 25 in 1750–75 and 20 in 1775–1800. This was much higher than that of other Caribbean islands. Barbados and the Leeward Islands, for instance, had a depletion rate of 12–15 per cent in the period 1775–1800.
8. E. A. Wrigley and R.S. Schofield, *The Population History of England, 1541–1871*, London: Edward Arnold, 1981, pp. 577 and 588.
9. B. W. Higman, *Slave Populations in the Caribbean, 1807-1834*, Baltimore: Johns Hopkins University Press, 1984, pp. 303–7.
10. Not all pronatalist measures were geared towards slave women. They also included such proposals as the encouragement of slave marriage and the pro-

vision of better housing. For more information on pronatalist proposals and their implementation, see B. Bush 'Hard labor: women, childbirth and resistance in British Caribbean slave societies', *History Workshop Journal* 36, 1993, pp. 83–99.
11. Genovese articulated the idea of paternalism most clearly in his *Roll, Jordan, Roll: the world the slaves made*, New York: Pantheon, 1974. His interpretation of paternalism has caused, and still causes, considerable controversy. For a recent debate, see 'Genovese Forum', *Radical History Review* 88, 2004, pp. 3–82.
12. For more information on the Slave Trade Committee, see J. Gratus, *The Great White Lie: slavery, emancipation, and changing racial attitudes*, New York: Monthly Review Press, 1973, chap. 3.
13. This cursory overview of childbirth practices before 1780 is based on the statements of Dr Jackson, Henry Coor, Lieutenant Baker-Davison, and William Fitzmaurice in S. Lambert (ed.), *House of Commons Sessional Papers of the Eighteenth Century* (hereafter, *Slave Trade Committee Report*), vol. 82, Wilmington, Del.: Scholarly Resources, 1975, pp. 55, 57, 89, 154, and 222; H. McNeill, *Observations on the Treatment of the Negroes in the Island of Jamaica*, London: G. J. and J. Robinson, 1788, p. 35; R. Renny, *A History of Jamaica*, London: Cawthorn, 1807, p. 208; G. Mathison, *Notices Respecting Jamaica in 1808–1809–1810*, London: John Stockdale, 1811, p. 29; and F. Cundall (ed.), *Lady Nugent's Journal: Jamaica one hundred years ago reprinted from a journal kept by Maria, Lady Nugent, from 1801 to 1815*, London: Adam and Charles Black, 1907, p. 164.
14. In 1824, the Unitarian missionary Thomas Cooper published an account of his stay on Hibbert's estate during the period 1817–1821 under the title *Facts Illustrative of the Condition of the Negro Slaves in Jamaica with Notes and an Appendix*, London: Hatchard. Hibbert's response led to further exchanges of pamphlets between the two men. For more information about their 'paper warfare', see D. C. Strange, 'Teaching the Means of Freedom', *Harvard Library Bulletin* 29, no. 4, 1981, pp. 403–19.
15. Various witnesses before the Slave Trade Committee provided similar accounts of childbirth practices as Tobin's. See, for instance, the statements by Lewis Cathbert and Simon Taylor in *House of Lords Sessional Papers* 1792, pp. 73 and 130; and *Slave Trade Committee Report*, vol. 72, p. 72. For other proslavery writings that echoed Tobin's account, see G. Francklyn, *Observations Occasioned by the Attempts Made in England to Affect the Abolition of the Slave Trade*, Kingston: J. Walker, 1788, pp. 36–7; *The Edinburgh Review and the West Indies*, Glasgow: John Smith and Son, 1816, p. 51; J. Stewart, *A View of the Past and Present State of the Island of Jamaica; with remarks on the moral and physical condition of the slaves and on the abolition of slavery in the colonies*, Edinburgh: Oliver and Boyd, 1823, p. 311; J. McQueen, *The West India Colonies; the calumnies and misrepresentations circulated against them by the Edinburgh Review, Mr Clarkson, Mr Cropper etc.*, London: Baldwin, Cradock and Joy, 1824, pp. 259–60; H. De La Beche, *Notes on the Present Condition of the Negroes in Jamaica*, London: T. Cadell, 1825, p. 12; R. Hibbert, *Hints to the Young Jamaica Sugar Planter*, London: T. and G. Underwood 1825, p. 13; A. Barclay, *A Practical View of the Present State of Slavery in the West Indies*, London: Smith, Elder and co., 1827, pp. 318 and 420; [A. Davis], *The West Indies*, London: James Cochrane and co., 1832, p. 37; and Cundall (ed.), *Lady Nugent's Journal*, p. 94.

184 Notes

16. McQueen, *The West India Colonies*, p. 257. This pamphlet was a direct refutation of Thomas Clarkson's *Thoughts on the Necessity of Improving the Condition of the Slaves in the British Colonies*, London: Hatchard, 1823, which was one of the first tracts advocating gradual emancipation. For more information on James McQueen, see E. Baigent, 'James MacQueen (1778–1870)', in *Oxford Dictionary of National Biography*, Oxford: Oxford University Press, 2004. Available at http://www.oxforddnb.com/view/article/17736 (accessed 9 September 2005).
17. The term 'indulgences', which was commonly used by pro- and antislavery writers, refers in this chapter and the next to proposed and implemented practices to ameliorate the condition of pregnant, lying-in, and nursing slave women.
18. [Tobin], *Cursory Remarks*, p. 80. For similar remarks, see Francklyn, *Observations Occasioned*, p. 36; and *Evidence upon Oath touching the Condition and Treatment of the Negro Population of the British West India Colonies, Part I*, London: Mrs. Ridgways, 1833, p. 18.
19. E. Shorter, *Women's Bodies: a social history of women's encounter with health, ill-health, and medicine* [1982], New Brunswick/London: Transaction Publishers, 1991, pp. 52 and 66.
20. Francklyn, *Observations Occasioned*, p. 36; De La Beche, *Notes on the Present Condition*, p. 12; and Cundall (ed.), *Lady Nugent's Journal*, pp. 93–4.
21. Francklyn, *Observations Occasioned*, p. 36; Hibbert, *Hints to the Young*, p. 13; and De La Beche, *Notes on the Present Condition*, p. 12.
22. McQueen, *The West India Colonies*, p. 259; and Cundall (ed.), *Lady Nugent's Journal*, pp. 93–4. This idea was a mere recycling of that found in many early travel accounts of Africa; namely, that women in 'Torrid zones' gave birth more easily than those in colder regions. See J. Morgan, *Laboring Women; reproduction and gender in New World slavery*, Philadelphia: University of Pennsylvania Press, 2004, p. 45.
23. *The Edinburgh Review*, p. 140.
24. J. Foot, *Observations Principally upon the Speech of Mr Wilberforce on His Motion in the House of Commons the 30th of May 1804*, London: T. Becket, 1805, p. 96. Foot had practised medicine in Nevis in the 1760s.
25. J. M. Adair, *Unanswerable Arguments against the Abolition of the Slave Trade with a Defence of the Proprietors of the British Sugar Colonies*, London: privately published, 1790, p. 131. Emphasis mine. Although based on his experiences in Antigua, the book aimed to defend all West Indian planters against the abolitionist attack on the slave trade. For a similar account, see J. Foot, *A Defence of the Planters in the West Indies Compromised in Four Arguments*, London: J. Debrett, 1792, p. 101.
26. M. G. Lewis, *Journal of a West India Proprietor: kept during a residence in the island of Jamaica* [1834], London: John Murray, 1838, p. 123. See, also Stewart, *A View of the Past*, p. 303. Some authors presented motherly neglect as a major contributing factor but did not attempt to explain it. See, for instance, *The Edinburgh Review*, p. 52; and Mathison, *Notices respecting Jamaica*, p. 92.
27. Lewis, *Journal of a West India Proprietor*, p. 123.
28. Ibid., pp. 96–7.
29. Ibid.
30. M. Harkin, 'Matthew Lewis's *Journal of a West India Proprietor*: surveillance and space on the plantation', *Nineteenth-Century Contexts* 24, no. 2, 2002, pp. 139–50. For another exploration of Lewis' engagement with the 'cult of sensibility', see K. A. Sandiford, *The Cultural Politics of Sugar:*

Caribbean slavery and narratives of colonialism, Cambridge: Cambridge University Press, 2000, chap. 6.
31. Lewis, *Journal of a West India Proprietor*, p. 321. Lewis also presented slave women as ignorant mothers in his account of various other 'prejudices' and 'misconceptions' of pregnant and lying-in women, such as their assumption that 'the eructation of the breath of a sucking child has something in it venomous' and the idea that miscarriages were caused by 'obeah' (witchcraft).
32. *House of Commons Parliamentary Papers* (hereafter, *PP*) 1831–32, XX, p. 467. See also, Adair, *Unanswerable Arguments*, p. 267; and Renny, *A History of Jamaica*, p. 208. The 1832 Select Committee's report played a crucial role in the public debate over slavery as extracts were published in pamphlets and referred to in speeches by abolitionists and M.P.s. For more information on the Committee, see D. Paton, 'Decency and the lash: gender and the British debate over slave emancipation, 1830–34', *Slavery and Abolition* 17, no. 3, 1996, pp. 164-5; and O. M. Blouet, 'Earning and learning in the British West Indies: an image of freedom in the pre-emancipation decade, 1823–33', *The Historical Journal* 34, no. 2, 1991, pp. 400–6.
33. Shorter, *Women's Bodies*, pp. 126–9.
34. [Dr Grainger], *An Essay on the More Common West-Indian Diseases; and the remedies which that country itself produces to which are added some hints on the management etc. of negroes by a physician in the West Indies*, London: T. Becker, 1814, p. 16; and D. Collins, *Practical Rules for the Management and Medical Treatment of Negro Slaves in the Sugar Colonies by a Professional Planter*, London: J. Barfield, 1803, p. 163. Collins had practised medicine in St. Vincent and Grainger in St. Kitts. In his statement before the Slave Trade Committee, former millwright Henry Coor also reflected on slave women's reliance on a slave wet nurse during the first nine days. He was keen to see this practice ended because the wet nurse seldom had sufficient milk for the infant, as she was 'exposed to hard work and poor living'. See *Slave Trade Committee Report*, vol. 82, p. 90. Like the practice of not changing a slave infant's clothes during the first nine days, the use of a wet nurse also stemmed from the slaves' assumption that a newborn child was a visitor from the underworld, who did not become part of the real world until it was nine days old. For more on this idea, see Bush, 'Hard labor', p. 94.
35. V.A. Fildes, *Breasts, Bottles and Babies: a history of infant feeding*, Edinburgh: Edinburgh University Press, 1986, chap. 2. This debate started in the first half of the eighteenth century and was initially directed at the upper echelons of society. By the end of the eighteenth century, the practice of immediate breastfeeding had begun to spread throughout English society. Both former estate doctors, then, presented slave women as not dissimilar from white, metropolitan women; they should also give up a practice that was not conducive to their own health and that of their infant.
36. *PP* 1803–4, X, p. 144. For a similar dismissive account of the slave midwife, see T. Roughley, *The Jamaica Planter's Guide; or, a system for planting and managing a sugar estate*, London: Longman, Hurst, Rees, Orme, and Brown, 1823, p. 91. The Assembly was composed of 45 members (two from each parish) and consisted besides planters also of attorneys, overseers, merchants, and professional men. A Council acted as the Upper House of the Legislature. It consisted of 12 members appointed by the Crown, who had to advice the governor and had the right to amend and issue bills. For more information on this system of government, see W. L. Burn, *Emancipation and Apprenticeship in the British West Indies*, London: Jonathan Cape, 1937, pp. 150–1.

37. Higman, *Slave Populations*, p. 319. The figure refers to the period 1807–34. The male infant mortality rate (298 per 1,000) was higher in Jamaica than the female mortality rate (248 per 1,000). Both rates compared unfavourably to those in England and Wales. During the period 1750–1799, the male infant mortality rate in the latter locality was 135 per 1,000 and the female infant mortality rate 122, see Wrigley and Schofield, *The Population History*, p. 249. The Jamaican slave infant mortality rate was, however, markedly lower than that of the eastern Caribbean islands. The mortality rate of slave boys in Barbados, for example, was 459 per 1,000 and that of slave girls 381, see Higman, *Slave Populations*, p. 319.
38. Renny, *A History of Jamaica*, p. 207; and Mathison, *Notices respecting Jamaica*, pp. 29 and 44.
39. Mathison, *Notices respecting Jamaica*, pp. 29 and 44. Mathison had returned to Jamaica in 1808 after a 13-year absence. During his stay in the island between 1808 and 1811, he had experimented with a variety of measures to counteract the negative effects arising from the abolition of the slave trade, which he recommended in his text to other (resident and absentee) planters.
40. W. A. Beckford, *Remarks upon the Situation of Negroes in Jamaica; impartially made from a local experience of nearly thirteen years in that island*, London: T. and J. Egerton, 1788, p. 24; and Adair, *Unanswerable Arguments*, pp. 131 and 198. This opinion was also expressed by several antislavery witnesses before the Slave Trade Committee, see, for instance, the statements of Captain Hall and Henry Coor in *Slave Trade Committee Report*, vol. 82, pp. 89 and 101.
41. Beckford, *Remarks upon the Situation*, pp. 24–5.
42. Hibbert, *Hints to the Young*, p. 13. See also Beckford, *Remarks upon the Situation*, p. 24.
43. Mathison, *Notices respecting Jamaica*, p. 44.
44. P. Gibbes, *Instructions for the Treatment of Negroes*, 2nd ed., London: Shepperson and Reynolds, 1788, p. 23. For another cash payment scheme, see the letter from the Duke of Portland to the governor of Jamaica, 23 April 1798 in *Slave Trade Committee Report*, vol. 122, p. 65.
45. John Baker Holroyd, 'Observations on the Project for Abolishing the Slave Trade and on the Reasonableness of Attempting Some Practical Mode of Relieving the Negroes' [1790] in P. Kitson (ed.), *Slavery, Abolition and Emancipation: writings in the British romantic period, vol. 2*, London: Pickering and Cato, 1992, p. 364. Holroyd also proposed a scheme to reward owners for successful births. He suggested that planters should be given ten pounds for every slave child born and reared to the age of eight years, paid for from a fund built up by duties paid on imported slaves. He was, in other words, of the opinion that natural increase required as much a change in the slave owners' as in the slave women's attitudes towards childbearing and childrearing.
46. On the appetite of metropolitan women for material, consumer pleasures, see Barker-Benfield, *The Culture of Sensibility*, pp. 191–3.
47. Absentee planter Henry De La Beche mentioned, for instance, that the dresses that slave women wore during the Christmas celebrations were 'often very expensive'. See his *Notes on the Present Condition*, p. 41. Remarks such as these about the slaves' material possessions served to convince the audience that the living and working conditions of the slaves were not as bad as abolitionists suggested. Antislavery writers also did their utmost to present slave women as active consumers. They argued that it showed that upon full freedom the ex-slaves would work in order to consume; and hence, that emanci-

pation would not lead to economic decline. See, Paton, 'Decency, dependence and the lash', pp. 166–7.
48. Hibbert, *Hints to the Young*, p. 14. For a similar proposal, see Beckford, *Remarks upon the Situation*, p. 24. On the Trinidad Ordinance, see Higman, *Slave Populations*, p. 350. Trinidad was a Crown Colony which meant that its Slave Law was designed by the Imperial Government. It is not surprising, then, that its Slave Law was more lenient than that of islands that had an independent legislature, such as Jamaica and Barbados.
49. Baker-Holroyd, *Observations on the Project*, pp. 364–5.
50. Collins, *Practical Rules*, p. 171. The Duke of Portland put forward a similar suggestion in his letter to the governor of Jamaica, 23 April 1798 in *Slave Trade Committee Report*, vol. 122, p. 66.
51. For abolitionist labour-release schemes, see Ramsay, *Essay on the Treatment*, p. 77; and Clarkson, *Essay in Impolicy*, p. 92.
52. M. Craton and J. Walvin, *A Jamaican Plantation: the history of Worthy Park, 1670–1970*, London/New York: W. H. Allen, 1970, p. 134.
53. Collins, *Practical Rules*, p. 171.
54. Beckford, *Remarks upon the Situation*, p. 24. Emphasis mine.
55. Shorter, *Women's Bodies*, pp. 49–53. Obstetric writings at the time only mentioned the impact of a pregnant woman's workload on the health of her infant.
56. Letter from the Duke of Portland to the governor of Jamaica, 23 April 1798 in *Slave Trade Committee Report*, vol. 122, p. 66.
57. Gibbes, *Instructions for the Treatment*, p. 14; Collins, *Practical Rules*, pp. 157–8; and W. Sells, *Remarks on the Condition of the Slaves in the Island of Jamaica* [1823], Shannon: Irish University Press, 1972, p. 17. Only Sells addressed the lying-in period, which he suggested should be between four and six weeks.
58. Gibbes, *Instructions for the Treatment*, p. 14.
59. P. Branca, *Women in Europe since 1750*, London: Croom Helm, 1978, p. 117; and Shorter, *Women's Bodies*, pp. 36–43 and 54. The following pro-slavery writings contain proposals for a lying-in room: Adair, *Unanswerable Arguments*, p. 247; Mathison, *Notices respecting Jamaica*, p. 29; Sells, *Remarks on the Condition*, p. 16; and Hibbert, *Hints to the Young*, p. 13.
60. Sells, *Remarks on the Condition*, p. 16.
61. Adair, *Unanswerable Arguments*, p. 247.
62. Mathsion, *Notices respecting Jamaica*, p. 91.
63. Hibbert, *Hints to the Young*, p. 13. Dr Collins gave the same recommendation for home births. See his *Practical Rules*, pp. 158–9.
64. R. Blackburn, *The Overthrow of Colonial Slavery, 1776–1848*, London: Verso, 1988, pp. 429–30.
65. See, for example, Adair, *Unanswerable Arguments*, p. 247; and the letter of the Duke of Portland to the governor of Jamaica, 23 April 1798 in *Slave Trade Committee Report*, vol. 122, p. 66; and Collins, *Practical Rules*, p. 159.
66. Mathison, *Notices respecting Jamaica*, p. 29. See also [Grainger], *An Essay on the More Common*, p. 72; and Sells, *Remarks on the Condition*, p. 18.
67. Roughley, *The Jamaica Planter's Guide*, p. 96. Some earlier writers also reflected on the power of the slave midwife, see for instance the statement by former estate doctor James Chisholme in *Slave Trade Committee Report*, vol. 69, p. 277.

68. See, for example, L. Mathurin, 'The arrival of black women', *Jamaica Journal* 9, nos. 2–3, 1975, pp. 5–6; and D. Gray White, *Ar'n't I a Woman?: female slaves in the plantation South*, New York: W.W. Norton, 1985, p. 116.
69. The summary of the debate about midwifery is based on: J. Donnison, *Midwives and Medical Men: a history of inter-professional rivalries and women's rights*, London: Heinemann, 1977, chap. 2; B. Brandon Schnorrenberg, 'Is childbirth any place for a woman?: the decline of midwifery in eighteenth-century England', in H.C. Payne (ed.), *Studies in Eighteenth-Century Culture*, vol. 10, Madison: University of Wisconsin Press, 1981, pp. 393–408; and Shorter, *Women's Bodies*, chaps. 3–4. It has been estimated that by the mid-eighteenth century, there were several hundred man-midwives practising in London alone and that there was one in every large town in Britain.
70. Roughley, *The Jamaica Planter's Guide*, p. 96.
71. Most of the midwifery training in the late-eighteenth and early-nineteenth centuries was provided by existing midwives and charities, usually in lying-in hospitals.
72. Collins, *Practical Rules*, pp. 159–60.
73. Mathison, *Notices respecting Jamaica*, p. 90. For a similar suggestion, see Sells, *Remarks on the Condition*, p. 16.
74. Jamaica differed in this respect from some other islands in the British Caribbean. The 1798 Slave Law of the Leeward Islands stipulated, for instance, that slave women should be given a lighter workload from the fifth month onwards. It was only marginal sugar producing islands or Crown Colonies that enacted measures to enhance the survival rate of the infants. See Higman, *Slave Populations*, p. 350.
75. Ibid., p. 350. This was an extension of the 1788 Slave Law, which stated that on estates that showed natural increase overseers were to be given 20 shillings for each slave child born. See the *Slave Trade Committee Report*, vol. 67, p. 213.
76. Parish churches provided its poorest members with a midwife and a lying-in nurse and also gave the women a bottle of gin or rum upon the delivery. See A. Wilson, 'Ceremony of childbirth and its interpretation', in V. Fildes (ed.), *Women as Mothers in Pre-Industrial England: essays in memory of Dorothy McLaren*, London/New York: Routledge, 1990, p. 81.
77. *House of Lords Sessional Papers*, 1792, p. 114.
78. For a striking account of this practice, see [A. Davis], *The West Indies*, p. 3.
79. Hibbert, *Hints to the Young*, p. 14. For a similar account, see *Evidence upon Oath*, p. 52.
80. Lewis, *Journal of a West India Proprietor*, p. 125. According to Lewis, then, material and monetary rewards were not enough to encourage slave women to give birth more often; it required also distinctions of honour and respect.
81. H. McD. Beckles, 'Female enslavement and gender ideologies in the Caribbean', in P.E. Lovejoy (ed.) *Identity in the Shadow of Slavery*, London: Continuum, 2000, p. 177.
82. J. R. Ward, 'The profitability of sugar planting in the British West Indies, 1650–1834', in H. Beckles and V. Shepherd (eds.), *Caribbean Slave Society and Economy: a student reader*, London; Ian Randle, 1991, p. 87.
83. Most planters, however, continued the material reward for successful births after 1827. James Kelly, for instance, mentioned that when he was a bookkeeper in the late 1820s and early 1830s, both the slave mother and the midwife shared an allowance of rum, salted meat, rice, sugar and cloth. See his *Voyage to Jamaica with Seventeen Years' Residence in that Island*, Belfast: J. Wilson, 1838, p. 34. It is possible that planters feared that if they were

to also discontinue the material reward, slave women would cause a major upheaval, which in turn would negatively affect their output levels. The fact that the material reward cost them relatively little may also have made them less inclined to discontinue this practice.
84. As mentioned in *The Consolidated Slave Law, Passed the 22nd December, 1826, Commencing on the 1st May, 1827 with a Commentary, Shewing the Differences between the New Law and the Repealed Enactment*, N. P., Courant Office, 1827 (hereafter, 1826 Slave Law), p. iv.
85. Higman, *Slave Populations*, p. 350.
86. R. S. Dunn, 'Sugar production and slave women in Jamaica', in I. Berlin and P. D. Morgan (eds.), *Cultivation and Sugar: labor and the shaping of slave life in the Americas*, Charlottesville: University Press of Virginia, 1993, p. 63.
87. *PP* 1818, XVII, p. 130.
88. Mathurin, 'The arrival of black women' p. 5. On the importance of motherhood in the slave community, see Bush, 'Hard labor'.
89. *PP* 1803–4, X, p. 145. An Assembly committee rejected this proposal in 1804 on the grounds that it was already 'universal custom'.
90. *PP* 1831–32, XX, p. 335; and Cundall (ed.), *Lady Nugent's Journal*, p. 94.
91. Some estates had already erected lying-in rooms in the late 1780s. See, for instance, the statement of Lewis Cuthbert in the *House of Lord Sessional Papers* 1792, p. 73. Monk Lewis mentioned that the slave women on his estate preferred to give birth in the lying-in room rather than in their own hut. See his *Journal of a West India Proprietor*, p. 96.
92. It seems that until the late 1780s most estates relied on several old slave women to deliver infants and that thereafter, they increasingly used one or two full-time midwives, who were in their late forties. See Dunn, 'Sugar production', pp. 64–5; and *PP* 1837–38, XLIX, p. 252.
93. See, for instance, *Negro Apprenticeship in the British Colonies*, London: Office of the Anti-Slavery Society, 1838, p. 20; and J. Sturge and T. Harvey, *The West Indies in 1837; being the journal of a visit to Antigua, Montserrat, Dominica, St. Lucia, Barbados and Jamaica*, London: Hamilton, Adams, 1838, p. 335.
94. Today pregnant and nursing women are given careful instructions about their diet. Pregnant women, for instance, are encouraged to gain 20 to 25 pound from foods rich in iron, protein, calcium, and other vitamins and minerals. See Shorter, *Women's Bodies*, p. 51.
95. In 1795 there were only 50 trained doctors in the island; that is, one doctor to every 1,500 slaves. See R. B. Sheridan, *Doctors and Slaves: a medical and demographic history of slavery in the British West Indies, 1680–1834*, Cambridge: Cambridge University Press, 1985, p. 276. In 1810, whites constituted 6.9 per cent of the total population in Jamaica. Because of the planters' policy to employ only single men as estate officers, few white Jamaicans lived in families. See Higman, *Slave Populations*, p. 77.
96. The birth rate was lower in Jamaica than in other islands in the British Caribbean. The old sugar colonies had the highest birth rate. Barbados, for instance, witnessed an average birth rate of 56 per 1,000 in the 1820s. But even, the newer sugar colonies had a birth rate that far exceeded Jamaica's and was much closer to that in the metropolitan society, which increased from 33.6 to 40 per 1,000 between 1760 and 1811. See Higman, *Slave Populations*, p. 308; and Wrigley and Schofield, *The Population History*, p. 230. There were some Jamaican estates, such as Worthy Park, that witnessed an increase in the birth rate during this period. The rises in their birth rate stemmed not

only from their owners' decision to implement more far-reaching methods to achieve natural increase but also from the make-up of their slave populations. Scholars have shown that locally born slave women were more fertile than their African-born counterparts. Hence estates with a high proportion of locally born slave women usually witnessed a higher birth rate than those with a large proportion of African-born slave women. See B. W. Higman, *Slave Population and Economy in Jamaica 1807–1834*, Cambridge: Cambridge University Press, 1976, pp. 115–7; and Craton and Walvin, *A Jamaican Plantation*, pp. 130 and 196.

97. The birth rates for the post-1807 period are based on data derived from the slave registration returns. The Jamaican Assembly passed a registration act in 1816 and the first return was provided in 1820. See Higman, *Slave Populations*, p. 8. The birth rate went up significantly after 1838, rising to 40 per 1,000 between 1844 and 1860. See G. W. Roberts, *The Population of Jamaica*, Cambridge: University Press, 1957, p. 269. Barbara Bush has argued that this rise suggests that the failure of the slave population to reproduce naturally was not just the result of 'harsh material conditions or adverse sex ratios' but also the result of slave women's 'deliberate management of their fertility', as conditions had not drastically improved in the immediate post-emancipation period. See her 'Hard labor', p. 95.

98. [P. H. Sligo], *Jamaica under the Apprenticeship System by a Proprietor*, London: J. Andrews, 1838, p. 91.

99. 'The negro apprenticeship', *Edinburgh Review*, January 1838, p. 498.

100. Based on: *A Report of the Proceedings of the Public Meeting Held at Exeter Hall on Thursday 23rd November 1837*, London: Central Emancipation Committee, 1837, p. 40; *A Statement of Facts Illustrating the Administration of the Abolition Law, and the Sufferings of the Negro Apprentices in the Island of Jamaica*, London, William Ball, 1837, p. 10; 'The negro apprenticeship', p. 483; Sturge and Harvey, *The West Indies*, p. 184; J. A. Thome and J. H. Kimball, *Emancipation in the West Indies: a six months' tour in Antigua, Barbadoes and Jamaica in the year 1837*, New York: American Anti-Slavery Society, 1838, p. 105; W. Lloyd, *Letters from the West Indies during a Visit in the Autumn of 1836 and the Spring of 1837*, London: Darton and Harvey, 1839, p. 195; W. F. Burchell, *Memoir of Thomas Burchell, Twenty-Two Years a Missionary in Jamaica*, London: Benjamin L. Green, 1849, p. 295; *PP* 1836, XV, pp. 37, 333, and 372; *PP* 1837, LIII, p. 329; and *PP* 1837–38, XLIX, p. 252.

101. *PP* 1836, XLVIII, p. 349; *PP* 1837, LIII, p. 75; and *PP* 1837-38, XLIX, p. 308. According to Mimi Sheller, the planters' idea that female apprentices were more troublesome than male apprentices was not unfounded. See her, 'Quasheba, mother, queen: black women's public leadership and political protest in post-emancipation Jamaica 1834–65', *Slavery and Abolition* 19, no. 3, 1998, pp. 94–7.

102. *PP* 1836, XLIVIII, p. 202; and *PP* 1837, LIII, pp. 69 and 123. For a similar argument, see Sturge and Harvey, *The West Indies*, p. 407.

103. *PP* 1836, XLVIII, p. 138. In order to obtain the compensation money, each island had to draw up a local Abolition Act which had to carry the 1833 Abolition Act into practical operation. The Jamaican Assembly completed its Act in December 1833. It was approved by the Colonial Office on the condition that the Assembly should draw up an Amending Act in order to remedy 'various serious defects', such as the clause that planters could imprison apprentices on their estates. The Amending Act was approved by the Colonial Office in January 1835. Its expiration in December 1835 led to the revival of the Aboli-

Notes 191

tion Act passed in December 1833. In November 1834, the Assembly passed a third Abolition Act. This Act, however, was disallowed on the grounds that it violated the 1833 Abolition Act. See *PP* 1836, XV, pp. 401–37.
104. *PP* 1836, XLVIII, p. 138.
105. Ibid., p. 139.
106. Sturge and Harvey, *The West Indies*, p. 11.
107. 'Circular 29 December 1837', *Public Record Office* (herafter, PRO), Colonial Office Records (hereafter, CO), 137/231. Sligo resigned in March 1836 after a conflict with the Colonial Office over S.M. Palmer who had made various accusations against planters and also against his fellow S.M.s. Sligo had called an inquiry to investigate Palmer's conduct towards an overseer and several other charges made against him. The fact that Palmer did not appear at the inquiry was for Sligo reason for his dismissal. The Colonial Office, however, did not agree and ordered Sligo to reinstate Palmer. As Sligo felt that this would weaken his already low prestige in the island, he resigned. His successor Lionel Smith did not take up office until September 1836. See Burn, *Emancipation and Apprenticeship*, pp. 240–9.
108. For more information on the Daughtrey and Gordon Commission, see Burn, *Emancipation and Apprenticeship*, pp. 256–60. Some of the statements made before the Commission have been included in a recent reprint of James Williams' narrative. See, J. Williams, *A Narrative of Events, Since the First of August, 1834, by James Williams, an Apprenticed Labourer in Jamaica* [1837], ed. Diana Paton, Durham, N.C.: Duke University Press, 2001.
109. *PP* 1837–38, XLIX, p. 189.
110. See, for instance, *PP* 1837–38, XLIX, pp. 177, 195, and 222–4. Many of the women who had lost their babies as a result of having been sent to the workhouse during the last stages of their pregnancy told the Daughtrey and Gordon Commission that workhouse officers had stubbornly refused their requests for more lenient treatment.
111. *A Statement of Facts*, pp. 11–2.
112. *PP* 1837, LIII, p. 330.
113. [Sligo], *Jamaica under the Apprenticeship*, p. 91.
114. Ibid., p. 138; and J. Sturge, *Horrors of the Negro Apprenticeship System in the British Colonies,* Glasgow: W. and W. Miller, 1837, p. 11.
115. S. Drescher, *The Mighty Experiment: free labor versus slavery in British Emancipation,* Oxford: Oxford University Press, 2002, pp. 147–8.
116. *PP* 1836, XV, p. 402.
117. The Anti-Slavery Society gave Jeremie a silver plate for his condemning account of the Jamaican Abolition Act, which had increased his reputation as a staunch supported of the anti-slavery cause. See Alexandra Franklin, 'Jeremie, Sir John (1795–1841)', in *Oxford Dictionary of National Biography*, Oxford: Oxford University Press, 2004. Available at http://www.oxforddnb.com/view/article/14773 (accessed 19 October 2004).
118. The 1836 Select Committee consisted of 15 members representing both the antislavery and the West India interests. Its report, completed on 13 August, raised several objections to the workings of apprenticeship in Jamaica but concluded that the 'great experiment' would succeed. For more information on the establishment and the workings of the 1836 Select Committee and on the reception of its report, see Burn, *Emancipation and Apprenticeship*, pp. 335–9.
119. *PP* 1836, XV, pp. 23, 402, and 413.
120. Ibid., p. 37.
121. Ibid., p. 413.

192 Notes

122. Ibid., p. 66.
123. *PP* 1837–38, XLIX, p. 185. For another striking violation of clause 11 of the 1833 Abolition Act, see Sturge and Harvey, *The West Indies*, p. 215.
124. Burn, *Emancipation and Apprenticeship*, p. 355.
125. Ibid., pp. 348–59. On 19 March 1838, Lord Glenelg proposed the Amendment Act in response to Lord Brougham's demand for an immediate abolition of apprenticeship. A proposal to include in the Amendment Act a clause to end apprenticeship in Jamaica on 1 January 1839 was opposed and defeated.
126. *PP* 1836, XV, p. 372. Each S.M. was allocated a particular district. The S.M. had to visit the properties in his district at regular intervals in order to hear complaints from the planters and/or overseers and also from the apprentices. Not only apprentices but also planters could be punished for not fulfilling the duties that the Abolition Act had bestowed upon them. For a good insight into the workings of the S.M.s' courts, see D. Paton, *No Bond but the Law: punishment, race, and gender in Jamaican state formation, 1780–1870*, Durham, N.C.: Duke University Press, 2004, chap. 2.
127. Blackburn, *Overthrow of Colonial Slavery*, p. 323; and Sells, *Remarks on the Condition*, p. 16.
128. Paton, *No Bond but the Law*, p. 12. Another colonial historian who has done much to undermine Foucault's account of disciplinary power is Ann L. Stoler. See in particular her *Race and the Education of Desire: Foucault's history of sexuality and the colonial order of things*, Durham, N.C.: Duke University Press, 1995.
129. A similar combination of modern and pre-modern power has been observed for the slave states in the Antebellum South. See, for instance, L. Stewart, 'Louisiana subjects: power, space and the slave body', *Ecumene* 2, no. 3, 1995, pp. 227–45.
130. R. Perry, 'Colonizing the breast: sexuality and maternity in eighteenth-century England', *Journal of the History of Sexuality* 2, no. 2, 1991, pp. 213–6.

CHAPTER 2

1. This metropolitan motherhood ideal is based on E. Shorter, *The Making of the Modern Family*, London: Collins, 1976, chap. 5; L. Davidoff and C. Hall, *Family Fortunes: men and women of the English middle class, 1780–1850* [1987], London: Routledge, 1992, chaps. 3 and 7; R. Perry, 'Colonizing the breast: sexuality and maternity in eighteenth-century England', *Journal of the History of Sexuality* 2, no. 2, 1991, pp. 213–6; and T. Bowers, *The Politics of Motherhood: British writing and culture, 1680-1760*, Cambridge: Cambridge University Press, 1996, pp. 25–8.
2. The term 'childrearing practices' refers in this chapter to the treatment that slave and apprenticed women bestowed upon their children from the moment they went back to work after the delivery until their children joined the third gang at the age of five.
3. J. Ramsay, *Essay on the Treatment and Conversion of African Slaves in the British Sugar Colonies*, Dublin: T. Walker and C. Jenking, 1784, p. 76. Two antislavery witnesses before the Slave Trade Committee also accused planters of grossly neglecting the condition of nursing women. See *Slave Trade Committee Report*, vol. 82, pp. 57 and 101.
4. See [Tobin], *Cursory Remarks upon the Reverend Mr Ramsay's Essay on the Treatment and Conversion of African Slaves in the Sugar Colonies: by a*

friend to the West India Colonies and their inhabitants, London: G. and T. Wilkie, 1785, p. 79; G. Francklyn, *Observations Occasioned by the Attempts Made in England to Affect the Abolition of the Slave Trade*, Kingston: J. Walker, 1788, p. 36; *The Edinburgh Review and the West Indies*, Glasgow: John Smith and son, 1816, p. 140; H. T. De La Beche, *Notes on the Present Condition of the Negroes in Jamaica*, London: T. Cadell, 1825, pp. 4–5 and 10; J. McQueen, *The West India Colonies; the calumnies and misrepresentations circulated against them by the Edinburgh Review, Mr Clarkson, Mr Cropper etc.*, London: Baldwin, Cradock and Joy, 1824, pp. 257–8; A. Barclay, *A Practical View of the Present State of Slavery in the West Indies*, London: Smith, Elder and co., 1827, pp. 318 and 433; C. R. Williams, *A Tour through the Island of Jamaica from the Western to the Eastern End in 1823*, London: Thomas Hurst, Edward Chance and co., 1827, p. 14; [A. Davis], *The West Indies*, London: James Cochrane and co., 1832, p. 37; and J. Kelly, *Voyage to Jamaica and Seventeen Years' Residence in that Island*, Belfast: J. Wilson, 1838, p. 33.
5. McQueen, *The West India Colonies*, p. 257.
6. Barclay, *A Practical View*, p. 322.
7. J. Stewart, *A View of the Past and Present State of the Island of Jamaica: with remarks on the moral and physical condition of the slaves and on the abolition of slavery in the colonies*, Edinburgh: Oliver and Boyd, 1823, p. 311.
8. Francklyn, *Observations Occasioned*, p. 37; and McQueen, *The West India Colonies*, pp. 257–8. According to Higman, slave women turned up two or three hours later than the rest of the field slaves. See his *Slave Populations in the Caribbean, 1807–1834*, Baltimore: Johns Hopkins University Press, 1984, p. 187.
9. W. A. Beckford, *Remarks upon the Situation of Negroes in Jamaica; impartially made from a local experience of nearly thirteen years in that island*, London: T. and J. Egerton, 1788, p. 24; and J. M. Adair, *Unanswerable Arguments against the Abolition of the Slave Trade with a Defence of the Proprietors of the British Sugar Colonies*, London: privately published, 1790, pp. 131 and 198.
10. Adair, *Unanswerable Arguments*, p. 131.
11. Beckford, *Remarks upon the Situation*, p. 24.
12. Ibid.
13. Collins, *Practical Rules for the Management and Medical Treatment of Negro Slaves in the Sugar Colonies by a Professional Planter*, London: J. Barfield, 1803, pp. 167–68. For similar suggestions, see P. Gibbes, *Instructions for the Treatment of Negroes*, 2nd ed., London: Shepperson and Reynolds, 1788, p. 14; and T. Roughley, *The Jamaica Planter's Guide; or, a system for planting and managing a sugar estate*, London: Longman, Hurst, Rees, Orme, and Brown, 1823, p. 103.
14. Roughley, *The Jamaica Planter's Guide*, p. 103.
15. Collins, *Practical Rules*, pp. 166–8.
16. P. Rabinow (ed.), *The Foucault Reader: an introduction to Foucault's thought* [1984], London: Penguin, 1991, p. 17.
17. V.A. Fildes, *Breasts, Bottles and Babies: a history of infant feeding*, Edinburgh: Edinburgh University Press, 1986, chaps. 8 and 10.
18. [Tobin], *Cursory Remarks*, p. 80
19. Roughley, *The Jamaica Planter's Guide*, p. 118. For similar explanations and dismissals of late weaning, see Adair, *Unanswerable Arguments*, p. 122; Collins, *Practical Rules*, p. 169; M. G. Lewis, *Journal of a West India Proprietor: kept during a residence in the island of Jamaica*, [1834], London:

John Murray, 1838, p. 322; *Evidence Upon Oath Touching the Condition and Treatment of the Negro Population of the British West India Colonies*, part 1, London: Mrs Ridgways, 1833, p. 19; and Kelly, *Voyage to Jamaica*, p. 34.
20. Higman, *Slave Populations*, pp. 353–4.
21. Fildes, *Breasts, Bottles and Babies*, p. 367. Fildes attributes the move towards early weaning in the eighteenth century to industrialisation; by weaning their children earlier, women were able to get back to work sooner.
22. See, for instance, Collins, *Practical Rules*, p. 169; and Roughly, *The Jamaica Planter's Guide*, p. 120. Some writers recommended an earlier weaning period, see for instance W. Sells, *Remarks on the Condition of the Slaves in the Island of Jamaica* [1823], Shannon: Irish University Press, 1972, p. 16.
23. Gibbes, *Instructions for the Treatment*, p. 20; Collins, *Practical Rules*, p. 170; and Lewis, *Journal of a West India Proprietor*, p. 406.
24. Collins, *Practical Rules*, p. 170.
25. Fildes, Breasts, *Bottles and Babies*, pp. 377–85.
26. Beckford, *Remarks upon the Situation*, p. 36; Gibbes, *Instructions for the Treatment*, pp. 16–20 and 35; Collins, *Practical Rules*, pp. 172–3; G. Mathison, *Notices Respecting Jamaica in 1808-1809-1810*, London: John Stockdale, 1811, pp. 91–2; and Roughley, *The Jamaica Planter's Guide*, p. 121. Planter Robert Hibbert also recommended that planters should not ignore children after they were weaned. He merely recommended, however, that they should provide children in the third gang with one well-cooked meal a day. See his *Hints to the Young Jamaica Sugar Planter*, London: T. and G. Underwood 1825, p. 14.
27. Gibbes, *Instructions for the Treatment*, p. 35. See also Roughley, *The Jamaica Planter's Guide*, p. 121.
28. Mathison, *Notices Respecting*, p. 92. This proposal supports the idea most clearly articulated by C.L.R. James in his *The Black Jacobins* (1938), that plantation slavery shaped and articulated the modernity of the Caribbean. It was not until the late 1810s before proposals were made in metropolitan society to set up schools for young children in industrials districts. See N. Whitbread, *The Evolution of the Nursery-Infant School: a history of infant and nursery education in Britain, 1800–1970*, London/Boston: Routledge and Kegan Paul, 1972, chap. 1.
29. *Slave Trade Committee Report*, vol. 82, p. 101.
30. Higman, *Slave Populations*, p. 187.
31. De La Beche, *Notes on the Present Condition*, p. 5; and Barclay, *A Practical View*, p. 318.
32. The following texts suggest that this was the most common nursing scheme in place after the turn of the century: *PP* 1836, XV, pp. 23, 61, 164, and 333; *PP* 1836, XLIVIII, p. 275; *PP* 1837, LIII, pp. 75 and 234; *PP* 1837–38, XLIX, pp. 157 and 292; *A Statement of Facts Illustrating the Administration of the Abolition Law, and the Sufferings of the Negro Apprentices in the Island of Jamaica*, London, William Ball, 1837, p. 7; J. Sturge, *Horrors of the Negro Apprenticeship System in the British Colonies*, Glasgow: W. and W. Miller, 1837, pp. 11 and 18; [P. H. Sligo], *Jamaica under the Apprenticeship System by a Proprietor*, London: J. Andrews, 1838, p. 92; J. Sturge and T. Harvey, *The West Indies in 1837; being the journal of a visit to Antigua, Montserrat, Dominica, St. Lucia, Barbados and Jamaica*, London: Hamilton, Adams, 1838, pp. 200, 335–6, and 401; and J. A. Thome and J. H. Kimball, *Emancipation in the West Indies: a six months' tour in Antigua, Barbadoes, and Jamaica in the year 1837*, New York: American Anti-Slavery Society, 1838,

p. 105. These accounts also indicate that by the turn of the century nursing women on most estates had been given a lighter workload.
33. Based on *PP* 1836, XV, pp. 24 and 377; *PP* 1837, LIII, p. 75; Sturge, *Horrors of the Negro*, p. 18; and Thome and Kimball, *Emancipation in the West Indies*, p. 105.
34. Fildes, *Breasts, Bottles and Babies*, p. 385.
35. Lewis, *Journal of a West India Proprietor*, p. 406.
36. *Evidence upon Oath*, p. 18.
37. See, for instance, Williams, *A Tour through the Island*, p. 14.
38. Higman, *Slave Populations*, p. 354.
39. *Evidence upon Oath*, p. 18.
40. Roughley, *The Jamaica Planter's Guide*, p. 118.
41. Higman, *Slave Populations*, p. 354.
42. Lewis, *Journal of a West India Proprietor*, pp. 331–2. Most of the attorneys were lawyers, clergymen and merchants. They visited the estates in their care once or twice a year and were paid a salary or a commission based on the annual yield. See O. Patterson, *The Sociology of Slavery: an analysis of the origins, development and structure of negro slave society in Jamaica*, London: MacGibbon and Kee, 1967, pp. 23 and 56–7.
43. Lewis, *Journal of a West India Proprietor*, p. 406.
44. Higman, *Slave Populations*, p. 216.
45. *A General History of Negro Slavery: collected from the most respectable evidence and unquestionable authorities*, Cambridge: Hatfield, 1826, p. 76.
46. *Slave Trade Committee Report*, vol. 81, p. 58.
47. *A Dialogue between a Well-Wisher and a Friend to the Slaves in the British Colonies by a Lady*, n. p., n. d. p. 4. For another use of this strategy, see [E. Rushton], *West Indian Eclogues*, London: J. Philips, 1787, p. 2. Female abolitionists published their works often anonymously. Like their male counterparts they focussed on the suffering of female slaves and the violation of family life under slavery and presented slave women as innocent victims in need of male protection. They differed from male abolitionists in that they expressed their views more often in imaginative literature than in critical analyses of the workings of the system of slavery. For more information on female abolitionist writings, see C. Midgley, *Women Against Slavery: the British campaigns 1780–1870*, London: Routledge, 1992; and M. Ferguson, *Subject to Others: British women writers and colonial slavery, 1670–1834*, London: Routlege, 1992.
48. T. Clarkson, *An Essay on the Impolicy of the African Slave Trade in Two Parts*, London; J. Phillips, 1788, p. 92. It was mainly Ramsay's work that had convinced Clarkson to devote himself to the abolitionist cause. For another proposal to reduce the workload of nursing women, see the statement of Captain George Young in *Slave Trade Committee Report*, vol. 73, p. 216.
49. Ramsay, *Essay on the Treatment*, p. 77.
50. As cited in J. Gratus, *The Great White Lie: slavery, emancipation and changing racial attitudes*, New York: Monthly Review Press, 1973, p. 76.
51. W. Wilberforce, *An Appeal to the Religion, Justice and Humanity of the Inhabitants of the British Empire on Behalf of Its Negro Slaves in the West Indies [1823]*, in P. Kitson (ed.), *Slavery, Abolition and Emancipation: writings in the British romantic period*, vol. 2, London: Pickering and Cato, 1999, p. 22.
52. *A General History of Negro Slavery*, p. 76. Emphasis mine. See also *Negro Slavery; or, a view of some of the more prominent features of that state of society, as it exists in the United States of America and in the colonies of the*

West Indies, especially in Jamaica, London: Hatchard and Son, 1823, p. 54; and *Plan for Effecting Emancipation by the Redemption of Female Slaves laid before Government in 1824*, in *Plans of Emancipation*, London: Baster and Thomas, [1824], pp. 5 and 7.

53. *The Consolidated Slave Law, Passed the 22nd December, 1826, Commencing on the 1st May, 1827 with a Commentary, Shewing the Differences between the New Law and the Repealed Enactment*, n. p.: Courant Office, 1827 (hereafter, 1826 Slave Law), p. 2. This change in the Slave Law will be discussed in more detail in chap. 4.

54. Rev. J. Riland (ed.), *Memoirs of a West India Planter; published from an original ms*, London: Hamilton, Adams and co., 1827, p. 83. Former missionary Richard Bickell also used the levy to demonstrate that slave women were naturally endowed with maternal affection in his *The West Indies as They Are; or, a real picture of slavery but more particular as it exists in the island of Jamaica, in three parts with notes*, London: Hatchard and son, 1825, p. 17. In case a planter did not succeed in paying his taxes, a levy on his slaves was usually issued. The marshal would gather the number of slaves with a value of the amount of tax owned and then sell them publicly. Under the 1826 Slave Law it was no longer possible for marshals to sell members of a slave family separately.

55. *1826 Slave Law*, p. 2.

56. *A Concise View of Colonial Slavery*, Newcastle: T. and J. Hodgson, 1830, p. 14. For similar accounts of a mother separated from her children through sale see, Rev. B. Godwin, *The Substance of a Course of Lectures on British Colonial Slavery Delivered at Bradford, York and Scarborough*, London: J. Hatchard and son, 1830, pp. 52–3; Riland (ed.), *Memoirs of a West India Planter*, pp. 87–8. For accounts of slave mothers who committed suicide or killed their nurselings on board of the slave ship, see *Slave Trade Committee Report*, vol. 69, pp. 126 and 137.

57. T. Cooper, *Facts Illustrative of the Condition of the Negro Slaves in Jamaica with Notes and an Appendix*, London: Hatchard, 1824, p. 14.

58. PP 1831–32, XX, p. 123; and R. Blackburn, *The Overthrow of Colonial Slavery, 1776–1848*, London: Verso, 1988, p. 422.

59. [Rev. Trew], *Nine Letters to his Grace the Duke of Wellington on Colonial Slavery*, London: William Stroker 1830, p. 54; and *Plan for Effecting*, pp. 8–9. Duncan dismissed such objections by arguing that planters at present did very little for young children and that parents were more than willing to work extra hours on their provision grounds or would find other ways to support their free infants because they knew that 'their children would be exempted from it [slavery]'. PP 1831–32, XX, pp. 122–3.

60. Godwin, *The Substance of a Course*, p. 157; *Nine Letters*, p. 54; and *Plan for Effecting*, pp. 5–9. The last two pamphlets doubted whether a scheme to free slave mothers would ever be implemented. They expected planters to ask such a high sum of compensation money that the Imperial government would not be able to afford the emancipation of slave women. The first pamphlet did not foresee any such problems but posed the question what impact the scheme would have on slave men, as they would not be able to fully support their wives.

61. *Plan for Effecting*, pp. 5–9.

62. Ibid., p. 5.

63. PP 1836, XV, pp. 23, 61, and 348; PP 1836, XLVIII, pp. 275 and 406; PP 1837, LIII, p. 75; PP 1837–38, XLIX, p. 292; *A Statement of Facts*, p. 7;

Sturge, *Horrors of the Negro*, pp. 10–1 and 18; and Sturge and Harvey, *The West Indies*, pp. 200 and 335.
64. *PP* 1837, LIII, pp. 137 and 234; *PP* 1837–38, XLIX, p. 157; and Sturge and Harvey, *The West Indies*, p. 200.
65. *PP* 1836, XLVIII, p. 115; and *PP* 1837, LIII, p. 279.
66. *PP* 1836, XV, pp. 413 and 419; and *PP* 1837, LIII, p. 65.
67. Two weeks after the onset of apprenticeship, Governor Sligo informed the colonial secretary that many planters had withdrawn the field nurse and allowed women little time to feed their children while they were at work in the field. See, *PP* 1835, L, p. 45.
68. Sturge, *Horrors of the Negro*, p. 17.
69. The publication of pamphlets increased after the publication of the 1836 Select Committee report. In November 1837, a Central Negro Emancipation Committee (CNEC) was set up to coordinate the campaign for the abolition of apprenticeship, whose main activities consisted of publishing pamphlets, lobbying M.P.s and forwarding petitions to government. For more information on CNEC, see W. L. Burn, *Emancipation and Apprenticeship in the British West Indies*, London: Jonathan Cape, 1937, pp. 344–7.
70. *A Statement of Facts*, pp. 7–8. See also Sturge, *Horrors of the Negro*, p. 18; and [Sligo], *Jamaica under the Apprenticeship*, p. 91.
71. Sturge, *Horrors of the Negro*, p. 18. For another example of this rhetorical strategy see, *An Appeal to the Christian Women of Sheffield from the Association for the Universal Abolition of Slavery*, Sheffield: R. Leader, 1837, pp. 11–2.
72. Sturge, *Horrors of the Negro*, p. 17.
73. Sturge and Harvey, *The West Indies*, p. 280; and Thome and Kimball, *Emancipation in the West Indies*, p. 105. For a similar account, see *A Report of the Proceedings of the Public Meeting held at Exeter Hall on Thursday 23rd of November 1837*, London: Central Emancipation Committee, 1837, p. 15.
74. Clauses 16 of the local Abolition Act stated that only apprentices were entitled to the customary allowances of food, clothes, housing and medical care, while clause 51 allowed for the 'extra-labour-for-medical-care schemes'. See *PP* 1836, XV, pp. 413 and 419.
75. *PP* 1836, XLVIII, p. 138. It is rather surprising that Governor Sligo deemed it essential to teach apprenticed women about the importance of contract because upon freedom they would not be able to engage in contracts if they were legally married.
76. Ibid., p. 139.
77. *PP* 1837, LIII, p. 329.
78. Ibid., p. 70. S.M. Moresby denied the abolitionists' prediction that ownership of their children would make slave women more affectionate mothers, by arguing that apprenticed women expressed the same degree of love for their free and apprenticed children. See, *PP* 1837, LIII, p. 344.
79. See, for instance, *An Appeal to the Christian*, p. 5.
80. *PP* 1837, LIII, p. 330. For similar remarks see also pp. 220, 253, 260, and 344.
81. Ibid., p. 253. Especially S.M.s Daughtrey and Moresby suggested that fathers raised most of the money by hiring themselves out for wages. See *PP* 1837, LIII, pp. 260 and 344.
82. *PP* 1836, XLVIII, p. 201; *PP* 1837, LIII, pp. 65 and 244; and *PP* 1837–38, XLIX, p. 313.
83. See, for instance, *PP* 1836, XLVIII, pp. 349 and 361; *PP* 1837, LIII, p. 214; and *PP* 1837–38, XLIX, p. 301.

84. *PP* 1836, XLVIII, p. 201. See also *PP* 1836, XV, p. 367; and *PP* 1837, LIII, p. 244. On the educational system during apprenticeship see, T. C. Holt, *The Problem of Freedom: race, labor and politics in Jamaica and Britain, 1832–1938*, Baltimore: Johns Hopkins University Press, 1992, pp. 72 and 151–2.
85. *PP* 1836, XLVIII, p. 201. See also *PP* 1837, LIII, p. 244.
86. Holt, *The Problem of Freedom*, pp. 43–4.
87. See in particular George Grey's remarks before the 1836 Select Committee in *PP* 1836, XV, p. 347.
88. Holt, *The Problem of Freedom*, p. 72.
89. Ibid., pp. 72–3.
90. Ibid., p. 194.
91. Sturge and Harvey, *The West Indies*, p. 349. Apprentices could buy their own or somebody else's discharge from apprenticeship against the wishes of the planter. The procedure to determine the purchase sum was so complicated that few apprentices were able to buy their own or another apprentice's discharge. The procedure will be discussed in more detail in chap. 4.
92. *PP* 1837, LIII, p. 322; and *PP* 1837-38, XLIX, p. 299. Domestic apprentices were to be freed in 1838 because they worked more hours per week than field labourers.
93. Davidoff and Hall, *Family Fortunes*, p. 171.
94. Sturge and Harvey, *The West Indies*, p. 349.
95. Thome and Kimball, *Emancipation in the West Indies*, p. 105; W. Lloyd, *Letters from the West Indies, during a Visit in the Autumn of 1836 and the Spring of 1837*, London: Darton and Harvey, 1839, p. 227; and *PP* 1836, XV, p. 376.
96. *PP* 1836, XV, pp. 402, 407, and 413.
97. Ibid., pp. 402 and 413.
98. J. Lane, *Apprenticeship in England, 1600-1914*, London: University College of London Press, 1996, pp. 81-5.
99. S. G. and E.O.A. Checkland (eds.), *The Poor Law Report of 1834*, Harmondsworth: Penguin, 1974, p. 467.
100. *PP* 1837–38, XLIX, p. 328. This circular letter aimed in particular to prevent S.M.s from sending pregnant women to the workhouse.
101. D. Eudell, *The Political Languages of Emancipation in the British Caribbean and the U.S. South*, Chapel Hill: The University of North Carolina Press, 2002, pp. 10–11.
102. *PP* 1837, LIII, p. 252. Emphasis mine.
103. Ibid. For another harrowing account, see *PP* 1837, LIII, p. 219.
104. *PP* 1837, LIII., p. 272. See also pp. 267, 326, and 335.
105. Ibid., p. 326.
106. Ibid., p. 92; and *PP* 1836, XV, p. 327. See also, *PP* 1836, XV, p. 325; *PP* 1836, XLVIII, pp. 362 and 369; and *PP* 1837, LIII, pp. 225, 246, and 268.
107. *PP* 1836, XLVIII, p. 115; and Burn, *Emancipation and Apprenticeship*, p. 176.
108. According to Burn, the various 'extra-labour-for-extra-indulgences schemes' that were in place on estates should therefore be seen as nothing but acts of 'narrow spitefulness on the part of the planters'. See, his *Emancipation and Apprenticeship*, p. 176.
109. *PP* 1836, XV, p. 327; and *PP* 1837, LIII, p. 226.
110. As cited in Eudell, *The Political Languages*, pp. 111–2.
111. Ibid., p. 111.
112. Collins, *Practical Rules*, p. 171.

113. For the gradual development of the idea that motherhood was incompatible with paid work outside the home, see K. Honeyman, *Women, Gender and Industrialisation in England, 1700–1870*, Houndsmill: Macmillan, 2000. For a good overview of recent feminist debates about motherhood, see S. Lawler, 'Motherhood and identity', in T. Cosslett, A. Easton, P. Summerfield (eds.), *Women, Power and Resistance: an introduction to women's studies*, Buckingham: Open University Press, 1996, pp. 154–64.
114. Most men saved the money they earned in order to buy land during or after apprenticeship. Their preference to spend their wages in this way will be discussed in more detail in chap. 4.
115. Even if they depicted slave and apprenticed women as bad or inapt mothers, the participants in the debate about childrearing practices on the estates saw them as having an innate capacity for nurturance, as opposed to men's inability to nurture.

CHAPTER 3

1. For a good overview of the shift in the norm of sexuality in the late eighteenth and early nineteenth centuries, see T. Laqueur, *Making Sex: body and gender from the Greeks to Freud*, Cambridge, Mass.: Harvard University Press, 1990; and J. Weeks, *Sex, Politics and Society: the regulation of sexuality since 1800* [1981], London: Longman, 1993.
2. This norm of male sexuality is based on L. Nead, *Myths of Sexuality: representations of women in Victorian Britain*, Oxford: Blackwell, 1988, p. 51; T. Hitchcock, 'Redefining sex in eighteenth-century England', *History Workshop Journal* 41, 1996, p. 81; T. Hitchcock, *English Sexualities, 1700–1800*, Basingstoke: Macmillan, 1997, pp. 100 and 108; and J. Tosh, *A Man's Place: masculinity and the middle-class home in Victorian England*, New Haven: Yale University Press, 1999, pp. 45–6.
3. H. Haste, *The Sexual Metaphor*, New York: Harvest Wheatsheaf, 1993, p. 167.
4. This norm of female sexuality is based on L. Davidoff and C. Hall, *Family Fortunes: men and women of the English middle class 1780–1850* [1987], London: Routledge, 1992, pp. 401–3; Nead, *Myths of Sexuality*, pp. 33–4; and G. J. Barker-Benfield, *The Culture of Sensibility: sex and society in eighteenth-century Britain*, Chicago: University of Chicago Press, 1992, pp. 325–47 and 366–73.
5. R. Perry, 'Colonizing the breast: sexuality and maternity in eighteenth-century England', *Journal of the History of Sexuality* 2, no. 2, 1991, pp. 210–3. Katherine Binhammer has argued that this redefinition of female sexuality was facilitated by the French Revolution and the wars with France. See her 'The sex panic of the 1790s', *Journal of the History of Sexuality* 6, no. 3, 1996, pp. 409–34. At times of war and other periods of great social and political unrest, ideas about women's sexual morality are mobilized to construct a strong group or national identity. At such times, women's sexuality tends to be represented as unruly and threatening social stability. For more information on the link between increased debates about sexual morality and threats to group or national identity, see S. O. Rose, 'Cultural analysis and moral discourses: episodes, continuities, and transformations', in V. E. Bonnell and L. Hunt (eds.), *Beyond the Cultural Turn: new directions in the study of culture and society*, Berkeley: University of California Press, 1999, pp. 217–38.

6. Two reasons seem to explain why slave women's relations with slave men received less attention than their relations with white men. First, both sides in the debate saw interslave sexual relations as less of a danger to their projects than interracial sexual encounters. And second, there was less information available for the authors about interslave sexual relations because these relations were carried out in the slave quarters, which were largely beyond the scope of white residents and visitors.
7. The few remarks about the sexual behaviour of female apprentices will be discussed in chaps 4 and 6.
8. See, for instance, *Considerations on the Expediency of an Improved Mode of Treatment of Slaves in the West Indian Colonies, Relatively to an Increase of Population*, London: published by the author, 1820, p. 11; W. Wilberforce, *An Appeal to the Religion, Justice and Humanity of the Inhabitants of the British Empire on Behalf of Its Negro Slaves in the West Indies* [1823], in P. Kitson (ed.), *Slavery, Abolition and Emancipation: writings in the British romantic period*, vol. 2, London: Pickering and Cato, 1999, p. 22; T. Cooper, *Facts Illustrative of the Condition of the Negro Slaves in Jamaica with Notes and an Appendix*, London: Hatchard, 1824, p. 14; *An Address on the State of Slavery in the West India Islands from the Committee of the Leicester Auxiliary Anti-Slavery Society*, London: Ellerton and Henderson, 1824, p. 11; R. Bickell, *The West Indies as They Are; or, a real picture of slavery, but more particular as it exists in the island of Jamaica in three parts with notes*, London: Hatchard and son, 1825, p. 17; and PP 1831–32, XX, pp. 71 and 112.
9. As articulated, amongst others, in J. Foot, *A Defence of the Planters in the West Indies Compromised in Four Arguments*, London: J. Debrett, 1792, p. 97; and M. G. Lewis, *Journal of a West India Proprietor: kept during a residence in the island of Jamaica* [1834], London: John Murray, 1838, p. 145. Between 1807 and 1834, almost 50 per cent of slave couples resided on different estates. This high ratio was not only the result of slave choice but also of the planters' practice to sell away husbands or wives and the sexual imbalance of slave imports (two thirds male and one third female). See B. W. Higman, *Slave Populations of the British Caribbean, 1807–1834*, Baltimore: Johns Hopkins University Press, 1984, pp. 364–73.
10. One of the first studies on the sexual coercion of Caribbean slave women was R. E. Reddock, 'Women and slavery in the Caribbean: a feminist perspective', *Latin American Perspectives* 12, 1985, pp. 63–80. The three monographs on Caribbean slave women that were published in the late 1980s and early 1990s have also paid considerable attention to the issue: H. McD. Beckles, *Natural Rebels: a social history of enslaved black women in Barbados*, London: Zen Books, 1989; B. Bush, *Slave Women in Caribbean Society, 1650–1838*, London: James Currey, 1990; and M. Morrissey, *Slave Women in the New World: gender stratification in the Caribbean*, Lawrence: University Press of Kansas, 1990. These studies largely followed the example of pioneering studies on American slave women's sexuality, such as A. Davis, *Women, Race and Class*, New York: Random House, 1981; and bell hooks, *Ain't I a Woman: black women and feminism*, Boston: South End Press, 1981.
11. M. Foucault, *The History of Sexuality*, vol. 1, London: Penguin, 1990, p. 106. It was harder for Caribbean than for American scholars to debunk the myth that slave women engaged in promiscuous and casual relations with both white and slave men because they lacked primary sources in which (ex) slave women described their sexual abuse. They did succeed, however, in providing an alternative account of slave women's sexuality by comparing

proslavery remarks about slave women's sexuality with abolitionist accounts and also with anthropological data.
12. See, for instance, B. Bush, '"Sable Venus", "she-devil" or "drudge"?: British slavery and the "fabulous fiction" of black women's identities, c. 1650–1838', *Women's History Review* 9, 2000, pp. 761–89; and K. Wilson, 'Empire, gender, and modernity in the eighteenth century', in P. Levine (ed.), *Gender and Empire*, Oxford: Oxford University Press, 2004, pp. 31–2. Both articles base their interpretations largely on the diary of the Jamaican overseer and planter Thomas Thistlewood. Trevor Burnard has written extensively on Thistlewood's long-term relationship with the slave woman Phibbah and also about his casual relationships with other slave women. Burnard's work also confirms the idea that many slave women used sex with white men to their own advantage. See, for example, his 'The sexual life of an eighteenth-century Jamaican slave overseer', in M. D. Smith (ed.), *Sex and Sexuality in Early America*, New York: New York University Press, 1998, pp. 163–89; 'Theatre of terror: domestic violence in Thomas Thistlewood's Jamaica', in C. Daniels and M. V. Kennedy (eds.), *Over the Threshold: intimate violence in early America*, London: Routledge, 1999, pp. 237–53; and *Mastery, Tyranny, and Desire: Thomas Thistlewood and his slaves in the Anglo-Jamaican world*, Chapel Hill: The University of North Carolina Press, 2004.
13. For studies on the image of the scheming Jezebel in proslavery writings, see H. McD. Beckles, 'Female enslavement and gender ideologies in the Caribbean', in P. E. Lovejoy (ed.), *Identity in the Shadow of Slavery*, London: Continuum, 2000, pp. 163–82; and V. A. Shepherd, 'Gender and representation in European accounts of pre-emancipation Jamaica', in V. A. Shepherd and H. McD. Beckles (eds.), *Caribbean Slavery in the Atlantic World: a student reader*, London: James Curry, 2000, pp. 702–12.
14. B. Edwards, *The History Civil and Commercial of the British Colonies in the West Indies vol. 1*, London: John Stockdale, 1793, p. 80.
15. *Marly; or, a planter's life in Jamaica*, Glasgow: Richard Griffin and co., 1828, p. 133.
16. Edwards, *The History Civil and Commercial*, p. 81. See also J. Foot, *Observations Principally upon the Speech of Mr Wilberforce on his Motion in the House of Commons the 30th of May 1804*, London: T. Becket, 1805, p. 96; and [J. Stewart], *An Account of Jamaica, and Its Inhabitants by a Gentleman Long Resident in the West Indies*, London: Longman, Hurst, Rees and Orme, 1808, p. 276.
17. [A. Davis], *The West Indies*, London: James Cochrane, 1832, p. 26.
18. J. B. Moreton, *West Indian Customs and Manners*, London: J. Parsons, 1793, p. 160. For similar remarks, see H. McNeill, *Observations on the Treatment of Negroes in the Island of Jamaica*, London: G. J. and J. Robinson, 1788, p. 41; and F. Cundall (ed.), *Lady Nugent's Journal: Jamaica one hundred years ago reprinted from a journal kept by Maria, Lady Nugent, from 1801 to 1815*, London: Adam and Charles Black, 1907, p. 118.
19. The term 'coloured' refers in this chapter not only to offspring of black-white unions but to all mixed offspring.
20. Lewis, *Journal of a West India Proprietor*, p. 78. For similar remarks, see McNeill, *Observations*, p. 41; Moreton, *West India Customs*, p. 77; and Cundall (ed.), *Lady Nugent's Journal*, p. 40.
21. Noticeably absent amongst the objections is the argument that long-term interracial relationships culturally tainted or 'blackened' white men. As R. Godbeer has shown in his *Sexual Revolution in Early America*, Baltimore: Johns Hopkins University Press, 2002, this was commonly articulated in the

North American colonies. Because white Jamaicans made up only 10 per cent of the total population and was predominantly male, white Jamaican men relied heavily upon black women for their survival.
22. See, for instance, [Stewart], *An Account*, p. 200.
23. G. Heuman, 'The social structure of the slave societies in the Caribbean', in F. W. Knight (ed.), *General History of the Caribbean*, vol. 3, Basingstoke: Macmillan, 1997, pp. 138–68.
24. McNeil, *Observations*, p. 42; [Stewart], *An Account*, p. 200; and Cundall (ed.), *Lady Nugent's Journal*, p. 118.
25. [Stewart], *An Account*, p. 200; and Moreton, *West India Customs*, p. 77.
26. In 1761, the local legislature limited the amount of property and wealth that white Jamaicans could leave to free blacks and coloureds. The wills of slaveholders show that this failed to prevent slaveholders from bequeathing wealth to their free coloured offspring and other free(d)men and that as a result metropolitan relatives of the slaveholders received less than expected. See G. Heuman, *Between Black and White: race, politics, and the free coloreds in Jamaica 1792–1865*, Oxford: Clio Press, 1981, pp. 6 and 28; Burnard, *Mastery, Tyranny, and Desire*, chap. 7; and C. Petley, 'Boundaries of rule, ties of dependency: Jamaican planters, local society and the metropole, 1800–1834', unpublished thesis, University of Warwick, 2003, chap. 7.
27. J. M. Adair, *Unanswerable Arguments against the Abolition of the Slave Trade with a Defence of the Proprietors of the British Sugar Colonies*, London: privately published, 1790, p. 121. See also, Foot, *A Defence*, p. 97; Collins, *Practical Rules for the Management and Medical Treatment of Negro Slaves in the Sugar Colonies by a Professional Planter*, London: J. Barfield, 1803, pp. 155–6; and [Dr Grainger], *An Essay on the More Common West India Diseases*, London: T. Becker, 1814, p. 14.
28. A. Barclay, *A Practical View of the Present State of Slavery in the West Indies*, London: Smith, Elder and co., 1827, p. 100. See also J. McQueen, *The West India Colonies: the calumnies and misrepresentations circulated against them by the Edinburgh Review, Mr Clarkson, Mr Cropper, etc.*, London: Baldwin, Cradock and Joy, 1824, pp. 230–3; and *Evidence upon Oath Touching the Condition and Treatment of the Negro Population of the British West India Colonies, part 1*, London: Mrs Ridgways, 1832, p. 37.
29. *Sketches and Recollections of the West Indies by a Resident*, London: Smith and Elder, 1827, p. 231.
30. [Davis], *The West Indies*, p. 70.
31. Rev. G. W. Bridges, *The Annals of Jamaica*, London: John Murray, 1826, p. 371.
32. C. R. Williams, *Tour Through the Island of Jamaica from the Western to the Eastern End in 1823*, London: Edward Chance and co., 1827, pp. 56 and 310.
33. Higman, *Slave Populations*, pp. 77, 149, and 380–4.
34. Ibid., p. 77.
35. Heuman, *Between Black and White*, chaps 2–3; and R. Blackburn, *Overthrow of Colonial Slavery, 1776–1848*, London: Verso, 1988, pp. 424–6.
36. This was enacted in 1733. See, Higman, *Slave Populations*, p. 147.
37. E. Brathwaite, *The Development of Creole Society in Jamaica 1770–1820*, Oxford: Clarendon Press, 1971, p. 167.
38. *Westminster Review*, April 1827, p. 445.
39. *Hamel, the Obeah Man* vol. 1, London: Hunt and Clarke, 1827, p. 77.
40. Ibid., p. 193. Emphasis mine.
41. *Hamel*, pp. 195–6.

42. J. Fahnestock, 'The heroine of irregular features: physiognomy and conventions of heroine description', *Victorian Studies* 24, no. 3, 1998, pp. 325–50.
43. See, for instance, Lewis, *Journal of a West India Proprietor*, p. 69; Williams, *Tour through the Island*, p. 324; and *Marly*, p. 180.
44. P. Mohammed, '"But most of all mi love me browning": the emergence in eighteenth and nineteenth century Jamaica of the mulatto woman as desired', *Feminist Review* 65, 2000, p. 43.
45. *Hamel*, pp. 83–8. Emphasis mine.
46. Moreton, *West India Customs*, p. 154. The song was quoted in various proslavery writings throughout the period 1780–1834. Michael Scott mentioned it in his book *Tom Cringle's Log*, London: J. M. Dent and Sons, 1836. His remark that 'I scarcely forgive myself for introducing it '[the song] here to polite society', suggests that the song served to convince readers of black slave women's deviation from the metropolitan ideal of female sexuality. On the various versions of the song and its popularity, see J. D'Costa and B. Lalla (eds.), *Voices in Exile: Jamaican texts of the eighteenth and nineteenth century*, Tuscaloosa: University of Alabama Press, 1989, p. 14.
47. Higman, *Slave Populations*, pp. 194–7.
48. The proslavery writers' hierarchy of the six races was one of several attempts at the time to theorize the differences between human beings based on visible and invisible signs. For more information on these attempts, see M. Banton, *The Idea of Race*, London: Tavistock Publishers, 1977, p. 5. As Roxann Wheeler has shown in her book *The Complexion of Race: categories of difference in eighteenth-century British culture*, Philadelphia: University of Philadelphia Press, 2000, many metropolitan men and women continued to rank human beings on the basis of older criteria, such as Christianity, civility and rank. By the mid-nineteenth century, however, these older theories were no longer in use and theories that explained human variety in terms of race drew increasingly upon science to explain and justify race hierarchies. It could be argued that the growth of the free coloured population in the 1820s helped to speed up the process in white Jamaican society of regarding skin colour as the most important marker of racial identity.
49. This is a rather problematic attempt to demonstrate the incidence of interracial sex. First, because it excludes the relations between white men and free(d) women. And second, because coloured slaves were not only the offspring of whites and members of the other five races but also the offspring of relations between blacks and quadroons, black and sambos, blacks and mulattos and blacks and mustees. Higman therefore suggests that whites fathered no more than half of all coloured slaves born between 1829 and 1834, see his *Slave Population and Economy in Jamaica 1807–1834*, Cambridge: Cambridge University Press, 1976, p. 139.
50. Ibid., pp. 139–53; and Higman, *Slave Populations*, pp. 147–8. It is difficult to establish a coloured slave/white adult male ratio because there are no accurate sources on the number of whites or the size of the coloured slave population at the time.
51. This calculation is based on the assumption of a 50/50 sex ratio and a 30/70 child/adult ratio in the white population. Figures of the white and slave population are for 1820 and are derived from: R. W. Fogel and S. L. Engerman, *Time on the Cross: the economics of American Negro slavery*, Boston: Little Brown, 1974, p. 132; W. Trotter, *The African American Experience, vol. 1*, Boston: Houghton Mifflin, 2001, appendix 13. The fertile female slave/white adult male ratio also supports the idea of a higher incidence of interracial sex in Jamaica than on the North American mainland. In Jamaica, there were

3.6 fertile slave women per one white adult male, whereas in North America there were only 0.19.
52. As Trevor Burnard has shown in his work on the Jamaican slaveholder Thomas Thistlewood, interracial sexual relations were more often forced than consensual. In order not to regard their sexual violation of slave women as a sin or as evidence of less than civilized instincts, white men must have told themselves that slave women were not human beings but lascivious savages indestructible under their assaults. In other words, the scheming Jezebel served as much to justify their interracial sexual encounters to themselves as to the outside world.
53. J. Stewart, *A View of the Past and Present State of the Island of Jamaica*, Edinburgh: Oliver and Boyd, 1823, p. 173.
54. *PP* 1831–32, XX, p. 393.
55. See, for example, Adair, *Unanswerable Arguments*, p. 161. Slaves were also married by nonconformist ministers. The differences between formal and nonconformist slave marriage and the legal standing of formal slave marriage will be discussed in detail in the next chapter.
56. J. R. Ward, 'The profitability of sugar planting in the British West Indies, 1650–1834', *Economic History Review* 31, no. 2, 1978, pp. 197–213.
57. E. Long, *History of Jamaica, or General Survey of the Antient and Modern State of that Island: with reflections on its situations, settlements, inhabitants, climate, products, commerce, laws, and government* [1774], London: Frank Cass, 1970, p. 330.
58. Adair, *Unanswerable Arguments*, p. 161.
59. Moreton, *West India Customs*, p. 155.
60. Most estates employed at any time between five and ten officers. Worthy Park Estate employed a total of 85 officers between 1783 and 1796. This clearly illustrates the high turnover-rate of white employees on Jamaican plantations. See, Heuman, 'Social structure', p. 154.
61. B. Bush, 'Hard labor: women, childbirth and resistance in British Caribbean slave societies', *History Workshop Journal* 36, 1993, p. 99. The first North American anti-miscegenation statute was passed in Virginia in 1661 and made 'fornication with a negro man or woman' a crime punishable by a fine. For more information on early North American anti-miscegenation legislation, see P. Finkelman, 'Crimes of love, misdemeanors of passion: the regulation of race and sex in the Colonial South', in C. Clinton and M. Gillespie (eds.), *The Devil's Lane: sex and race in the early South*, New York: Oxford University Press, 1997, pp. 127–31.
62. *The Consolidated Slave Law, Passed the 22nd December, 1826, Commencing on the 1st May, 1827 with a Commentary, Shewing the Differences between the New Law and the Repealed Enactment*, N. P.: Courant Office, 1827 (hereafter, 1826 Slave Law), p. 10.
63. In the American South, for example, only slave girls were legally protected against rape, while the sexual abuse of an adult slave woman could only come to court if the claimant was the woman's owner and the defendant another white man. See C. Clinton, '"Southern dishonor": flesh, blood, race and bondage', in C. Bleser (ed.), *In Joy and Sorrow: women, family and marriage in the Victorian South, 1830–1900*, New York: Oxford University Press, 1991, p. 65.
64. The act was based on a rape act which had been in place in the mother country for several centuries. That only few cases of rape were brought before metropolitan courts of justice stemmed largely from the fact that the courts looked for evidence of the victim's character and past life. Most of the cases

that came to court were exceptional cases where there was no doubt about the victim's character, such as cases where a witness had interrupted a rape or where medical help was obtained. The number of rape and attempted rape cases brought to court increased slightly after 1750. This should not be seen as an indication that the number of rapes increased but as evidence that women were more willing to prosecute their sexual attackers and also as evidence of a heightened sensitivity and anxiety about sexual violence at the time. See, J. M. Beatie, *Crime and the Courts in England, 1660–1800*, Oxford: Clarendon Press, 1986, pp. 125–31.

65. Blackburn, *Overthrow of Colonial Slavery*, p. 422.
66. PP 1824, XXIV, pp. 427 and 452. The Assembly's opposition to the amelioration proposals was largely based on copies of a confidential dispatch of Lord Bathurst, which had circulated as a result of a leak in the Colonial Office and which contained the statement that Parliament would impose its will on the colonies if local legislatures did not voluntarily adopt the proposals. For more on the Assembly's response to the proposals, see L. J. Ragatz, *The Fall of the Planter Class in the British Caribbean, 1763–1833* [1927], New York: Octagon Books, 1963, p. 417.
67. The rape act was included in the 1826 Slave Law. The latter was disallowed, however, as it met neither the letter nor the spirit of the ameliorative proposals set out in Lord Bathurst's dispatch to colonial governors in July 1823. A rewritten version was disallowed in 1829 and it was not until 1831 before the Colonial Office finally approved a revised Slave Law. See, Ragatz, *The Fall of the Planter Class*, p. 419.
68. This estimate of the white sex ratio is based on parish records from the late eighteenth and early nineteenth centuries and was provided to the author by Christer Petley.
69. Finkelman, 'Crimes of love', pp. 129–38; and C. Degler, *Neither Black nor White: slavery and race relations in Brazil and the United States*, New York: Macmillan, 1971, pp. 238–9.
70. The decline increased rapidly in the 1820s when planters put increasing pressure on their slaves in order to combat declining profits. The annual rate of natural decrease rose from –0.25 in 1818 to –1 in 1830. See Blackburn, *Overthrow of Colonial Slavery*, p. 428.
71. *Address to the Public on the Present State of the Question Relative to Negro Slavery in the British Colonies*, York: W. Alexander and son, 1828, p. 13. For a very similar account, see *A Plan for the Abolition of Slavery Consistently with the Interests of All Parties Concerned*, London: George Sidford, 1828, p. 5.
72. Cooper, *Facts Illustrative*, pp. 9, 14, and 42. For other antislavery accounts of interslave relations, see Wilberforce, *An Appeal to the Religion*, p. 22; *An Address on the State*, p. 32; Bickell, *The West Indies*, p. 17; *The Negro's Memorial; or abolitionist's catechism by an abolitionist*, London: Hatchard, 1825, p. 60; and *A Plan for the Abolition*, p. 5. Several former missionaries addressed the promiscuity of interslave relations in memoirs published after emancipation in order to demonstrate the moral progress made by the ex-slave population. See, for example, J. M. Phillippo, *Jamaica: its past and present state*, London: John Snow, 1843, p. 218; and H. M. Waddell, *Twenty-Nine Years in the West Indies and Central Africa: a review of missionary work and adventure, 1829–1858* [1863], London: Frank Cass, 1970, p. 40.
73. This criticism will be discussed in detail in chap. 4.
74. G. H. Rose, *A Letter on the Means and Importance of Converting the Slaves in the West Indies to Christianity*, London: Murray, 1823, p. 32. See also J.

Ramsay, *Essay on the Treatment and Conversion of African Slaves in the British Sugar Colonies*, Dublin: T. Walker, C. Jenking, 1784, p. 243; Wilberforce, An Appeal to Religion, p. 22; and Cooper, *Facts Illustrative*, p. 13.
75. *The Negro's Memorial*, p. 60; *A Plan for the Abolition*, p. 5; and *PP* 1831–32, XX, p. 71.
76. *Considerations on the Expediency*, pp. 10–11. For another rare remark about slave women's natural chastity in the debate about interslave relations, see T. S. Winn, *Emancipation; or practical advice to British slaveholders with suggestions for the general improvement of West India affairs*, London: W. Phillips, 1824, p. 38.
77. The first argument was most clearly expressed by John Barry in his statement before the 1832 Select Committee in *PP* 1831–32, XX, p. 70. For an example of the second argument, see T. Clarkson, *Thoughts on the Necessity of Improving the Condition of the Slaves in the British Colonies; with a view to their ultimate emancipation,* London: Hatchard, 1824, pp. iv and 9.
78. Rev. B. Godwin, *Substance of a Course of Lectures on British Colonial Slavery Delivered at Bradford, York and Scarborough*, London: J. Hatchard and son, 1830, p. 139.
79. Ibid., p. 9; and R. Wedderburn, *The Horrors of Slavery; exemplified in the life and history of the Rev. Robert Wedderburn*, London: n. p., 1824, pp. 6–7; B. M'Mahon, *Jamaica Plantership*, London: Effingham Wilson, 1839, p. 292; *Slave Trade Committee Report*, vol. 82, p. 181; and *PP* 1831–32, XX, p. 305.
80. Ramsay, *Essay on the Treatment*, p. 204; and *The Negro's Memorial*, p. 52.
81. Nead, *Myths of Sexuality*, p. 94.
82. T. Henderson, *Disorderly Women in Eighteenth-Century London: prostitution and control in the metropolis 1730–1830*, London: Longman, 1999, chap. 7.
83. M. Chase, 'Wedderburn, Robert (1762-1835/6?)', in *Oxford Dictionary of National Biography,* Oxford: Oxford University Press. Available at http://www.oxforddnb.com/view/article/47210 (accessed 8 July 2005).
84. Wedderburn, *The Horrors of Slavery*, pp. 5 and 7.
85. *Slave Trade Committee Report*, vol. 82, p. 194.
86. As cited in *Negro Slavery; or, a view of some of the more prominent features of that state of society, as it exists in the United States of America and in the colonies of the West Indies, especially in Jamaica*, London: Hatchard and son, 1823, pp. 79–80.
87. M'Mahon, *Jamaica Plantership*, pp. 69–71.
88. [E. Rushton], *West Indian Eclogues*, London: J. Philips, 1787, p. 21; and E. Helme, *The Farmer of Inglewood Forest; or, an affecting portrait of virtue and vice*, London: George Virtue, 1824, p. 393. Contrary to proslavery fiction writers, antislavery fiction writers in the 1820s featured both light-skinned and dark-skinned slave women in their accounts of interracial sex. The dark-skinned Mimba in *The Koromantyn Slaves*, London: n. p., 1823, for example, is singled out by a neighbouring owner for dishonest purposes. By concentrating on both categories of slave women, antislavery writers argued that all slave women ran the risk of sexual abuse.
89. R. Bage, *Man As He Is* [1792], in S. Aravamudan (ed.), *Slavery, Abolition and Emancipation: writings in the British romantic period*, vol. 6, London: Pickering and Cato, 1999, pp. 137–42.
90. Higman, *Slave Populations*, p. 112.
91. Burnard, *Mastery, Tyranny and Desire*, pp. 45–46.

92. *Slave Trade Committee Report*, vol. 82, p. 194. See also, *The Negro's Memorial*, p. 52.
 93. On the sexual abuse of married slave women, see *Negro Slavery*, pp. 79–80; [Rev. Trew], *Nine Letters to his Grace the Duke of Wellington on Colonial Slavery*, London: William Stroker 1830, p. 39; and T. Jackson, *Britain's Burden; or the intolerable evils of colonial slavery exposed*, Cambridge: Metcalfe, 1832, p. 18. On the sexual abuse of young slave girls, see Ramsay, *Essay on the Treatment*, p. 204; Clarkson, *Thoughts on the Necessity*, p. iv; *The Negro's Friend; or the Sheffield anti-slavery album*, Sheffield: Blackwell, 1826, p. 37; and M'Mahon, *Jamaica Plantership*, pp. 51 and 69.
 94. M'Mahon, *Jamaican Plantership*, p. 135. For another striking account of incest, see Ramsay, *Essay on the Treatment*, p. 204.
 95. Cooper as cited in Rev. J. Riland (ed.), *Memoirs of a West India Planter; published from an original ms*, London: Hamilton, Adams and co., 1827, p. 203. See also, *An Address on the State*, p. 11.
 96. Riland (ed.), *Memoirs of a West India Planter*, p. 128.
 97. Wedderburn, *Horrors of Slavery*, pp. 6–7.
 98. C. Petley, '"Legitimacy" and social boundaries: free people of colour and the social order in Jamaican slave society', *Social History* 30, no. 4, 2005, pp. 488–94.
 99. Davidoff and Hall, *Family Fortunes*, p. 329.
100. P. Langford, *Englishness Identified: manners and characters 1650–1850*, Oxford: Oxford University Press, 2000, p. 111.
101. A notable exception to this rule is the Reverend Benjamin Godwin. See his *Substance of a Course*, p. 9.
102. Riland (ed.), *Memoirs of a West India Planter*, p. 128.
103. Ramsay, *Essay on the Treatment*, p. 204; *Negro Slavery*, p. 54; and *The Negro's Friend*, p. 37.
104. M'Mahon, *Jamaica Plantership*, p. 183.
105. Clarkson, *Thoughts on the Necessity*, p. iv.
106. See, for example, *Slave Trade Committee Report*, vol. 82, p. 98; and M'Mahon, *Jamaica Plantership*, p. 51.
107. See, for instance, the short story 'Zangara, or the Negro slave', in *The Negro's Friend*, p. 37; and Captain Marjoribanks, *Slavery; an essay in verse*, Edinburgh: J. Robertson, 1802, p. 24.
108. [Rushton], *West Indian Eclogues*, pp. 53–4; Bage, *Man as He Is*, p. 143; and Helme, *The Farmer of Inglewood Forest*, p. 475.
109. The abolitionists' attitude towards direct slave action is more complicated, however, than outlined here. Their pacifist principles led them to dissociate themselves from the three major revolts that plagued the region in the early nineteenth-century: Barbados 1816, Demerara 1823, and Jamaica 1831–32. They expressed some support for the rebellious slaves by emphasizing that their action stemmed from the planters' inhumane treatment and also by comparing the revolts to strikes in the mother country. For more information on the abolitionist reactions to the revolts, see G. Matthews, 'The other side of slave revolts', in S. Courtman (ed.), *Beyond the Blood, the Beach and the Banana: new perspectives in Caribbean studies*, Kingston: Ian Randle Publishers, 2004, pp. 49–70.
110. The following texts address consensual interracial sexual relations: Ramsay, *Essay on the Treatment*, p. 204; Wilberforce, *An Appeal to the Religion*, p. 25; *Negro Slavery*, p. 53; Wedderburn, *Horrors of Slavery*, pp. 8–9; Godwin, *Substance of a Course*, p. 68; and *PP* 1831-32, XX, pp. 70–4.
111. *PP* 1831-32, XX, p. 71.

112. Ibid., p. 101; Ramsay, *Essay on the Treatment*, p. 204; and Wilberforce, *An Appeal to the Religion*, pp. 23–4.
113. American abolitionists articulated more clearly than their English counterparts the common denominator of prostitution and slavery: the sale in bodies. For an examination of their attempts to compare and contrast prostitution and slavery, see A. Dru Stanley, *From Bondage to Contract: wage labor, marriage and the market in the age of slave emancipation*, Cambridge: Cambridge University Press, 1998, chap. 6.
114. It is possible that this concern about the blurring of the colour line was triggered by a fear that offspring of free coloured-white unions would migrate to Britain and there pose a threat to racial purity. Felicity Nussbaum's analysis of fiction and plays from the late eighteenth and early nineteenth centuries suggests that there was a heightened public concern about interracial intimacy in metropolitan society around the turn of the century. See her *The Limits of the Human: fictions of anomaly, race, and gender in the long eighteenth century*, Cambridge: Cambridge University Press, 2003, p. 249. On the abolitionists' contradictory relationship to power, see R. McGowen, 'Power and humanity, or Foucault among the historians', in C. Jones and R. Porter (eds.), *Reassessing Foucault: power, medicine and the body*, London: Routledge, 1994, pp. 102–10.
115. Wedderburn, *The Horrors of Slavery*, p. 9.
116. See, for example, *Slave Trade Committee Report*, vol. 82, p. 97; and Rose, *A Letter on the Means*, p. 32.
117. J. Anderson, *Observations on Slavery; particularly with a view to its effects on the British colonies in the West Indies*, Manchester: J. Harrop, 1789, p. 17.
118. E. Burke, *Sketch of the Negro Code* [1792], in P. Kitson (ed.), *Slavery, Abolition and Emancipation: writings in the British romantic period, vol. 2*, London: Pickering and Cato, 1999, p. 203. This proposal not only aimed to civilize the slaves but also to achieve natural increase.
119. Beatie, *Crime and the Courts*, p. 127. The death penalty in rape cases was repealed in 1841. The statement of former missionary Robert Young before the 1832 Select Committee supports this interpretation, see *PP* 1831–32, XX, p. 426.
120. Bickell, *The West Indies*, p. 55; Wilberforce, *An Appeal to the Religion*, p. 23; and Cooper as cited in Riland (ed.), *Memoirs of a West India Planter*, p. 203. In the early nineteenth century, planters provided their slaves with clothes, needles, threads and scissors to make their own clothing in addition to ready-made jackets, hats, and caps. The amount of cloth and clothing handed out to children under 14 was very small, however, so that most children wore, as Bickell suggested, little more than a shift. See Higman, *Slave Populations*, pp. 223–4.
121. *Remarks upon the Injustice and Immorality of Slavery in Eight Letters by the Rev. George Whitfield*, London: John Stephens, 1830, pp. 4–5.
122. Nead, *Myths of Sexuality*, p. 33. Interestingly, the 1824 *Plan for Effecting Emancipation by the Redemption of Female Slaves* discussed in the previous chapter did not suggest that emancipating slave women under 45 was a means to ensure the sexual purity of African Jamaican women on the plantations.
123. *1826 Slave Law*, p. 4.
124. W. L. Burn, *Emancipation and Apprenticeship in the British West Indies*, London: Jonathan Cape, 1937, p. 95; Blackburn, *Overthrow of Colonial Slavery*, pp. 432–3; and M. Turner, *Slaves and Missionaries: the disintegration of Jamaican slave society 1787–1834*, Urbana: University of Illinois

Press, 1982, p. 16. Between 1802 and 1828, planters tried to limit the exposure of slaves to religious instruction by enacting that missionaries had to apply for a licence to preach.
125. S. Gilman, *Difference and Pathology: stereotypes of sexuality, race and madness*, London: Cornell University Press, 1985.
126. Pamela Scully has shown that European colonisers in South Africa often drew upon the representation of the scheming Jezebel to define African women as inferior. See her 'Rape, race and colonial culture', *American Historical Review* 100, no. 2, 1995, pp. 335–59. On the long-lasting effects of this process, see E. Brooks-Higginbotham, 'African-American women's history and the metalanguage of race', *Signs* 17, no. 2, 1992, pp. 251–74.
127. See, for instance, Davis, *Women, Race and Class*; and B. Bush, 'History, memory, myth?: reconstructing the history (or histories) of black women in the African diaspora', in S. Newell (ed.), *Images of African and Caribbean Women: migration, displacement, diaspora*, Stirling: Centre of Commonwealth Studies, 1996, pp. 3–28.
128. See, for example, D. Spurr, *The Rhetoric of Empire: colonial discourse in journalism, travel writing, and imperial administration*, Durham, N.C.: Duke University Press, 1996, chap. 5.
129. O. Patterson, *The Sociology of Slavery: an analysis of the origins, development and structure of negro slave society in Jamaica*, London: MacGibbon and Kee, 1967, p. 167.
130. hooks, *Ain't I a Woman*, pp. 20–2.
131. H. Beckles, 'Black masculinity in Caribbean slavery', in R. E. Reddock (ed.), *Interrogating Caribbean Masculinities: theoretical and empirical analyses*, Kingston: University of the West Indies Press, 2004, pp. 225–43.
132. On the rise of skin colour as a marker of human difference in the eighteenth century, see Wheeler, *The Complexion of Race*; Nussbaum, *The Limits of the Human*; and K. Wilson, *The Island Race: Englishness, empire and gender in the eighteenth century*, London: Routledge, 2002.
133. Also in a more indirect way did antislavery writings reinforce the metropolitan discourse on racial hierarchy. The challenge that they posed to this discourse instilled in many people a fear that if abolitionists were to succeed in ending the system of slavery, there would be a larger influx of people of African descendent into the mother country, which in turn would threaten the racial purity of the group that formed the apex of the social hierarchy in the country: whites. This fear led some to publish accounts that provided evidence of a 'natural' hierarchy of races. See, Nussbaum, *Limits of the Human*, pp. 18–9.
134. The most common 'sexual sins' of slave women dealt with by missionaries was sex outside of marriage, including premarital sex and adultery with white and black men. 'Diaries Moravian missionaries', *Jamaica Archives*, Moravian Archives H/6; Q/8; and Q/9.

CHAPTER 4

1. S. Parker, *Informal Marriage: cohabitation and the Law, 1750–1989*, Houndsmills: Macmillan, 1990, chap. 3; and D. Lemmings, 'Marriage and the law in the eighteenth century: Hardwick's Marriage Act of 1753', *The Historical Journal* 39, no. 2, 1996, pp. 344–6. The Act aimed primarily to counteract bigamy and clandestine marriages of children of good families with social and economic inferiors. It did not apply to marriages of the Royal

Family, Quakers and Jews, nor to marriages performed outside of England and Wales.
2. This ideal is based on: L. Davidoff and C. Hall, *Family Fortunes: men and women of the English middle class 1780–1850* [1987], London: Routledge, 1992, chap. 7; A. Clarke, *The Struggle for the Breeches: gender and the making of the British working class*, Berkeley: University of California Press, 1995, chap. 5; and R. B. Shoemaker, *Gender in English Society 1650–1850: the emergence of separate spheres?*, London: Longman, 1998, chap. 4.
3. Several scholars, most notably Lawrence Stone in his *The Family, Sex and Marriage in England 1500–1800* (1977) have argued that in the course of the eighteenth century relations between spouses became more equal because spouses showed more affection towards one another. I would argue that the increased show of affection between spouses should not be confused with equality. In fact, after the turn of the century the emphasis on affection was increasingly accompanied by an emphasis on the husband's role as the head of the household and the wife's duty to unconditionally support her husband.
4. J. R. Gillis, *For Better, For Worse: British marriages, 1600-to the present*, Oxford: Oxford University Press, 1985, chap. 4; and J. Weeks, *Sex, Politics and Society: the regulation of sexuality since 1800* [1981], London: Longman, 1993, chap. 1. On the lower classes' gradual acceptance of the middle-class marriage ideal, see Clark, *The Struggle for the Breeches,* chaps 11–14.
5. The following is a rather brief sketch of the relational lives of the slaves, as Caribbean historians have not yet explored in great detail the nature of slave marriage. This stems not only from the fact that they lack sources that provide an insight into the slaves' intimate world but also because they have been more interested in dispelling the myth instigated by contemporary observers that the slave family was overwhelmingly matrifocal and instable than in the quality of the slaves' intimate relationships. For some early studies on the Caribbean slave family and household, see B. W. Higman, 'African and creole slave family patterns in Trinidad', *Journal of Family History* 3, no. 2, 1978, pp. 163–80; M. Craton, 'Changing patterns of slave families in the British West Indies', *Journal of Interdisciplinary History* 10, no. 1, 1979, pp. 1–35; and O. Patterson, 'Persistence, continuity and change in the Jamaican working-class family', *Journal of Family History* 7, no. 2, 1982, pp. 135–61. Historians working on American slavery have in recent years begun to focus on the quality of slave relationships, using predominantly accounts by slaves and ex-slaves. For a recent study, see E. West, *Chains of Love*, Urbana: University of Illinois Press, 2004. Although scholars working on Caribbean slavery lack (ex) slave narratives, there are various sources that they can use to construct a more detailed picture of the slaves' relational lives, such as missionary reports, punishment records, and statements made by apprentices before S.M.s.
6. 'Return of numbers of marriages legally solemnized between slaves', in *PP* 1823, XCIII, pp. 320–1.
7. The Moravian missionaries performed, for instance, 189 marriages between 1827 and 1834. See, B. W. Higman, *Slave Populations of the British Caribbean, 1807-1834*, Baltimore: Johns Hopkins University Press, 1984, p. 116.
8. For a description of this type of slave marriage, see, for instance, J. B. Moreton, *West India Customs and Manners*, London: J. Parsons, 1793, p. 159.
9. Barbara Bush has argued that it was especially slave women who preferred informal marriage because it placed less emphasis than an Anglican or a nonconformist marriage on male domination and female submission. See

her *Slave Women in Caribbean Society, 1650–1838*, London: James Currey, 1990, pp. 101–2.
10. Gillis, *For Better, For Worse*, p. 110.
11. [Rev. Trew], *Nine Letters to his Grace the Duke of Wellington on Colonial Slavery by Ignotus*, London: William Stroker, 1830, p. 38.
12. Craton, 'Changing Patterns', p. 31.
13. H. McD. Beckles, *Natural Rebels: a social history of enslaved black women in Barbados*, London: Zen Books, 1989, p. 131; and M. Morrissey, Slave *Women in the New World: gender stratification in the Caribbean*, Lawrence: University Press of Kansas, 1989, p. 93. There is some evidence to support this argument. Planter Robert Scott, for example, told the 1832 Select Committee that he never separated formally married slaves upon sale. See *PP* 1831–32, XX, p. 341. As chapter 5 will illustrate, there is more evidence to suggest that the majority of the planters did not treat slaves differently on the basis of their marital status.
14. B. W. Higman, *Slave Population and Economy in Jamaica 1807–1834*, Cambridge: Cambridge University Press, 1976, pp. 164–5.
15. Ibid., p. 71; and Higman, *Slave Populations*, p. 116. That planters purchased more male than female slaves stemmed largely from the make-up of the slave ships: three males to two females. The sex ratios of the plantations gradually worked themselves out after the abolition of the slave trade. By 1832, there were 94 slave men per 100 slave women.
16. Until the mid-1810s, these two bans significantly reduced the pool of potential mates because they not only applied to real siblings and cousins but also to shipmates who were regarded as brothers and sisters (and their children as cousins). See Higman, *Slave Population*, p. 73; and P. D. Curtin, *Two Jamaicas: the role of ideas in a tropical colony, 1830–65*, Cambridge, Mass.: Harvard University Press, 1955, p. 26.
17. *The Consolidated Slave Law, Passed the 22nd December, 1826, Commencing on the 1st May, 1827 with a Commentary, Shewing the Differences between the New Law and the Repealed Enactment*, N.P.: Courant Office, 1827 (hereafter, 1826 Slave Law), pp. 13–4; J. Foot, *A Defence of the Planters in the West Indies Compromised in Four Arguments*, London: J. Debrett, 1792, pp. 96–7; and A. Thompson, *Substance of the Speech Delivered at the Meeting of the Edinburgh Society for the Abolition of Slavery on October 19, 1830*, Edinburgh: Whyte and co., 1830, p. 7.
18. *PP* 1831–32, XX, p. 18. A marriage of two free(d)men, on the other hand, had the same legal status as that of white islanders.
19. M. Turner, *Slaves and Missionaries: the disintegration of Jamaican slave society, 1787–1834*, Urbana: University of Illinois Press, 1982, p. 21.
20. This summary is based on: Turner, *Slaves and Missionaries*, p. 83; and *Jamaica Archives* (hereafter, *JA*), Moravian Archives, H/6, H/7, J/19, Q/7, Q/8, Q/9, and Q/10.
21. Bush, *Slave Women in Caribbean Society*, chap. 6.
22. This gendered division of labour comes most clearly to the fore in the court case relating to the death of a slave child by drowning. See *Public Record Office* (hereafter, *PRO*), Colonial Office Records (hereafter, CO), 137/171.
23. Parker, *Informal Marriage*, pp. 48–70.
24. *1826 Slave Law*, p. 2.
25. *PP* 1824, XXIV, p. 439.
26. *PP* 1826, XXIX, p. 7; and *PP* 1826–27, XXV, pp. 61–4 and 179. This also lends support to C.L.R. James' idea that plantation slavery shaped and

articulated the modernity of the Caribbean because such changes in marriage law were not adopted in the mother country until the late 1830s.
27. J. Ramsay, *Essay on the Treatment and Conversion of African Slaves in the British Sugar Colonies*, Dublin: T. Walker and C. Jenking, 1784, p. 19; and W. Wilberforce, *An Appeal to the Religion, Justice and Humanity of the Inhabitants of the British Empire on Behalf of Its Negro Slaves in the West Indies* [1823], in P. Kitson (ed.), *Slavery, Abolition and Emancipation: writings in the British romantic period, vol. 2*, London: Pickering and Cato, 1999, p. 19.
28. Ramsay, *Essay on the Treatment*, p. 243.
29. E. Burke, *Sketch of the Negro Code* [1792], in P. Kitson (ed.), *Slavery, Abolition and Emancipation: writings in the British romantic period, vol. 2*, London: Pickering and Cato, 1999, pp. 202–7. A year before the publication of this pamphlet, Burke had supported Wilberforce's motion for the abolition of the slave trade. The pamphlet clearly reflects that events in France in the second half of 1792 led Burke to drastically change his views on reforms, including the abolition of the slave trade. For more information on Burke's ideas about the slave trade, see R. Blackburn, *The Overthrow of Colonial Slavery, 1776–1848*, London: Verso, 1988, pp. 147–50.
30. On the home as the incubator of good moral behaviour, see C. Hall, *White, Male and Middle Class: explorations in feminism and history*, Cambridge: Polity Press, 1992, chap. 3.
31. Early antislavery writers made little or no distinction between formal and nonconformist slave marriage. As we shall see, later antislavery writers wanted slaves to opt for a formal slave marriage and were keen to see this type of slave marriage to become fully legal.
32. Captain Marjoribanks, *Slavery: an essay in verse*, Edinburgh: J. Robertson, 1802, p. 21. Emphasis mine.
33. Ramsay, *Essay on the Treatment*, p. 243; and Burke, *Sketch of the Negro Code*, p. 203.
34. *The Koromantyn Slaves*, London: n. p., 1823, p. 11. Emphasis mine.
35. Hall, *White, Male and Middle class*, p. 236. On the dual attitude of the missionaries, see also J. H. Proctor, 'Scottish missionaries and Jamaican slaveholders', *Slavery and Abolition* 25, no. 1, 2004, pp. 51–70.
36. *JA*, Moravian Archives, H/6.
37. *PP* 1831–32, XX, pp. 112 and 157. Duncan was not the only nonconformist missionary who advised slave couples to marry in an Anglican church. These missionaries merely followed the practice of nonconformist ministers in the metropolitan society, see Gillis, *For Better, For Worse*, p. 205.
38. [Rev. Trew], *Nine Letters*, p. 40.
39. See, for instance, *Address to the Public on the Present State of the Question Relative to Negro Slavery in the British Colonies*, York: W. Alexander and son, 1828, p. 9; and H. Bleby, *Death Struggles of Slavery: being a narrative of facts and incidents which occurred in a British colony during the last two years immediately preceding Negro emancipation*, London: Hamilton, Adams and co., 1853, p. 90.
40. See, for example, *PP* 1831–32, XX, p. 74; R. Bickell, *The West Indies as They Are; or, a real picture of slavery: but more particular as it exists in the island of Jamaica in three parts with notes*, London: Hatchard, 1823, p. 34; and *Remarks upon the Injustice and Immorality of Slavery in Eight Letters by the Rev. George Whitfield*, London: John Stephens, 1830, p. 34.
41. See, for example, statements by John Barry and William Knibb before the 1832 Select Committee in *PP* 1831–32, XX, pp. 74 and 284.

42. A few early antislavery writers called for compulsory manumission but limited it to a small number of cases: free men who wanted to purchase their wife's freedom and married slave men with three or more children. See, for example, J. Anderson, *Observations on Slavery: particularly with a view to its effects on the British colonies in the West Indies*, Manchester: J. Harrop, 1789, p. 19; and Burke, *Sketch of a Negro Code*, p. 207.
43. Bickell, *The West Indies*, p. 34.
44. L. Forman Cody, 'The politics of illegitimacy in an age of reform: women, reproduction and political economy in England's new poor law of 1834', *Journal of Women's History* 11, no. 4, 2000, pp. 133–6. According to Belinda Meteyard, the 1753 Marriage Act largely explains the increase in illegitimacy rates in the late eighteenth and early nineteenth centuries because it redefined the notion of illegitimacy and changed perceptions of responsibility in sexual relations. See her 'Illegitimacy and marriage in eighteenth-century England', *Journal of Interdisciplinary History* 10, no. 3, 1980, pp. 479–89.
45. *Slave Trade Committee Report*, vol. 82, p. 51. Emphasis mine. There are no statistics available for the number of slaves who made the Atlantic crossing with a partner or a family member. It can safely be assumed, however, that few slave families made the crossing together because it was not common for entire families to be caught in slave raids, while those who were caught together were usually separated during the voyage to the coast. I want to thank Audra Diptee and Jelmer Vos for sharing this information with me.
46. J. R. Ward, *British West Indian Slavery 1750–1834: the process of amelioration*, Oxford: Clarendon Press, 1988, chap. 3.
47. *The Speech of James Losh, esq., in the Guildhall, Newcastle-upon-Tyne on the 31st March 1824*, Newcastle: T. and J. Hodgson, 1824, p. 3.
48. *JA*, Moravian Archives, Q/9.
49. See, for instance, William Taylor's statement before the 1832 Select Committee in *PP* 1831–32, XX, pp. 56–7.
50. On American slave women's preference to live separated from their husbands, see West, *Chains of Love*.
51. Thomson, *Substance of a Speech*, p. 7. For similar accounts, see *A Dialogue between a Well-Wisher and a Friend to the Slaves in the British Colonies by a Lady*, n.p: n.d., p. 9; and T. Cooper, *Facts Illustrative of the Condition of the Negro Slaves in Jamaica with Notes and an Appendix*, London: Hatchard, 1824, p. 32. Slaves who had run away for less than five days were punished by their owner with a severe flogging or confinement in the stocks. Those who had run away for more than five days were brought before two Justices of the Peace. They were given a severe flogging or were confined to hard labour. Slaves harbouring runaways were tried at a special slave court or at a quarter session. See *1826 Slave Law*.
52. *Slave Trade Committee Report*, vol. 82, p. 98.
53. As cited in G. Jackson, *A Memoir of the Rev. John Jenkins late a Wesleyan Missionary in the island of Jamaica* 2nd ed., London: Rev. J. Mason, n.d., p. 120. See also, Cooper as cited in Rev. J. Riland (ed.), *Memoirs of a West India Planter; published from an original ms*, London: Hamilton, Adams and co., 1827, p. 201; and *PP* 1831–32, XX, p. 57.
54. Burke, *Sketch of a Negro Code*, pp. 204 and 207. For a similar proposal, see Captain Young's statement in *Slave Trade Committee Report*, vol. 73, p. 217.
55. Anderson, *Observations on Slavery*, p. 19. It was not until 1823 before easier manumission laws became abolitionist policy. See, Blackburn, *Overthrow of Colonial Slavery*, p. 422.

56. Anderson, *Observations on Slavery*, pp. 16–7. This plan was based on Anderson's experiences as a farmer. One of his male employees, whose wife was heavily pregnant, had asked him if he could also do the work of his wife so that she could stay at home.
57. *Slave Trade Committee Report*, vol. 73, p. 217.
58. *Plan for Effecting Emancipation by the Redemption of Female Slaves Laid before Government in 1824, in Plans of Emancipation*, London: Baster and Thomas, [1824], pp. 5 and 8.
59. T. Clarkson, *Thoughts on the Necessity of Improving the Condition of the Slaves in the British Colonies*, London: Hatchard, 1824, pp. iv and 9; *Review of the Quarterly Review; or, an exposure of the erroneous opinions promulgated in that work on the subject of colonial slavery*, London: Hatchard, 1824, p. 27; Cooper as cited in Riland (ed.), *Memoirs of a West India Planter*, pp. 200–3; and Rev. G. W. Craufurd as cited in T. Jackson, *Britain's Burden; or, the intolerable evils of colonial slavery exposed*, Cambridge: Metcalfe, 1832, p. 18.
60. Cooper as cited in Riland (ed.), *Memoirs of a West India Planter*, p. 201. Cooper responded here to G. W. Bridges' *A Voice from Jamaica; in reply to William Wilberforce*, London: Longman and co., 1823.
61. Ibid., p. 202.
62. J. Tosh, *A Man's Place: masculinity and the middle-class home in Victorian England*, New Haven: Yale University Press, 1999, p. 60.
63. M. Edgeworth, *The Grateful Negro* [1804], in S. Aravaduman (ed.), *Slavery, Abolition and Emancipation: writings in the British romantic period*, vol. 6, London: Pickering and Cato, 1999, pp. 295–325. Previous studies of this novel have tried to assess the extent to which Edgeworth displayed antislavery sympathies by concentrating on her depiction of Caesar's and Clara's masters and the rebellious slaves. See, for instance, G. Boulukos, 'Maria Edgeworth's "Grateful Negro" and the sentimental argument for slavery', *Eighteenth-Century Life* 23, no. 1, 1999, pp. 12–29; and F. R. Botkin, 'Questioning the "necessary order of things": Maria Edgeworth's "The Grateful Negro", plantation slavery, and the abolition of the slave trade', in B. Carey, M. Ellis and S. Salih (eds.), *Discourses of Slavery and Abolition: Britain and its colonies, 1760–1838*, Basingstoke: Palgrave Macmillan, 2004, pp. 194–208.
64. Cooper, *Facts Illustrative*, p. 41. Cooper attributed this inability mainly to the lack of religious instruction. His account of slave marriage, then, is another example of the shifts in missionary writings between the languages of equality and difference.
65. A. Dru Stanley, *From Bondage to Contract: wage labor, marriage and the market in the age of slave emancipation*, Cambridge: Cambridge University Press, 1998, chap. 1.
66. Another important method through which slaves could develop a bond with the law was the so-called Council of Protection. This institution will be discussed in the next chapter.
67. Burke, *Sketch of a Negro Code*, pp. 202–3.
68. *A Plan for the Abolition of Slavery Consistently with the Interests of All Parties Concerned*, London: George Sidford, 1828, p. 20. The author was in favour of gradual rather than immediate emancipation and wanted slave marriage to be encouraged or, if necessary, 'enforced by law'.
69. Burke, *Sketch of A Negro Code*, p. 204.
70. Cooper, *Facts Illustrative*, p. 10; and *Address to the Public*, p. 9.
71. T. Clarkson, *An Essay on the Impolicy of the African Slave Trade in Two Parts*, London: J. Phillips, 1788, p. 100.

72. There is little evidence in the primary sources of domestic discord. Because of the nature of the institution of slavery as well as the personalities of the spouses, however, physical and verbal violence must have regularly broken out between slave husbands and wives.
73. *PP* 1833, IV, pp. 209 and 212. This clause also applied to the separation of children from their parents. The local Abolition Act, however, did not include a remedy for a wife, husband, parent, or child who had by mistake or by omission from the S.M., been separated from his or her family.
74. See my '"To wed or not to wed?": the struggle to define Afro-Jamaican relationships, 1834–38', *Journal of Social History* 38, no. 1, 2004, pp. 81–111.
75. A notable exception is Edward Eliot who believed that after August 1834 formal marriage had become a voluntary and fully binding contract between two parties. See his *Christian Responsibilities Arising out of the Recent Changes in Our West India Colonies: in five discourses, four preached in the West Indies and one in England,* London: J. W. Parker, 1836, pp. 54–5.
76. 'Minutes of the House of Assembly 15 December 1835', PRO, CO 140/126. This 'rush to marriage' can largely be explained by the fact that written permission from the owner or overseer was no longer needed. It is likely that there were apprentices amongst those who married in the first year of apprenticeship, who simply married in order to avail themselves of one of the new rights bestowed on them, and thereby give expression to the change in their legal status.
77. *PP* 1835, L, p. 84; *PP* 1836, XLVIII p. 154; and *PP* 1837, LIII, pp. 83, 94 and 269.
78. *PP* 1836, XLVIII, p. 231. See also Lord Glenelg's remark in *PP* 1835, L, p. 135.
79. See, for instance, *PP* 1835, L, pp. 84 and 153; *PP* 1836, XLVIII, p. 140; and *PP* 1837, LIII, p. 94.
80. *PP* 1836, XLVIII, p. 123.
81. Ibid. Critics also argued that the stability of the estates would be enhanced by the promotion of marriage. See, for instance, *PP* 1835, L, p. 84; and *PP* 1837, LIII, p. 260.
82. S.M. Marlton's report from June 1835 shows most clearly that the critics' calls upon the planters to promote apprenticed marriage had fallen upon deaf ears. See *PP* 1835, L, p. 153.
83. The bill, which was passed early 1836 and took effect in 1837, also allowed for civil marriage and the central registration of every marriage. For its various provisions and the factors that led to the bill, see Parker, *Informal Marriage*, chap. 4.
84. *PP* 1836, XLVIII, p. 61. For a similar argument, see Richard Matthews' analysis of the marriage laws in the colonies in *PP* 1836, XV, p. 641. On the eve of apprenticeship there were about 50 Anglican ministers in the island, each serving around 18,000 people. See N. Ortmayer, 'Church, marriage and legitimacy in the British West Indies (nineteenth and twentieth centuries)', *The History of the Family* 2, no. 2, 1997, p. 143.
85. *PP* 1836, XLVIII, p. 61.
86. Ibid., pp. 61 and 641. A similar debate took place in the American South during Reconstruction. It was eventually decided that not only church-sanctioned but also informal marriages performed during slavery should be regarded as legal. This decision aimed to increased the number of legitimate children and therefore reduce the demands upon state support. It also had to make it easier to transfer property across the generations. See, L. F. Edwards, *Gendered*

Strife and Confusion: the political culture of Reconstruction, Urbana: University of Illinois Press, 1997, chap. 1.
87. *PP* 1836, XV, p. 646.
88. *PP* 1836, XLVIII, p. 60.
89. *PP* 1836, XV, p. 6.
90. Glenelg supported his recommendation amongst others with the argument that because of the paucity of Anglican ministers in the islands, nonconformist missionaries had a great influence over the apprentices and that they could thus easily promote 'a due reverence among their converts for the institution of marriage', which in turn would 'confer the most essential benefits on society at large'. *PP* 1836, XLVIII, p. 60. This argument is not surprising, considering that it was generally argued in the metropolitan debate about proposed changes in the 1753 Hardwick Act that religious nonconformity was beneficial for society. See, Parker, *Informal Marriage*, p. 49.
91. J. Sturge and T. Harvey, *The West Indies in 1837; being the journal of a visit to Antigua, Montserrat, Dominica, St. Lucia, Barbados and Jamaica*, London: Hamilton, Adams, 1838, p. 349; and *PP* 1837, LIII, pp. 217, 220, 259, and 320.
92. *PP* 1837, LIII, pp. 220 and 264. Most of the women released from apprenticeship by their husbands were field workers.
93. J. A. Thome and J. H. Kimball, *Emancipation in the West Indies: a six months' tour in Antigua, Barbadoes, and Jamaica in the year 1837*, New York: American Anti-Slavery Society, 1838, p. 103.
94. The three valuators were presented with witnesses who remarked upon the apprentice's services before and after 1 August 1834. Thereafter, they determined individually how much the apprentice would be worth if hired by the year. From this amount they then deducted a sum to cover the 'contingencies' (such items as the costs of clothing which a master was bound to supply) and multiplied this by the number of years or parts of years that apprenticeship was still to run. The impact of this complicated procedure can be concluded from the fact that between August 1834 and August 1836 only 893 of the 1,385 apprentices who were valued eventually paid the sum fixed. See W. L. Burn, *Emancipation and Apprenticeship in the British West Indies*, London: Jonathan Cape, 1937, p. 276.
95. *PP* 1836, XLVIII, pp. 65 and 386–7. The second suggestion was already in place in British Guyana. See Burn, *Emancipation and Apprenticeship*, p. 279.
96. Burn, *Emancipation and Apprenticeship*, p. 277; and *PP* 1836, XLVIII, p. 431
97. Burn, *Emancipation and Apprenticeship*, p. 330. Apprentices employed in the first gang were valued at £15; those in the second at £10; and those in the third at £7.
98. Ibid., p. 278; and T. C. Holt, *The Problem of Freedom: race, labor and politics in Jamaica and Britain, 1832–1938*, Baltimore: Johns Hopkins University Press, 1992, p. 145.
99. *PP* 1837, LIII, p. 264.
100. Holt, *The Problem of Freedom*, pp. 73–5.
101. As cited in Holt, *The Problem of Freedom*, p. 77.
102. As cited in D. L. Eudell, *The Political Languages of Emancipation in the British Caribbean and the U.S. South*, Chapel Hill: The University of North Carolina Press, 2002, pp. 79–80.
103. On the extent of interracial sex after August 1834, see the statement of Augustus Beaumont before the 1836 Select Committee in *PP* 1836, XV, p. 242; and

B. M'Mahon, *Jamaica Plantership*, London: Effingham Wilson, 1839, pp. 120–1. Planters were by law only allowed to put recalcitrant apprentices in the dungeon in order to await the arrival of the S.M. Many planters, however, put apprentices in the dungeon without calling upon the S.M. Planters could be tried for disobeying this and other rules that forbade them to punish their apprentices. If proven guilty, they were usually required to pay a fine. See Burn, *Emancipation and Apprenticeship*, p. 274.
104. *PP* 1837, LIII, p. 235. The 1826 rape act was continued after August 1834. It is not known how many rape cases appeared before a Grand Jury.
105. To uphold the idea that apprentices would become law-abiding citizens, critics had to omit accounts of apprentices who used non-legal means to improve their condition, such as arson or strike. See D. Paton, *No Bond but the Law: punishment, race and gender in Jamaican state formation, 1780–1870*, Durham, N.C.: Duke University Press, 2004, p. 81.
106. Thome and Kimball, *Emancipation in the West Indies*, p. 100; and Captain Studholme Hodgson, *Truths from the West Indies: including a sketch from Madeira in 1833*, London: William Ball, 1838, p. 158.
107. *A Statement of Facts Illustrating the Administration of the Abolition Law, and the Sufferings of the Negro Apprentices in the Island of Jamaica*, London, William Ball, 1837, p. 25.
108. Rev. W. Bevan, *The Operation of the Apprenticeship System in the British Colonies*, Liverpool: D. Marple and co. 1838, p. 26.
109. This summary of the legal and extra-legal practices that made it difficult for abroad apprenticed and free-apprenticed couples to visit one another is based on: *PP* 1835, L, p. 236; *PP* 1836, XV, pp. 402, 414, 416, and 422; and *PP* 1837–38, XLIX, p. 170.
110. *PP* 1837, LIII, p. 217.
111. Ibid.
112. *A Statement of Facts*, p. 39. For other accounts of difficulties faced by apprentices to visit their apprenticed or free spouse, see *An Appeal to the Christian Women of Sheffield from the Association for the Universal Abolition of Slavery*, Sheffield: R. Leader, 1837, p. 11; Bevan, *The operation of the Apprenticeship*, p. 26; and Sturge and Harvey, *The West Indies*, p. 407.
113. *A Statement of Facts*, p. 39.
114. On this right as a 'natural right', see *PP* 1836, XV, p. 63; *PP* 1837, LIII, p. 217; and *PP* 1837–38, XLIX, p. 284.
115. *PP* 1836, XV, pp. 104 and 424.
116. *PP* 1835, L, p. 136. Emphasis mine. Glenelg expressed a similar opinion in a letter to Governor Lionel Smith in October 1837, see *PP* 1837–38, XLIX, p. 284.
117. Tosh, *A Man's Place*, p. 89.
118. *PP* 1835, L, p. 136. For a similar interpretation of visiting rights, see John Jeremie's statement before the 1836 Select Committee in *PP* 1836, XV, p. 104.
119. *PP* 1837, LIII, p. 336.
120. *PP* 1837–38, XLIX, p. 284.
121. *PP* 1836, XV, pp. 104 and 414; and *PP* 1837, LIII, p. 217.
122. *PP* 1837–38, XLIX, p. 284.
123. 'Circular 13 June 1836', *JA*, Thomas Davies Special Magistrate, 4/47.
124. *PP* 1837, LIII, p. 217.
125. H. McNeill, *Observations on the Treatment of Negroes in the Island of Jamaica*, London: G. J. and J. Robinson, 1788, p. 35.

218   Notes

126. J. Foot, *A Defence of the Planters in the West Indies Compromised in Four Arguments*, London: J. Debrett, 1782, p. 100
127. McNeill, *Observations on the Treatment*, p. 41; and J. M. Adair, *Unanswerable Arguments against the Abolition of the Slave Trade with a Defence of the Proprietors of the British Sugar Colonies*, London: privately published, 1790, p 161.
128. J. Foot, *Observations Principally upon the Speech of Mr. Wilberforce on his Motion in the House of Commons, the 30th of May 1804*, London: T. Becket, 1805, p. 96.
129. See, for instance, Adair, *Unanswerable Arguments*, p. 157; and P. Gibbes, *Instructions for the Treatment of Negroes*, 2nd ed., London: Shepperson and Reynolds, 1788, p. 21.
130. Foot, *A Defence of the Planters*, p. 98.
131. Ibid., pp. 97–9.
132. Adair, *Unanswerable Arguments*, p. 158. Adair nevertheless praised slave women in abroad marriages for carrying out their wifely duties. He emphasized, for instance, that they cooked for their husbands.
133. F. Cundall (ed.), *Lady Nugent's Journal: Jamaica one hundred years ago reprinted from a journal kept by Maria, Lady Nugent, from 1801 to 1815*, London: Adam and Charles Black, 1907, p. 307. See also, Adair, *Unanswerable Arguments*, p. 161.
134. It was not until the 1830s that the ideal of the home was raised to the level of a cultural norm. See Tosh, *A Man's Place*, p. 30. Only Foot expressed some concern about the latter when he argued that non-residence increased the chances of desertion.
135. B. Edwards, *The History Civil and Commercial of the British Colonies in the West Indies, vol. 1*, London: John Stockdale, 1793, p. 81. For a similar account, see E. Long, *The History of Jamaica, or General Survey of the Antient and Modern State of that Island: with reflections on its situations, settlements, inhabitants, climate, products, commerce, laws, and government* [1774], London: Frank Cass, 1970, p. 415.
136. [J. Stewart], *An Account of Jamaica, and Its Inhabitants by a Gentleman Long resident in the West Indies*, London: Longman, Hurst, Rees and Orme, 1808, p. 277.
137. Ibid.
138. [Tobin], *Cursory Remarks upon the Reverend Mr. Ramsay's Essay on the Treatment and Conversion of African Slaves in the Sugar Colonies: by a friend to the West India colonies and their inhabitants*, London: G. and T. Wilkie, 1785, p. 96; W. A. Beckford, *Remarks upon the Situation of Negroes in Jamaica; impartially made from a local experience of nearly thirteen years in that island*, London: T. and J. Egerton, 1788, p. 278; G. Francklyn, *Observations Occasioned by the Attempts Made in England to Affect the Abolition of the Slave Trade*, Kingston: J.Walker, 1788, p. 35; Moreton, *West Indian Customs*, p. 150; and *Slave Trade Committee Report*, vol. 69, p. 213.
139. Moreton, *West India Customs*, p. 150.
140. [Tobin], *Cursory Remarks*, p. 96; Beckford, *Remarks upon the Situation*, p. 278; and Francklyn, *Observations Occasioned*, p. 35.
141. J. McQueen, *The West India Colonies; the calumnies and misrepresentations circulated against them by the Edinburgh Review, Mr Clarkson, Mr Cropper etc.*, London: Baldwin, Cradock and Joy, 1824, p. 279. For similar contradictory arguments, see H. De La Beche, *Notes on the Present Condition of the Negroes in Jamaica*, London: T. Cadell, 1825, pp. 17 and 48; and A. Barclay,

A Practical View of the Present State of Slavery in the West Indies, London: Smith, Elder and co., 1827, pp. 101–2.
142. Barclay, *A Practical View*, p. 102. Only one proslavery writer in the 1820s proposed an increase in religious instruction as a means to prepare the slaves for marriage. See J. Stewart, *A View of the Past and Present State of the Island of Jamaica; with remarks on the moral and physical condition of the slaves and on the abolition of slavery in the colonies*, Edinburgh: Oliver and Boyd, 1823, p. 310.
143. McQueen, *The West India Colonies*, p. 301; and T. Foulks, *Eighteen Months in Jamaica with Recollections of the Late Rebellion*, London: Whittaker, Treacher and Arnott, 1833, p. 102. This argument was also articulated by some early defenders of slavery, see, for example, Long, *The History of Jamaica*, p. 414; and *Slave Trade Committee Report*, vol. 72, p. 162.
144. C. R. Williams, *Tour Through the Island of Jamaica from the Western to the Eastern End in 1823*, London: Edward Chance and co., 1827, p. 224.
145. [A. Davis], *The West Indies*, London: James Cochrane, 1832, p. 72. The question whether slaves would work for wages played a central role in the 1832 Select Committee. See D. Paton, 'Decency, dependence, and the lash: gender and the British debate over slave emancipation, 1830-34', *Slavery and Abolition* 17, no. 3, 1996, pp. 178–9.
146. McQueen, *The West India Colonies*, p. 271; Barclay, *A Practical View*, p. 55; and *PP* 1831–32, XX, p. 341.
147. McQueen, *The West India Colonies*, p. 271; J. Hakewill, *A Picturesque Tour of the Island of Jamaica: from drawings made in the years 1820 and 1821*, London: Hurst and Robinson, 1825, p. 8; and *Marly; or, a planter's life in Jamaica*, Glasgow: Richard Griffin and co., 1828, p. 99.
148. *The Edinburgh Review and the West Indies*, Glasgow: John Smith and son, 1816, p. 144; *Evidence upon Oath Touching the Condition and Treatment of the Negro Population of the British West India Colonies, part 1*, London: Mrs Ridgways, 1832, p. 26; and *PP* 1831–32, XX, p. 55. Middle-class metropolitan society at the time deemed it essential that houses contained separate rooms for adults and children. See Davidoff and Hall, *Family Fortunes*, chap. 8.
149. *Evidence upon Oath*, p. 26.
150. Barclay, *A Practical View*, p. 420. See also *PP* 1831–32, XX, p. 39.
151. Barclay, *A Practical View*, pp. 420–2.
152. Ibid., p. 101. For similar remarks, see McQueen, *The West India Colonies*, p. 279; and *Evidence upon Oath*, p. 44.
153. Captain Henderson, *A Brief View of the Actual Condition and Treatment of the Negro Slaves in the British Colonies in a Letter to a Member of the Imperial Parliament*, London: Baldwin, Cradock and Joy, 1816, p. 20.
154. *PP* 1831–32, XX, p. 57.
155. 'Minutes West India Committee April 1823', *Institute of Commonwealth Studies* (hereafter, *ICS*), West India Committee, planters-merchants 1822–1829. This proposal to increase the marriage rate was part of a series of ameliorative proposals very similar to those presented by the Canning Government in May 1823 and which also included a ban on female flogging (see chap. 5). The West India Committee was convinced by 1823 that only amelioration on a grant scale could prevent or postpone emancipation. Throughout the 1820s and early 1830s, it put considerable pressure on planters to change their practices. In 1833, it defended the planters' interests during the various discussions about emancipation. It was largely as a result of its pressure that the Imperial government raised the compensation for owners from 15

220 *Notes*

to 20 million pounds. Throughout the apprenticeship period, the Committee did little to defend the interests of the planters. For more information on the activities of the West India Committee in the 1820s and 1830s, see L. J. Ragatz, *The Fall of the Planter Class in the British Caribbean, 1763–1833* [1927], New York: Octagon Books, 1963, pp. 411–2.

156. *1826 Slave Law*, p. 5.
157. *PP* 1826–27, XXV, p. 64; and *PP* 1828, XXVII, p. 100.
158. *PP* 1826–27, XXV, p. 76.
159. *PP* 1836, XV, p. 306–7. Shirley had arrived in Jamaica shortly before the onset of apprenticeship in order to directly manage his properties. The Assembly's formal justification for the rejection of this provision to legalize nonconformist marriages was that only the government at home had the right to enact such a marriage bill.
160. Turner, *Slaves and Missionaries*, pp. 75 and 83.
161. Slave religion was thus clearly a double-edge sword. It made the slaves more docile on the one hand, while it increased their desire for freedom on the other.
162. That opponents of apprenticeship did not focus extensively on this issue seems to stem largely from the fact that marriage, like motherhood, did not provide them with very strong arguments to demonstrate that apprenticeship would not achieve its most important aim: turning the ex-slaves into wage labourers. The existence of numerous obstacles that planters put in the way of apprenticed couples to exercise their conjugal duties made it furthermore practically impossible for opponents to deny the critics' accusation regarding the lack of protection afforded to apprenticed marriage.
163. *Kingston Chronicle*, 7 September 1835, in PRO, CO 142/3. With its 55 paid subscribers, the paper represented only a moderate opposition to apprenticeship. Burn, *Emancipation and Apprenticeship*, p. 273.
164. *PP* 1835, L, p. 367. He reiterated this remark in his report from March 1836, see *PP* 1836, XLVIII, p. 378.
165. Eudell, *The Political Languages*, p. 107.
166. A husband's ability to take his provider role seriously was an important criterium used in metropolitan society at the time to argue in favour of or against an extension of male suffrage. See, Clark, *The Struggle for the Breeches*, p. 221.
167. *PP* 1837, LIII, p. 69.
168. Ibid.
169. U. R. Q. Henriques, 'Bastardy and the new poor law', *Past and Present* 37, 1967, p. 114.
170. *PP* 1837, LIII, p. 69.
171. The bastardy clauses in the Poor Law, which firmly placed the liability of the maintenance of an illegitimate child on its mother, were supported with an image that was very different from the one used by Dillon: a woman who was the cause of her own misery because she had failed to exercise sexual restraint. For more information on the bastardy clauses and their changes over time, see S. G. and E. O. A. Checkland (eds.), *The Poor Law Report of 1834*, London: Penguin 1974, pp. 258–74 and 472–83.
172. *PP* 1837, LIII, p. 200.
173. Ibid.
174. Henriques, 'Bastardy', p. 111.
175. The evidence that antislavery writers presented to support their demand for a change in manumission laws gave their readers the idea that it was only free(d) men who tried to buy their enslaved partner. There is evidence, how-

ever, that there were also many free(d) women who tried to buy their enslaved partner's freedom. See, for example, Bleby, *Death Struggles of Slavery*, p. 90.
176. As mentioned, for instance, by Mary Wollstonecraft in her *Vindication of the Rights of Women* (1792).
177. This was also largely achieved by ignoring the realities of marital life on the plantations. In accounts of abroad relations, for example, it is nearly always the husband who does the visiting.
178. This process has been excellently described by John Gilles in his *For Better, For Worse*.

CHAPTER 5

1. 'The 1788 Slave Law' in *Slave Trade Committee Report*, vol. 67, p. 210. If the stipulation of the maximum number of lashes was not observed, a planter had to pay a fine of ten pounds. The clause remained valid, albeit with some minor alterations, until 1834. Some research has been carried out into the floggings inflicted by the Jamaican slave courts. See, for instance, D. Paton, 'Punishment, crime and the bodies of slaves in eighteenth-century Jamaica', *Journal of Social History* 34, 2001, pp. 923–54. Thus far, however, no detailed study has been published on the punishment regime in force on Jamaican plantations during slavery.
2. 'The 1788 Slave Law' in *Slave Trade Committee Report*, vol. 67, p. 209. The clause that set out the Council of Protection also stipulated that courts could order the complainant's discharge of slavery as a means of 'future protection'. Assizes were held three times a year in each county and were the highest level of criminal court in the island. Quarter sessions functioned below this and took place every three months in every parish. There were also petty sessions, which took place whenever the required number of magistrates decided to hold court but which did not deal with such serious crimes as excessive violence against slaves. See, D. Paton, *No Bond but the Law: punishment, race and gender in Jamaican state formation, 1780–1870*, Durham, N.C.: Duke University Press, 2004, p. 63.
3. See, for example, H. De La Beche, *Notes on the Present Condition of the Negroes in Jamaica*, London: T. Cadell, 1825, pp. 20 and 45; and M. G. Lewis, *Journal of a West India Proprietor: kept during a residence in the island of Jamaica* [1834], London: John Murray, 1838, p. 119.
4. *PP* 1831–32, XX, p. 428.
5. One of the first studies to describe and explain the shift in the late eighteenth century away from public forms of punishment that aimed at the body towards private forms of punishment that tried to reach the offender's soul was Michel Foucault's *Discipline and Punish* [1977], London: Penguin, 1991. Various studies on punishment in the modern period have been influenced by and have also critiqued Foucault's work, such as R. McGowen, 'The body and punishment in eighteenth-century England', *Journal of Modern History* 59, 1987, pp. 651–79, which largely informs the last section of this chapter.
6. Early antislavery writings provide, however, numerous accounts of female flogging on the slave ships. For an analysis of these writings, see M.A. Favret, 'Flogging: the anti-slavery movement writes pornography', *Essay and Studies*, 1998, pp. 19–43; and M. Wood, *Blind Memory: visual representations of slavery in England and America 1780–1865*, Manchester, Manchester University Press, 2000, chap. 5.

7. J. Campbell, *A Letter to Sir Robert Peel on the Subject of British Colonial Slavery*, Edinburgh: Colston, 1830, p. 53.
8. Captain Studholme Hodgson, *Truths from the West Indies: including a sketch from Madeira in 1833*, London: William Ball, 1838, p. 144. The most horrific descriptions of female flogging during both slavery and apprenticeship can be found in B. M'Mahon, *Jamaica Plantership*, London: Effingham Wilson, 1839. Former bookkeeper Benjamin M'Mahon concentrated in his descriptions on what the slave woman's body felt rather than what the woman said. His horrific descriptions of female flogging and those of other writers served also to enhance the virtue of the readers by allowing them to feel compassion for the suffering of others. On this process of 'spectatorial sympathy', see K. Halttunen, 'Humanitarianism and the pornography of pain in Anglo-American Culture', *American Historical Review* 100, no. 2, 1995, pp. 304–34.
9. R. Bickell, *The West Indies as They Are; or, a real picture of slavery: but more particular as it exists in the island of Jamaica in three parts with notes*, London: Hatchard, 1823, p. 29.
10. As cited in G. Jackson, *A Memoir of the Rev. John Jenkins late a Wesleyan Missionary in the island of Jamaica*, 2nd ed., London: Rev. J. Mason, n. d., p. 112.
11. Some scholars have interpreted the emphasis on the exposure of the flogged female body as evidence that antislavery writers eroticized the suffering of the slaves. See, for instance, Halttunen, 'Humanitarianism', p. 324; and Favret, 'Flogging', p. 24.
12. Goderich's letter to J. C. Smyth, 25 July 1831 in *PP* 1832, XLVI, p. 3. Goderich had strong links with the abolitionist movement and played an educational and propagandist role in the emancipation of the slaves by exposing abuses of planters and exerting pressure on them. See W. L. Burn, *Emancipation and Apprenticeship in the British West Indies*, London: Jonathan Cape, 1937, p. 62.
13. *The Death Warrant of Negro Slavery throughout the British Dominions*, London: Hatchard, 1829, p. 33.
14. M'Mahon, *Jamaica Plantership*, pp. 52–3.
15. Bickell, *The West Indies as They Are*, p. 49.
16. *The Negro's Memorial: or, abolitionist's catechism, by an abolitionist*, London: Hatchard, 1825, p. 60.
17. Female purity had both a sexual and a moral component. It involved not only the absence of sexual thoughts and experiences but also behaviour that did not excite sexual feelings in others or otherwise caused shame or shock. See R. B. Shoemaker, *Gender in English Society 1650–1850: the emergence of separate spheres?*, London: Longman, 1998, p. 23.
18. H. Bleby, *Death Struggles of Slavery: being a narrative of facts and incidents which occurred in a British colony during the last two years immediately preceding Negro emancipation*, London: Hamilton, Adams and co., 1853, p. 188.
19. Hodgson, *Truths from the West Indies*, p. 145.
20. See, for example, *Memoirs of Charles Campbell at Present Prisoner in the Jail of Glasgow: including his adventures as a seaman, and as an overseer in the West Indies written by himself*, Glasgow: James Duncan and co., 1828, p. 20; and Campbell, *A Letter to Sir Robert Peel*, p. 53.
21. Trew as cited in Jackson, *A Memoir*, p. 113.
22. Ibid., p. 120.

23. Ibid., p. 112; *A General History of Negro Slavery: collected from the most respectable evidence and unquestionable authorities*, Cambridge: Hatfield, 1826, p. 88; and *PP* 1831–32, XX, p. 428.
24. *The Negro's Memorial*, p. 60.
25. Captain Majoribanks, *Slavery: an essay in verse*, Edinburgh: J. Robertson, 1802, p. 13. The slave man who acquiesced in his partner's flogging was a more common image in fictional accounts of female flogging than the slave man who actively tried to protect his partner against flogging. For an example of the latter, see [E. Rushton], *West Indian Eclogues*, London: J. Philips, 1787, p. 2.
26. *A Letter to John Bull: to which is added the sketch of a plan for the safe, speedy, and effectual abolition of slavery by a free-born Englishman*, London: Hatchard, 1823, p. 12.
27. Planters appointed several slave men to head the first and second gang on the basis of their intelligence, ability, and knowledge of planting. These drivers received their orders directly from the overseer and had to report to him on completion of work. Most drivers were allowed to use the whip on their own authority and were bestowed with favours and privileges, such as larger allowances of food and clothing. Slaves often applied to drivers to adjust differences in an extra-legal court of arbitration, while the drivers often pleaded with the management on behalf of the slave community. See P.D. Curtin, *Two Jamaicas: the role of ideas in a tropical colony, 1830–65*, Cambridge, Mass.: Harvard University Press, 1955, pp. 19–20; and O. Patterson, *The Sociology of Slavery: an analysis of the origins, development and structure of negro slave society in Jamaica*, London: MacGibbon and Kee, 1967, p. 63.
28. Hodgson, *Truths from the West Indies*, p. 144.
29. H. Whiteley, *Excessive Cruelty to Slaves: three months in Jamaica in 1832, comprising a residence of seven weeks on a sugar plantation*, London: Hatchard, 1833, p. 10. Whiteley narrated in this pamphlet nearly all the floggings he had witnessed during his stay. The pamphlet was one of the most popular antislavery publications. During the first two weeks, it sold some 200,000 copies abroad alone. Burn, *Emancipation and Apprenticeship*, pp. 60 and 97.
30. W. Wilberforce, *An Appeal to the Religion, Justice and Humanity of the Inhabitants of the British Empire on Behalf of Its Negro Slaves in the West Indies* [1823], in P. Kitson (ed.), *Slavery, Abolition and Emancipation: writings in the British romantic period, vol. 2*, London: Pickering and Cato, 1999, pp. 17–8. Wilberforce also argued that drivers used their power to persuade slave women into having sex with them.
31. Bleby, *Death Struggles*, p. 3.
32. See Bickell, *The West Indies As They Are*, p. 29; [Rushton], *West Indian Eclogues*, p. 2; and *A Dialogue between a Well-Wisher and a Friend to the Slaves in the British Colonies by a Lady*, N. p.: n. d., p. 4.
33. See, for instance, *Slave Trade Committee Report*, vol. 82, pp. 77 and 205.
34. *Anti-Slavery Reporter*, February 1831, p. 129. The journal was set up by the Anti-Slavery Society in 1825 and served as a means for debating the objectives of abolitionism and for conducting the Society's propaganda. Its scope extended beyond the West Indies; it also included articles on the Atlantic slave trade and on slavery in other parts of the Americas. See R. Blackburn, *The Overthrow of Colonial Slavery, 1776–1848*, London: Verso, 1988, pp. 422–3.

224 Notes

35. Whiteley, *Excessive Cruelty*, p. 4. For other striking examples of floggings committed by white estate officers, see Hodgson, *Truths from the West Indies*, p. 144; and Bleby, *Death Struggles*, p. 188.
36. Rev. B. Godwin, *Substance of a Course of Lectures on British Colonial Slavery Delivered at Bradford, York and Scarborough*, London: J. Hatchard and son, 1830, p. 49.
37. *PP* 1830–31, XVI, p. 231. In April 1829, Kitty appealed to a local magistrate who considered her complaint grounded and set up a Council of Protection. The Council decided by 13 votes to 4 not to prosecute Bridges. After a letter from a local antislavery society, Goderich ordered the Jamaican Attorney General to prepare an indictment against Bridges. The Grand Jury, however, refused to find a true bill. See Burn, *Emancipation and Apprenticeship*, p. 62.
38. *PP* 1830–31, XVI, p. 231.
39. *PP* 1831–32, XLVII, p. 387. Mr Jackson, the custos of Port Royal, and his wife had abused the mother and daughter for more than five months before a complaint about their treatment was made to magistrate Dr Palmer. The latter established a Council of Protection in June 1831, which decided that there were no grounds for prosecution. Two months later, a Grand Jury threw out a bill of indictment against Mr Jackson. See Burn, *Emancipation and Apprenticeship*, pp. 62–4.
40. Goderich stated repeatedly that female flogging fostered 'base and unmanly aspects in the other sex'. See, for instance, *PP* 1831–32, XLVI, p. 3. On men and violence in early nineteenth-century England, see Shoemaker, *Gender in English Society*, pp. 15 and 29.
41. Bleby, *Death Struggles*, p. 74. See also the letter of a local antislavery activist cited in *PP* 1830–31, XVI, pp. 202–3.
42. Knibb as cited in C. Hall, *White, Male and Middle Class: explorations in feminism and history*, Cambridge: Polity Press, 1992, p. 213. This was one of several speeches that Knibb held in England following his statement before the 1832 Select Committee on the slave rebellion and the role of Baptist missionaries within it. For more information on Knibb's role in the slavery debate, see C. Hall, *Civilising Subjects: metropole and colony in the English imagination 1830–1867*, Cambridge: Policy Press, 2002, chap. 1.
43. Only a small percentage of white women in the island were slaveholders. Most of the mistresses referred to by the antislavery writers were urban slaveholding women or the wives of planters who were responsible for the domestic slaves. See B. W. Higman, *Slave Populations of the British Caribbean, 1807–1834*, Baltimore: Johns Hopkins University Press, 1984, p. 107. For information on the way white slaveholding women treated their female slaves, see H. Beckles, 'White women and slavery in the Caribbean', *History Workshop Journal* 36, 1993, pp. 66–82.
44. *Slave Trade Committee Report*, vol. 82, p. 52.
45. See, for instance, *Negro Slavery: or, a view of some of the more prominent features of that state of society, as it exists in the United States of America and in the colonies of the West Indies, especially in Jamaica*, London; Hatchard and son, 1823, p. 42. On the link between women's finer sensibilities and their role as guardians of morality, see Shoemaker, *Gender in English Society*, pp. 23–4; and J. Tosh, *A Man's Place: masculinity and the middle-class home in Victorian England*, New Haven: Yale University Press, 1999, p. 44.
46. *A Word from the Bible, Common Prayer Book, and Laws of England, on Behalf of Enslaved British Subjects*, London: L. B. Seeley and sons, 1829, p.

55; and *Slave Trade Committee Report*, vol. 82, p. 152. For a fictive account of a white mistress flogging her slave women, see C. Smith, *The Wanderings of Warwick*, London: J. Bell, 1794, p. 54.
47. See, for instance, Campbell, *A Letter to Sir Robert Peel*, p. 53; Cooper as cited in *The Edinburgh Review*, February 1823, p. 174; and *Word from the Bible*, p. 54.
48. Bickell as cited in A. Barclay, *A Practical View of the Present State of Slavery in the West Indies*, London: Smith, Elder and co., 1827, p. 446.
49. *PP* 1831–32, XLVII, p. 385. She had ordered, or inflicted herself, a variety of corporal punishments, ranging from flogging and beating to confinement in the stocks. The women had suffered far more at her hands than at her husband's. Because of the common law doctrine of coverture, however, Mrs Jackson could not be sued for mistreating the slave women.
50. L. Davidoff and C. Hall, *Family Fortunes: men and women of the English middle class 1780–1850* [1987], London: Routledge, 1992, pp. 388–96.
51. *The Speech of James Losh, esq., in the Guildhall, Newcastle-upon-Tyne on the 31st March 1824*, Newcastle: T. and J. Hodgson, 1824, p. 10; and Trew as cited in Jackson, *A Memoir*, p. 113.
52. See, for instance, *The Edinburgh Review*, October-January 1824-25, p. 213; and *The Anti-Slavery Reporter*, February 1831, p. 29.
53. The term 'criminal justice system' refers here to the laws and the lawyers and judges in the island who interpreted and enforced them and decided upon punishments for those who transgressed them.
54. Bleby, *Death Struggles*, p. 79. Goderich argued that biased magistrates were also the main reason why the Council of Protection had dismissed the claim of Kate and Ann Whitfield. See *PP* 1831–32, XLVII, p. 385.
55. Bickell, *The West Indies as They Are*, p. 31; and *PP* 1831–32, XX, p. 266.
56. *PP* 1831–32, XLVI, p. 313. Shortly after this Council of Protection dismissed the case, the Colonial Office issued an investigation into the behaviour of the various magistrates and vestrymen who had sat on it.
57. Ibid., pp. 311–3. As a result of the postponements, one of the key witnesses had seen chance to leave the island.
58. *PP* 1831–32, XX, p. 266. From 1831 onwards slave evidence was only admitted in certain criminal cases against whites and was subject to several conditions. See *The Consolidated Slave Law, Passed the 22nd December, 1826, Commencing on the 1st May, 1827 with a Commentary, Shewing the Differences between the New Law and the Repealed Enactment*, N. p.: Courant Office, 1827 (hereafter, *1826 Slave Law*), p. 37.
59. *A General History*, p. 111. It was not only grand juries who dismissed slave evidence but also Councils of Protection and local justices, who were faced with slaves that claimed excessive flogging. See, for instance, Campbell, *Letter to Sir Robert Peel*, pp. 53–4; and *The Anti-Slavery Reporter*, February 1831, p. 135.
60. *PP* 1831–32, XVI, p. 230.
61. On this antislavery notion of freedom, see T. C. Holt, *The Problem of Freedom: race, labor and politics in Jamaica and Britain, 1832–1938*, Baltimore: Johns Hopkins University Press, 1992, pp. xxii and 26.
62. On the importance of this attribute in the definition of Englishness, see P. Langford, *Englishness Identified: manners and characters 1650–1850*, Oxford: Oxford University Press, 2000, pp. 138–56.
63. See, for instance, D. Lambert, '"True lovers of religion": Methodist persecution and white resistance to anti-slavery in Barbados, 1823–1825', *Journal of Historical Geography* 28, no. 2, 2002, pp. 216–36; S. Swaminathan,

'Developing the West Indian proslavery position after the Somerset decision', *Slavery and Abolition* 24, no. 3, 2003, pp. 40–60; D. Lambert, 'Producing/contesting whiteness: rebellion, anti-slavery and enslavement in Barbados, 1816', *Geoforum* 36, 2005, pp. 29–43; D. Lambert, *White Creole Culture, Politics and Identity during the Age of Abolition*, Cambridge: Cambridge University Press, 2005; and C. Petley, 'Slavery, emancipation and the creole world view of Jamaican colonists, 1800–1834', *Slavery and Abolition* 26, no. 1, 2005, pp. 91–114. This chapter draws especially on David Lambert's work on Barbados, which adds to earlier studies on the link between the slavery debate and Englishness, such as Linda Colley's *Britons: forging the nation, 1707–1837*, New Haven: Yale University Press, 1992 and Catherine Hall's, *White, Male and Middle Class*, in that it shows that this debate was not just a site where ideas about Englishness were employed and produced but also a place where they were contested.

64. De La Beche, *Notes on the Condition*, p. 32.
65. *Quarterly Review* 32, no. 64, 1825, p. 536.
66. Ibid.; and Lewis, *Journal of a West India Proprietor*, p. 119; and De La Beche, *Notes on the Condition*, p. 33.
67. *Marly; or, a planter's life in Jamaica*, Glasgow: Richard Griffin and co., 1828, p. 156.
68. See, for example, *Quarterly Review* 32, no. 64, 1825, p. 537.
69. Lewis, *Journal of a West India Proprietor*, p. 119.
70. 'Minutes West India Committee June 1823', *Institute of Commonwealth Studies* (hereafter, *ICS*), West India Committee, planters-merchants 1822–1829; and L. J. Ragatz, *The Fall of the Planter Class in the British Caribbean, 1763–1833* [1927], New York: Octagon Books, 1963, pp. 411–2.
71. PP 1824, XXIV, p. 443. Various other local legislatures refused to pass a ban on female flogging. For the Barbados legislature's attitude towards female flogging, see H. McD. Beckles, *Natural Rebels: a social history of enslaved black women in Barbados*, London: Zed Books, 1989, pp. 39–42.
72. PP 1826, XXIX, pp. 11–12; and *Quarterly Review* 32, no. 64, 1825, p. 537. The West India Committee was very active in the 1820s and early 1830s. It defended the slave system in periodicals, such as *Blackwood's Edinburgh Magazine*, and in its own journal *The West India Reporter* and in a wide range of pamphlets. Like the antislavery movement, it also organized lecture tours and held rallies. See Ragatz, *The Fall of the Planter Class*, pp. 426–9 and 447–9.
73. Blackburn, *The Overthrow of Colonial Slavery*, 433. On the Order in Council's ban on female flogging, see PP 1826–27, XXV, pp. 76–7.
74. PP 1826–27, XXV, p. 117. It was only after the Assembly was dissolved in March 1826 and a new Assembly had been appointed that the various clauses in the Order in Council for Trinidad were seriously considered for local implementation.
75. PP 1828, XXVII, p. 110.
76. PP 1836, XV, p. 224. The bill was accompanied by two other far-reaching measures: compulsory manumission and the establishment of a committee to investigate emancipation.
77. Various proposals were adopted besides the encouragement of slave marriage, including the admission of slave evidence in courts of law, the abolition of Sunday markets as a means to promote religious instruction, and the recognition of the slaves' personal property.
78. Some of these authors, however, favoured some degree of moderation in the practice, such as substituting the whip by rods or exempting pregnant women from the whip. See, for instance, [A. Davis], *The West Indies*, London: James

Cochrane, 1832, p. 65; and Jackson, *A Memoir*, p. 113. For metropolitan writers who opposed a ban on female flogging, see, for instance, the statements of Robert Scott and William Shand before the 1832 Select Committee in *PP* 1831–32, XX, pp. 337 and 481.
79. This strategy reflects the authors' influence by sentimental literature, which regarded the body as a reliable sign of one's identity. See K. Sanchez-Eppler, *Touching Liberty: abolition, feminism and the politics of the body*, Berkeley: University of California Press, 1997, p. 27.
80. C. R. Williams, *Tour Through the Island of Jamaica from the Western to the Eastern End in 1823*, London: Edward Chance and co., 1827, pp. 296–7.
81. Ibid., p. 13.
82. *State of Society and Slavery in Jamaica: in a reply to an article in the Edinburgh Review*, London: James Ridgway, 1824, p. 9. For a similar remark, see *Evidence upon Oath Touching the Condition and Treatment of the Negro Population of the British West India Colonies, part 1*, London: Mrs Ridgways, 1832, p. 17.
83. *Quarterly Review* 32, no. 64, 1825, p. 536.
84. [Davis], *The West Indies*, p. 59.
85. Barclay, *A Practical View*, p. 75. Emphasis mine.
86. Williams, *A Tour through the Island*, p. 131; and *PP* 1831–32, XX, p. 350.
87. [J. Stewart], *An Account of Jamaica, and Its Inhabitants by a Gentleman Long Resident in the West Indies*, London: Longman, Hurst, Rees and Orme, 1808, p. 152.
88. W. Sells, *Remarks on the Condition of the Slaves in the Island of Jamaica* [1823], Shannon: Irish University Press, 1972, p. 39.
89. *PP* 1831–32, XLVIII, pp. 380–1.
90. Barclay, *A Practical View*, p. 76. This court case from 1818 was not the best to combat the antislavery argument because the judge had reduced Boyden's sentence on the grounds of insufficient proof of excessive flogging.
91. [Davis], *The West Indies*, p. 35.
92. *Evidence upon Oath*, p. 37. For another confirmation of Davis' idea, see *PP* 1831–32, XLVII, p. 367.
93. Lambert, '"True lovers"', p. 222.
94. On the role of pain and suffering in humanitarian reform, see Halttunen, 'Humanitarianism'; and T. W. Laqueur, 'Bodies, details and the humanitarian narrative', in L. Hunt (ed.), *The New Cultural History*, Berkeley: University of California Press, 1989, pp. 176–204. On abolitionism as a humanitarian reform movement, see R. McGowen, 'Power and humanity, or Foucault among the historians', in C. Jones and R. Porter (eds.), *Reassessing Foucault: power, medicine and the body*, London: Routledge, 1994, pp. 91–112.
95. On the impact of the eighteenth-century 'cult of sensibility' on humanitarian reform, see G. J. Barker-Benfield, *The Culture of Sensibility: sex and society in eighteenth-century Britain*, Chicago: University of Chicago Press, 1992, pp. 224–31.
96. M. J. Wiener, *Reconstructing the Criminal: culture, law and policy in England, 1830–1914*, Cambridge: Cambridge University Press, 1990, pp. 93 and 100.
97. For more information on the antislavery concept of power, see McGowen, 'Power and humanity', pp. 106–7.

CHAPTER 6

1. *PP* 1836, XV, p. 409.

2. Male apprentices usually received a flogging of up to 39 lashes for minor offences and were for the more serious offences, such as violating the property of the employer, sentenced to time and labour in the workhouse. A return of punishments meted out by S.M.s between August 1834 and August 1835 suggests that it was mainly on account of 'neglect of duty', 'disobedience' and 'insolence' that female apprentices were sentenced to the workhouse. See *PP* 1836, XV, p. 560. The first workhouses were erected in the major sugar growing areas in the 1770s. By the 1820s, most parishes had a workhouse that housed runaway slaves, slaves privately committed by their owners, and slaves given prison sentences by the courts. For more information on the workhouses during slavery, see D. Paton, *No Bond but the Law: punishment, race, and gender in Jamaican state formation, 1780–1870*, Durham, N.C.: Duke University Press, 2004, chap. 1.
3. P.D. Curtin, *Two Jamaicas: the role of ideas in a tropical colony, 1830-65*, Cambridge, Mass.: Harvard University Press, 1955, pp. 74–5; W. L. Burn, *Emancipation and Apprenticeship in the British West Indies*, London: Jonathan Cape, 1937, pp. 279–80; and *PP* 1835, XV, pp. 506–34. The V.L.M.s and the members of the workhouse committees were mostly planters and other members of the local elite.
4. The treadmill was usually placed in the workhouse's courtyard and cells were arranged around it. The adoption of the treadmill in the island's workhouses was not only the result of pressure put on the Assembly by Governor Sligo. Influenced by metropolitan penal theories, some local magistrates were convinced that the mill could help to instil in apprentices the skills and habits required of wage labourers. They also believed that the hard labour carried out by workhouse inmates was so similar to work on the estates that only the treadmill could sufficiently act as a deterrent. As early as July 1834, adverts appeared in local papers directed at parish vestries and encouraging them to install treadmills in the workhouses. See, *PP* 1835, L, p. 73; Burn, *Emancipation and Apprenticeship*, p. 193; and Paton, *No Bond but the Law*, chap. 3.
5. For more information on the experiences of female apprentices in the workhouses, see my 'Slavery by another name: apprenticed women in Jamaican workhouses in the period 1834–38', *Social History* 26, no. 1, 2001, pp. 39–59.
6. [P. H. Sligo], *Jamaica under the Apprenticeship System by a Proprietor*, London: J. Andrews, 1838, p. 27.
7. The term 'abolitionists' refers in this chapter to those critics of apprenticeship whose writings were directly mobilized in the campaign to end apprenticeship and were usually published by or with strong support of the Anti-Slavery Society or the Central Negro Emancipation Committee.
8. W. Lloyd, *Letters from the West Indies, during a Visit in the Autumn of 1836 and the Spring of 1837*, London: Darton and Harvey, 1839, p. 164.
9. This is how Governor Sligo described the flogging of female workhouse inmates in one his reports from 1836. See *PP* 1836, XV, p. 47.
10. Ibid., pp. 6–7 and 314; and Burn, *Emancipation and Apprenticeship*, pp. 338–9. The Anti-Slavery Society was extremely disappointed in the report. Four antislavery writers (Joseph Sturge, Thomas Harvey, John Scoble, and William Lloyd) went to the West Indies in the autumn of 1836 to investigate the workings of apprenticeship for themselves. Their investigations resulted in two books: Lloyd's *Letters from the West Indies* and J. Sturge and T. Harvey's, *The West Indies in 1837: being the journal of a visit to Antigua, Montserrat, Dominica, St. Lucia, Barbados and Jamaica*, London: Hamilton, Adams, 1838.

11. As cited in J. H. Hinton, *Memoir of William Knibb: missionary in Jamaica*, London: Houlston and Stoneman, 1847, p. 232. See also the letters of the Baptist missionary Thomas Burchell to his brother published in W. F. Burchell, *Memoir of Thomas Burchell: twenty-two years a missionary in Jamaica*, London: Benjamin L. Green, 1849.
12. Based on the rules of 15 workhouses in *PP* 1836, XV, pp. 506–34. These additional practices lend further support to the idea that modern power in the colonial context worked through both the body and the soul.
13. [Sligo], *Jamaica under the Apprenticeship*, p. 23. Sligo mentioned this in response to the cutting off of the women's hair upon entering the workhouse.
14. H. Stern, *A Statement of Facts Submitted to the Right Hon. Lord Glenelg*, London: J.C. Chappell, 1837, p. 247. For other horrid descriptions, see *Statement and Observations on the Workings of the Laws for the Abolition of Slavery Throughout the British Colonies*, London: Anti-Slavery Society, 1836, p. 32; J. Sturge, *Horrors of the Negro Apprenticeship System in the British Colonies*, Glasgow: W. and W. Miller, 1837, p. 10; and Captain Studholme Hodgson, *Truths from the West Indies: including a sketch from Madeira in 1833*, London: William Ball, 1838, p. 322.
15. Sturge and Harvey, *The West Indies*, p. 336.
16. Statements made by apprentices before the Daughtrey and Gordon Commission suggest that apprenticed women strongly resisted the workhouse's disciplinary practices. Leanty Thomas' daughter, for instance, begged the workhouse supervisor to give her mother time to catch up on the mill. See *PP* 1837–38, XLIX, p. 194.
17. It is not surprising that abolitionists did not address the impact of the abuse on the women's partners and children because most of the abuse took place within the walls of the workhouse. The only spectators of the abuse were the officers who committed the crime, the V.L.M.s, and the other inmates.
18. Although often used as a euphemism for chastity, modesty referred at the time to a general pattern of reserved behaviour and self-effacement. See R. B. Shoemaker, *Gender in English Society, 1650–1850: the emergence of separate spheres?*, London: Longman, 1998, p. 23.
19. *An Appeal to the Christian Women of Sheffield from the Association for the Universal Abolition of Slavery*, Sheffield: R. Leader, 1837, p. 13.
20. *PP* 1836, XLVI, p. 62.
21. This particular indecency of the mill was also conveyed in an engraving of the treadmill that was included in editions of *A Narrative of Events, Since the First of August, 1834, by James Williams an Apprenticed Labourer in Jamaica* (1837) and was also sold separately. For an excellent analysis of this engraving, see Paton, *No Bond but the Law*, pp. 106–9.
22. Sturge and Harvey, *The West Indies*, pp. 155 and 219.
23. As cited in Burn, *Emancipation and Apprenticeship*, p. 284. Oldrey served as an anti-slavery witness before the 1836 Select Committee.
24. Paton, *No Bond but the Law*, p. 108.
25. Burn, *Emancipation and Apprenticeship*, p. 284.
26. This additional 'benefit' of the treadmill comes to the fore in statements made before the Daughtrey and Gordon Commission. See in particular the statements by Mary Ann Shaw, Lavinia Reynolds, Eleanor Howell and Elizabeth Bartley in *PP* 1837–38, XLIX, pp. 190–1.
27. *PP* 1836, XV, p. 7.
28. [Sligo], *Jamaica under the Apprenticeship*, p. 22. Emphasis mine.
29. Paton, *No Bond but the Law*, pp. 96–7.

230   Notes

30. [Sligo], *Jamaica under the Apprenticeship*, p. 23; and *PP* 1836, XV, p. 529. The 1836 Select Committee used a similar argument to denounce chaining. See *PP* 1836, XV, pp. 7 and 221.
31. *PP* 1836, XV, pp. 171 and 268. Newspaper proprietor and former Assembly member Beaumont had opposed the abolition of slavery but by the time he testified before the 1836 Select Committee, he had become a supporter of abolition of apprenticeship as well as a stern opponent of the Jamaican Assembly. See Burn, *Emancipation and Apprenticeship*, p. 337.
32. For a detailed account of how the mill injured women, see Sturge, *Horrors*, p. 11.
33. *Statement and Observations*, p. 32.
34. *PP* 1837, LIII, p. 127.
35. *PP* 1836, XV, p. 47; *PP* 1837, LIII, p. 46; and [Sligo], *Jamaica under the Apprenticeship*, pp. 27–30. During his time in office, Sligo regularly asked antislavery writers in England to undertake action to ensure that apprenticeship would correspond with the ideal described in the 1833 Abolition Act. In July 1835, for instance, he sent Lord Suffield information about female flogging and asked him to use it but without mentioning its source. See Burn, *Emancipation and Apprenticeship*, p. 335.
36. *PP* 1835, L, p. 73.
37. Ibid.
38. During the last year of his governorship, Sligo moved away from ensuring that apprenticeship would instil in apprentices the skills and habits required of docile and hardworking labourers and towards protecting the apprentices' newfound rights. See Curtin, *Two Jamaicas*, pp. 90–4.
39. As cited in *Statement and Observations*, p. 33. Emphasis mine. The newspaper had been instrumental in ending slavery by siding with antislavery writers and attacking the caste system in the island. See G. Heuman, *Between Black and White: race, politics, and the free coloreds in Jamaica, 1792–1865*, Oxford: Clio Press, 1981, p. 98. For other striking accounts of the impact of the practices on the officers' sensibility, see *PP* 1836, XLVIII, p. 63; and *A Statement of Facts Illustrating the Administration of the Abolition Law, and the Sufferings of the Negro Apprentices in the Island of Jamaica*, London, William Ball, 1837, p. 12.
40. Hodgson, *Truths from the West Indies*, p. 322. Various witnesses before the Daughtrey and Gordon Commission confirmed Hodgson's conclusion that only a small number of women consented to the drivers' wishes. For an interpretation of their statements and more information about the sexual abuse of female workhouse inmates, see my 'Slavery by another name:" p. 53; and Paton, *No Bond but the Law*, pp. 100–3.
41. [Sligo], *Jamaica under the Apprenticeship*, p. 20.
42. *PP* 1837, LIII, p. 46.
43. Sterne, *A Statement of Facts*, p. 216.
44. Ibid.
45. Sturge and Harvey, *The West Indies*, p. 226. The term 'Buckra' was used by slaves and apprentices to denote white men.
46. S.M.s could visit the workhouse but had no authority to change the rules or give orders to workhouse officers. They could only rectify instances of abuse in the workhouse by informing the governor about it. For a particularly strong denunciation of this inability of S.M.s to improve the workhouse discipline, see the statement of William Oldrey before the 1836 Select Committee in *PP* 1836, XV, p. 169.
47. *The Edinburgh Review*, January 1838, p. 519.

Notes 231

48. See, for instance, *PP* 1836, XV, p. 221.
49. *A Report of the Proceedings of the Public Meeting Held at Exeter Hall on Thursday 23rd of November 1837 to Take into Consideration the Present Condition of the Negro Apprentices in the British Colonies*, London: Central Negro Emancipation Committee, 1837, p. 26. For information on the Exeter Hall meeting, see Burn, *Emancipation and Apprenticeship*, pp. 344–6.
50. *PP* 1836, XLVIII, p. 66.
51. Chaining and the cutting off of hair were only mentioned in the 1834 Jamaica Gaols Act.
52. As cited in Rev. W. Bevan, *The Operation of the Apprenticeship System in the British Colonies*, Liverpool: D. Marple and co., 1838, p. 39. O'Connell had voted against the Abolition of Slavery Bill in May 1833 because he disapproved of the compensation proviso and considered the apprentices' rights to be too limited. See R. Blackburn, *The Overthrow of Colonial Slavery, 1776–1848*, London: Verso, 1988, p. 457. For similar statements, see *PP* 1836, XV, pp. 88, 169, and 314; Sturge and Harvey, *The West Indies*, p. 336; and Hinton, *Memoir of William Knibb*, p. 229.
53. *PP* 1836, XV, p. 46. For more information on the ways in which clause 17 was interpreted, see Burn, *Emancipation and Apprenticeship*, pp. 284–6.
54. The Assembly also failed to incorporate in the local Abolition Act the suggestion mentioned in clause 16 of the 1833 Abolition Act, namely that regulations be adopted for the 'prevention and punishment of cruelty, injustice or other wrongs or injury by the employer'. See *PP* 1836, XV, p. 409.
55. See, for example, *The Edinburgh Review*, January 1838, p. 519.
56. Sterne, *A Statement of Facts*, pp. 247–51.
57. Ibid., p. 251.
58. [Sligo], *Jamaica under the Apprenticeship*, p. 31.
59. Ibid., p. 28.
60. Ibid.
61. Ibid., pp. cxxii–cvxxiii. This bill was rejected on the grounds that four of the six affidavits denied the principal charge.
62. Ibid., p. 30.
63. Or, as one abolitionist pamphlet argued: 'It is utterly hopeless to depend . . . on the integrity and good faith of the Jamaica House of Assembly . . . not one atom of power will they ever, by their own acts and deed, be induced to surrender.' *A Statement of Facts*, pp. 42–3.
64. [Sligo], *Jamaica under the Apprenticeship*, pp. 29–30. The same idea was expressed in *A Statement of Facts*, p. 39.
65. Burn, *Emancipation and Apprenticeship*, p. 355.
66. *Speech of George Thompson at a Great Meeting for the Extinction of Negro Apprenticeship Held in the Town Hal, Devonport on Wednesday May 2nd 1838*, London: Central Negro Emancipation Office, 1838, p. 43.
67. As mentioned by Israel Lemon, the president of the workhouse committee of St. Ann, in his statement before the Daughtrey and Gordon Commission. *PP* 1837–38, XLIX, p. 193.
68. *PP* 1836, XV, p. 221.
69. *PP* 1836, XLVIII, p. 65; and *PP* 1836, XV, p. 394.
70. *PP* 1836, XLVIII, p. 335.
71. *PP* 1837-38, XLIX, pp. 193–4.
72. Henry Taylor, a senior clerk in the Colonial Office. As cited in Burn, *Emancipation and Apprenticeship*, p. 281.
73. *PP* 1836, XLVIII, p. 42. Burge referred here to the case of Mary Hennessy. As she had been sentenced to be confined in the workhouse rather than sentenced

232 *Notes*

to the penal gang and/or treadmill her hair should not have been shaven off. For other dismissals of Sligo's accusation that female flogging was a widespread practice, see *PP* 1836, XV, pp. 218 and 280; and *PP* 1836, XLVIII, p. 332.
74. *PP* 1836, XLVIII, p. 335.
75. *PP* 1837-38, XLIX, p. 198. Drake's successor, Alexander Levi, blamed in turn the mill overseer for any injuries sustained by women on the mill. See *PP* 1837–38, XLIX, pp. 132–3.
76. *PP* 1836, XLVIII, p. 420.
77. *PP* 1837-38, XLIX, p. 193.
78. On the use of this strategy with regards to chaining, see *PP* 1836, XV, pp. 221 and 281.
79. *PP* 1836, XLVIII, p. 331.
80. Ibid., p. 64.
81. Ibid., p. 334.
82. *PP* 1837, LIII, p. 132. On the use of this argument with regards to the cutting off of hair, see *PP* 1836, XLVIII, p. 64; and *PP* 1837, LIII, pp. 47–9.
83. See, for instance, the case of driver John Gordon and supervisor Sloly from the Falmouth workhouse in *PP* 1836, XV, p. 394.
84. *PP* 1836, XV, p. 396. Emphasis mine.
85. For a more detailed account of the ways in which the workhouse served as a means for the planters to regain some of their former power, see my 'Slavery by another name'.
86. The average hire of a workhouse inmate was 1s. and 3d. a day. *PP* 1836, XV, p. 511.
87. *PP* 1837–38, XLIX, p. 180.
88. On the planters' idea that the workhouse could transform apprentices into efficient and docile wage labourers, see Paton, *No Bond but the Law*, pp. 86–7.
89. Burn, *Emancipation and Apprenticeship*, pp. 279–80. The change in metropolitan prison legislation followed the 1835 report into the prison system in England and Wales. For more information on this change, see R. McGowen, 'The well-ordered prison: England, 1780–1865', in N. Morris and D. J. Rotman (eds.). *The Oxford History of the Prison: the practices of punishment in Western society*, New York: Oxford University Press, 1995, pp. 100–1; and M. Ignatieff, *A Just Measure of Pain: the penitentiary in the industrial revolution, 1750–1850*, London: Macmillan, 1978, p. 177.
90. Sligo's letter to the Assembly from June 1836 in which he mentioned 24 cases of illegal female flogging was primarily based on reports of such investigations. See *PP* 1836, XV, p. 394.
91. The investigation carried out by S.M. Bourne in March 1836 led, for instance, to three bills of indictment. See *PP* 1836, XV, p. 34; and *PP* 1836, XLVIII, pp. 402 and 414.
92. *PP* 1836, XLVIII, p. 417.
93. See, for instance, the demand of the St. John workhouse committee in *PP* 1837, LIII, p. 128.
94. As cited in Burn, *Emancipation and Apprenticeship*, p. 287.
95. Ibid.
96. In his response to one of the cases of female flogging mentioned by Sligo, Glenelg replied that the flogging of female apprentices for offences not connected to apprenticeship could be legal, such as disobeying orders of workhouse officers. See Burn, *Emancipation and Apprenticeship*, p. 284.

97. The governors simultaneously tried to prosecute workhouse officers accused of flogging female apprentices. For more information about this strategy, see my 'Slavery by another name', p. 56.
98. Especially Sligo put a lot of pressure on the Assembly. Smith, who assumed office in September 1836, was initially very conciliatory towards the Assembly. During his second year in office, however, he came to favour a policy of coercion. See Burn, *Emancipation and Apprenticeship*, p. 332.
99. PP 1836, XLVIII, p. 62. See also [Sligo], *Jamaica under the Apprenticeship*, p. 28.
100. As cited in Burn, *Emancipation and Apprenticeship*, p. 285.
101. PP 1836, XV, p. 177. Sligo referred here to the local Abolition Act, which interpreted clause 17 of the 1833 Abolition Act in clause 21.
102. Ibid., p. 173.
103. Ibid., p. 522.
104. Ibid., pp. 174–5.
105. PP 1836, XLVIII, p. 414.
106. PP 1836, XV, p. 395.
107. Ibid., p. 394.
108. These reports provided a less rose-coloured picture of the workhouses than the inquiry into the island's penal system, which was carried out by Sligo on the orders of the Colonial Office between December 1835 and February 1836 and used a written questionnaire. PP 1836, XV, p. 506.
109. PP 1837–38, XLIX, p. 272.
110. Ibid.
111. As mentioned in Paton, *No Bond but the Law*, p. 90.
112. The former campaign began in November 1835 and the latter in June 1836.
113. Workhouse committees and the courts formed the planters' second line of defence. The committees confirmed the Assembly's standpoint by refusing to change their rules, whereas the courts ensured that officers accused of abusing female workhouse inmates were acquitted and that there was thus no deterrent for officers to carry out specific wishes of local planters or otherwise transgress the workhouse rules.
114. Burn, *Emancipation and Apprenticeship*, p. 361; and Paton, *No Bond but the Law*, p. 118. In February 1838, the Colonial Office had already called for such an act. It drew heavily upon the recommendations mentioned in Captain Pringle's report of the West India prison system. Following the 1836 Select Committee report and various other bad reports from the island, the Colonial Office appointed Captain Pringle in August 1837 to investigate the penal system in Jamaica and several other islands.
115. Paton, *No Bond but the Law*, p. 118. The West India Prisons Act led to a huge clash between the Imperial government and the Jamaican Assembly. Various people spoke out in favour of colonial autonomy, while the Imperial government contemplated imposing direct rule on the island. The Imperial government eventually suspended the Jamaican assembly. It was not restored until June 1839 after it had passed remedial legislation. For more information on the debate surrounding the West India Prisons Act, see T. C. Holt, *The Problem of Freedom: race, labor and politics in Jamaica and Britain, 1832–1938*, Baltimore: Johns Hopkins University Press, 1992, pp. 108–12; and Paton, *No Bond but the Law*, pp. 118–20.
116. Sterne, *A Statement of Facts*, p. vii.
117. McGowen, 'The well-ordered Prison', pp. 85–97. Another abolitionist who played a crucial role in the metropolitan prison reform campaign was Joseph

234 Notes

   Sturge. He made a tour of American penal institutions in order to devise an appropriate discipline system for British prisons.
118. Paton, *No Bond but the Law*, p. 88.
119. On the penal reformers' accusations of prison officers, see McGowen, 'The well-ordered prison', p. 82.
120. For more information on these features of the metropolitan prison system, see McGowen, 'The well-ordered Prison', pp. 79–110; and J. Briggs, C. Harrison, A. McInnes and D. Vincent, *Crime and Punishment in England: an introductory history*, London: University College of London Press, 1996, pp. 159–61.
121. As is most clearly expressed in [Sligo], *Jamaica under the Apprenticeship*, p. 24.

CONCLUSION

1. W. A. Beckford, *Remarks upon the Situation of Negroes in Jamaica; impartially made from a local experience of nearly thirteen years in that island*, London: T. and J. Egerton, 1788, p. 24.
2. A. Barclay, *A Practical View of the Present State of Slavery in the West Indies*, London: Smith, Elder and co., 1827, p. 422.
3. For studies that have examined this process mainly based on contemporary comparisons between metropolitan middle-class women and their social superiors and inferiors, see L. Davidoff and C. Hall, *Family Fortunes: men and women of the English middle class 1780–1850* [1987], London: Routledge, 1992; and J. Perkin, *Women and Marriage in Nineteenth-century England*, London: Routledge, 1989. It is mainly in studies that explore the maturation of the metropolitan, middle-class womanhood ideal in the latter part of the nineteenth century that references are made to women in the colonies. See, for example, A. Davin, 'Imperialism and motherhood', *History Workshop Journal 5*, 1978, pp. 9–65; and various articles in P. Levine (ed.), *Gender and Empire*, Oxford: Oxford University Press, 2004; and C. Midgeley (ed.), *Gender and Imperialism*, Manchester: Manchester University Press, 1995.
4. The discourses of slavery and abolition mirror in this respect other colonial discourses. As Homi K. Bhabha has argued 'the construction of the colonial subject in discourse, and the exercise of colonial power through discourse demands an articulation of forms of difference — racial and sexual. Such an articulation becomes crucial if it is held that the body is always simultaneously inscribed in both the economy of pleasure and desire and the economy of discourse, domination and power'. 'The other question: difference, discrimination, and the discourse of colonialism', in R. Ferguson, M. Gever, T. T. Minn-ha and C. West (eds.), *Out There: marginalization and contemporary cultures*, Cambridge, Mass.: MIT press, 1990, p. 72.
5. *PP* 1836, XV, p. 71.
6. See, for instance, W. L. Burn, *Emancipation and Apprenticeship in the British West Indies*, London: Jonathan Cape, 1937, p. 289; and P. D. Curtin, *Two Jamaicas: the role of ideas in a tropical colony 1830–1865*, Cambridge, Mass.: Harvard University Press, 1955, p. 94.
7. *PP* 1836, XV, p. 425.
8. E. B. Higginbotham, 'African-American women's history and the metalanguage of race', *Signs* 17, no. 2, 1992, p. 253.

9. R. Wheeler, *The Complexion of Race: categories of difference in eighteenth-century British culture*, Philadelphia: University of Philadelphia Press, 2000, p. 7.
10. See, for instance, S. Wilmott, '"Females of abandoned character"?: women and protest in Jamaica 1838–65', in V. Shepherd, B. Brereton, and B. Bailey (eds.), *Engendering History: Caribbean women in historical perspective*, Kingston: Ian Randle, 1995, pp. 279–95; M. Sheller, 'Quasheba, mother, queen: black women's public leadership and political protest in post-emancipation Jamaica 1834–65', *Slavery and Abolition* 19, no. 3, 1998, pp. 90–117; and B. Brereton, 'Family strategies, gender, and the shift to wage labor in the British Caribbean', in B. Brereton and K. Yelvington (eds.), *The Colonial Caribbean in Transition: essays on post-emancipation social and cultural history*, Mona, Jamaica: University of the West Indies Press, 1999, pp. 77–107.
11. The participants in this debate were not that dissimilar from those in the debates about slavery and abolition and included missionaries, colonial officials, members of parliament, and abolitionists. Catherine Hall has explored the missionaries' accounts of the progress of the ex-slaves in various works, including 'White visions, black lives: the free villages of Jamaica', *History Workshop Journal* 36, 1993, pp. 100–32 and *Civilising Subjects: metropole and colony in the English imagination 1830–1867*, Cambridge: Polity Press, 2002. Howard Temperley has examined the attitudes of the British and Foreign Anti-Slavery Society to the progress of emancipation in his *British Antislavery, 1833–1870*, London: Longman, 1972.

Bibliography

PRIMARY SOURCES

Manuscript sources

      Public Record Office (PRO), The National Archives, Kew, U.K.
CO 137. Original Correspondence, Jamaica.
CO 140. Sessional Papers, Jamaica.
CO 142. Miscellanea, Jamaica.
      Jamaica Archives (JA), Spanish Town.
Moravian Archives. H/6-H7, J/19, and Q7-10.
Thomas Davis Special Magistrate. 4/47.
      Institute of Commonwealth Studies (ICS), London.
West India Committee. Minutes of Planters and Merchants, 1822–29.

Parliamentary papers (PP)

1818, XVII, 'Papers Relating to Treatment of Slaves in the Colonies'.
1823, XVIII, 'Papers Relative to Slave Population of Jamaica, St. Christopher's and Bahamas'.
1824, XXVI, 'Papers in Explanation of Measures for Melioration of Condition of Slave Population in West Indies and South America'.
1826, XXIX, 'Papers in Explanation of Measures for Melioration of Condition of Slave Population in West Indies and South America'.
1826–27, XXV, 'Papers in Explanation of Measures for Melioration of Condition of Slave Population in West Indies and South America'.
1826–27, XXVI, 'Papers in Explanation of Measures for Melioration of Condition of Slave Population in West Indies and South America'.
1828, XXII, 'Papers in Explanation of Measures adopted for Melioration of Condition of Slave Population in H.M. Possessions in West Indies, South America and Mauritius'.
1830, XXI, 'Papers in Explanation of Measures adopted for Melioration of Condition of Slave Population in H.M. Possessions in West Indies, South America and Mauritius'.
1830–31, XVI, 'Information from Jamaica Respecting Inquiry into Treatment of Female Slave'.
1831–32, XX, 'Report of the Select Committee on Extinction of Slavery in British Dominions'.

1831–32, XLVI, 'Papers in Explanation of Measures for Melioration of Condition of Slave Population in H.M. Possessions in West Indies, South America, Cape of Good Hope and Mauritius'.
1831–32, XLVII, 'Correspondence Relative to Punishment of Two Female Slaves at Port Royal, Jamaica'.
1833, IV, 'Bill for Abolition of Slavery throughout British Colonies, for Promoting Industry of Manumitted Slaves, and for Compensating Owners'.
1835, L, 'Papers in Explanation of Measures to Give Effect to Act for Abolition of Slavery, Part I and II'.
1836, XV, 'Report of Select Committee on Negro Apprenticeship in Colonies'.
1836, XLVIII, 'Papers in Explanation of Measures to Give Effect to Act for Abolition of Slavery, Part III'.
1837, LIII, 'Papers in Explanation of Measures to Give Effect to Act for Abolition of Slavery, Part IV'.
1837–38, XLIX, 'Papers in Explanation of Measures to Give Effect to Act for Abolition of Slavery, Part V'.

Other official documents

Lambert, S. (ed.), *House of Commons Sessional Papers of the Eighteenth Century (Slave Trade Committee Report)*, vols 69, 70, 72, 82, and 122, Wilmington, Del.: Scholarly Resources, 1975.
The Consolidated Slave law, Passed the 22nd December 1826, Commencing on the 1st May 1827 with a Commentary Shewing the Differences between the New Law and the Repealed Enactment (1826 Slave Law), N.p.: Courant Office, 1827.

Periodicals

Anti-Slavery Reporter, 1831.
Edinburgh Review, 1823–1825 and 1838.
Quarterly Review, 1825.
Westminster Review, 1827.

Printed primary sources

A Concise View of Colonial Slavery, Newcastle: T. and J. Hodgson, 1830.
Adair, J. M., *Unanswerable Arguments against the Abolition of the Slave Trade with a Defence of the Proprietors of the British Sugar Colonies*, London: privately published, 1790.
Address to the Public on the Present State of the Question Relative to Negro Slavery in the British Colonies, York: W. Alexander and son, 1828.
A Dialogue between a Well-Wisher and a Friend to the Slaves in the British Colonies by a Lady, N.p.: n.d.
A General History of Negro Slavery: collected from the most respectable evidence and unquestionable authorities, Cambridge: Hatfield, 1826.
A Letter to John Bull: to which is added the sketch of a plan for the safe, speedy, and effectual abolition of slavery by a free-born Englishman, London: Hatchard, 1824.
An Address on the State of Slavery in the West India Islands from the Committee of the Leicester Auxiliary Anti-Slavery Society, London: Hamilton, 1824.

An Address to the Christian Women of Sheffield from the Association for the Universal Abolition of Slavery, Sheffield: R. Leader, 1837.
An Appeal to Common Sense on Behalf of Justice, Humanity, and Religion in a Letter Addressed to Henry Bright, m.p., Bristol: Barry and son, 1823.
Anderson, J., *Observations on Slavery: particularly with a view to its effects on the British colonies in the West Indies*, Manchester: J. Harrop, 1789.
Anecdotes of Africans, London: Harvey and Darton, 1827.
A Plan for the Abolition of Slavery Consistently with the Interests of All Parties Concerned, London: George Sidford, 1828.
A Report of the Proceedings of the Public Meeting held at Exeter Hall on Thursday 23rd of November 1837 to Take into Consideration the Present Condition of the Negro Apprentices in the British Colonies, London: Central Negro Emancipation Committee, 1837.
A Statement of Facts Illustrating the Administration of the Abolition Law and the Sufferings of the Negro Apprentices in the Island of Jamaica, London: William Ball, 1837.
A Word from the Bible, Common Prayer Book, and Laws of England on Behalf of Enslaved British Subjects, London: L. B. Seeley and sons, 1829.
Bage, R., *Man as He Is* [1792], in S. Aravamudan (ed.), *Slavery, Abolition and Emancipation: writings in the British romantic period*, vol. 6, London: Pickering and Cato, 1999.
Barclay, A., *A Practical View of the Present State of Slavery in the West Indies*, London: Smith, Elder and co., 1827.
Beckford, W., *Remarks upon the Situation of Negroes in Jamaica; impartially made from a local experience of nearly thirteen years in that island*, London: T. and J. Egerton, 1788.
Bevan, W., *The Operation of the Apprenticeship System in the British Colonies*, Liverpool: D. Marple and co., 1838.
Bickell, R., *The West Indies as They Are; or, a real picture of slavery but more particularly as it exists in the island of Jamaica in three parts with notes*, London: J. Hatchard and son, 1825.
Bleby, H., *Death Struggles of Slavery: being a narrative of facts and incidents which occurred in a British colony, during the two years immediately preceding Negro emancipation*, London: Hamilton, Adams and co., 1853.
Bridges, G. W., *The Annals of Jamaica*, London: John Murray, 1826.
Burchell, W. F., *Memoir of Thomas Burchell, Twenty-Two Years a Missionary in Jamaica*, London: Benjamin L. Green, 1849.
Burke, E., *Sketch of the Negro Code* [1792], in P. Kitson (ed.) *Slavery, Abolition and Emancipation: writings in the British romantic period*, vol. 2, London: Pickering and Cato, 1999.
[Campbell, C.], *Memoirs of Charles Campbell at Present Prisoner in the Jail of Glasgow: including his adventures as a seaman, and as an overseer in the West Indies written by himself*, Glasgow: James Duncan and co., 1828.
Campbell, J., *A Letter to Sir Robert Peel on the Subject of British Colonial Slavery*, Edinburgh: Colston, 1830.
Clarkson, T., *An Essay on the Impolicy of the African Slave Trade in Two Parts*, London: J. Phillips, 1788.
———, *Thoughts on the Necessity of Improving the Condition of the Slaves in the British Colonies: with a view to their ultimate emancipation*, London: Hatchard, 1824.
Collins, *Practical Rules for the Management and Medical Treatment of Negro Slaves in the Sugar Colonies by a Professional Planter*, London: J. Barfield, 1803.

Considerations on the Expediency of an Improved Mode of Treatment of Slaves in the West Indian Colonies Relatively to an Increase of Population, London: Spragg, 1820.

Cooper, T., *Facts Illustrative of the Condition of the Negro Slaves in Jamaica with Notes and an Appendix*, London: Hatchard, 1824.

Cundall, F. (ed.), *Lady Nugent's Journal: Jamaica one hundred years ago reprinted from a journal kept by Maria, Lady Nugent, from 1801 to 1815 issued for private circulation in 1839*, London: Adam and Charles Black, 1907.

[Davis, A.], *The West Indies*, London: James Cochrane and co., 1832.

De La Beche, H. T., *Notes on the Present Condition of the Negroes in Jamaica*, London: T. Cadell, 1825.

Edgeworth, M., *The Grateful Negro* [1804], in S. Aravamudan (ed.), *Slavery, Abolition and Emancipation: writings in the British romantic period*, vol. 6, London: Pickering and Cato, 1999.

Edwards, B., *The History Civil and Commercial of the British Colonies in the West Indies 2 vols.*, London: John Stockdale, 1793.

Eliot, E., *Christian Responsibilities Arising out of the Recent Change in Our West India Colonies: in five discourses, four preached in the West Indies and one in England*, London: J. W. Parker, 1836.

Evidence upon Oath Touching the Condition and Treatment of the Negro Population of the British West India Colonies, part I, London: Mrs Ridgways, 1833.

Foot, J., *A Defence of the Planters in the West Indies Comprised in Four Arguments*, London: J. Debrett, 1792.

———, *Observations Principally upon the Speech of Mr. Wilberforce on his Motion in the House of Commons the 30th of May 1804*, London: T. Becket, 1805.

Foulks, T., *Eighteen Months in Jamaica with Recollections of the Late Rebellion*, London: Whittaker, Treacher, Arnott, 1833.

Francklyn, G., *Observations Occasioned by the Attempts Made in England to Affect the Abolition of the Slave Trade*, Kingston: J. Walker, 1788.

Gibbes, P., *Instructions for the Treatment of Negroes*, London: Shepperson and Reynolds, 1788.

Godwin, B., *The Substance of a Course of Lectures on British Colonial Slavery Delivered at Bradford, York and Scarborough*, London: J. Hatchard and son, 1830.

[Grainger], *An Essay on the More Common West Indian Diseases: and the remedies which that country itself produces to which are added some hints on the management of the Negroes by a physician in the West Indies*, London: T. Becker, 1804.

Hakewill, J., *A Picturesque Tour of the Island of Jamaica from Drawings Made in the Years 1820 and 1821*, London: Hurst and Robinson, 1825.

Hamel, The Obeah Man 2 vols., London: Hunt and Clarke, 1827.

Helme, E., *The Farmer of Inglewood Forest; or, an affecting portrait of virtue and vice*, London: George Virtue, 1824.

Henderson., *A Brief View of the Actual Condition and Treatment of the Negro Slaves in the British Colonies in a Letter to a Member of the Imperial Parliament*, London: Baldwin, Cradock, Joy, 1816.

Hibbert, R., *Hints to the Young Jamaica Sugar Planter*, London: T. and G. Underwood, 1825.

Hinton, J. H., *Memoir of William Knibb, Missionary in Jamaica*, London: Houlston and Stoneman, 1847.

Hodgson, S., *Truths from the West Indies: including a sketch of Madeira in 1833*, London: William Ball 1838.

Holroyd, J. B., *Observations on the Project for Abolishing the Slave Trade and on the Reasonableness of Attempting Some Practical Mode of Relieving the Negroes* [1790], in P. Kitson (ed.), *Slavery, Abolition and Emancipation: writings in the British romantic period*, vol. 2, London: Pickering and Cato, 1999.

Jackson, G., *A Memoir of the Rev. John Jenkins late a Wesleyan Missionary in the Island of Jamaica: including characteristic notices of West Indian slavery etc.*, London: Rev. J. Mason, n. d.

Jackson, T., *Britain's Burden; or, the intolerable evils of colonial slavery exposed*, Cambridge: Metcalfe, 1832.

Kelly, J., *Voyage to Jamaica and Seventeen Years' Residence in that Island*, Belfast: J. Wilson, 1838.

Lewis, M. G., *Journal of a West India Proprietor; kept during a residence in the island of Jamaica* [1834], London: John Murray, 1838.

Lloyd, W., *Letters from the West Indies during a Visit in the Autumn of 1836 and the Spring of 1837*, London: Darton and Harvey, 1839.

Long, E., *History of Jamaica, or General Survey of the Antient and Modern State of that Island: with reflections on its situations, settlements, inhabitants, climate, products, commerce, laws, and government* [1774], London: Frank Cass, 1970.

M'Mahon, B., *Jamaica Plantership*, London: Effingham Wilson, 1839.

McNeill, H., *Observations on the Treatment of the Negroes in the Island of Jamaica: including some account of their temper and character*, London: G. J. and J. Robinson, 1788.

McQueen, J., *The West Indian Colonies: the calumnies and misrepresentations circulated against them by the Edinburgh Review, Mr. Clarkson, Mr. Cropper etc.*, London: Baldwin, Cradock and Joy, 1824.

Marjoribanks., *Slavery: an essay in verse*, Edinburgh: J. Robertson, 1802.

Marly; or, a planter's life in Jamaica, Glasgow: Richard Griffin and co., 1828.

Mathison, G., *Notices Respecting Jamaica in 1808–1809–1810*, London: John Stockdale, 1811.

Moreton, J. B., *West India Customs and Manners*, London: J. Parson, 1793.

Negro Apprenticeship in the British Colonies, London: Office of the Anti-Slavery Society, 1838.

Negro Slavery; or, a view of some of the more prominent features of that state of society as it exists in the United States of America and in the colonies of the West Indies, especially in Jamaica, London: Hatchard and son, 1823.

Paton, D. (ed.), *A Narrative of Events, Since the First of August, 1834, by James Williams, an Apprenticed labourer in Jamaica* [1837], Durham, N.C.: Duke University Press, 2001.

Phillippo, J., *Jamaica: its past and present state*, London: John Snow, 1843.

Plan for Effecting Emancipation by the Redemption of Female Slaves Laid before Government in 1824, in Plans of Emancipation, London: Baster and Thomas, 1824.

Ramsay, J., *Essay on the Treatment and Conversion of African Slaves in the British Sugar Colonies*, Dublin: T. Walker and C. Jenking, 1784.

Remarks on the Injustice and Immorality of Slavery in Eight Letters by the Rev. George Whitfield, London: John Stephens, 1830.

Renny, R., *A History of Jamaica with Observations*, London: Cawthorn, 1807.

Review of the Quarterly Review; or, an exposure of the erroneous opinions promulgated in that work on the subject of colonial slavery, being a substance of a series of letters which appeared in the 'New Times' of September and October 1824, London: Hatchard, 1824.

Riland, J. (ed.), *Memoirs of a West India Planter: published from an original ms*, London: Hamilton, Adams and co., 1827.

Rose, G. H., *A Letter on the Means and Importance of Converting the Slaves in the West Indies to Christianity*, London: Murray, 1823.

Roughley, T., *The Jamaica Planter's Guide; or, a system for planting and managing a sugar estate*, London: Longman, Hurst, Rees, Orme and Brown, 1823.

[Rushton, E.], *West Indian Eclogues*, London: J. Phillips, 1787.

Scott, M., *Tom Cringle's Log*, London: J. M. Dent and sons, 1836.

Sells, W., *Remarks on the Condition of the Slaves in the Island of Jamaica* [1823], Shannon: Irish University Press, 1972.

Sketches and Recollections of the West Indies by a Resident, London: Smith and Elder, 1828.

[Sligo, P. H.], *Jamaica under the Apprenticeship System by a Proprietor*, London: J. Andrew, 1838.

Smith, C., *The Wanderings of Warwick*, London: J. Bell, 1794.

Speech of George Thompson at a Great Meeting for the Extinction of Negro Apprenticeship Held in the Town Hall Devonport on Wednesday May 2nd 1838, London: Central Negro Emancipation Office, 1838.

Statements and Observations on the Workings of the Laws for the Abolition of Slavery Throughout the British Colonies and the Present State of the Negro Condition, London: Anti-Slavery Society, 1836.

State of Society and Slavery in Jamaica: in a reply to an article in the Edinburgh Review, London: James Ridgway, 1824.

Sterne, H., *A Statement of Facts Submitted to the right hon. Lord Glenelg*, London: J. C. Chappell, 1837.

[Stewart, J.], *An Account of Jamaica and Its Inhabitants by a Gentleman, Long Resident in the West Indies*, London: Longman, Hurst, Rees and Orme, 1808.

——, *A View of the Past and Present State of the Island of Jamaica: with remarks about the moral and physical condition of the slaves and on the abolition of slavery in the colonies*, Edinburgh: Oliver and Boyd, 1823.

Sturge, J., *Horrors of the Negro Apprenticeship System in the British Colonies*, Glasgow: W. and W. Miller, 1837.

——, and Harvey, T., *The West Indies in 1837; Being the Journal of a Visit to Antigua, Montserrat, Dominica, St. Lucia, Barbados and Jamaica*, London: Hamilton, Adams and co., 1838.

The Death Warrant of Negro Slavery Throughout the British Dominions, London: Hatchard, 1829.

The Edinburgh Review and the West Indies: with observations on the pamphlets of Messrs Stephen, Macauly, and remarks on the slave registry bill by colonist, Glasgow: John Smith and son, 1816.

The Koromantyn Slaves, London: J. Hatchard, 1823.

The Negro's Friend; or, the Sheffield anti-slavery album, Sheffield: Blackwell, 1826.

The Negro's Memorial; or, abolitionist's catechism, by an abolitionist, London: Hatchard 1825.

The Speech of James Losh, esq. in the Guildhall Newcastle-upon-Tyne on the 31st March 1824, Newcastle: T. and J. Hodgson, 1824.

Thome, J. A. and Kimball, J. H., *Emancipation in the West Indies, a Six Months' Tour in Antigua, Barbadoes, and Jamaica, in the Year 1837*, New York: American Anti-Slavery Society, 1838.

Thomson, A., *Substance of the Speech Delivered at the Meeting of the Edinburgh Society for the Abolition of Slavery on October 19, 1830*, Edinburgh: Whyte and co., 1830.

[Tobin], *Cursory Remarks upon the Reverend Mr. Ramsay's Essay on the Treatment and Conversion of African Slaves in the Sugar Colonies by a Friend of the West Indian Colonies and their Inhabitants*, London: G. and T. Wilkie, 1785.
[Trew], *Nine Letters to His Grace the Duke of Wellington on Colonial Slavery by Ignotus*, London: William Stroker, 1830.
[Turnbull, G.], *An Apology for Negro Slavery; or, the West India planters vindicated from the charge of inhumanity by the author of letters to a young planter*, London: Stuart and Stevenson, 1786.
Waddell, H. M., *Twenty-Nine Years in the West Indies and Central Africa: a review of missionary work and adventure, 1829–1858* [1863], London: Frank Cass, 1970.
Wedderburn, R., *The Horrors of Slavery; exemplified in the life and history of the Rev. Robert Wedderburn*, London: R. Carlile, 1824.
Whiteley, H., *Excessive Cruelty to Slaves: three months in Jamaica in 1832, comprising a residence of seven weeks on a sugar plantation*, London: Hatchard, 1833.
Wilberforce, W., *An Appeal to the Religion, Justice and Humanity of the Inhabitants of the British Empire on Behalf of Its Negro Slaves in the West Indies* [1823], in P. Kitson (ed.), *Slavery, Abolition and Emancipation: writings in the British romantic period, vol. 2*, London: Pickering and Cato, 1999.
Williams, C. R., *A Tour Through the Island of Jamaica from the Western to the Eastern End in the Year 1823*, London: Thomas Hurst, Edward Chance and co., 1827.
Winn, T. S., *Emancipation; or, practical advice to British slaveholders with suggestions for the general improvement of West India affairs*, London: W. Phillips, 1824.

SECONDARY SOURCES

Altink, H. 'Slavery by another name: apprenticed women in Jamaican workhouses in the period 1834–8', *Social History* 26, no. 1, 2001, pp. 40–59.
———, '"To wed or not to wed?": the struggle to define Afro-Jamaican relationships, 1834–38', *Journal of Social History* 38, no. 1, 2004, pp. 81–111.
———, 'More than producers and reproducers', in S. Courtman (ed.), *Beyond the Blood, The Beach and the Banana: new perspectives in Caribbean studies*, Kingston: Ian Randle, 2004, pp. 71–90.
Baigent, E., 'James MacQueen (1778–1870)', in *Oxford Dictionary of National Biography*, Oxford: Oxford University Press, 2004. Available at http://www.oxforddnb.com/view/article/17736 (accessed 9 September 2005).
Banton, M., *The Idea of Race*, London: Tavistock Publishers, 1977.
Barker-Benfield, G. J., *The Culture of Sensibility: sex and society in eighteenth-century Britain*, Chicago: University of Chicago Press, 1992.
Beattie, J. M., *Crime and the Courts in England, 1660–1800*, Oxford: Clarendon Press, 1986.
Beckles, H. McD., *Natural Rebels: a social history of enslaved black women in Barbados*, London: Zed Books, 1989.
———, 'White women in slavery in the Caribbean', *History Workshop Journal* 36, 1993, pp. 66–82.
———, 'Sex and gender in the historiography of Caribbean slavery', in V. Shepherd, B. Brereton, and B. Bailey (eds.), *Engendering History: Caribbean women in historical perspective*, New York: St. Martin's Press, 1995, pp. 125–40.

―――, 'Female enslavement and gender ideologies in the Caribbean', in P. E. Lovejoy (ed.), *Identity in the Shadow of Slavery*, London: Continuum, 2000, pp. 163–82.

―――, 'Black masculinity in Caribbean slavery', in R. E. Reddock (ed.), *Interrogating Caribbean Masculinities: theoretical and empirical analyses*, Kingston: University of the West Indies Press, 2004, pp. 225–43.

Bhabha, H. K., 'The other question: difference, discrimination, and the discourse of colonialism', in R. Ferguson, M. Gever, T. T. Minn-ha, and C. West (eds.), *Out There: marginalization and contemporary cultures*, Cambridge, Mass.: MIT Press, 1990, pp. 71–87.

Binhammer, K., 'The sex panic of the 1790s', *Journal of the History of Sexuality* 6, no. 3, 1996, pp. 409–34.

Blackburn, R., *The Overthrow of Colonial Slavery, 1776–1848*, London: Verso, 1988.

Blouet, O. M., 'Earning and learning in the British West Indies: an image of freedom in the pre-emancipation decade 1823–1833', *The Historical Journal* 34, no. 2, 1991, pp. 391–409.

Borris, E. and Janssens, A., 'Complicating categories: an introduction', *International Review of Social History* 44, 1999, pp. 1–12.

Botkin, F. R., 'Questioning the "necessary order of things": Maria Edgeworth's "The Grateful Negro", plantation slavery, and the abolition of the slave trade', in B. Carey, M. Ellis, and S. Salih (eds.), *Discourses of Slavery and Abolition: Britain and its colonies, 1760–1838*, Basingstoke: Palgrave Macmillan, 2004, pp. 194–208.

Boulukos, G., 'Maria Edgeworth's "Grateful Negro" and the sentimental argument for slavery', *Eighteenth-Century Life* 23, no. 1, 1999, pp. 12–29.

Bowers, T., *The Politics of Motherhood: British writing and culture 1680–1760*, Cambridge: Cambridge University Press, 1996.

Branca, P., *Women in Europe since 1750*, London: Croom Helm, 1978.

Brathwaite, E., *The Development of Creole Society in Jamaica 1770–1820*, Oxford: Clarendon Press, 1971.

Brereton, B., 'Family strategies, gender, and the shift to wage labor in the British Caribbean', in B. Brereton and K. Yelvington (eds.), *The Colonial Caribbean in Transition: essays on post-emancipation social and cultural history*, Mona: University of the West Indies Press, 1999, pp. 77–107.

Briggs, J., Harrison C., McInnes, A., and Vincent, D., *Crime and Punishment in England: an introductory history*, London: University College of London Press, 1996.

Burn, W. L., *Emancipation and Apprenticeship in the British West Indies*, London: Jonathan Cape, 1937.

Burnard, T., 'The sexual life of an eighteenth-century Jamaican slave overseer', in M. D. Smith (ed.), *Sex and Sexuality in Early America*, New York: New York University Press, 1998, pp. 163–89.

―――, 'Theatre of terror: domestic violence in Thomas Thistlewood's Jamaica', in C. Daniels and M. V. Kennedy (eds.), *Over the Threshold: intimate violence in early America*, London: Routledge, 1999, pp. 237–53.

―――, *Mastery, Tyranny, and Desire: Thomas Thistlewood and his slaves in the Anglo-Jamaican world*, Chapel Hill: The University of North Carolina Press, 2004.

Bush, B., *Slave Women in Caribbean Society, 1650–1838*, London: James Currey, 1990.

―――, 'Hard labor: women, childbirth and resistance in British Caribbean slave societies', *History Workshop Journal* 36, 1993, pp. 83–99.

——, 'History, memory, myth?: reconstructing the history or (histories) of black women in the African Diaspora', in S. Newell (ed.), *Images of African and Caribbean Women: migration, displacement and Diaspora*, Stirling: Centre of Commonwealth Studies, 1996, pp. 3–28.

——, '"Sable Venus", "she devil" or "drudge"?: British slavery and the "fabulous fiction" of black women's identities, c. 1650–1838', *Women's History Review* 9, no. 4, 2000, pp. 761–89.

——. 'From slavery to freedom: black women, cultural resistance and identity in Caribbean plantation society', in T. Bremer and U. Fleishmann (eds.), *History and Histories in the Caribbean*, Frankfurt am Main: Vervuert, 2001, pp. 115–59.

Carey, B., Ellis, M. and Salih, S. (eds.), *Discourses of Slavery and Abolition: Britain and its colonies, 1760–1838*, Basingstoke: Palgrave Macmillan, 2004.

Chartier, R., *Cultural History*, Oxford: Polity Press, 1988.

Chase, M., 'Wedderburn, Robert (1762–1835/6?)', in *Oxford Dictionary of National Biography*, Oxford: Oxford University Press. Available at http://www.oxforddnb.com/view/article/47210 (accessed 8 July 2005).

Checkland, S. G. and Checkland, E. O. A. (eds.), *The Poor Law Report of 1834*, London: Penguin, 1974.

Clarke, A., *The Struggle for the Breeches: gender and the making of the British working class*, Berkeley: University of California Press, 1995.

Clinton, C., '"Southern dishonor": flesh, blood, race and bondage', in C. Bleser (ed.), *In Joy and Sorrow: women, family and marriage in the Victorian South 1830–1900*, New York: Oxford University Press, 1991.

Cody, L. F., 'The politics of illegitimacy in an age of reform: women, reproduction and political economy in England's new poor law of 1834', *Journal of Women's History* 11, no. 4, 2000, pp. 131–56.

Coleman, D., *Romantic Colonization and British Anti-Slavery*, Cambridge: Cambridge University Press, 2005.

Colley, L., *Britons: forging the nation, 1707–1837*, New Haven: Yale University Press, 1992.

Cooper, F. and Stoler, A. L., *Tensions of Empire: colonial cultures in a bourgeois world*, Berkeley: University of California Press, 1997.

Craton, M., 'Changing patterns of slave families in the British West Indies', *Journal of Interdisciplinary History* 10, no. 1, 1979, pp. 1–35.

——, and Walvin, J., *A Jamaican Plantation: the history of Worthy Park*, New York: W. H. Allen, 1970.

Cunningham, H., *Children and Childhood in Western Society since 1500*, London: Longman, 1995.

Curtin, P. D., *Two Jamaicas: the role of ideas in a tropical colony, 1830–1865*, Cambridge, Mass.: Harvard University Press, 1955.

Dadzie, S., 'Searching for the invisible woman: slavery and resistance in Jamaica', *Race and Class* 32, no. 2, 1990, pp. 21–38.

Davidoff, L. and Hall, C., *Family Fortunes: men and women of the English middle class, 1780–1850* [1987], London: Routledge, 1992.

Davies, K., 'A moral purchase: femininity, commerce and abolition, 1788–1792', in E. Eger, C. Grant, C.O. Gallchoir and P. Warburton (eds.), *Women, Writing and the Public Sphere, 1700–1830*, Cambridge: Cambridge University Press, 2001, pp. 133–59.

Davin, A., 'Imperialism and motherhood', *History Workshop Journal* 5, 1978, pp. 9–65.

Davis, A., *Women, Race and Class*, New York: Random House, 1981.

Bibliography

Davis, D. B., *The Problem of Slavery in the Age of Revolution*, Ithaca: Cornell University Press, 1975.

D'Costa, L. and Lalla, B. (eds.), *Voices in Exile: Jamaican texts of the eighteenth and nineteenth century*, Tuscaloosa: University of Alabama Press, 1989.

Donnison, J., *Midwives and Medical Men: a history of inter-professional rivalries and women's rights*, London: Heinemann, 1977.

Drescher, S., *The Mighty Experiment: free labor versus slavery in British emancipation*, Oxford: Oxford University Press, 2002.

Dunn, R. S., 'Sugar production and slave women in Jamaica', in I. Berlin and P. D. Morgan (eds.), *Cultivation and Sugar: labor and the shaping of slave life in the Americas*, Charlottesville: University Press of Virginia, 1993, pp. 49–72.

Edwards, L., *Gendered Strife and Confusion: the political structure of reconstruction*, Urbana: University of Illinois Press, 1997.

Engerman, S. L. and Fogel, R. W., *Time on the Cross: the economics of American Negro slavery*, Boston: Little Brown, 1974.

Eudell, D. L., *The Political Languages of Emancipation in the British Caribbean and the U.S. South*, Chapel Hill: University of North Carolina Press, 2002.

Fahnestock, J., 'The heroine of irregular features: physiognomy and conventions of heroine descriptions', *Victorian Studies* 24, no. 3, 1981, pp. 325–50.

Favret, M. A., 'Flogging: the anti-slavery movement writes pornography', *Essays and Studies*, 1998, pp. 19–43.

Ferguson, M., *Subject to Others: British women writers and colonial slavery 1670–1834*, London: Routledge, 1992.

Fildes, V.A., *Breasts, Bottles and Babies: a history of infant feeding*, Edinburgh: Edinburgh University Press, 1986.

Finkelman, P., 'Crimes of love, misdemeanors of passion: the regulation of sex in the Colonial South', in C. Clinton and M. Gillespie (eds.), *The Devil's Lane: sex and race in the Early South*, New York: Oxford University Press, 1997, pp. 124–38.

Foucault, M., *Discipline and Punish: the birth of the prison* [1977], London: Penguin, 1991.

——, *The History of Sexuality, vol. 1*, London: Penguin, 1990.

Franklin, A., 'Jeremie, Sir John (1795–1841)' in *Oxford Dictionary of National Biography*, Oxford: Oxford University Press, 2004. Available http://www.oxforddnb.com/view/article/14773 (accessed 19 October 2004).

Genovese, E., *Roll, Jordan, Roll: the world the slaves made*, New York: Pantheon, 1974.

'Genovese Forum', *Radical History Review* 88, 2004, pp. 3–82.

Gillis, J. R., *For Better, For Worse: British marriages 1600–to the present*, Oxford: Oxford University Press, 1985.

Gilman, S., *Difference and Pathology: stereotypes of sexuality, race and madness*, London: Cornell University Press, 1985.

Godbeer, R., *Sexual Revolution in Early America*, Baltimore: Johns Hopkins University Press, 2002.

Gould, P., *Barbaric Traffic: commerce and antislavery in the eighteenth-century Atlantic world*, Cambridge, Mass.: Harvard University Press, 2003.

Gratus, J., *The Great White Lie: slavery, emancipation, and changing radical attitudes*, New York: Monthly Review Press, 1973.

Green, W. A., *British Slave Emancipation: the sugar colonies and the great experiment, 1830–1865*, Oxford: Clarendon Press, 1996.

Greene, J. P., 'Liberty, slavery and the transformation of British identity in the eighteenth-century West Indies', *Slavery and Abolition* 21, no. 1, 2000, pp. 10–31.
Halbersleben, K. L., *Women's Participation in the British Antislavery Movement, 1824–65*, Lewiston/Queenston/Lampeter: The Edwin Mellon Press, 1993.
Hall, C., *White, Male and Middle Class: explorations in feminism and history*, Cambridge: Polity Press, 1992.
——, 'White visions, black lives: the free villages of Jamaica', *History Workshop Journal* 36, 1993, pp. 100–32.
——, *Civilising Subjects: metropole and colony in the English imagination 1830–1867*, Cambridge: Polity Press, 2002.
Hall, S. and Du Gay, P. (eds.), *Questions of Cultural Identity*, London: Sage, 1996.
Halttunen, K., 'Humanitarianism and the pornography of pain in Anglo-American culture', *American Historical Review* 100, no. 2, 1995, pp. 304–34.
Harkin, M., 'Matthew Lewis's *Journal of a West India Proprietor*: surveillance and space on the plantation', *Nineteenth-Century Contexts* 24, no. 2, 2002, pp. 139–50.
Haste, H., *The Sexual Metaphor*, New York: Harvest Wheatsheaf, 1993.
Henderson, T., *Disorderly Women in Eighteenth-Century London: prostitution and control in the metropolis, 1730–1830*, London: Longman, 1999.
Henriques, U. R. Q., 'Bastardy and the new poor law', *Past and Present* 37, 1967, pp. 103–29.
Heuman, G. J., *Between Black and White: race, politics, and the free coloreds in Jamaica, 1792–1865*, Oxford: Clio Press, 1981.
——, 'The social structure of the slave societies in the Caribbean', in F. W. Knight (ed.), *General History of the Caribbean, vol. 3*, Basingstoke: Macmillan, 1997, pp. 138–68.
Higginbotham, E. B., 'African-American women's history and the metalanguage of race', *Signs* 17, no. 2, 1992, pp. 251–74.
Higman, B. W., *Slave Population and Economy in Jamaica, 1807–1834*, Cambridge: Cambridge University Press, 1976.
——, 'African and creole slave family patterns in Trinidad', *Journal of Family History* 3, no. 2, 1978, pp. 163–80.
——, *Slave Populations in the Caribbean, 1807–1834*, Baltimore: Johns Hopkins University Press, 1984.
Hitchcock, T., 'Redefining sex in eighteenth-century England', *History Workshop Journal* 41, 1996, pp. 72–90.
——, *English Sexualities, 1700–1800*, Basingstoke: Macmillan, 1997.
Hochshild, A., *Bury the Chains: the British struggle to abolish slavery*, London: Macmillan, 2005.
Holt, T. C., *The Problem of Freedom: race, labor, and politics in Jamaica and Britain, 1832–1938*, Baltimore: Johns Hopkins University Press, 1992.
Honeyman, K., *Women, Gender and Industrialisation in England, 1700–1870*, Houndsmill: Macmillan, 2000.
hooks, b., *Ain't I a Woman: black women and feminism*, Boston: South End Press, 1981.
Hurwitz, S. J. and Hurwitz, E. F., *Jamaica: a historical portrait*, London: Pall Mall Press, 1971.
Ignatieff, M., *A Just Measure of Pain: the penitentiary in the Industrial Revolution, 1750–1850*, London: Macmillan, 1978.
Jennings, J., *The Business of Abolishing the British Slave Trade*, London: Frank Cass, 1997.

Kiple, K., *The Caribbean Slave: a biological history*, Cambridge: Cambridge University Press, 1984.

Kitson, P., '"Bales of living anguish": representations of race and the slave in romantic writing', *English Literary History* 67, no. 2, 2000, pp. 515–37.

Lalla, B., *Defining Jamaican Fiction: marronage and the discourse of survival*, Tuscaloosa: University of Alabama Press, 1996.

Lambert, D., '"True lovers of religion": Methodist persecution and white resistance to anti-slavery in Barbados, 1823–1825', *Journal of Historical Geography* 28, no. 2, 2002, pp. 216–36.

———, 'Producing/contesting whiteness: rebellion, antislavery and enslavement in Barbados, 1816', *Geoforum* 36, 2005, pp. 29–43.

———, *White Creole Culture, Politics and Identity during the Age of Abolition*, Cambridge: Cambridge University Press, 2005.

Lane, J., *Apprenticeship in England 1600–1914*, London: University College of London Press, 1996.

Langford, P., *Englishness Identified: manners and characters 1650–1850*, Oxford: Oxford University Press, 2000.

Laqueur, T. W., 'Bodies, details, and the humanitarian narrative', in L. Hunt (ed.), *The New Cultural History*, Berkeley: University of California Press, 1989, pp. 176–204.

———, *Making Sex: body and gender from the Greeks to Freud*, Cambridge, Mass.: Harvard University Press, 1990.

Lawler, S., 'Motherhood and identity', in T. Cosslett, A. Easton, and P. Summerfield (eds.), *Women, Power and Resistance: an introduction to women's studies*, Buckingham: Open University Press, 1996, pp. 154–64.

Lemmings, D., 'Marriage and the law in the eighteenth century: Hardwicke's marriage act of 1753', *The Historical Journal* 39, no. 2, 1996, pp. 339–60.

Loomba, A., *Colonialism-Postcolonialism*, London: Routledge, 1998.

McGowen, R., 'The body and punishment in eighteenth-century England', *Journal of Modern History* 59, 1987, pp. 651–79.

———, 'Power and humanity, or Foucault among the historians', in C. Jones and R. Porter (eds.), *Reassessing Foucault: power, medicine and the body*, London: Routledge, 1994, pp. 91–112.

———, 'The well-ordered prison: England 1780–1865', in N. Morris and D. J. Rotman (eds.), *The Oxford History of the Prison: the practices of punishment in Western society*, New York: Oxford University Press, 1995, pp. 79–110.

Mair, L. M., 'The arrival of black women', *Jamaica Journal* 9, nos 2–3, 1975, pp. 2–7.

———, *The Rebel Woman in the British West Indies during Slavery*, Kingston: IOJ, 1975.

———, *Women Field Workers in Jamaica during Slavery*, Mona: Department of History, 1987.

Malik, K., *The Meaning of Race: race, history and culture in Western society*, London: Macmillan, 1996.

Mathieson, W. L., *British Slavery and Its Abolition 1823–1838*, London: Longman, 1926.

Matthews, G., 'The other side of slave revolts', in S. Courtman (ed.), *Beyond the Blood, the Beach and the Banana: new perspectives in Caribbean Studies*, Kingston: Ian Randle Publishers, 2004, pp. 49–70.

Meteyard, B., 'Illegitimacy and marriage in eighteenth-century England', *Journal of Interdisciplinary History* 10, no. 3, 1980, pp. 479–89.

Midgley, C., *Women Against Slavery: the British campaigns 1780–1870*, London: Routledge, 1992.

———, (ed.), *Gender and Imperialism*, Manchester: Manchester University Press, 1995.
Mill, S. *Discourse*, London: Routledge, 1997.
Mohammed, P., '"But most of all mi love me browning": the emergence in eighteenth and nineteenth century Jamaica of the mulatto woman as desired', *Feminist Review* 65, 2000, pp. 22–48.
Morgan, J., *Laboring Women: reproduction and gender in New World slavery*, Philadelphia, University of Pennsylvania Press, 2004.
Morrissey, M., *Slave Women in the New World: gender stratification in the Caribbean*, Lawrence: University Press of Kansas, 1989.
Nead, L., *Myths of Sexuality: representations of women in Victorian Britain*, Oxford: Blackwell, 1988.
Nussbaum, F., *The Limits of the Human: fictions of anomaly, race, and gender in the long eighteenth century*, Cambridge: Cambridge University Press, 2003.
Oldfield, J. R., *Popular Politics and British Anti-Slavery: the mobilisation of public opinion against the slave trade, 1787–1807*, Manchester: Manchester University Press, 1995.
———, (ed.), *The British Atlantic Slave Trade, vol. 3*, London: Pickering and Chatto, 2003.
Ortmayer, N., 'Church, marriage and legitimacy in the British West Indies (nineteenth and twentieth centuries)', *The History of the Family* 2, no. 2, 1997, pp. 141–70.
O'Shaughenessy, A. J., *An Empire Divided: the American revolution and the British Caribbean*, Philadelphia: University of Pennsylvania Press, 2000.
Parker, S., *Informal Marriage: cohabitation and the law, 1750–1989*, Houndsmills: Macmillan, 1990.
Paton, D., 'Decency, dependence and the lash: gender and the British debate over slave emancipation, 1830–34', *Slavery and Abolition* 17, no.3, 1996, pp. 163–84.
———, 'Punishment, crime and the bodies of slaves in eighteenth-century Jamaica', *Journal of Social History* 34, no. 4, 2001, pp. 923–54.
———, *No Bond but the Law: punishment, race, and gender in Jamaican state formation, 1780–1870*, Durham, N.C.: Duke University Press, 2004.
Patterson, O., *The Sociology of Slavery: an analysis of the origins, development and structure of Negro slave society in Jamaica*, London: MacGibbon and Kee, 1967.
———, 'Persistence, continuity and change in the Jamaican working-class family', *Journal of Family History* 7, no. 2, 1982, pp. 135–61.
Perkin, J., *Women and Marriage in Nineteenth-century England*, London: Routledge, 1989.
Perry, R., 'Colonizing the breast: sexuality and maternity in eighteenth-century England', *Journal of the History of Sexuality* 2, no. 2, 1991, pp. 204–34.
Petley, C., 'Boundaries of rule, ties of dependency: Jamaican planters, local society and the metropole 1800–1834', unpublished thesis, University of Warwick, 2003.
———, 'Slavery, emancipation and the creole world view of Jamaican colonists, 1800–1834', *Slavery and Abolition* 26, no. 1, 2005, pp. 93–114.
———, '"Legitimacy" and social boundaries: free people of colour and the social order in Jamaican slave society', *Social History* 30, no. 4, 2005, pp. 481–98.
Proctor, J. H., 'Scottish missionaries and Jamaican slaveholders', *Slavery and Abolition* 25, no. 1, 2004, pp. 51–70.
Rabinow, P. (ed.), *The Foucault Reader: an introduction to Foucault's thoughts* [1984], London: Penguin, 1991.

Ragatz, L. J., *The Fall of the Planter Class in the British Caribbean, 1765–1833* [1927], New York: Octagon Books, 1963.
Reddock, R. E., 'Women and slavery in the Caribbean: a feminist perspective', *Latin American Perspectives* 12, no. 1, 1985, pp. 63–80.
Roberts, G. W., *The Population of Jamaica*, Cambridge: University Press, 1957.
Rose, S. O., 'Cultural analysis and moral discourse: episodes, continuities, and transformations', in V. E. Bonnell and L. Hunt (eds.), *Beyond the Cultural Turn: new directions in the study of culture and society*, Berkeley: University of California Press, 1999, pp. 217–38.
Sanchez-Eppler, K., *Touching Liberty: abolition, feminism and the politics of the body*, Berkeley: University of California Press, 1997.
Sandiford, K. A., *The Cultural Politics of Sugar: Caribbean slavery and narratives of colonialism*, Cambridge: Cambridge University Press, 2000.
Schnorrenberg, B. B., 'Is childbirth any place for a woman?: the decline of midwifery in eighteenth-century England', in H.C. Payne (ed.), *Studies in Eighteenth-Century Culture*, vol. 10, Madison: University of Wisconsin Press, 1981, pp. 393–408.
Scully, P., 'Rape, race, and colonial culture', *American Historical Review* 100, no. 2, 1995, pp. 335–59.
Sheller, M., 'Quasheba, mother, queen: black women's public leadership and political protest in post-emancipation Jamaica 1834–65', *Slavery and Abolition* 19, no. 3, 1998, pp. 90–117.
Shepherd, V. A. (ed.), *Women in Caribbean History*, London: James Currey, 1999.
———, 'Gender and representation in European accounts of pre-emancipation Jamaica', in V. A. Shepherd and H. McD. Beckles (eds.), *Caribbean Slavery in the Atlantic World: a student reader*, London: James Currey, 2000, pp. 702–12.
Sheridan, R. B., *Doctors and Slaves: a medical and demographic history of slavery in the British West Indies, 1680–1834*, Cambridge: Cambridge University Press, 1985.
Shoemaker, R. B., *Gender in English Society, 1650–1850: the emergence of separate spheres?*, London: Longman, 1998.
Shorter, E., *The Making of the Modern Family*, London: Collins, 1976.
———, *Women's Bodies: a social history of women's encounter with health, ill-health and medicine*, London: Transaction Publishers, 1991.
Simms, R., 'Controlling images and the gender ideologies of enslaved African women', *Gender and Society* 15, no. 6, 2001, pp. 879–97.
Spurr, D., *The Rhetoric of Empire: colonial discourse in journalism, travel writing, and imperial administration*, Durham, N.C.: Duke University Press, 1993.
Stanley, A. D., *From Bondage to Contract: wage labor, marriage and the market in the age of slave emancipation*, Cambridge: Cambridge University Press, 1998.
Steel, M. J., 'A philosophy of fear: the world view of the Jamaican plantocracy in a comparative perspective', *Journal of Caribbean History* 7, 1993, pp. 1–20.
Stewart, L., 'Louisiana subjects: power, space and the slave body', *Ecumene* 2, no. 3, 1995, pp. 227–45.
Stoler, A. L., *Race and the Education of Desire: Foucault's history of sexuality and the colonial order of things*, Durham, N.C.: Duke University Press, 1995.
Stone, L., *The Family, Sex and Marriage in England, 1500–1800* [1977], London: Penguin, 1990.
Strange, D. C., 'Teaching the means of freedom', *Harvard Library Bulletin* 29, no. 4, 1981, pp. 403–19.

Swaminathan, S., 'Developing the West Indian proslavery position after the Somerset decision', *Slavery and Abolition* 24, no. 3, 2003, pp. 40–60.
Temperley, H., *British Antislavery, 1833–1870*, London: Longman, 1972.
Thomas, N., *Colonialism's Culture: anthropology, travel and government*, Oxford: Polity Press, 1994.
Tosh, J., *A Man's Place: masculinity and the middle-class home in Victorian England*, New Haven: Yale University Press, 1999.
Trotter, W., *The African American Experience, vol. 1*, Boston: Houghton Mifflin, 2001.
Turley, D., *The Culture of English Antislavery, 1780–1860*, London: Routledge, 1991.
Turner, M., *Slaves and Missionaries: the disintegration of Jamaican slave society, 1787–1834*, Urbana: University of Illinois Press, 1982.
———, 'The 11 o'clock flog: women, work and labour law in the British Caribbean', *Slavery and Abolition* 20, no. 1, 1999, pp. 38–58.
Ward, J. R., 'Profitability of sugar planting in the British West Indies, 1650–1834', *Economic History Review* 31, no. 2, 1978, pp. 197–213.
———, *British West Indian Slavery, 1750–1834: the process of amelioration*, Oxford: Clarendon Press, 1988.
Weeks, J., *Sex, Politics and Society: the regulation of sexuality since 1800* [1981], London: Longman, 1993.
West, E., *Chains of Love*, Urbana: University of Illinois Press, 2004.
Wheeler, R., *The Complexion of Race: categories of difference in eighteenth-century British culture*, Philadelphia: University of Philadelphia Press, 2000.
Whitbread, N., *The Evolution of the Nursery-Infant School: a history of infant and nursery education in Britain, 1800–1970*, London: Routledge and Kegan Paul, 1972.
White, D. G., *Ar'n't I a Woman?: female slaves in the plantation South*, New York: W.W. Norton, 1985.
White, H., *The Content of Form: narrative discourse and historical representation*, Baltimore: Johns Hopkins University Press, 1987.
Wiener, M., *Reconstructing the Criminal: culture, law and policy in England, 1830–1914*, Cambridge: Cambridge University Press, 1990.
Wilmot, S., 'Not "full free": the ex-slaves and the apprenticeship system in Jamaica, 1834–1838', *Jamaica Journal* 17, 1984, pp. 2–10.
———, '"Females of abandoned character"?: women and protest in Jamaica 1838–65', in V. Shepherd, B. Brereton, and B. Bailey (eds.), *Engendering History: Caribbean women in historical perspective*, Kingston: Ian Randle, 1995, pp. 279–95.
Wilson, A., 'Ceremony of childbirth and its interpretation', in V. Fildes (ed.), *Women as Mothers in Pre-Industrial England: essays in memory of Dorothy McLaren*, London: Routledge, 1990, pp. 68–107.
Wilson, K., *The Island Race: Englishness, empire and gender in the eighteenth century*, London: Routledge, 2002.
———, 'Empire, gender, and modernity in the eighteenth century', in P. Levine (ed.), *Gender and Empire*, Oxford: Oxford University Press, 2004, pp. 14–45.
Wood, M., *Blind Memory: visual representations of slavery in England and America, 1780–1865*, Manchester: Manchester University Press, 2000.
Wrigley, E. A. and Schofield, R. S., *The Population History of England, 1541–1871*, London: Edward Arnold, 1981.

Index

Page numbers in italics refer to figures or tables.

A
Act for the Abolition of Slavery in the British Colonies, 2
- apprenticed marriage, 10
- childbearing practices, 12, 31
- clause 17, 156, 157–158
- co-residence, 106–107
- flogging, 34, 147
- planters' deliberate violation, 147–148
- planters' social status, 34–36, 173–174
- slave marriage, 10, 106–107

Act to Amend the Act for the Abolition of Slavery in the British Colonies, 36
- apprenticeship, 59

Adoption, 29

Antislavery discourse
- apprenticeship, 148–158
  - 1833 Abolition Act, 156
  - actors, 150–151
  - chaining, 151–152
  - criminal justice system, 157
  - disciplinary practices, 149–150
  - illegality of abuse, 150
  - illegal practices, 156
  - indecency, 151
  - inmates, 152
  - lack of gender order, 151
  - legal protection, 155
  - metropolitan norm of masculinity, 155
  - missionaries, 149
  - physical suffering, 152
  - planters, 149–150
  - resistance, 150
  - society's lack of civilization, 152–153
  - Special Magistrates, 154–155
  - taste for cruelty, 153–154
  - treadmills, 149, 153
  - workhouse abuse of female apprentices, 148–158
  - workhouse committee members, 154–155
  - workhouse officers, 154
- changing discourse, 6
- childrearing practices, 48–64
  - condition of nursing women, 48
  - early accounts, 49
  - freeing of slave mothers, 51–52
  - Imperial Government, 52
  - improved nursing practices, 49
  - later accounts, 49–50
  - local assemblies, 51
  - nursing, 49
  - risk of being separated from their infants, 50–51
  - slave women's maternal affection, 50
- contradictory nature, 6
- flogging, 130
  - calls for ban, 137–138
  - descriptions, 131–132
  - deviated from civilized English society, 138–139
  - exposure of women's bodies, 130
  - female sexual purity, 132
  - as indecent practice, 131–139
  - legally allowed number of lashes, 129, 135–136
  - local magistrates, 138
  - man of sensibility, 134
  - metropolitan ideal of manhood, 136
  - metropolitan ideal of womanhood, 133

Antislavery discourse (*continued*)
　moral degradation, 130
　moral qualities of their husbands and children, 132
　potential humanity of slaves, 134–135
　pregnant women, 135
　problem for partners and children, 133–134
　slave evidence, 138
　slavery corrupted, 134–135
　white Jamaican society, 136
　white mistress, 136–137
metropolitan ideal of womanhood, 169–176
proslavery discourse, mutual influence, 7
slave marriage
　1826 Slave Law, 95–96
　　clause 4, 95–96
　changes in status, 95–96
　co-residence, 97, 100, 101
　denunciation of planters, 98–99
　husband's role, 101–102
　illegitimate births, 100
　improved moral condition, 96–97
　lives of lower classes, 96
　metropolitan ideal of husband-protector, 102
　metropolitan ideal of marriage, 96–98
　obtaining enslaved partners' freedom, 100
　primarily as moral institution, 96–97
　residence on nearby estates, 101
　separation of married slave couples, 100–101
　separation of married slave couples by sale, 101
　taking care of husband's and children's needs, 102–104
　voluntary manumission, 99
slave men's sexuality, 66
slave women
　centrality of, 6
　like middle-class, English women, 169–170
　suffering, innocent, and passive woman as dominant image, 170–171
slave women's sexuality, 78–87
　abused slave women as asexual, 81
　accounts of unsuccessful resistance, 80–81
　consensual interracial sex, 84
　emerging discourse of fatherhood, 83
　estate officers, 81–82
　forced interracial sex, 81, 83–84
　male slave as emasculated man, 83–84
　metropolitan norm of masculine sexual restraint, 82–83
　naturally chaste, 80
　owners' disregard of slave marriage, 79
　potentially virtuous slave women, 79
　prostitutes, 84
　reform proposals, 85–87
　relations between whte men and free coloured women, 84
　sexual behaviour, 66
　skin colour, 84–85
　slave women's resistance, 80–81
　slave women's status as commodity, 79–80
workhouses, 148–158
　1833 Abolition Act, 156
　actors, 150–151
　chaining, 151–152
　criminal justice system, 157
　disciplinary practices, 149–150
　illegality of abuse, 150
　illegal practices, 156
　indecency, 151
　inmates, 152
　lack of gender order, 151
　legal protection, 155
　metropolitan norm of masculinity, 155
　missionaries, 149
　physical suffering, 152
　planters, 149–150
　resistance, 150
　society's lack of civilization, 152–153
　Special Magistrates, 154–155
　taste for cruelty, 153–154
　treadmills, 149, 153
　workhouse abuse of female apprentices, 148–158
　workhouse committee members, 154–155
　workhouse officers, 154

Anti-slavery movement, 1
Anti-Slavery Society, 1–2
Apprenticeship, 2, 7, 30–32
 1838 Amendment Act, 59
 antislavery discourse, 148–158
  1833 Abolition Act, 156
  actors, 150–151
  chaining, 151–152
  criminal justice system, 157
  disciplinary practices, 149–150
  illegality of abuse, 150
  illegal practices, 156
  indecency, 151
  inmates, 152
  lack of gender order, 151
  legal protection, 155
  metropolitan norm of masculinity, 155
  missionaries, 149
  physical suffering, 152
  planters, 149–150
  resistance, 150
  society's lack of civilization, 152–153
  Special Magistrates, 154–155
  taste for cruelty, 153–154
  treadmills, 149, 153
  workhouse abuse of female apprentices, 148–158
  workhouse committee members, 154–155
  workhouse officers, 154
 childbirth practices, 31–32
  pregnant apprentices as troublemakers, 31–32
 childrearing practices
  after 1834, 53
  apprenticed mother's lack of maternal affection, 60
  apprenticed mothers opposing voluntary apprenticeship of free children, 56–57
  difference from white metropolitan mothers, 60
  education, 57, 58
  field labour force, 58
  free children's lack of access to medical care, 55
  loving mothers, 56
  metropolitan gender ideal, 56
  motherhood incompatible with paid work, 58
  not providing free children with food, clothes and medical care, 53–54, 60
  nursing, 52–53
  pay back time lost in looking after sick child, 55–56
  withdrawal of indulgences for nursing women, 53–54
 conciliatory policy, 173–174
 co-residence, 114
 "different body" site of cultural and political contestation, 171–172
 female flogging, 10
 flogging, 148
 land ownership, 110
 male apprentice
  land ownership, 110
  wage labour, 110
 marriage, 10, 107–115, 124–125
  1833 Abolition Act, 10
  Anglican ministers, 108
  female victims, 125
  mainly economic arguments, 107
  nonconformist marriages, 108–109
  provider role, 124–125
  visiting rights, 112–115
 metropolitan ideal of middle-class marriage, 92
 motives, 8
 natural troublemakers, 158–159
 proslavery discourse
  1833 Abolition Act, 161–162
  denied abuse, 159–160
  disciplinary practices justified, 159
  disciplinary practices legal, 160–161
  flogging, 162–164
  governor and colonial secretary, 162–163
  moderate punishments, 160
  planters' power, 161–162
  treadmills, 164–165
  who should control workhouse, 165
 rape, 111
  impact on women's husbands, 111–112
 sexual and physical abuse, 111
  impact on women's husbands, 111–112
 slavery
  continuities, 8
  contrasted, 171–172
  valuation procedure, 109–110
  workhouses, 147–148

Index

Assertiveness, free population
  distinguished behaviours among six races in Jamaica, 71–74
  growth, 71
  lack of sexual restraint, 74
  proposals to regulate slave women's excessive sexuality, 75–78

B
Breast-feeding, 18
British abolitionism, 1
  slave women, 2

C
Caring mother, 5–6
Chaining, 151–152
Childbirth practices, 11, 13–14
  1833 Abolition Act, 12, 31
  apprenticeship, 31–32
    pregnant apprentices as troublemakers, 31–32
  legislation, 27–37
  natural decrease, 12
  proslavery discourse, 13–20
    adoption, 29
    after 1834, 33
    allowances and indulgences, 34–35
    apprenticeship, 30–32
    breast-feeding, 18
    deserted attention, 16
    economic motives, 34
    engagement with metropolitan discourse, 16
    hygiene during home deliveries, 17–18
    improvements in quality of delivery, 23
    inattention of mother, 16
    lacked intrinsic affection, 28–29
    lighter workload, 29–30
    lower-class counterparts, 15
    lying-in rooms, 17–18, 23–24
    manumitting as incentive to childbirth, 22
    maternity as duty and responsibility, 32
    measures of exceptional fertility, 20–21
    medical care, 14
    midwives, 18, 24–26, 30
    monetary reward, 20, 27–28
    motherly neglect, 16–17
    natural increase, 15
    planters as civilized, 19–20
    practices allegedly universally adopted, 14–15
    profitability of estates, 26–27
    proposals to change, 20–27
    proposals to exempt slave women from hard work, 21
    remarks about planters, 19
    semi-autonomous spaces, 23–24
    sentencing pregnant women to workhouse, 31–33
    slave women as both producers and reproducers, 20
    slave women as different from whites, 15–17
    slave women clung to own childbirth practices, 16
    time off before and after delivery, 14–15, 22–23
    white estate doctor, 26
  proslavery focus on, 11–12
  rhetoric, 37–38
  rose-coloured accounts, 11–12
  sources, 13
Childrearing practices, 39–64
  antislavery discourse, 48–64
    condition of nursing women, 48
    early accounts, 49
    freeing of slave mothers, 51–52
    Imperial Government, 52
    improving nursing practices, 49
    later accounts, 49–50
    local assemblies, 51
    nursing, 49
    risk of being separated from their infants, 50–51
    slave women's maternal affection, 50
  apprenticeship
    after 1834, 53
    apprenticed mothers lack of maternal affection, 60
    apprenticed mothers opposing voluntary apprenticeship of free children, 56–57
    difference from white metropolitan mothers, 60
    education, 57, 58
    field labour force, 58
    loving mothers, 56
    metropolitan gender ideal, 56
    motherhood incompatible with paid work, 58

not providing free children with food, clothes and medical care, 53–55
nursing, 52–53
paying back time lost in looking after sick child, 55–56
withdrawal of indulgences for nursing women, 53–54
women's refusal to provide their free children with medical care, 60
proslavery discourse
breast-feeding, 41, 43–44, 44–45
defined motherhood, 42
exempted from particular tasks, 43
extra food, 45
feeding-on-demand schemes, 46–47
feeding-on-supply schemes, 46
indulgences for nursing women, 44
labour-reducing arrangements, 42
maternal affection, 42
metropolitan ideal of motherhood, 45–46
metropolitan medical texts, 44
mother's duty to show affection, 45–46
natural increase, 40–41
raising healthy children, 42
reduced workloads of nursing women, 46
rose-coloured accounts, 41–42
weaned children, 48
weaning, 41, 44–45
weaning early, 46–47
weaning early-infant mortality link, 47
Civilization, sexuality, 78
Colonial discourse, 5
heterogeneity, contradiction, and ambivalence, 5
Consensual sexual relationships, 67
Co-residence, 97, 100, 101, 117
1833 Abolition Act, 106–107
apprenticeship, 114

D
Disciplinary power, 37

E
Education, 58
Endogamy, 71–74
Estate doctor, 26

F
Female purity, 9–10
Fictive writings, 6–7
Field labour, 8–9
slave wife, 103
Flogging, 129–145
1833 Abolition Act, 34, 147
antislavery discourse, 130
calls for ban, 137–138
descriptions, 131–132
deviated from civilized English society, 138–139
exposure of women's bodies, 130
female sexual purity, 132
as indecent practice, 131–139
legally allowed number of lashes, 129, 135–136
local magistrates, 138
man of sensibility, 134
metropolitan ideal of manhood, 136
metropolitan ideal of womanhood, 133
moral degradation, 130
moral qualities of their husbands and children, 132
potential humanity of slaves, 134–135
pregnant women, 135
problem for partners and children, 133–134
slave evidence, 138
slavery corrupted, 134–135
white Jamaican society, 136
white mistress, 136–137
apprenticeship, 148
legal redress, 129–130
mode, 129, 130
natural troublemaker, 159
proslavery discourse, 130–131, 139–145
ban, 140–141
criminal justice system, 143
impediment to slave civilization, 139–140
Jamaican society as English society, 142
men of sensibility, 143
metropolitan-based proslavery authors, 143
metropolitan gender ideals, 142
morally corrupting influence, 140
plantation discipline, 139, 141–142

Flogging (*continued*)
  rule of law, 142
  slave women as potentially virtuous, 140
  white mistress, 142–143
  regulation, 129
  workhouses, 148
Free children, 53
  apprenticed mothers opposing voluntary apprenticeship of free children, 56–57
  food, clothing, and medical care, 53–55
  voluntary apprenticeship, 54
Freedom, 172–173
  freeing of slave mothers, 51–52
  manumitting as incentive to childbirth, 22
  obtaining enslaved partners' freedom, 100
  voluntary manumission, 99
Free population, assertiveness growth, 71
  lack of sexual restraint, 74
  proposals to regulate slave women's excessive sexuality, 75–78
  by six races of Jamaica, 71–74

G
Gender, metropolitan discourse, 4

H
Hamel, the Obeah Man, 71–74
Husband
  metropolitan ideal of husband-protector, 102
  role, 91

I
Identities, 3–4
Images of apprenticed women, 7–8
Images of slave women, 3–4
Indifferent mother, 5, 6
Infant mortality rate, 11

J
Jamaica, 8
  characterized, 8
  Christmas Day rebellion, 9
  persecuted missionaries, 9
  slave population, natural decrease, 12
Jezebel, 4

L
Land ownership, apprenticeship, 110
Lying-in room, 23–24

M
Mammy, 4
Marriage, 91–128
  1753 Marriage Act, 95
  1836 Marriage Act, 95
  apprenticeship, 107–115, 124–125
    Anglican ministers, 108
    female victims, 125
    mainly economic arguments, 107
    nonconformist marriages, 108–109
    provider role, 124–125
    visiting rights, 112–115
  middle classes' norms, 91
Marriage Act of 1753, 91, 95
Marriage contract, wage contract, link, 107
Metropolitan discourse, 3
  gender, 4
  slave women's sexuality, 89
  race, 4
  sexuality, 4, 65
  norm, 78
Metropolitan ideal of husband-protector, 102
Metropolitan ideal of marriage, 96–98, 118–119
  apprenticeship, 92
  middle class, 91–92
  slaves, 92
Metropolitan ideal of masculinity, marker of Englishness, 137
Metropolitan ideal of motherhood, 9, 62
  characterized, 39
  combination of motherhood and work, 62–63
Metropolitan ideal of womanhood, 170
  antislavery discourse, 169–176
  proslavery discourse, 169–176
Midwives, 18, 24–26, 30
Missionaries, 149, 175–176
  persecuted, 9
  slave marriage, 94–95
  workhouses, 149
Motherhood, 9, *see also* Childbirth practices; Childrearing practices
  indifferent mother, 5, 6
  slave women's maternal affection, 50

Index

N
Non-fictive writings, 6–7

P
Paternalism, 13
Physical punishment, *see* Flogging
Planters, 147–148
  slave marriage, 98–99
  socio-economic status
    1833 Abolition Act, 34–36, 173–174
    slave marriage, 125–126
    workhouses, 149–150, 161–162
Primary materials, 4
Proslavery discourse
  antislavery discourse, mutual influence, 7
  apprenticeship
    1833 Abolition Act, 161–162
    denied abuse, 159–160
    disciplinary practices justified, 159
    disciplinary practices legal, 160–161
    flogging, 162–164
    governor and colonial secretary, 162–163
    moderate punishments, 160
    planters' power, 161–162
    treadmills, 164–165
    who should control workhouse, 165
  childbirth practices, 13–20
    adoption, 29
    allowances and indulgences, 34–35
    apprenticeship, 30–32
    breast-feeding, 18
    deserted attention, 16
    economic motives, 34
    engagement with metropolitan discourse, 16
    hygiene during home deliveries, 17–18
    improvements in quality of delivery, 23
    inattention of mother, 16
    lacked intrinsic affection, 28–29
    lighter workload, 29–30
    lower-class counterparts, 15
    lying-in rooms, 17–18, 23–24
    manumitting as incentive to childbirth, 22
    maternity as a serious duty and responsibility, 32
    measures of exceptional fertility, 20–21
    medical care, 14
    midwives, 18, 24–26, 30
    monetary reward, 27–28
    monetary reward for successful deliveries, 20
    motherly neglect, 16–17
    natural increase, 15
    planters as civilized, 19–20
    practices allegedly universally adopted, 14–15
    profitability of estates, 26–27
    proposals to change, 20–27
    proposals to exempt slave women from hard work, 21
    punish rather than indulge pregnant and lying-in women after 1834, 33
    remarks about planters, 19
    semi-autonomous spaces, 23–24
    sentencing pregnant women to workhouse, 31–33
    slaves as different from whites, 15–16
    slave women as both producers and reproducers, 20
    slave women clung to their own childbirth practices, 16
    slave women's natural difference, 15–17
    time off, 14–15
    time off before and after delivery, 22–23
    white estate doctor, 26
  childrearing practices
    breast-feeding, 41, 43–44
    breast-feeding period, 44–45
    defined motherhood, 42
    exempted from particular tasks, 43
    extra food, 45
    feeding-on-demand schemes, 46–47
    feeding-on-supply schemes, 46
    indulgences for nursing women, 44
    labour-reducing arrangements, 42
    link between early weaning and infant mortality rates, 47
    maternal affection, 42
    metropolitan medical texts, 44
    metropolitan motherhood ideal, 45–46
    mother's duty to show affection, 45–46

Proslavery discourse (continued)
  natural increase, 40–41
  raising healthy children, 42
  reduced workloads of nursing women, 46
  rose-coloured accounts, 41–42
  weaned children, 48
  weaning, 41, 44–45
  weaning early, 46–47
 flogging, 130–131, 139–145
  ban, 140–141
  criminal justice system, 143
  impediment to slave civilization, 139–140
  Jamaican society as English society, 142
  men of sensibility, 143
  metropolitan-based proslavery authors, 143
  metropolitan gender ideals, 142
  morally corrupting influence, 140
  plantation discipline, 139, 141–142
  rule of law, 142
  slave women as potentially virtuous, 140
  white mistress, 142–143
 metropolitan ideal of womanhood, 169–176
 rose-coloured accounts
  comparing slave women to lower-class English women, 169
  comparing slave women to rural English women, 169
  comparing slave women to white metropolitan women, 169
 slave marriage, 104–106, 115–126
  1826 Slave Law, clause 4, 122
  affection, 117–118
  apprenticed couples failing to carry out their gendered roles, 124
  church-sanctioned, 117, 118–119
  co-residence, 117, 120–121
  early proslavery writers, 116–119
  as economic institution, 116–126
  facilitating third party, 121
  formal marriage voluntary and binding contract, 123–124
  later proslavery writers, 119–126
  marriage to free man, 119–120
  metroplitan marriage ideal, 118–119
  monogamy, 116, 117
  natural increase, 116–117
  nonconformist marriage, 122–123
  opposition to formal slave marriage, 122, 123
  provider role, 120
  scheme to increase marriage rate, 121–122, 124
  separation by sale, 120
  slave huts, 120–121
  slave men's inability to provide, 120
  socio-economic status of planters, 125–126
  workload, 121
 slave men's sexuality, 66
  social stability, 66
 slave women's sexuality
  activity at early age, 68
  deviant from metropolitan model, 68
  external pressures, 68
  free coloureds, 69
  growth of free population, 71
  housekeeper, 69
  inheritances, 69
  interracial sexual relations, 70–71
  multiple partners, 68
  natural decrease, 69–70
  naturally promiscuous, 68
  obsession with infertility, 69–70
  potentially virtuous slave women, 70–71
  prostitution, 68, 69
  sexual relations with white men, 68–69
  theories of slave women's sexual deviance, 67–69
  as threatening deviants, 67–68
 uses, 4, 5
 varied, changing, inconsistent, and contradictory, 5–6
workhouses
 1833 Abolition Act, 161–162
 denied abuse, 159–160
 disciplinary practices justified, 159
 flogging, 162–164
 governor and colonial secretary, 162–163
 moderate punishments, 160
 planters' power, 161–162
 treadmills, 164–165
 who should control workhouse, 165

Index

R
Race, metropolitan discourse, 4
Rape, apprenticeship, 111
  impact on women's husbands, 111–112

S
Scheming Jezebel, 67
Select Committee on the Extinction of Slavery throughout the British Dominions, 2
Semi-autonomous spaces, 23–24
Sexual and physical abuse, female apprentice, 111
  impact on women's husbands, 111–112
Sexual exploitation, slave women's sexuality, 67
Sexuality, 65–90
  changes in norm of female, 65
  civilization, 78
  Foucault's argument, 67
  metropolitan discourse, 4
  metropolitan society, 65
  passive model of female sexuality, 65–66
  polluting power, 78
  sexual relationships, 9–10
Skin colour, 71–74, 90
Slave husband, 99–102, 117
  as wife's protector, 99–102
Slave hut, 120–121
Slave marriage, 10, 93
  1833 Abolition Act, 10, 106–107
  antislavery discourse
    1826 Slave Law, 95–96
      clause 4, 95–96
    changes in status, 95–96
    co-residence, 97, 100, 101
    denunciation of planters, 98–99
    husband's role, 101–102
    illegitimate births, 100
    lives of lower classes, 96
    marriage improved people's moral condition, 96–97
    marriage primarily as moral institution, 96–97
    metropolitan ideal of husband-protector, 102
    metropolitan ideal of marriage, 96–98
    obtaining enslaved partners' freedom, 100
    residence on nearby estates, 101
    separation of married slave couples, 100–101
    taking care of husband's and children's needs, 102–104
    voluntary manumission, 99
  church-sanctioned, 93–94
  informal, 93–94
  missionaries, 94–95
  mixed marriage, 94
  proslavery discourse, 104–106, 115–126
    1826 Slave Law, clause 4, 122
    affection, 117–118
    apprenticed couples' gendered roles, 124
    church-sanctioned, 117, 118–119
    co-residence, 117, 120–121
    early proslavery writers, 116–119
    as economic institution, 116–126
    facilitating third party, 121
    formal marriage voluntary and binding contract, 123–124
    later proslavery writers, 119–126
    marriage to free man, 119–120
    metropolitan ideal of marriage, 118–119
    monogamy, 116, 117
    natural increase, 116–117
    nonconformist marriage, 122–123
    opposition to formal slave marriage, 122, 123
    provider role, 120
    scheme to increase marriage rate, 121–122, 124
    separation by sale, 120, 191
    slave huts, 120–121
    slave men's inability to provide, 120
    socio-economic status of planters, 125–126
    workload, 121
  slave couples residing on different estates, 94
  slaves married to free black or coloured person, 94
Slave men's sexuality, 66
  antislavery discourse, 66
  proslavery discourse, 66
  social stability, 66
Slave registration, 1
Slavery, apprenticeship, continuities, 8
Slave trade, 1

Slave wife, 117
  field labour, 103
  role as career of family, 102–104
Slave women, 2–3
  antislavery discourse, similar to middle-class, English women, 169–170
  apprenticeship, contrasted, 171–172
  from bearers of children to economic burdens, 27–36
  British abolitionism, 2
  "different body" site of cultural and political contestation, 171–172
  paternalistic attitude towards, 13
Slave women's sexuality, 65–90
  antislavery discourse, 66, 78–87
    abused slave women as asexual, 81
    accounts of unsuccessful resistance, 80–81
    consensual interracial sex, 84
    emerging discourse of fatherhood, 83
    estate officers, 81–82
    forced interracial sex, 81, 83–84
    male slave as emasculated man, 83–84
    metropolitan norm of masculine sexual restraint, 82–83
    naturally chaste, 80
    owners' disregard of slave marriage, 79
    potentially virtuous slave women, 79
    prostitutes, 84
    reform proposals, 85–87
    relations between whte men and free coloured women, 84
    skin colour, 84–85
    slave women's resistance, 80–81
    slave women's status as commodity, 79–80
  images, 67
  metropolitan discourse on gender, 89
  proslavery discourse
    activity at early age, 68
    deviant from metropolitan model, 68
    external pressures, 68
    free coloureds, 69
    growth of free population, 71
    housekeeper, 69
    inheritances, 69
    interracial sexual relations, 70–71
    multiple partners, 68
    natural decrease, 69–70
    naturally promiscuous, 68
    obsession with infertility, 69–70
    potentially virtuous slave women, 70–71
    prostitution, 68, 69
    sexual relations with white men, 68–69
    theories of slave women's sexual deviance, 67–69
    as threatening deviants, 67–68
  sexual exploitation, 67
Sovereign power, 37
Special Magistrates, 7
  workhouses, 154–155
Stereotypical images, 4, 67

T
Treadmills, 147, 149, 153, 164–165

V
Voluntary manumission, 99

W
Wage contract, marriage contract, link, 107
Wage labour, male apprentice, 110
War of representation, 3
White estate doctor, 26
Wife, role, 91
Women
  defined, 169
  female purity, 9–10
  flogging, 10
    apprenticeship, 10
  metropolitan, middle-class norm, 169
  role, 169
Workhouses, 147
  antislavery discourse, 148–158
  1833 Abolition Act, 156
  abuse of female apprentices in, 148–158
  actors, 150–151
  chaining, 151–152
  criminal justice system, 157
  disciplinary practices, 149–150
  illegal practices, 150, 156
  indecency, 151
  inmates, 152
  lack of gender order, 151
  legal protection, 155

metropolitan norm of masculinity, 155
apprenticeship, 147–148
flogging, 148
missionaries, 149
physical suffering, 152
planters, 149–150
proslavery discourse
  1833 Abolition Act, 161–162
  denied abuse, 159–160
  disciplinary practices justified, 159
  flogging, 162–164
  governor and colonial secretary, 162–163
  moderate punishments, 160
  planters' power, 161–162
  treadmills, 164–165
  who should control workhouse, 165
resistance, 150
society's lack of civilization, 152–153
Special Magistrates, 154–155
taste for cruelty, 153–154
treadmills, 149, 153
workhouse committee members, 154–155
workhouse officers, 154